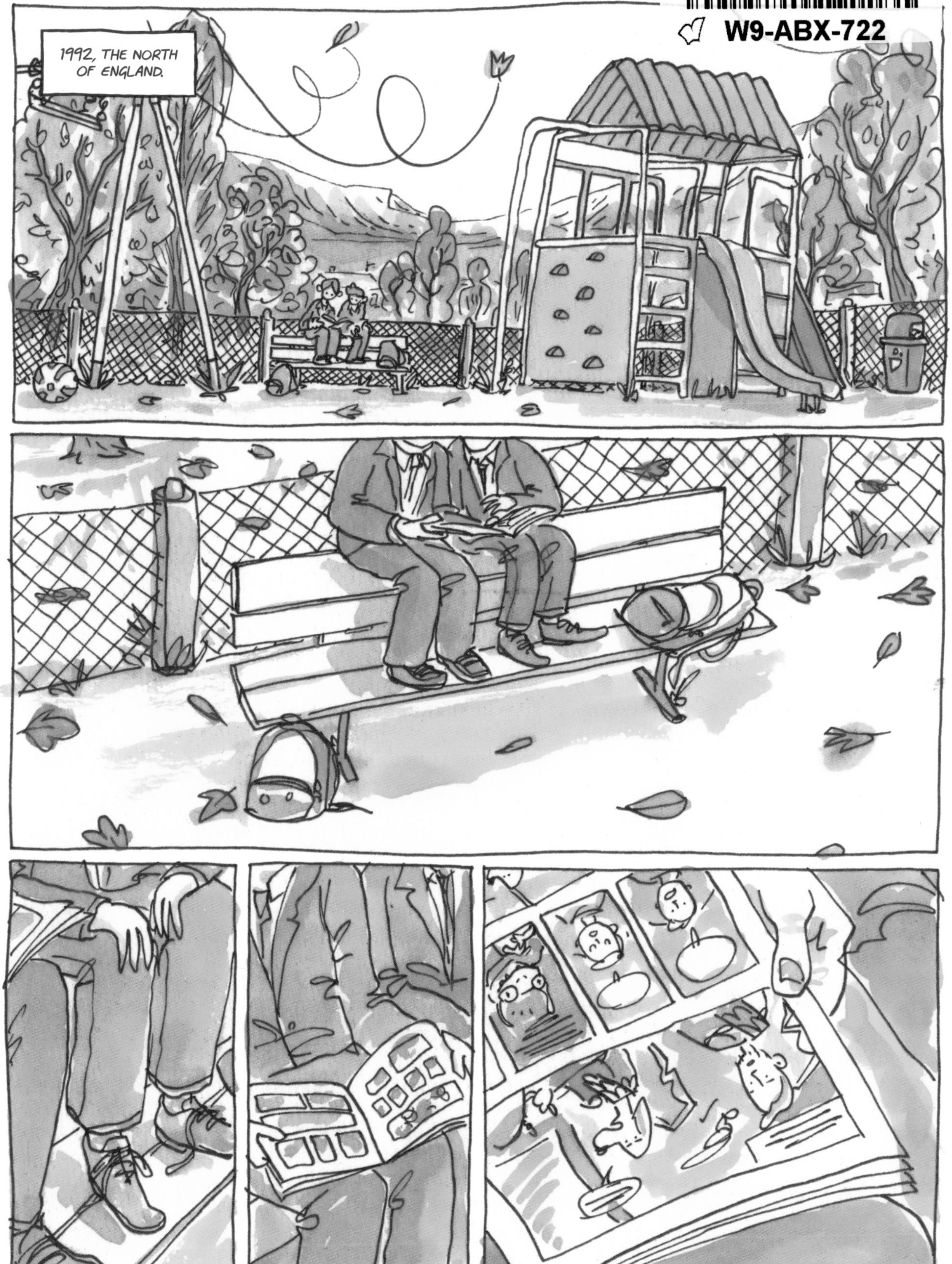
1992, THE NORTH OF ENGLAND.

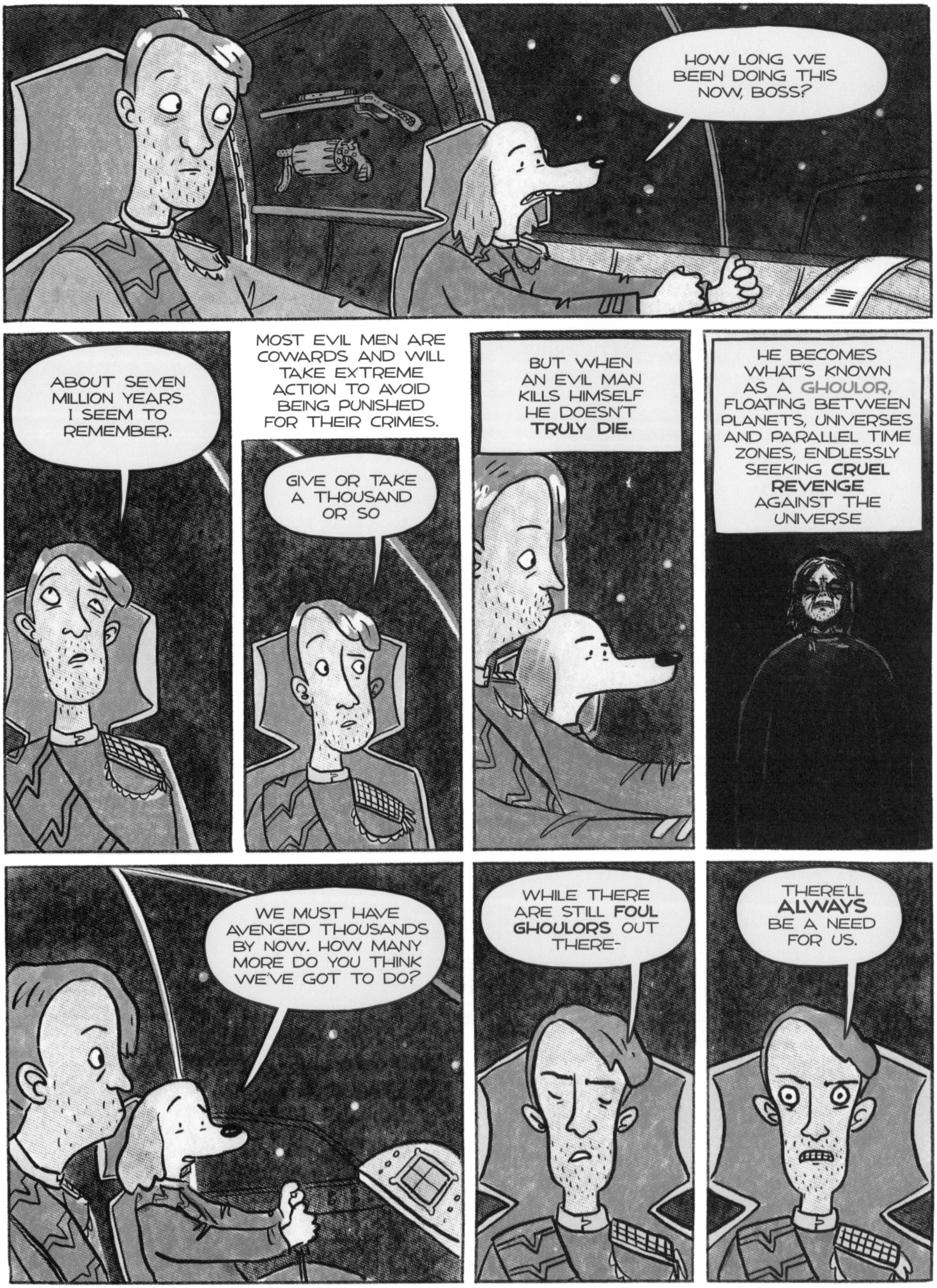
HOW LONG WE BEEN DOING THIS NOW, BOSS?
ABOUT SEVEN MILLION YEARS I SEEM TO REMEMBER.
MOST EVIL MEN ARE COWARDS AND WILL TAKE EXTREME ACTION TO AVOID BEING PUNISHED FOR THEIR CRIMES.
GIVE OR TAKE A THOUSAND OR SO
BUT WHEN AN EVIL MAN KILLS HIMSELF HE DOESN'T TRULY DIE.
HE BECOMES WHAT'S KNOWN AS A GHOULOR, FLOATING BETWEEN PLANETS, UNIVERSES AND PARALLEL TIME ZONES, ENDLESSLY SEEKING CRUEL REVENGE AGAINST THE UNIVERSE
WE MUST HAVE AVENGED THOUSANDS BY NOW. HOW MANY MORE DO YOU THINK WE'VE GOT TO DO?
WHILE THERE ARE STILL FOUL GHOULORS OUT THERE-
THERE'LL ALWAYS BE A NEED FOR US.

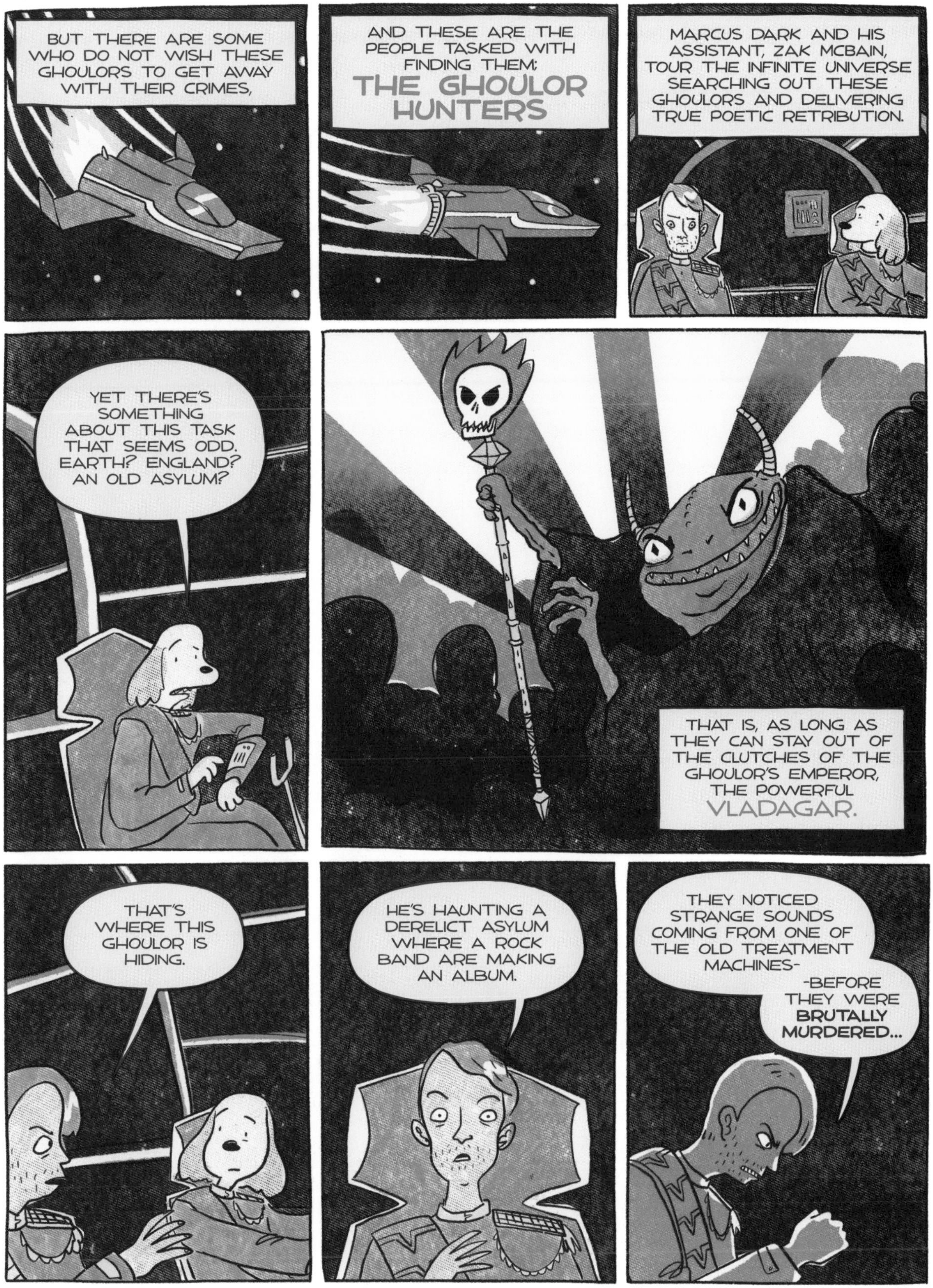
BUT THERE ARE SOME WHO DO NOT WISH THESE GHOULORS TO GET AWAY WITH THEIR CRIMES,
AND THESE ARE THE PEOPLE TASKED WITH FINDING THEM; THE GHOULOR HUNTERS
MARCUS DARK AND HIS ASSISTANT, ZAK MCBAIN, TOUR THE INFINITE UNIVERSE SEARCHING OUT THESE GHOULORS AND DELIVERING TRUE POETIC RETRIBUTION.
YET THERE'S SOMETHING ABOUT THIS TASK THAT SEEMS ODD. EARTH? ENGLAND? AN OLD ASYLUM?
THAT IS, AS LONG AS THEY CAN STAY OUT OF THE CLUTCHES OF THE GHOULOR'S EMPEROR, THE POWERFUL VLADAGAR.
THAT'S WHERE THIS GHOULOR IS HIDING.
HE'S HAUNTING A DERELICT ASYLUM WHERE A ROCK BAND ARE MAKING AN ALBUM.
THEY NOTICED STRANGE SOUNDS COMING FROM ONE OF THE OLD TREATMENT MACHINES-
-BEFORE THEY WERE BRUTALLY MURDERED...

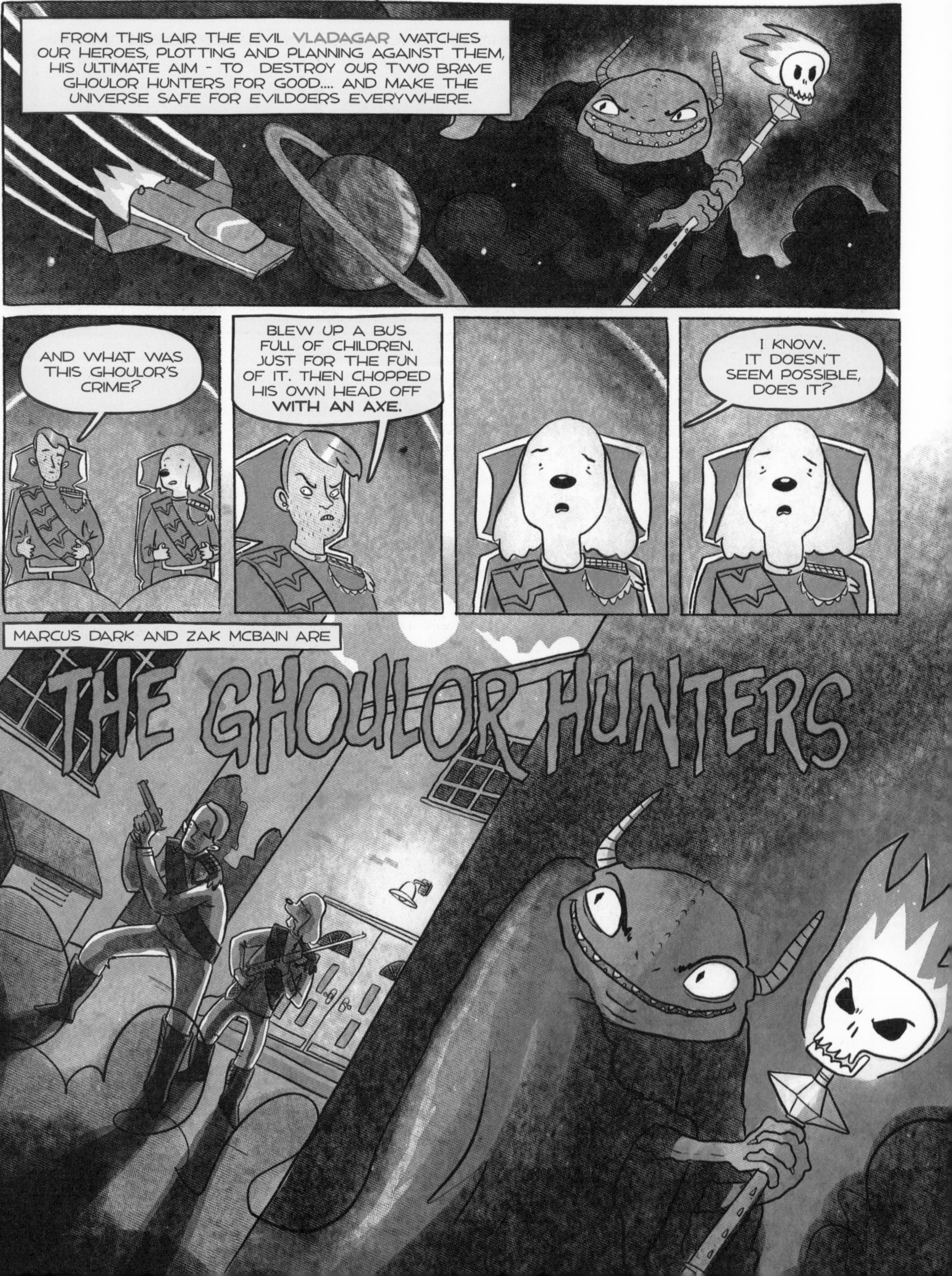
FROM THIS LAIR THE EVIL VLADAGAR WATCHES OUR HEROES, PLOTTING AND PLANNING AGAINST THEM, HIS ULTIMATE AIM - TO DESTROY OUR TWO BRAVE GHOULOR HUNTERS FOR GOOD.... AND MAKE THE UNIVERSE SAFE FOR EVILDOERS EVERYWHERE.
AND WHAT WAS THIS GHOULOR'S CRIME?
BLEW UP A BUS FULL OF CHILDREN. JUST FOR THE FUN OF IT. THEN CHOPPED HIS OWN HEAD OFF WITH AN AXE.
I KNOW. IT DOESN'T SEEM POSSIBLE, DOES IT?
MARCUS DARK AND ZAK MCBAIN ARE
THE GHOULOR HUNTERS

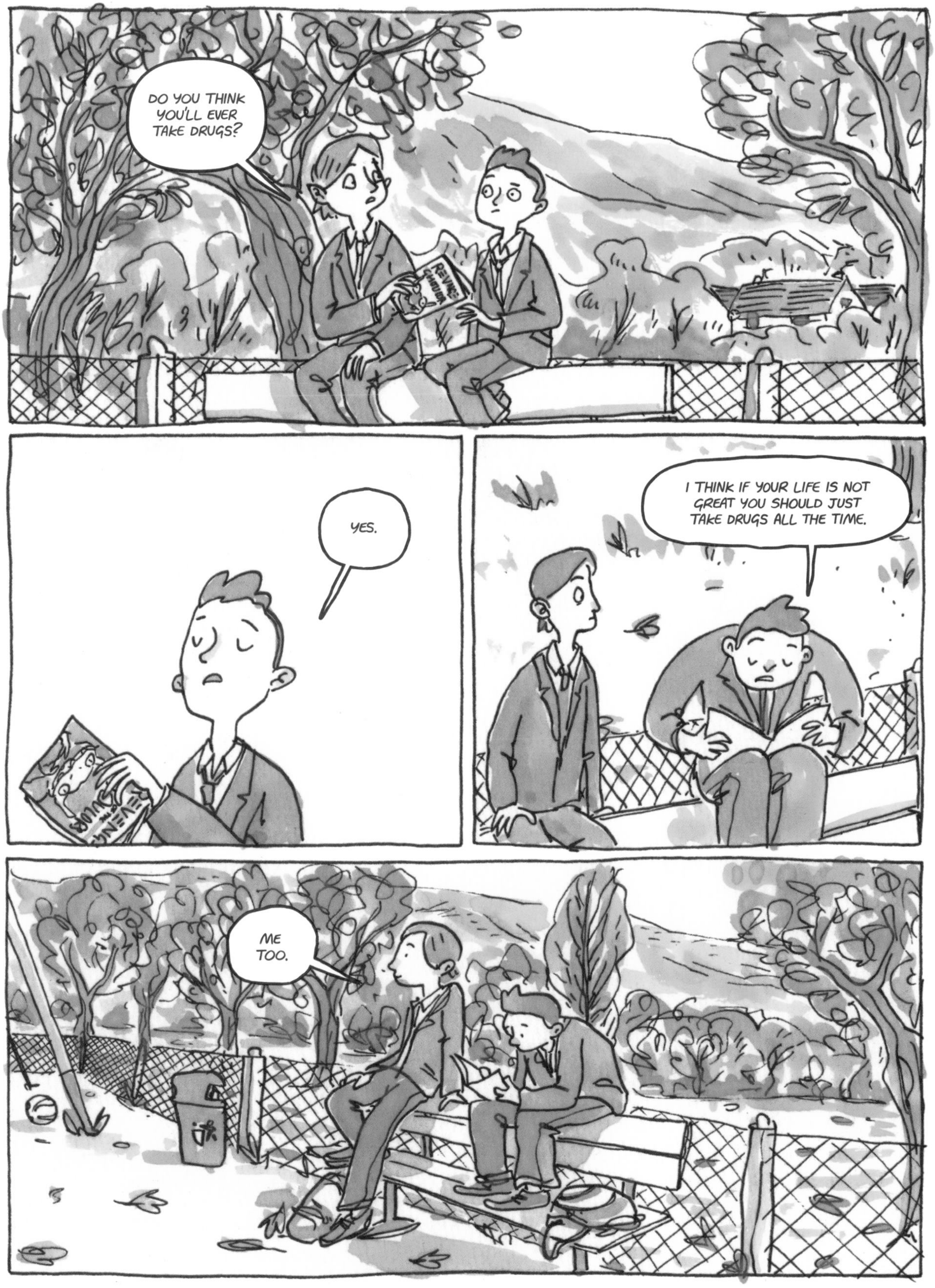
DO YOU THINK YOU'LL EVER TAKE DRUGS?
YES.
I THINK IF YOUR LIFE IS NOT GREAT YOU SHOULD JUST TAKE DRUGS ALL THE TIME.
ME TOO.

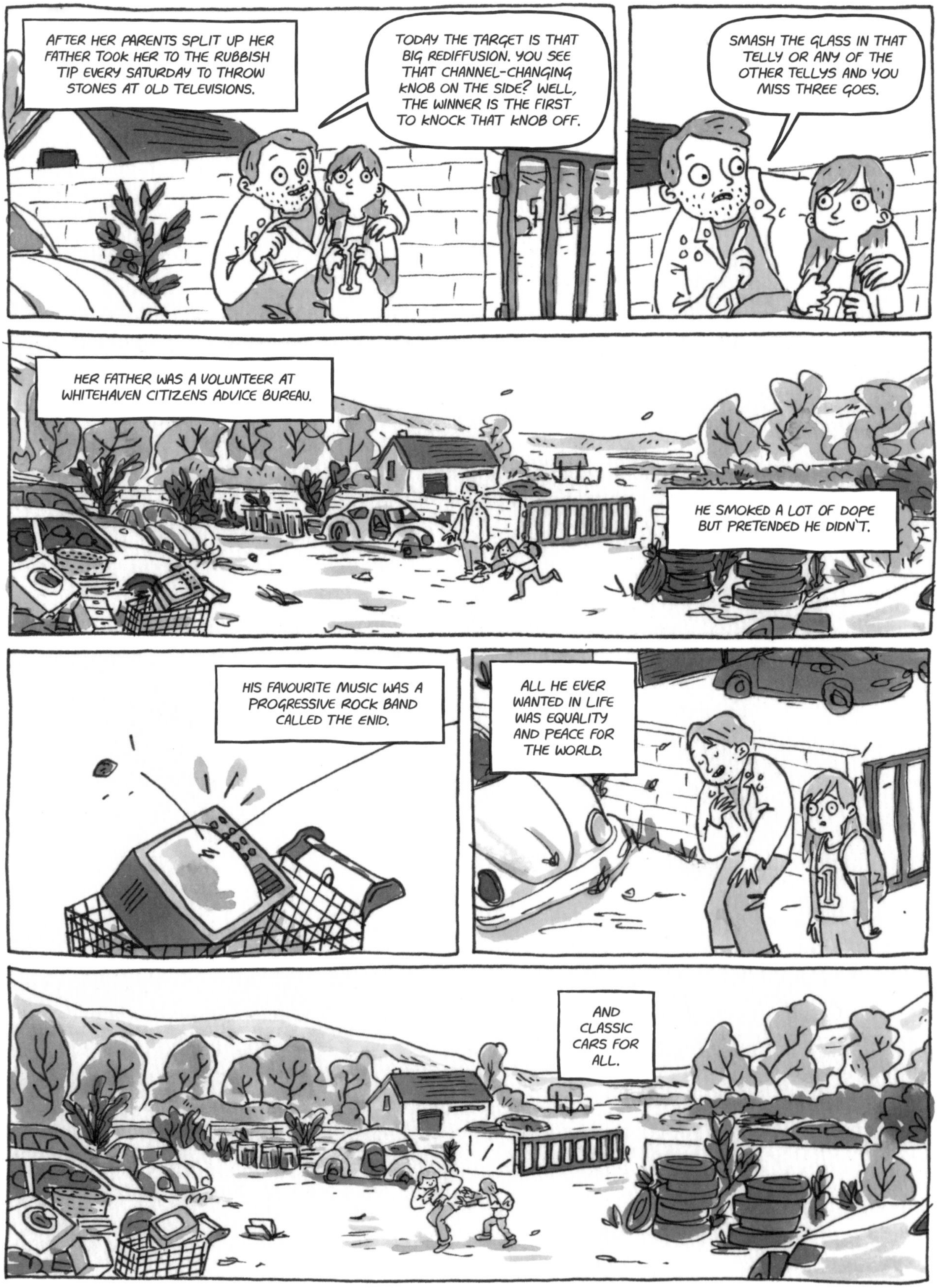
AFTER HER PARENTS SPLIT UP HER FATHER TOOK HER TO THE RUBBISH TIP EVERY SATURDAY TO THROW STONES AT OLD TELEVISIONS.
TODAY THE TARGET IS THAT BIG REDIFFUSION. YOU SEE THAT CHANNEL-CHANGING KNOB ON THE SIDE? WELL, THE WINNER IS THE FIRST TO KNOCK THAT KNOB OFF.
SMASH THE GLASS IN THAT TELLY OR ANY OF THE OTHER TELLYS AND YOU MISS THREE GOES.
HER FATHER WAS A VOLUNTEER AT WHITEHAVEN CITIZENS ADVICE BUREAU.
HE SMOKED A LOT OF DOPE BUT PRETENDED HE DIDN'T.
HIS FAVOURITE MUSIC WAS A PROGRESSIVE ROCK BAND CALLED THE ENID.
ALL HE EVER WANTED IN LIFE WAS EQUALITY AND PEACE FOR THE WORLD.
AND CLASSIC CARS FOR ALL.

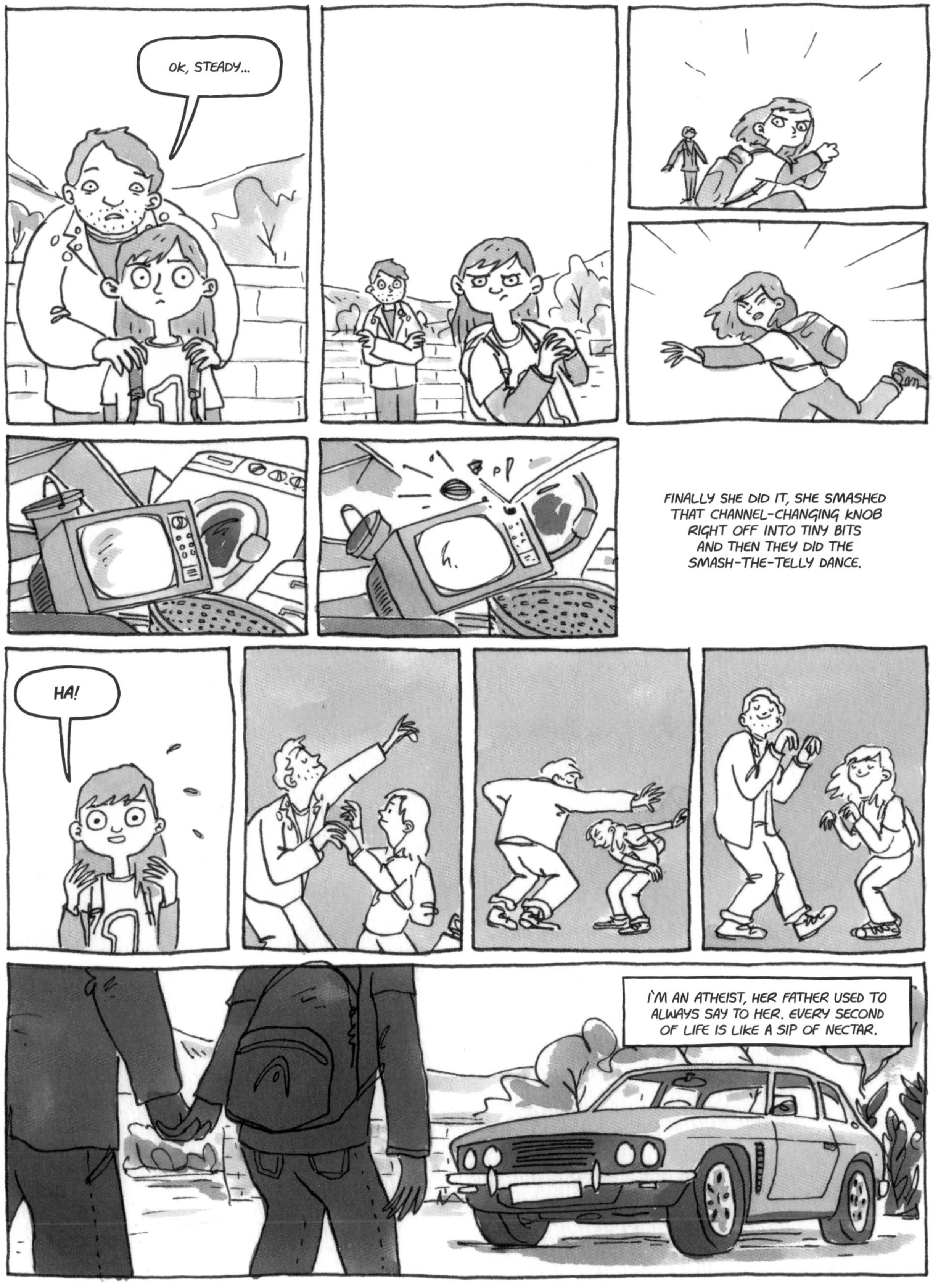
OK, STEADY...
FINALLY SHE DID IT, SHE SMASHED THAT CHANNEL-CHANGING KNOB RIGHT OFF INTO TINY BITS AND THEN THEY DID THE SMASH-THE-TELLY DANCE.
HA!
I'M AN ATHEIST, HER FATHER USED TO ALWAYS SAY TO HER. EVERY SECOND OF LIFE IS LIKE A SIP OF NECTAR.

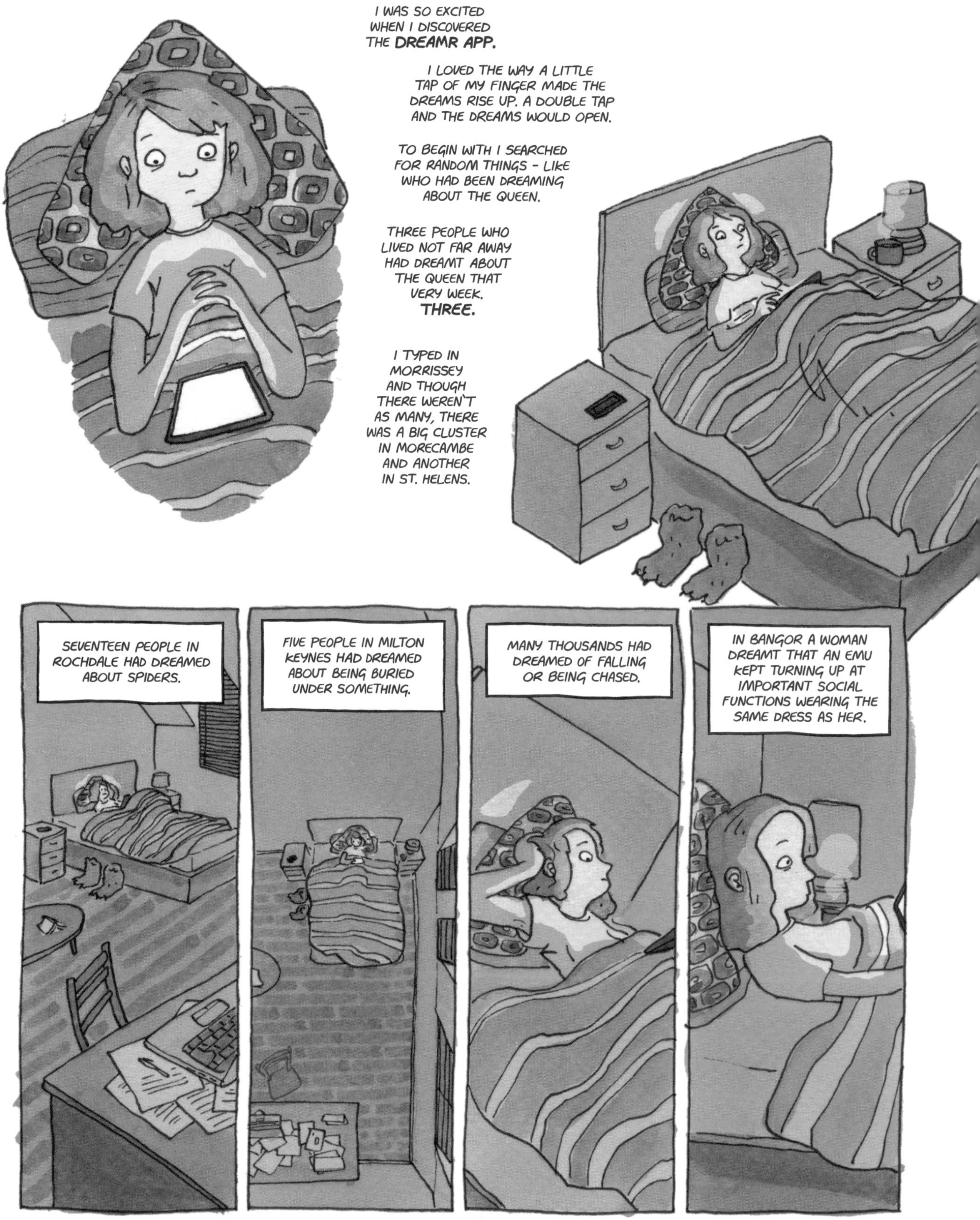

I WAS SO EXCITED WHEN I DISCOVERED THE **DREAMR APP.**
I LOVED THE WAY A LITTLE TAP OF MY FINGER MADE THE DREAMS RISE UP. A DOUBLE TAP AND THE DREAMS WOULD OPEN.
TO BEGIN WITH I SEARCHED FOR RANDOM THINGS - LIKE WHO HAD BEEN DREAMING ABOUT THE QUEEN.
THREE PEOPLE WHO LIVED NOT FAR AWAY HAD DREAMT ABOUT THE QUEEN THAT VERY WEEK.
THREE.
I TYPED IN MORRISSEY AND THOUGH THERE WEREN'T AS MANY, THERE WAS A BIG CLUSTER IN MORECAMBE AND ANOTHER IN ST. HELENS.
SEVENTEEN PEOPLE IN ROCHDALE HAD DREAMED ABOUT SPIDERS.
FIVE PEOPLE IN MILTON KEYNES HAD DREAMED ABOUT BEING BURIED UNDER SOMETHING.
MANY THOUSANDS HAD DREAMED OF FALLING OR BEING CHASED.
IN BANGOR A WOMAN DREAMT THAT AN EMU KEPT TURNING UP AT IMPORTANT SOCIAL FUNCTIONS WEARING THE SAME DRESS AS HER.

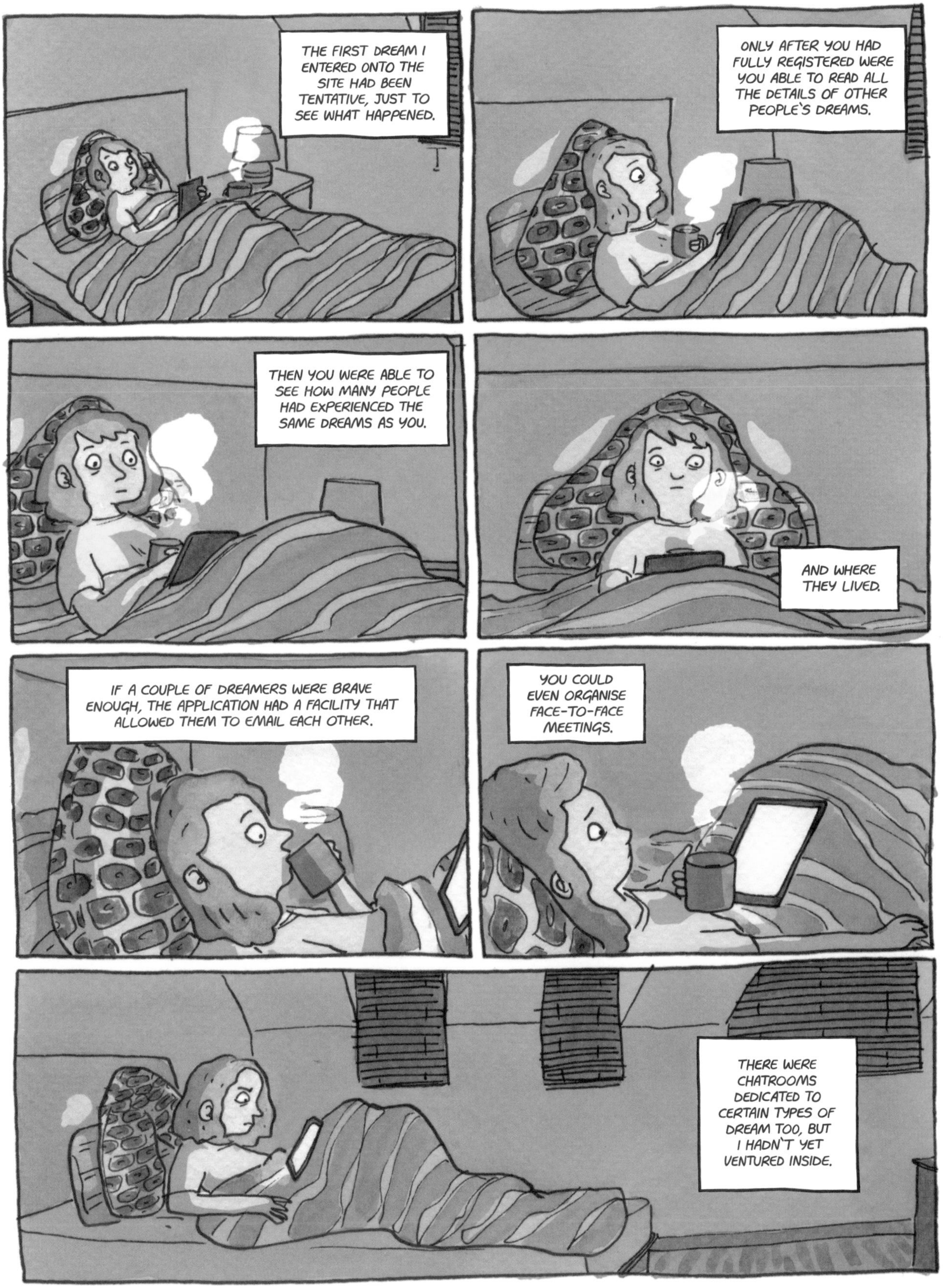
THE FIRST DREAM I ENTERED ONTO THE SITE HAD BEEN TENTATIVE, JUST TO SEE WHAT HAPPENED.
ONLY AFTER YOU HAD FULLY REGISTERED WERE YOU ABLE TO READ ALL THE DETAILS OF OTHER PEOPLE'S DREAMS.
THEN YOU WERE ABLE TO SEE HOW MANY PEOPLE HAD EXPERIENCED THE SAME DREAMS AS YOU.
AND WHERE THEY LIVED.
IF A COUPLE OF DREAMERS WERE BRAVE ENOUGH, THE APPLICATION HAD A FACILITY THAT ALLOWED THEM TO EMAIL EACH OTHER.
YOU COULD EVEN ORGANISE FACE-TO-FACE MEETINGS.
THERE WERE CHATROOMS DEDICATED TO CERTAIN TYPES OF DREAM TOO, BUT I HADN'T YET VENTURED INSIDE.

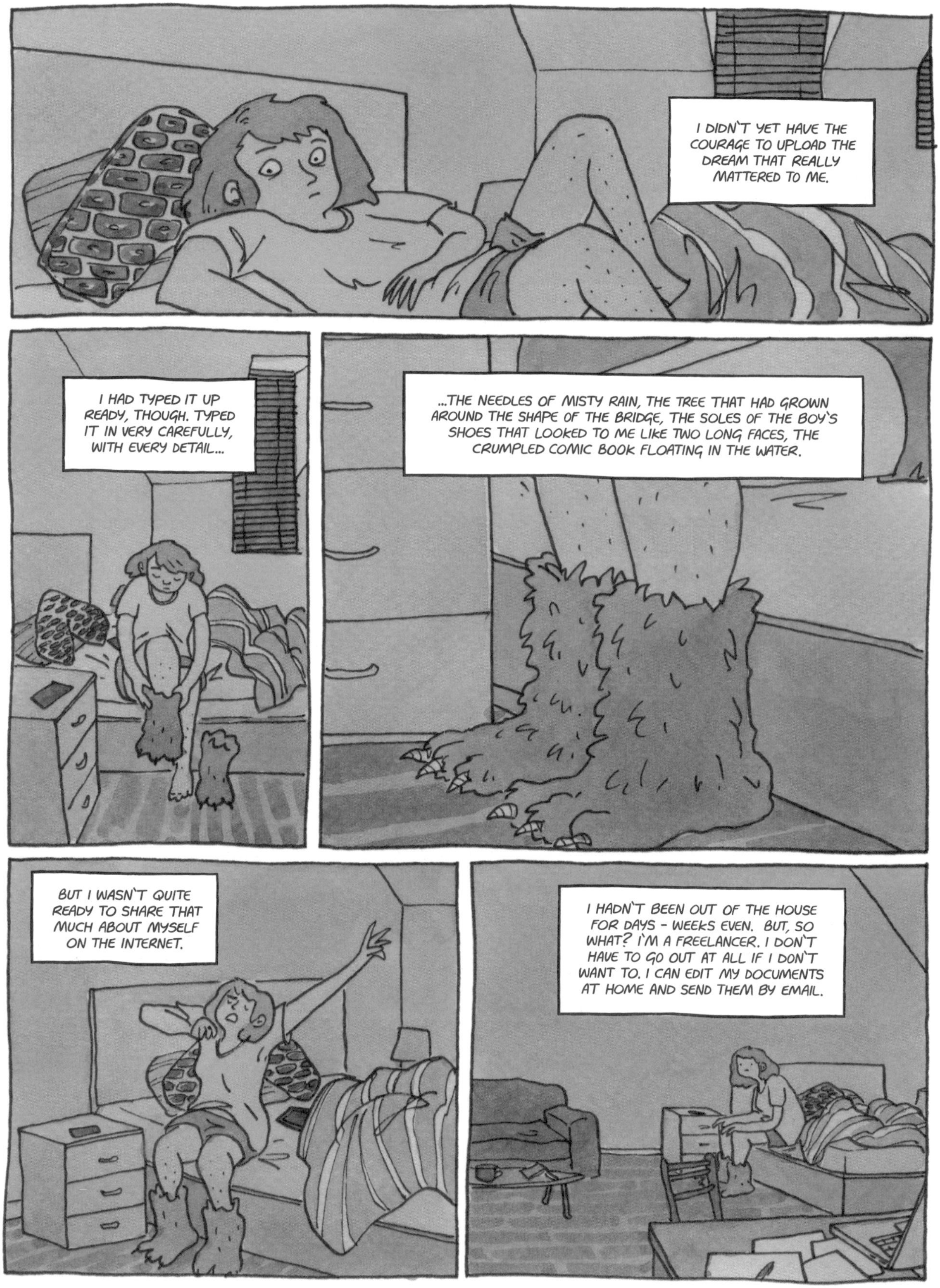
I DIDN'T YET HAVE THE COURAGE TO UPLOAD THE DREAM THAT REALLY MATTERED TO ME.
I HAD TYPED IT UP READY, THOUGH. TYPED IT IN VERY CAREFULLY, WITH EVERY DETAIL...
...THE NEEDLES OF MISTY RAIN, THE TREE THAT HAD GROWN AROUND THE SHAPE OF THE BRIDGE, THE SOLES OF THE BOY'S SHOES THAT LOOKED TO ME LIKE TWO LONG FACES, THE CRUMPLED COMIC BOOK FLOATING IN THE WATER.
BUT I WASN'T QUITE READY TO SHARE THAT MUCH ABOUT MYSELF ON THE INTERNET.
I HADN'T BEEN OUT OF THE HOUSE FOR DAYS - WEEKS EVEN. BUT, SO WHAT? I'M A FREELANCER. I DON'T HAVE TO GO OUT AT ALL IF I DON'T WANT TO. I CAN EDIT MY DOCUMENTS AT HOME AND SEND THEM BY EMAIL.

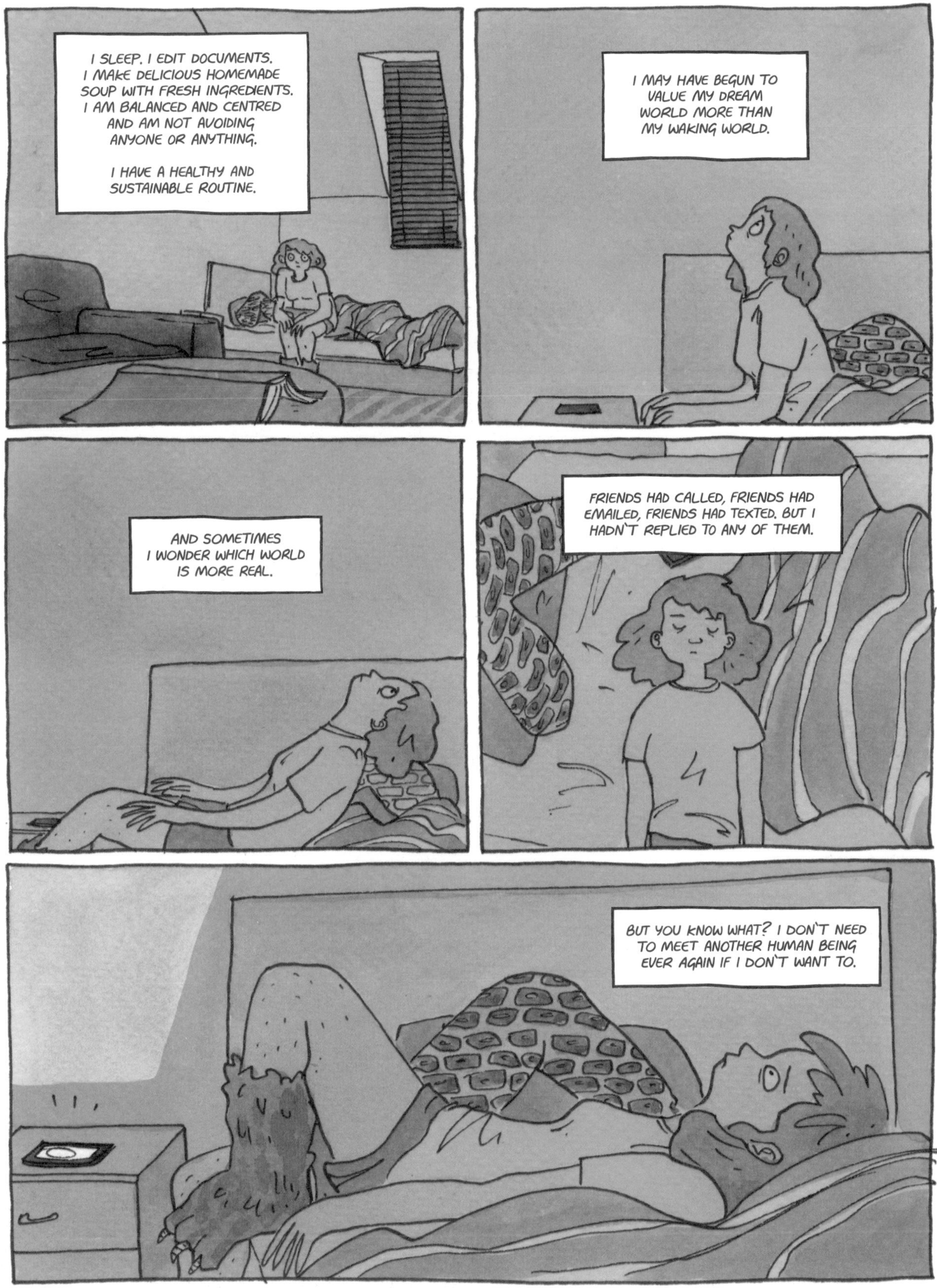
I SLEEP. I EDIT DOCUMENTS. I MAKE DELICIOUS HOMEMADE SOUP WITH FRESH INGREDIENTS. I AM BALANCED AND CENTRED AND AM NOT AVOIDING ANYONE OR ANYTHING.
I HAVE A HEALTHY AND SUSTAINABLE ROUTINE.
I MAY HAVE BEGUN TO VALUE MY DREAM WORLD MORE THAN MY WAKING WORLD.
AND SOMETIMES I WONDER WHICH WORLD IS MORE REAL.
FRIENDS HAD CALLED, FRIENDS HAD EMAILED, FRIENDS HAD TEXTED. BUT I HADN'T REPLIED TO ANY OF THEM.
BUT YOU KNOW WHAT? I DON'T NEED TO MEET ANOTHER HUMAN BEING EVER AGAIN IF I DON'T WANT TO.

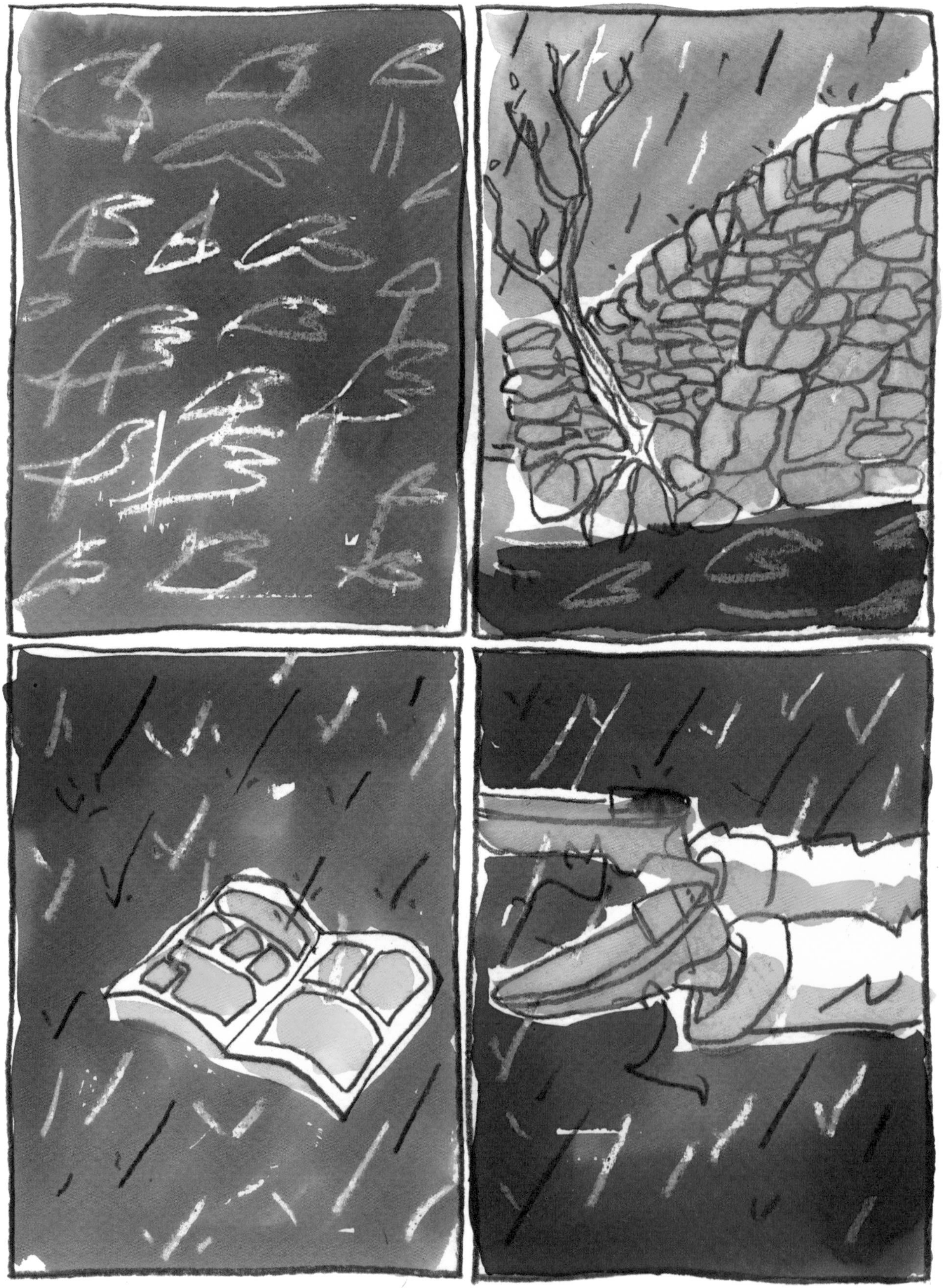

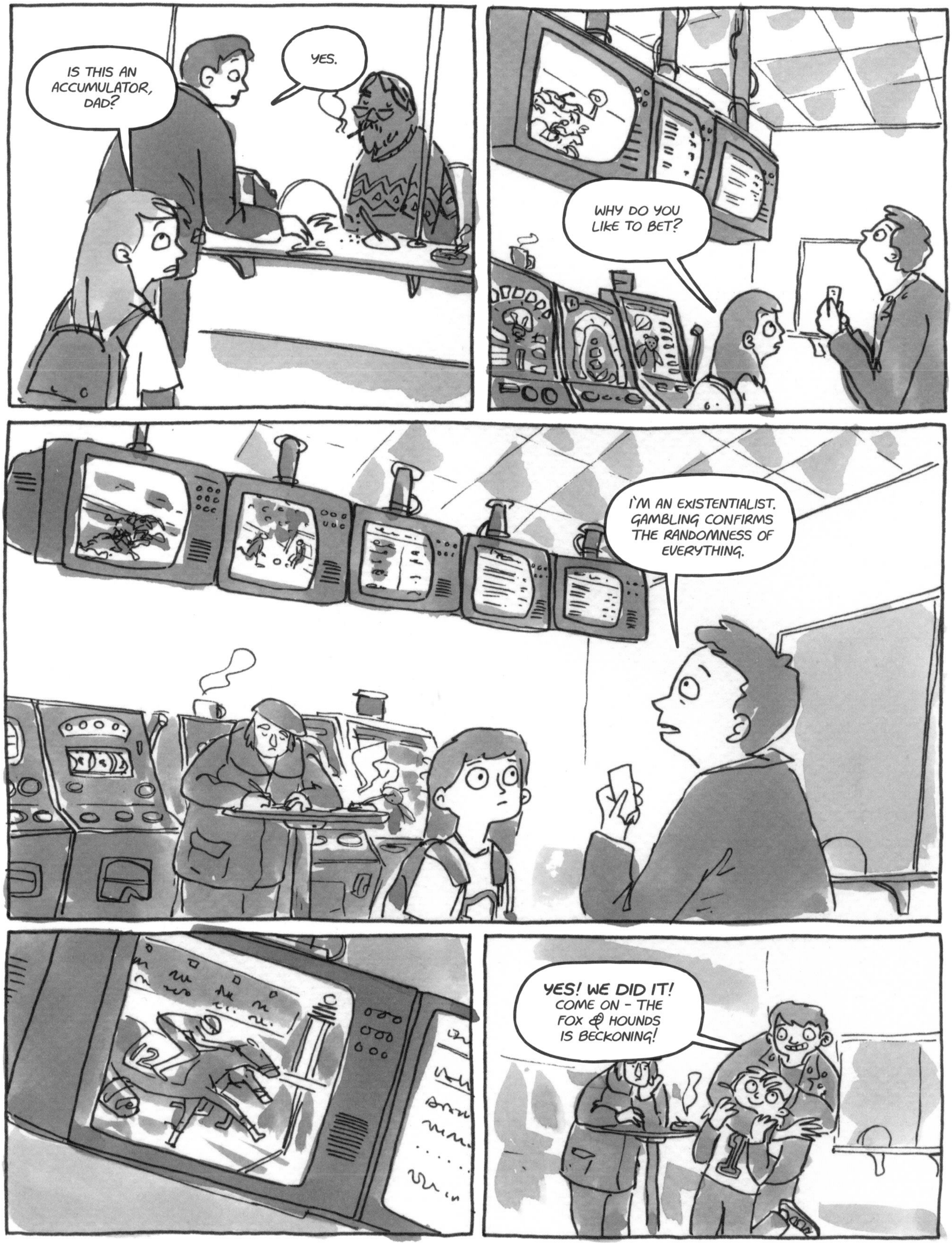
IS THIS AN ACCUMULATOR, DAD?
YES.
WHY DO YOU LIKE TO BET?
I'M AN EXISTENTIALIST. GAMBLING CONFIRMS THE RANDOMNESS OF EVERYTHING.
YES! WE DID IT! COME ON - THE FOX & HOUNDS IS BECKONING!

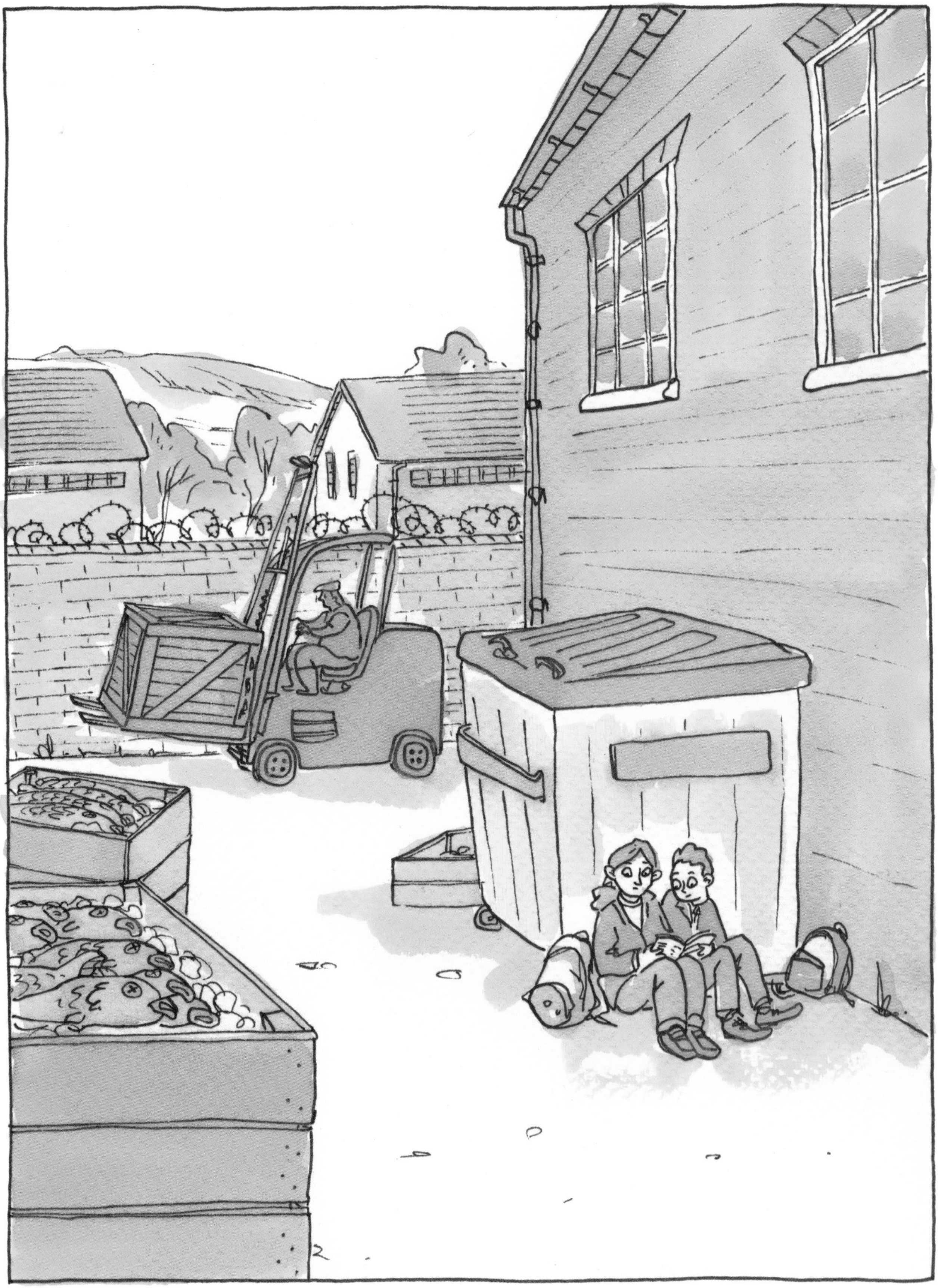

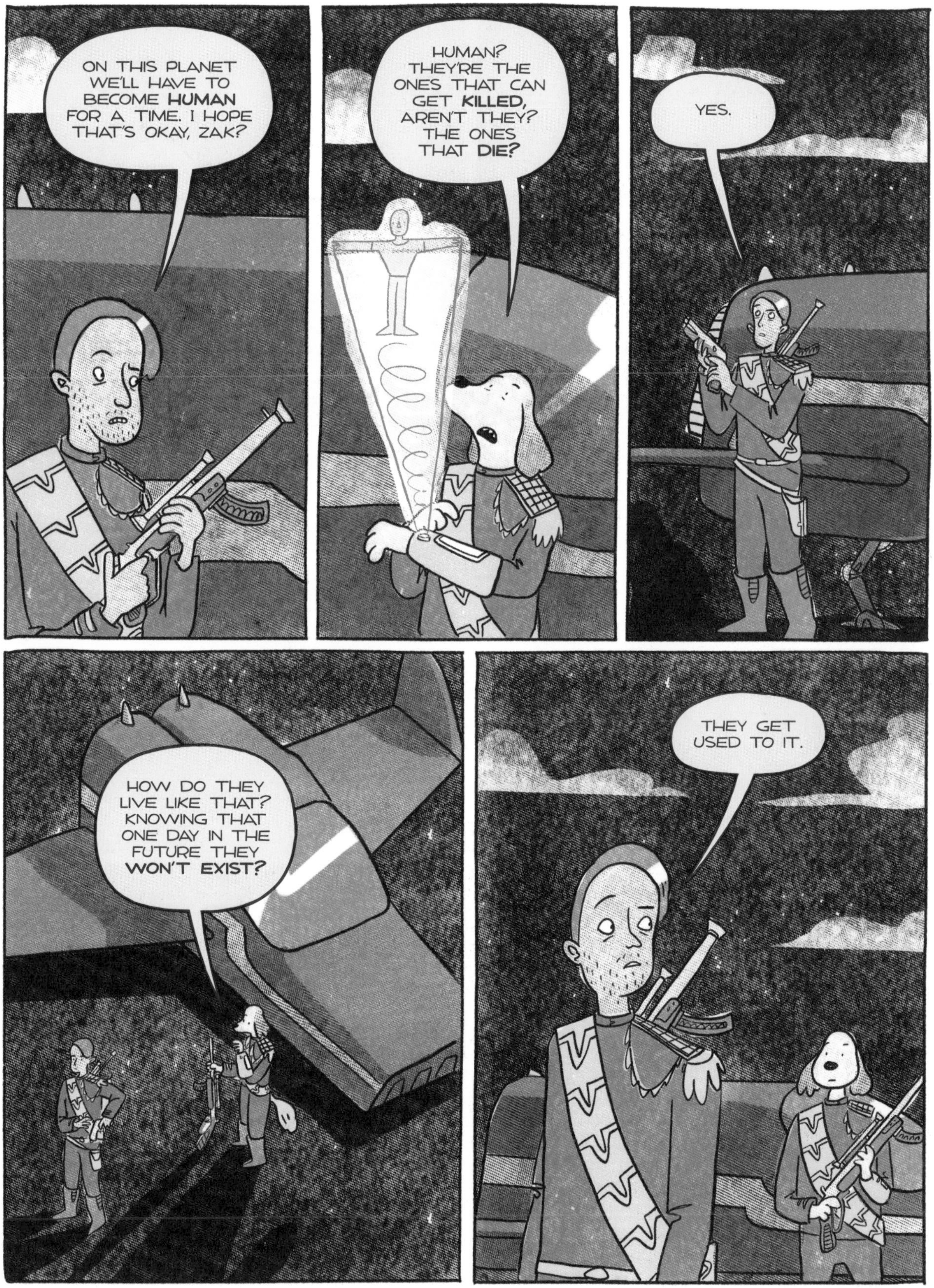
ON THIS PLANET WE'LL HAVE TO BECOME **HUMAN** FOR A TIME. I HOPE THAT'S OKAY, ZAK?
HUMAN? THEY'RE THE ONES THAT CAN GET **KILLED,** AREN'T THEY? THE ONES THAT **DIE?**
YES.
HOW DO THEY LIVE LIKE THAT? KNOWING THAT ONE DAY IN THE FUTURE THEY **WON'T EXIST?**
THEY GET USED TO IT.

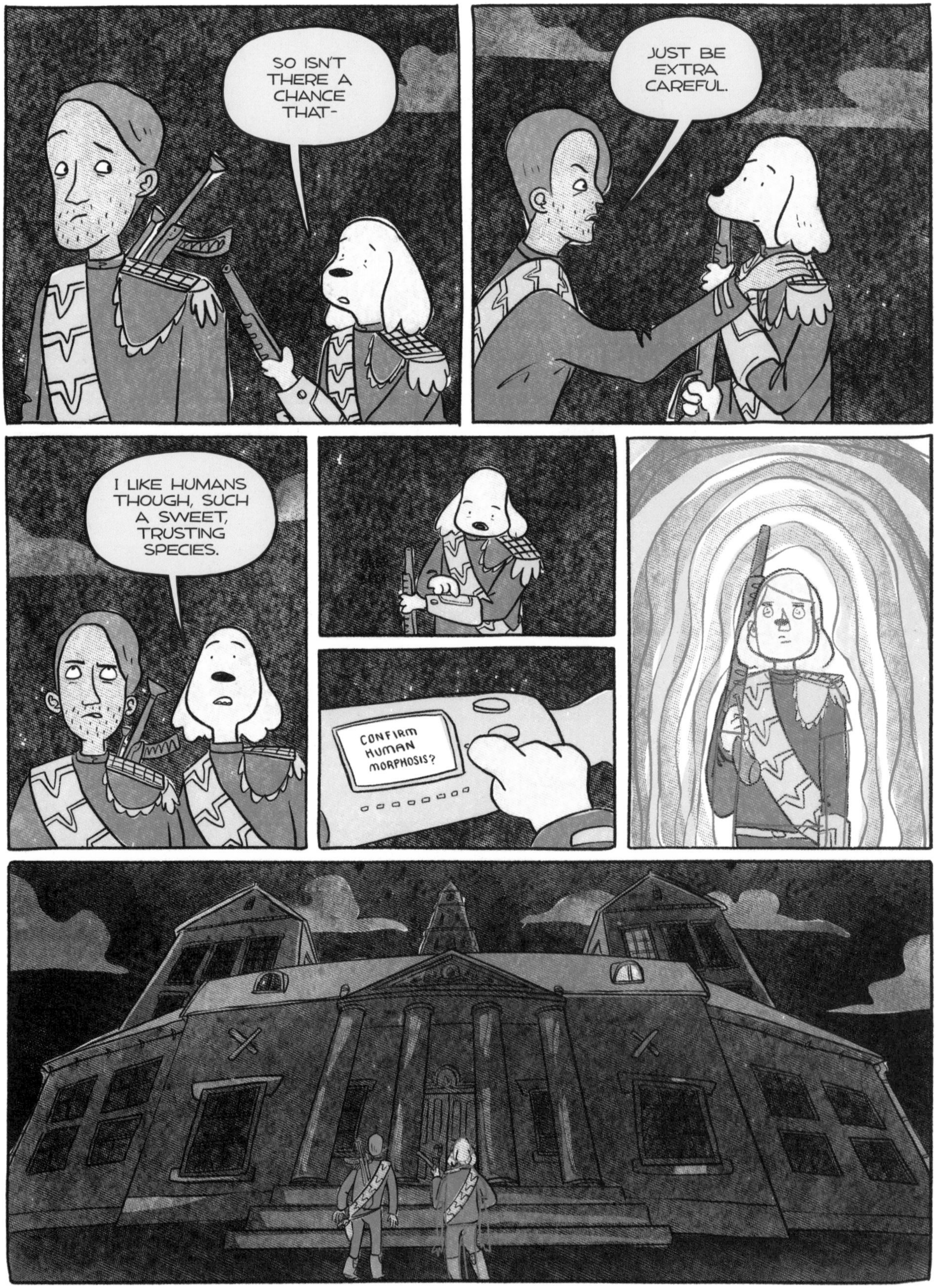
SO ISN'T THERE A CHANCE THAT-
JUST BE EXTRA CAREFUL.
I LIKE HUMANS THOUGH, SUCH A SWEET, TRUSTING SPECIES.
CONFIRM HUMAN MORPHOSIS?

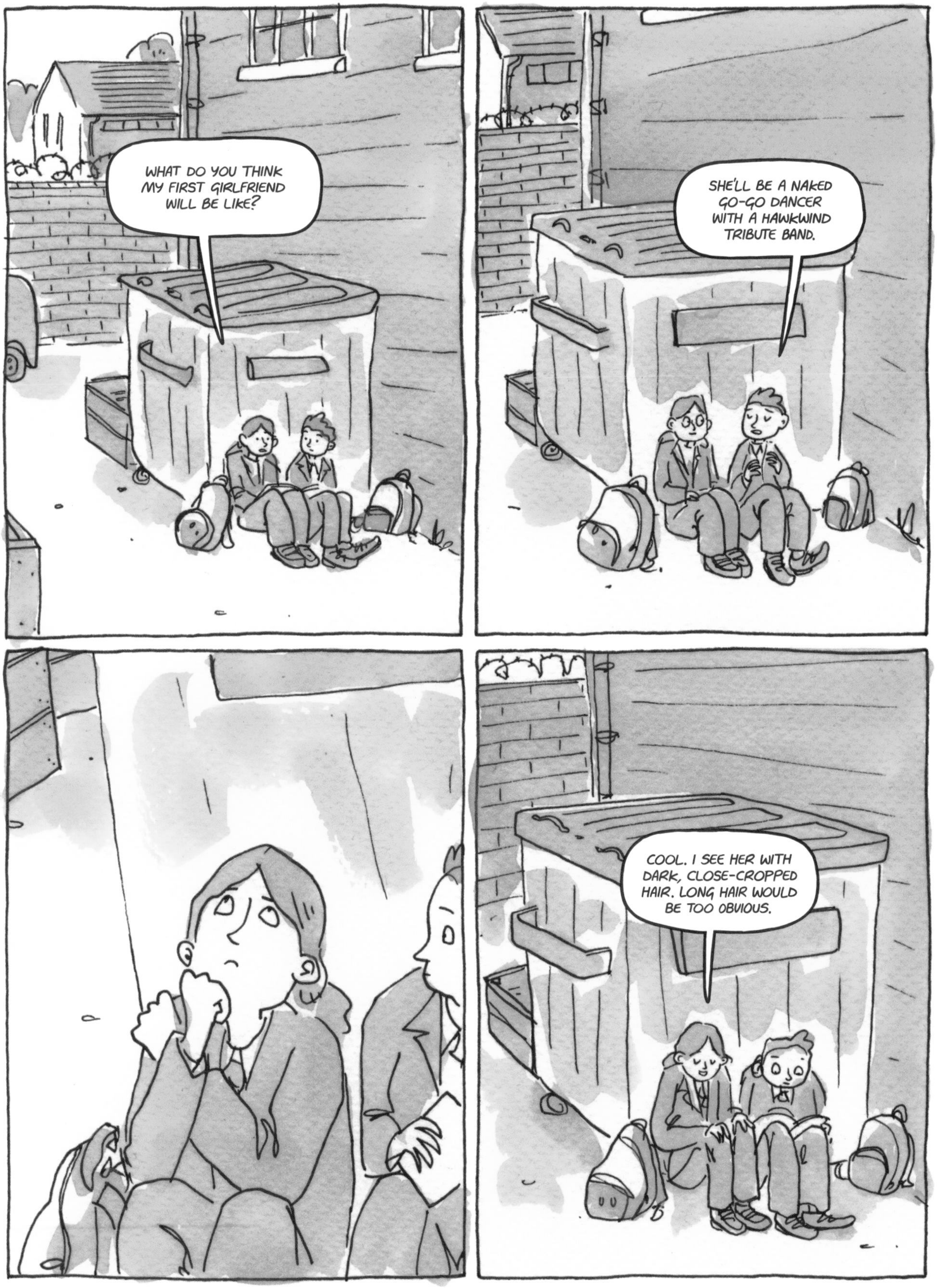
WHAT DO YOU THINK MY FIRST GIRLFRIEND WILL BE LIKE?
SHE'LL BE A NAKED GO-GO DANCER WITH A HAWKWIND TRIBUTE BAND.
COOL. I SEE HER WITH DARK, CLOSE-CROPPED HAIR. LONG HAIR WOULD BE TOO OBVIOUS.

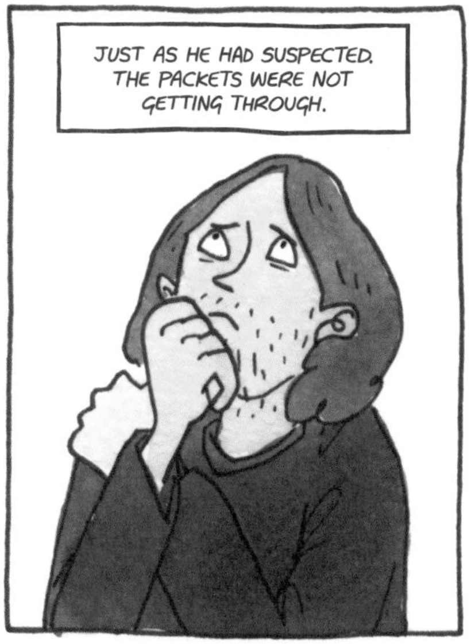
JUST AS HE HAD SUSPECTED. THE PACKETS WERE NOT GETTING THROUGH.

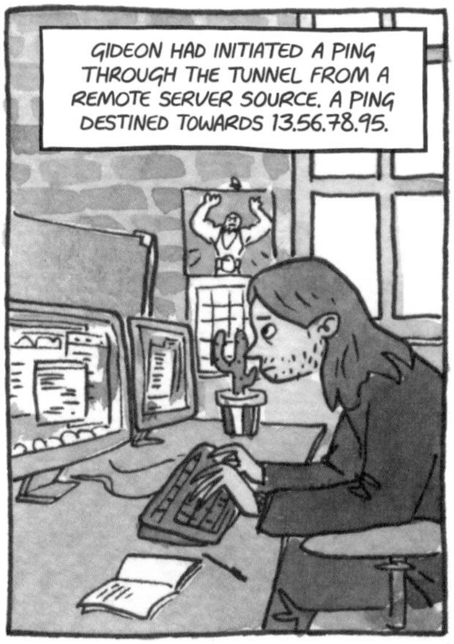
GIDEON HAD INITIATED A PING THROUGH THE TUNNEL FROM A REMOTE SERVER SOURCE. A PING DESTINED TOWARDS 13.56.78.95.

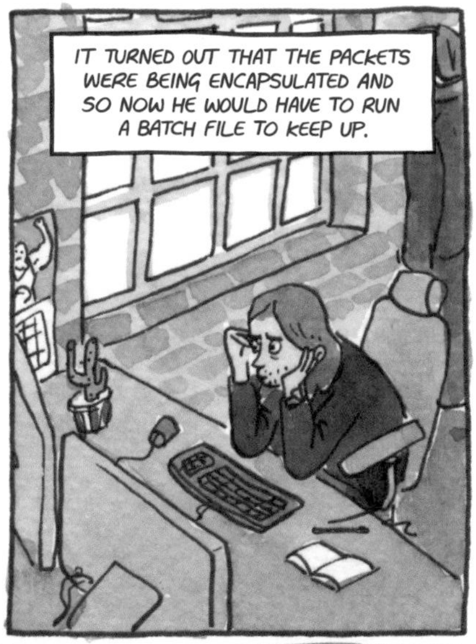
IT TURNED OUT THAT THE PACKETS WERE BEING ENCAPSULATED AND SO NOW HE WOULD HAVE TO RUN A BATCH FILE TO KEEP UP.

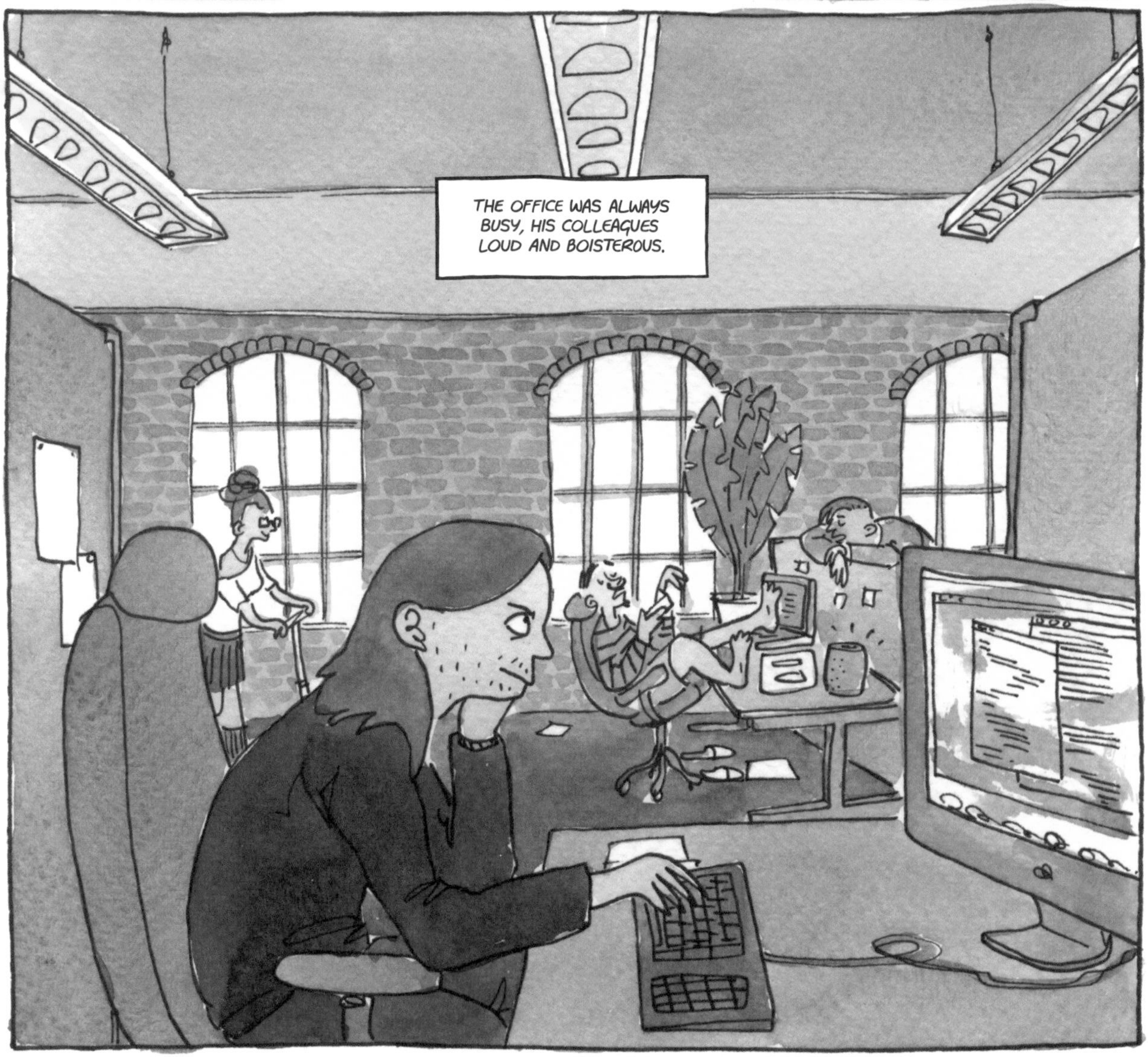
THE OFFICE WAS ALWAYS BUSY, HIS COLLEAGUES LOUD AND BOISTEROUS.

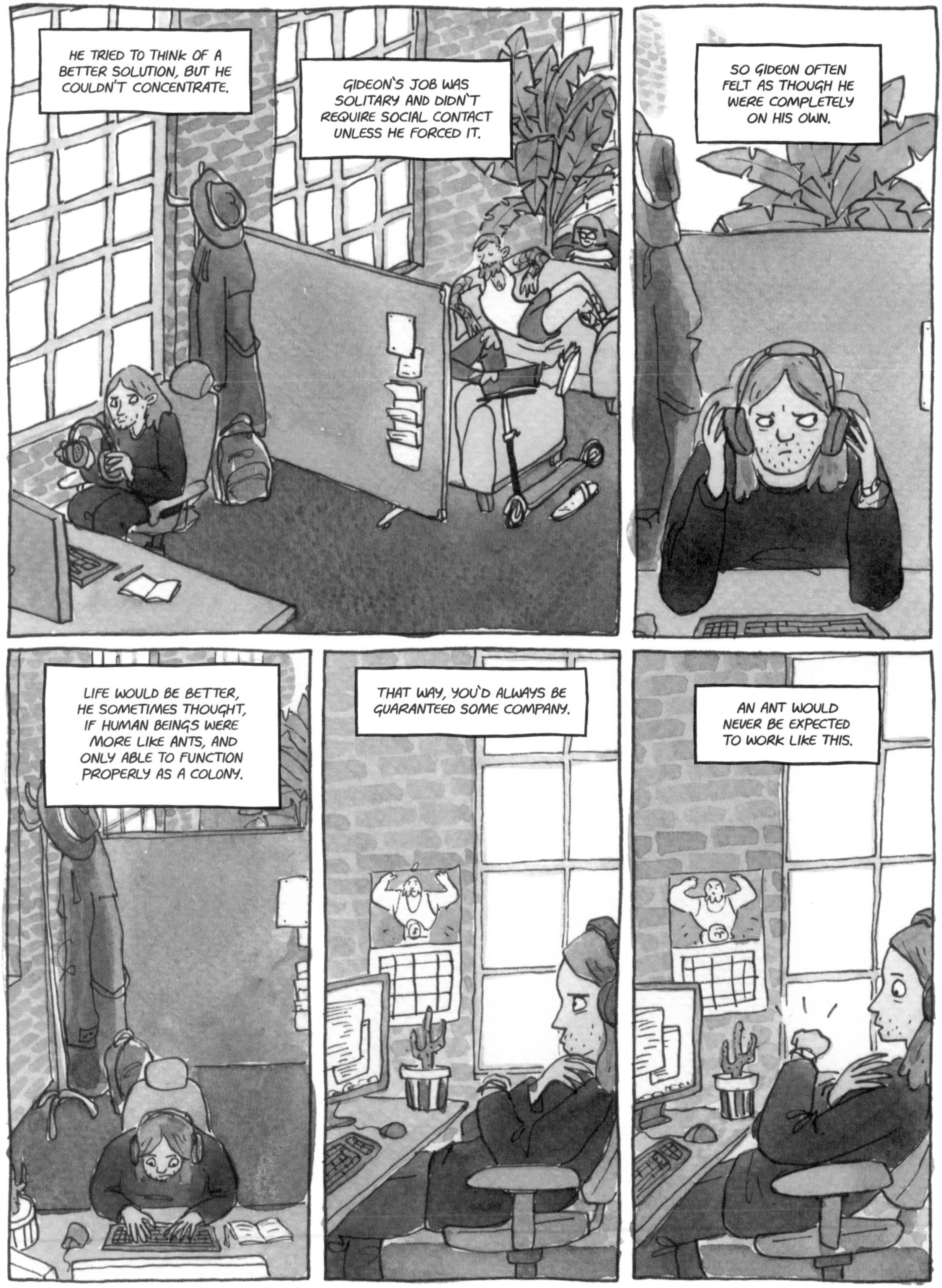

HE TRIED TO THINK OF A BETTER SOLUTION, BUT HE COULDN'T CONCENTRATE.
GIDEON'S JOB WAS SOLITARY AND DIDN'T REQUIRE SOCIAL CONTACT UNLESS HE FORCED IT.
SO GIDEON OFTEN FELT AS THOUGH HE WERE COMPLETELY ON HIS OWN.
LIFE WOULD BE BETTER, HE SOMETIMES THOUGHT, IF HUMAN BEINGS WERE MORE LIKE ANTS, AND ONLY ABLE TO FUNCTION PROPERLY AS A COLONY.
THAT WAY, YOU'D ALWAYS BE GUARANTEED SOME COMPANY.
AN ANT WOULD NEVER BE EXPECTED TO WORK LIKE THIS.

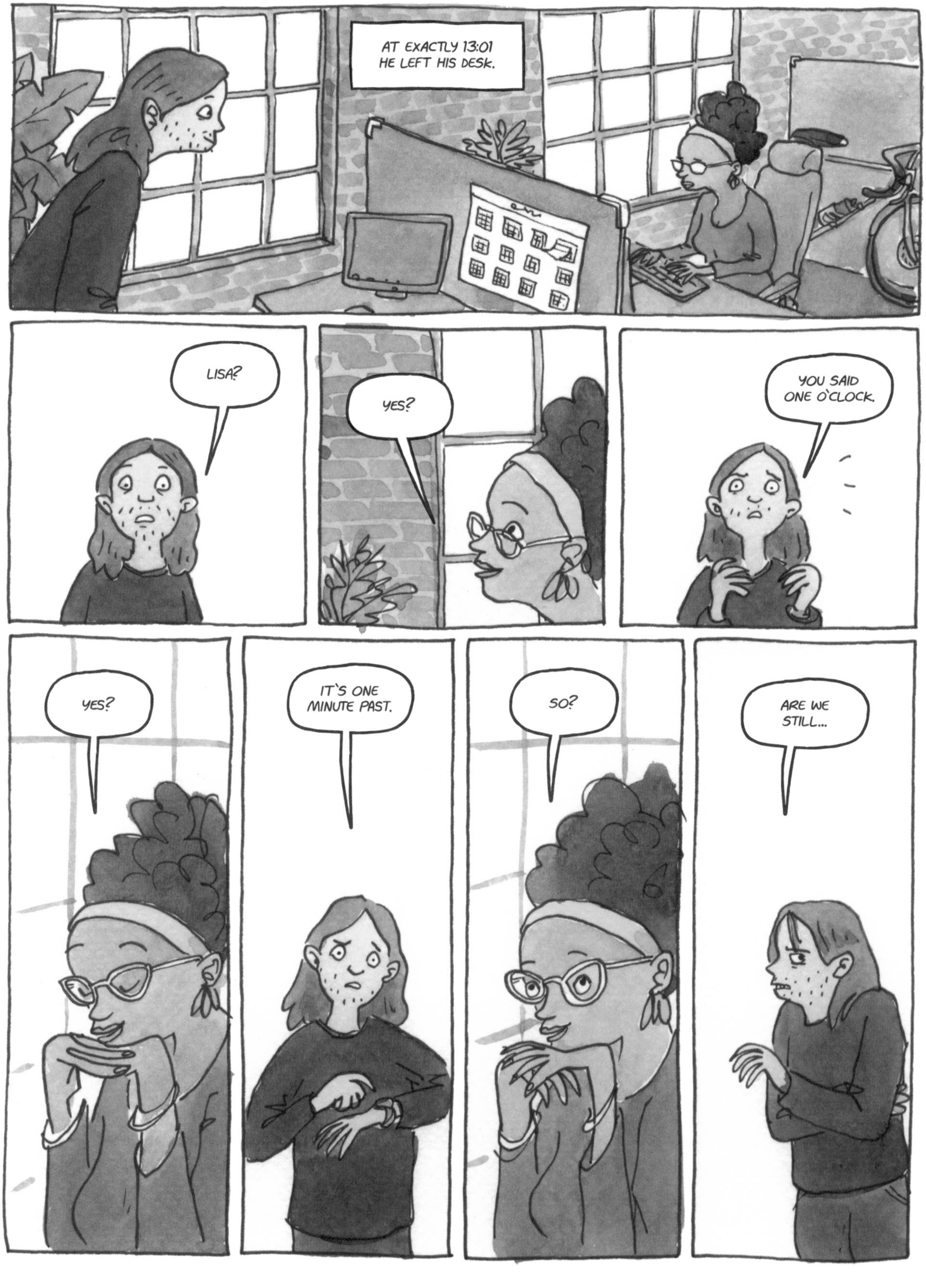
AT EXACTLY 13:01
HE LEFT HIS DESK.
LISA?
YES?
YOU SAID ONE O'CLOCK.
YES?
IT'S ONE MINUTE PAST.
SO?
ARE WE STILL...

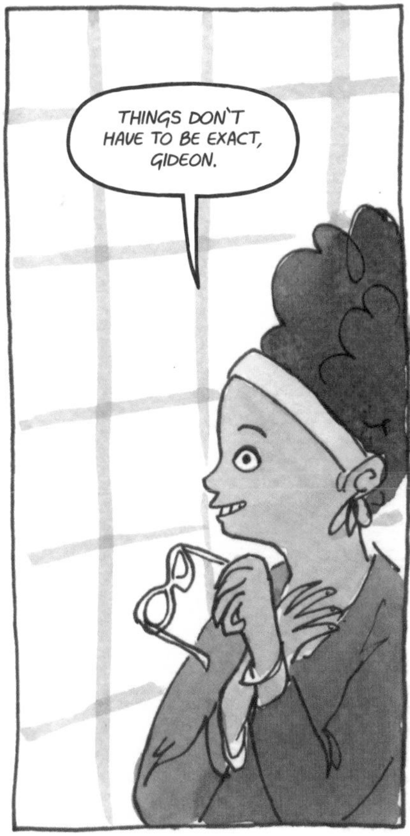
THINGS DON'T HAVE TO BE EXACT, GIDEON.

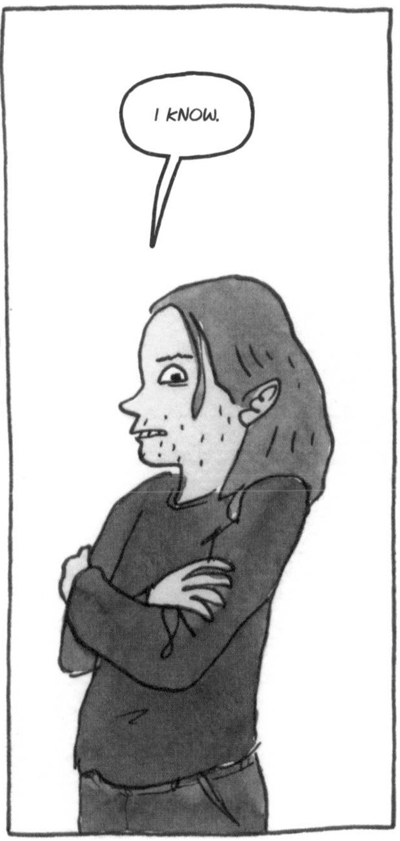
I KNOW.

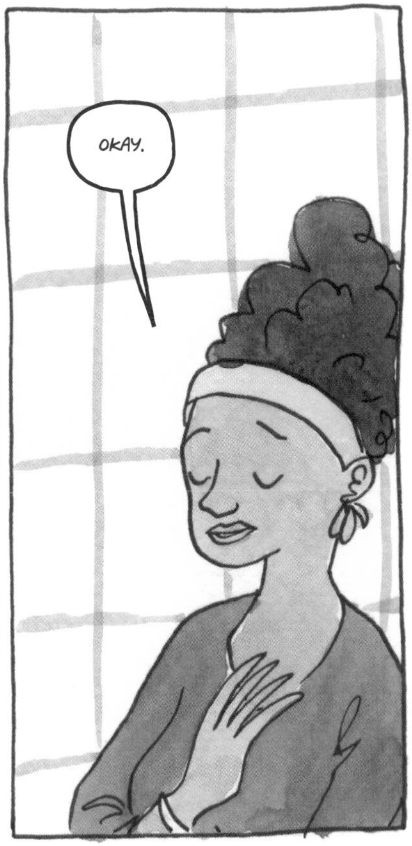
OKAY.

HE LOOKED AT HER GIANT WHITE PLASTIC SPECTACLES, WHICH WERE LYING NEXT TO HER KEYBOARD. SHE WAS ALWAYS TAKING THEM ON AND OFF, HE HAD NO IDEA WHY.

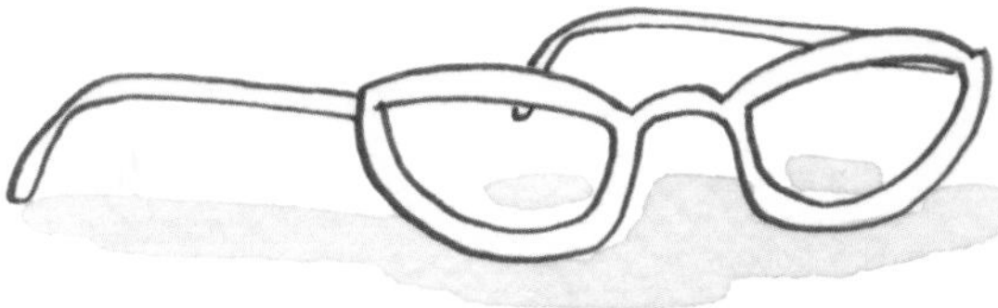

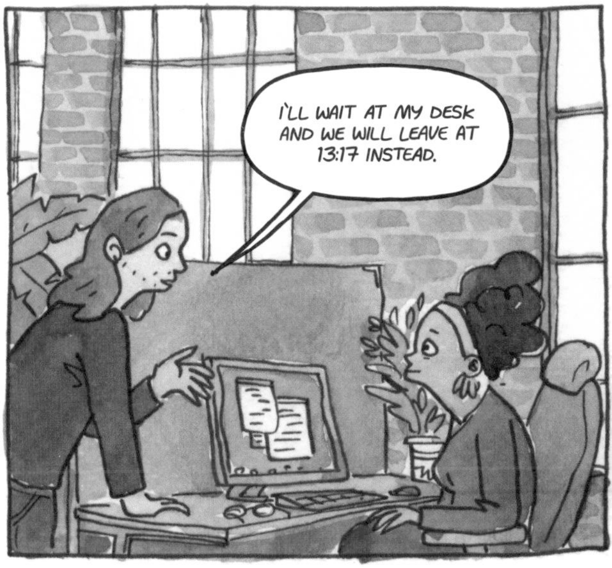
I'LL WAIT AT MY DESK AND WE WILL LEAVE AT 13:17 INSTEAD.

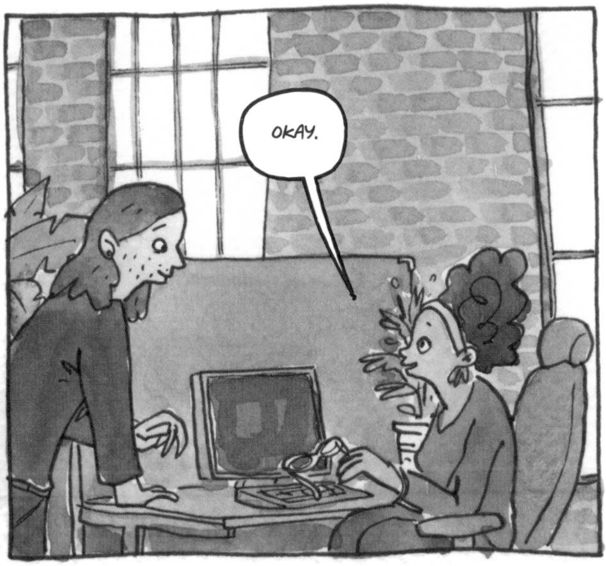
OKAY.

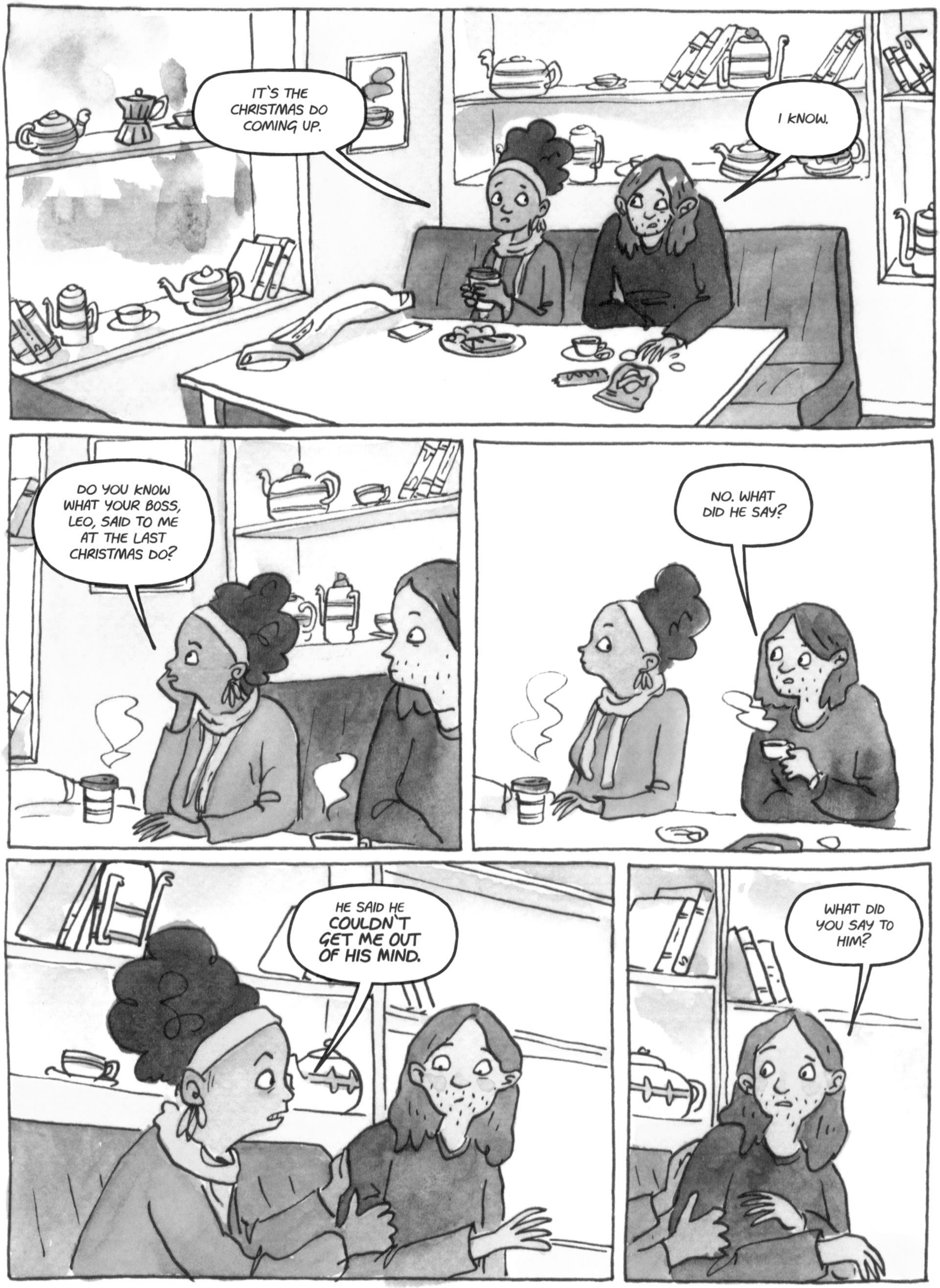
IT'S THE CHRISTMAS DO COMING UP.
I KNOW.
DO YOU KNOW WHAT YOUR BOSS, LEO, SAID TO ME AT THE LAST CHRISTMAS DO?
NO. WHAT DID HE SAY?
HE SAID HE COULDN'T GET ME OUT OF HIS MIND.
WHAT DID YOU SAY TO HIM?

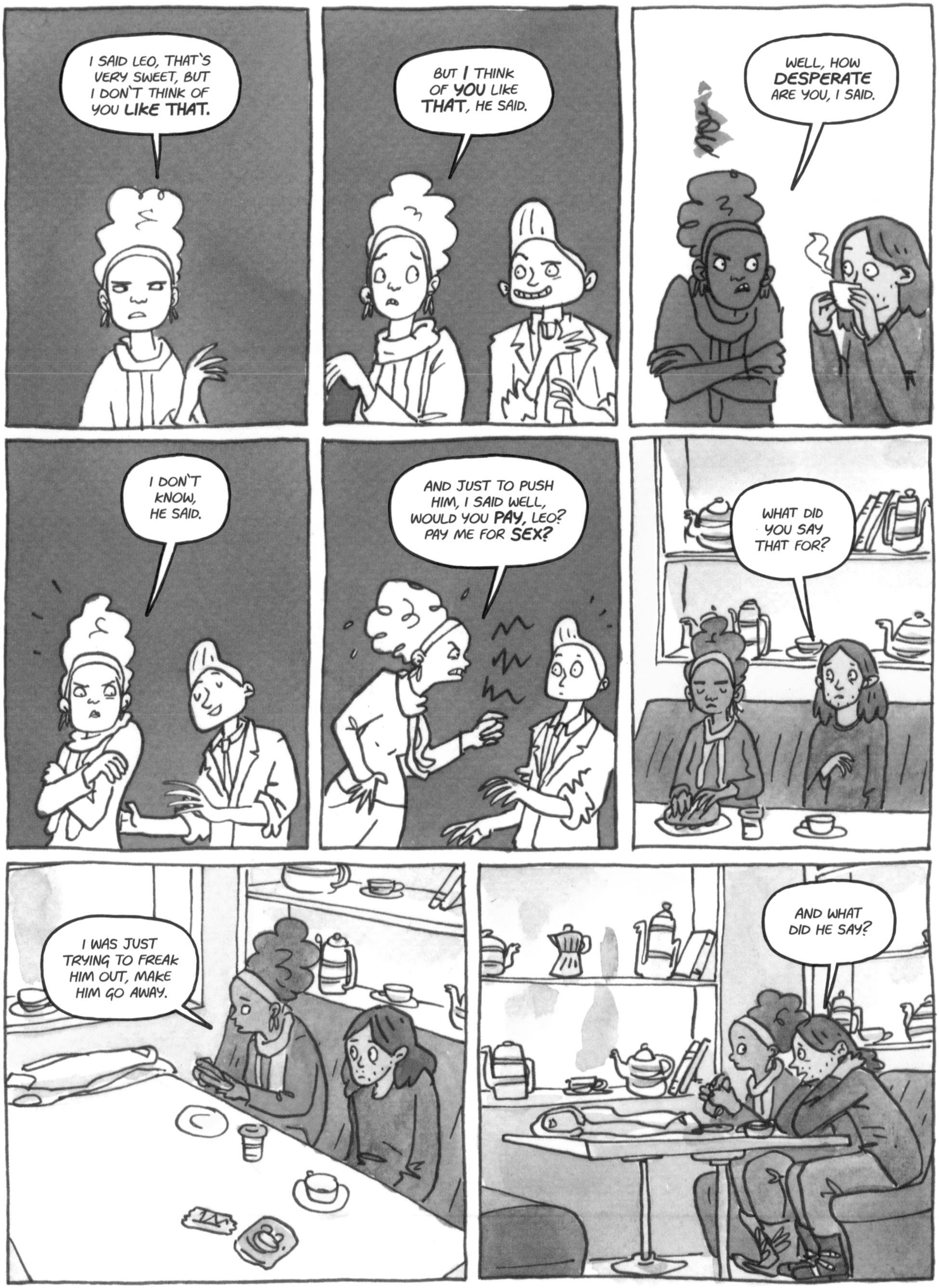
I SAID LEO, THAT`S VERY SWEET, BUT I DON`T THINK OF YOU LIKE THAT.
BUT I THINK OF YOU LIKE THAT, HE SAID.
WELL, HOW DESPERATE ARE YOU, I SAID.
I DON`T KNOW, HE SAID.
AND JUST TO PUSH HIM, I SAID WELL, WOULD YOU PAY, LEO? PAY ME FOR SEX?
WHAT DID YOU SAY THAT FOR?
I WAS JUST TRYING TO FREAK HIM OUT, MAKE HIM GO AWAY.
AND WHAT DID HE SAY?

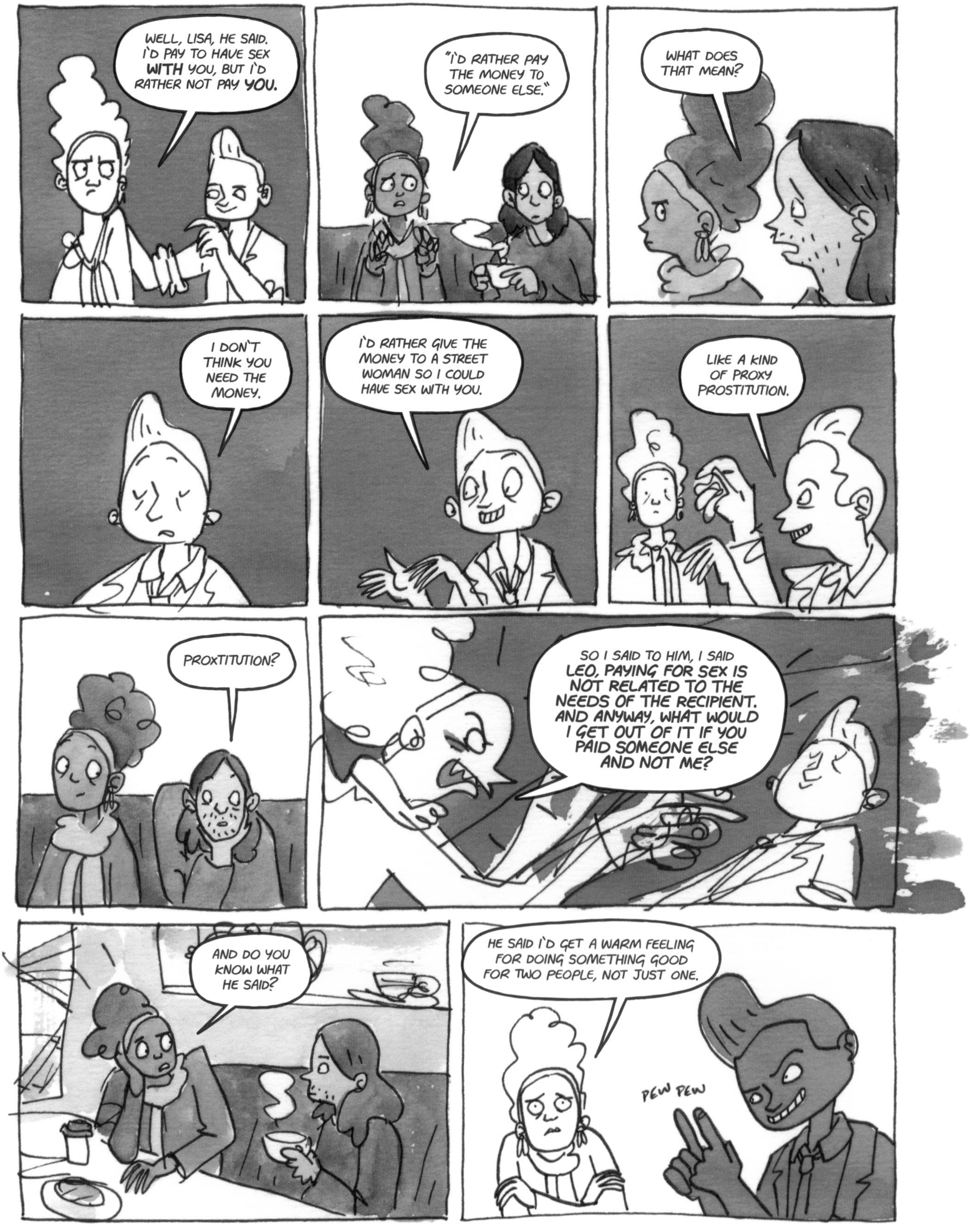
WELL, LISA, HE SAID. I'D PAY TO HAVE SEX **WITH** YOU, BUT I'D RATHER NOT PAY **YOU.**
"I'D RATHER PAY THE MONEY TO SOMEONE ELSE."
WHAT DOES THAT MEAN?
I DON'T THINK YOU NEED THE MONEY.
I'D RATHER GIVE THE MONEY TO A STREET WOMAN SO I COULD HAVE SEX WITH YOU.
LIKE A KIND OF PROXY PROSTITUTION.
PROXTITUTION?
SO I SAID TO HIM, I SAID **LEO, PAYING FOR SEX IS NOT RELATED TO THE NEEDS OF THE RECIPIENT. AND ANYWAY, WHAT WOULD I GET OUT OF IT IF YOU PAID SOMEONE ELSE AND NOT ME?**
AND DO YOU KNOW WHAT HE SAID?
HE SAID I'D GET A WARM FEELING FOR DOING SOMETHING GOOD FOR TWO PEOPLE, NOT JUST ONE.
PEW PEW

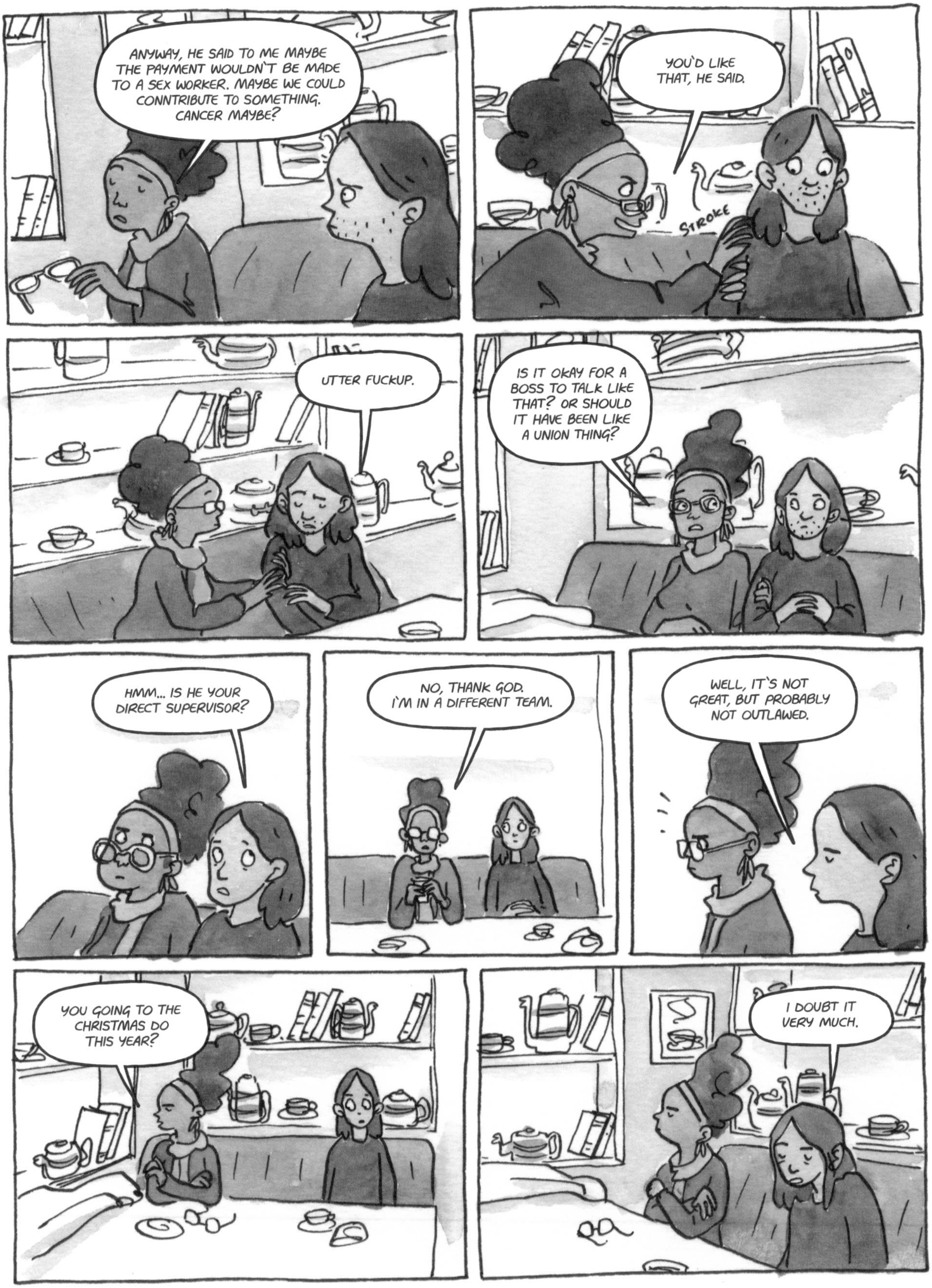
ANYWAY, HE SAID TO ME MAYBE THE PAYMENT WOULDN'T BE MADE TO A SEX WORKER. MAYBE WE COULD CONNTRIBUTE TO SOMETHING. CANCER MAYBE?
YOU'D LIKE THAT, HE SAID.
STROKE
UTTER FUCKUP.
IS IT OKAY FOR A BOSS TO TALK LIKE THAT? OR SHOULD IT HAVE BEEN LIKE A UNION THING?
HMM... IS HE YOUR DIRECT SUPERVISOR?
NO, THANK GOD. I'M IN A DIFFERENT TEAM.
WELL, IT'S NOT GREAT, BUT PROBABLY NOT OUTLAWED.
YOU GOING TO THE CHRISTMAS DO THIS YEAR?
I DOUBT IT VERY MUCH.

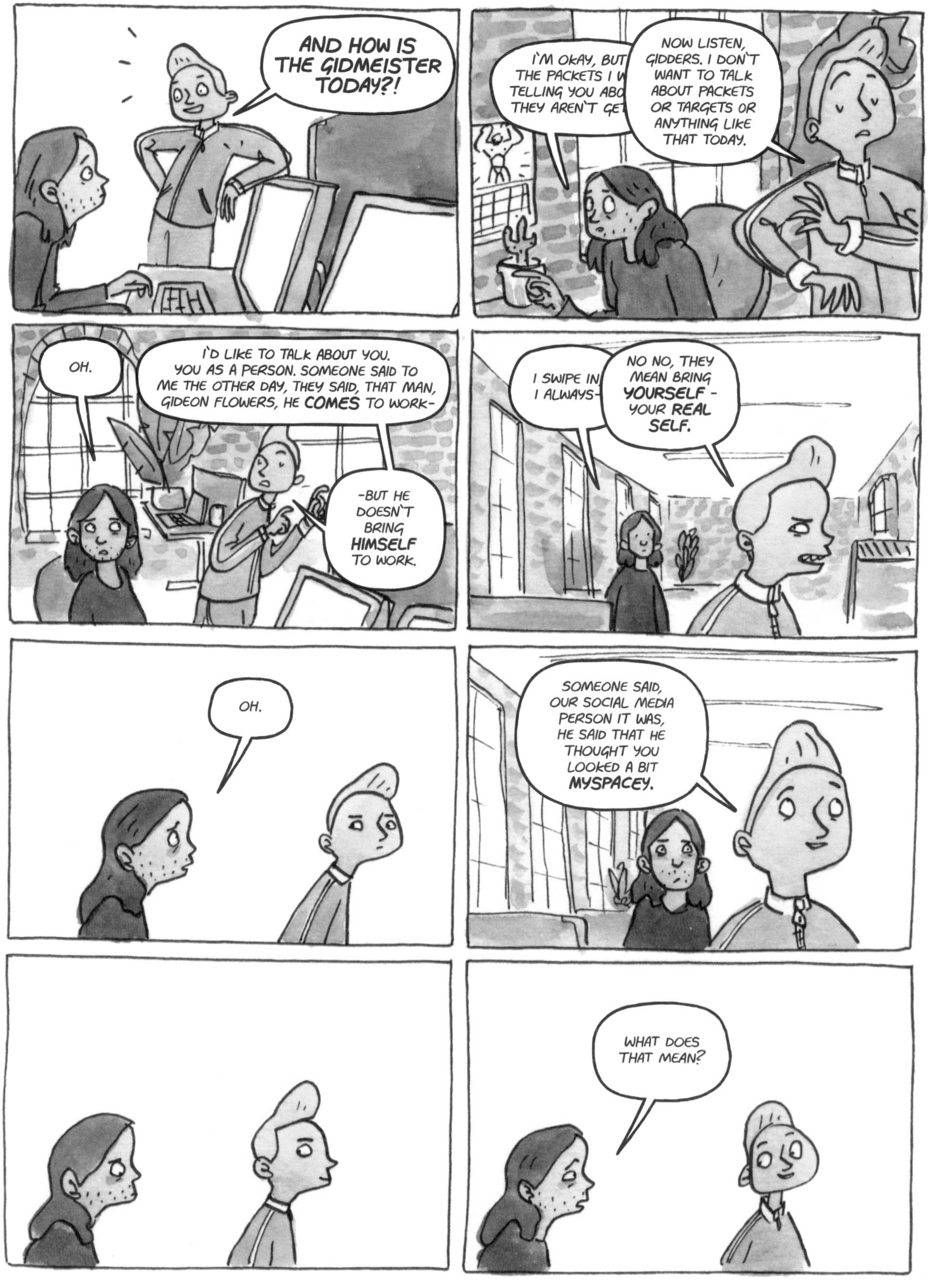
AND HOW IS THE GIDMEISTER TODAY?!
I'M OKAY, BUT THE PACKETS I W TELLING YOU ABO THEY AREN'T GE
NOW LISTEN, GIDDERS. I DON'T WANT TO TALK ABOUT PACKETS OR TARGETS OR ANYTHING LIKE THAT TODAY.
OH.
I'D LIKE TO TALK ABOUT YOU. YOU AS A PERSON. SOMEONE SAID TO ME THE OTHER DAY, THEY SAID, THAT MAN, GIDEON FLOWERS, HE COMES TO WORK-
-BUT HE DOESN'T BRING HIMSELF TO WORK.
I SWIPE IN I ALWAYS-
NO NO, THEY MEAN BRING YOURSELF - YOUR REAL SELF.
OH.
SOMEONE SAID, OUR SOCIAL MEDIA PERSON IT WAS, HE SAID THAT HE THOUGHT YOU LOOKED A BIT MYSPACEY.
WHAT DOES THAT MEAN?

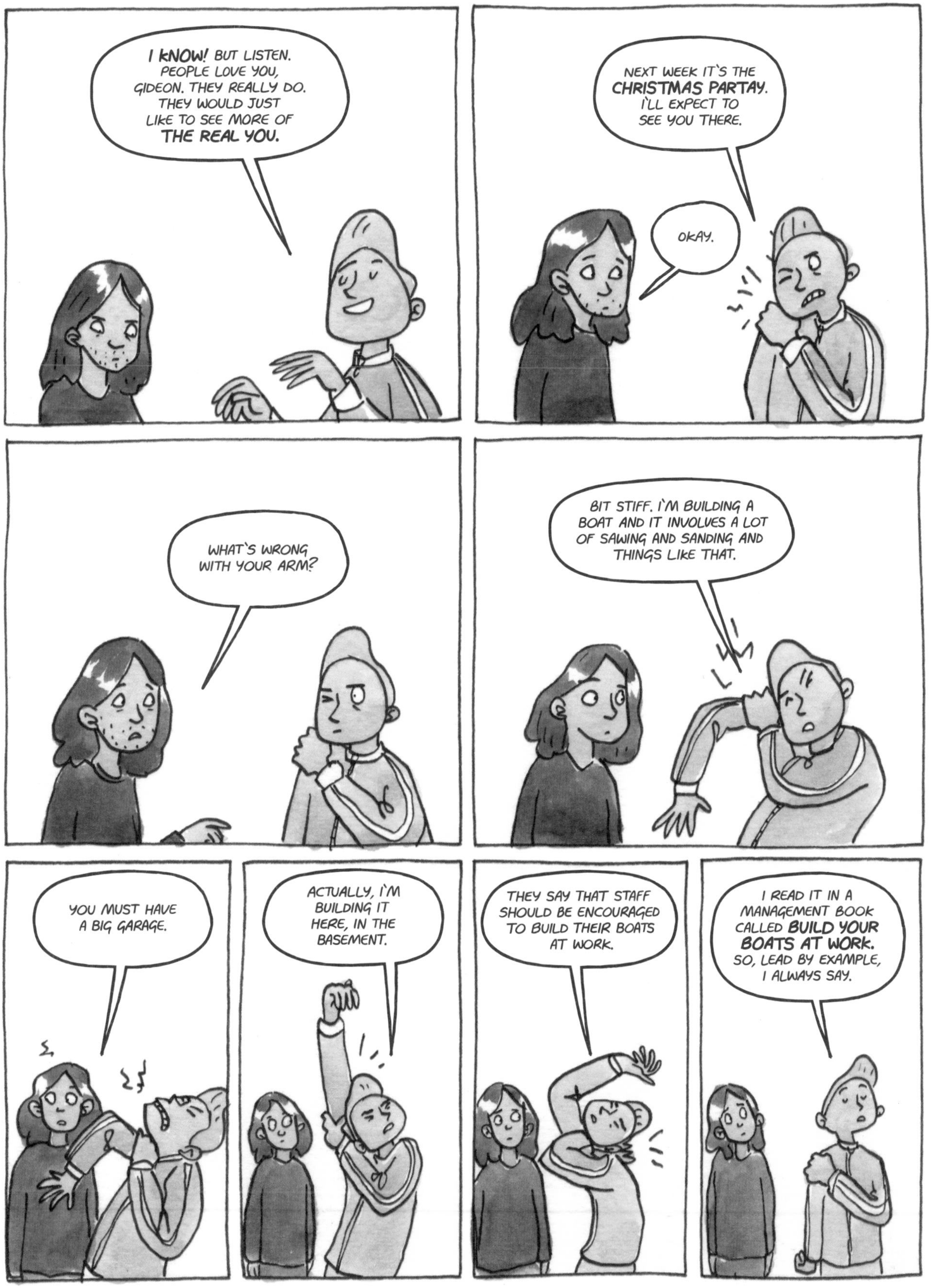
I KNOW! BUT LISTEN. PEOPLE LOVE YOU, GIDEON. THEY REALLY DO. THEY WOULD JUST LIKE TO SEE MORE OF THE REAL YOU.
NEXT WEEK IT'S THE CHRISTMAS PARTAY. I'LL EXPECT TO SEE YOU THERE.
OKAY.
WHAT'S WRONG WITH YOUR ARM?
BIT STIFF. I'M BUILDING A BOAT AND IT INVOLVES A LOT OF SAWING AND SANDING AND THINGS LIKE THAT.
YOU MUST HAVE A BIG GARAGE.
ACTUALLY, I'M BUILDING IT HERE, IN THE BASEMENT.
THEY SAY THAT STAFF SHOULD BE ENCOURAGED TO BUILD THEIR BOATS AT WORK.
I READ IT IN A MANAGEMENT BOOK CALLED BUILD YOUR BOATS AT WORK. SO, LEAD BY EXAMPLE, I ALWAYS SAY.

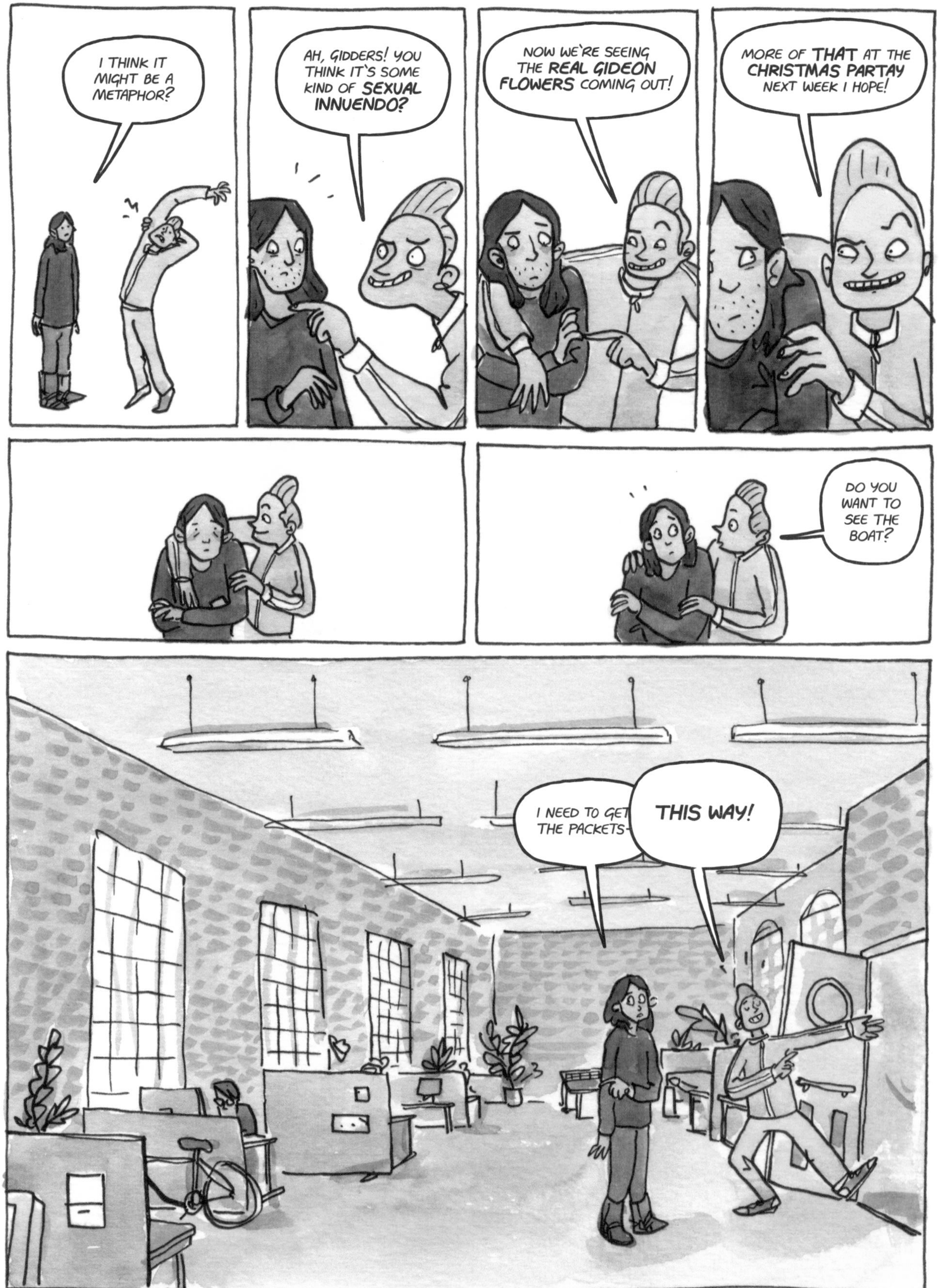
I THINK IT MIGHT BE A METAPHOR?
AH, GIDDERS! YOU THINK IT'S SOME KIND OF SEXUAL INNUENDO?
NOW WE'RE SEEING THE REAL GIDEON FLOWERS COMING OUT!
MORE OF THAT AT THE CHRISTMAS PARTAY NEXT WEEK I HOPE!
DO YOU WANT TO SEE THE BOAT?
I NEED TO GET THE PACKETS-
THIS WAY!

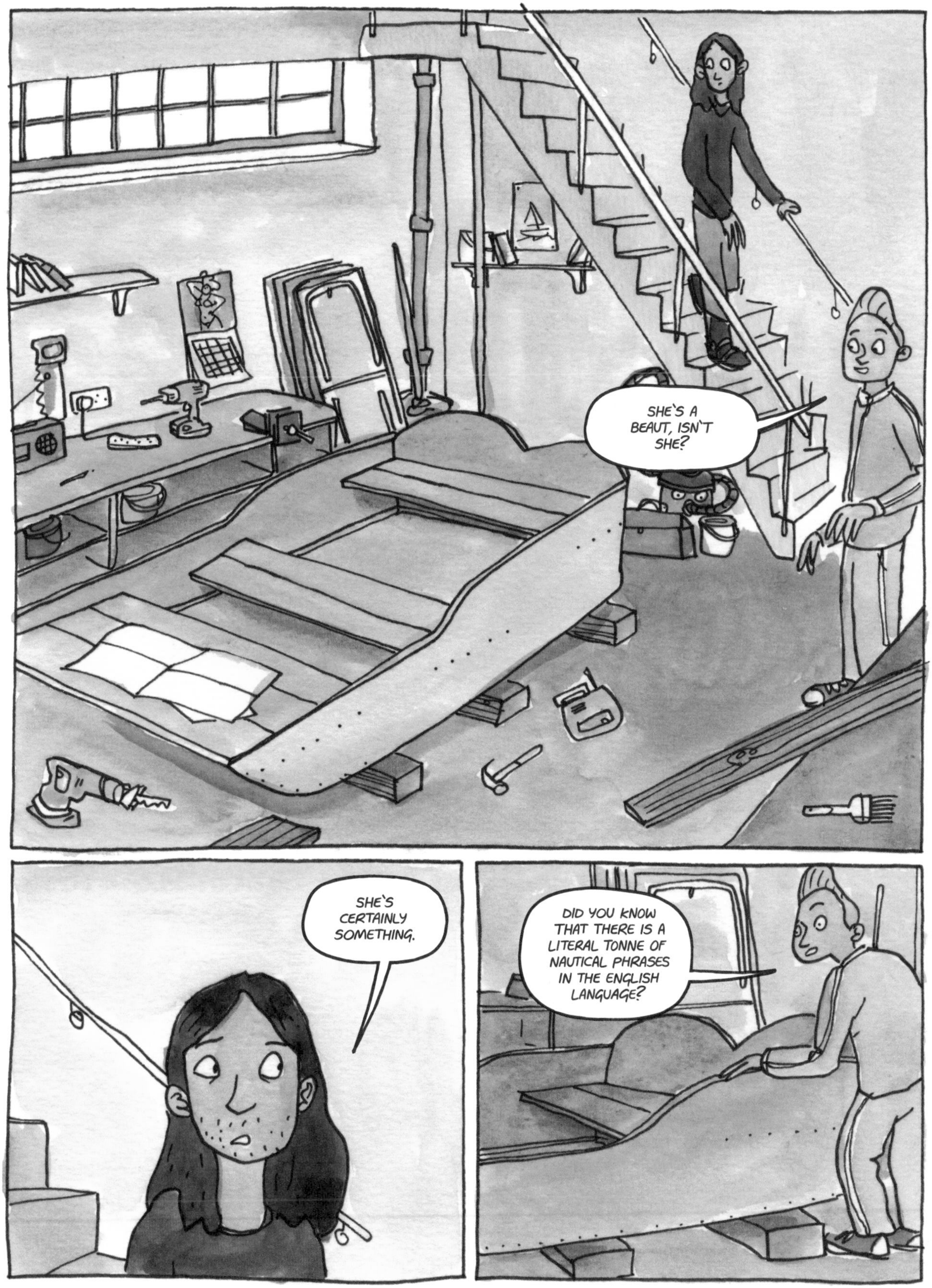
SHE'S A BEAUT, ISN'T SHE?
SHE'S CERTAINLY SOMETHING.
DID YOU KNOW THAT THERE IS A LITERAL TONNE OF NAUTICAL PHRASES IN THE ENGLISH LANGUAGE?

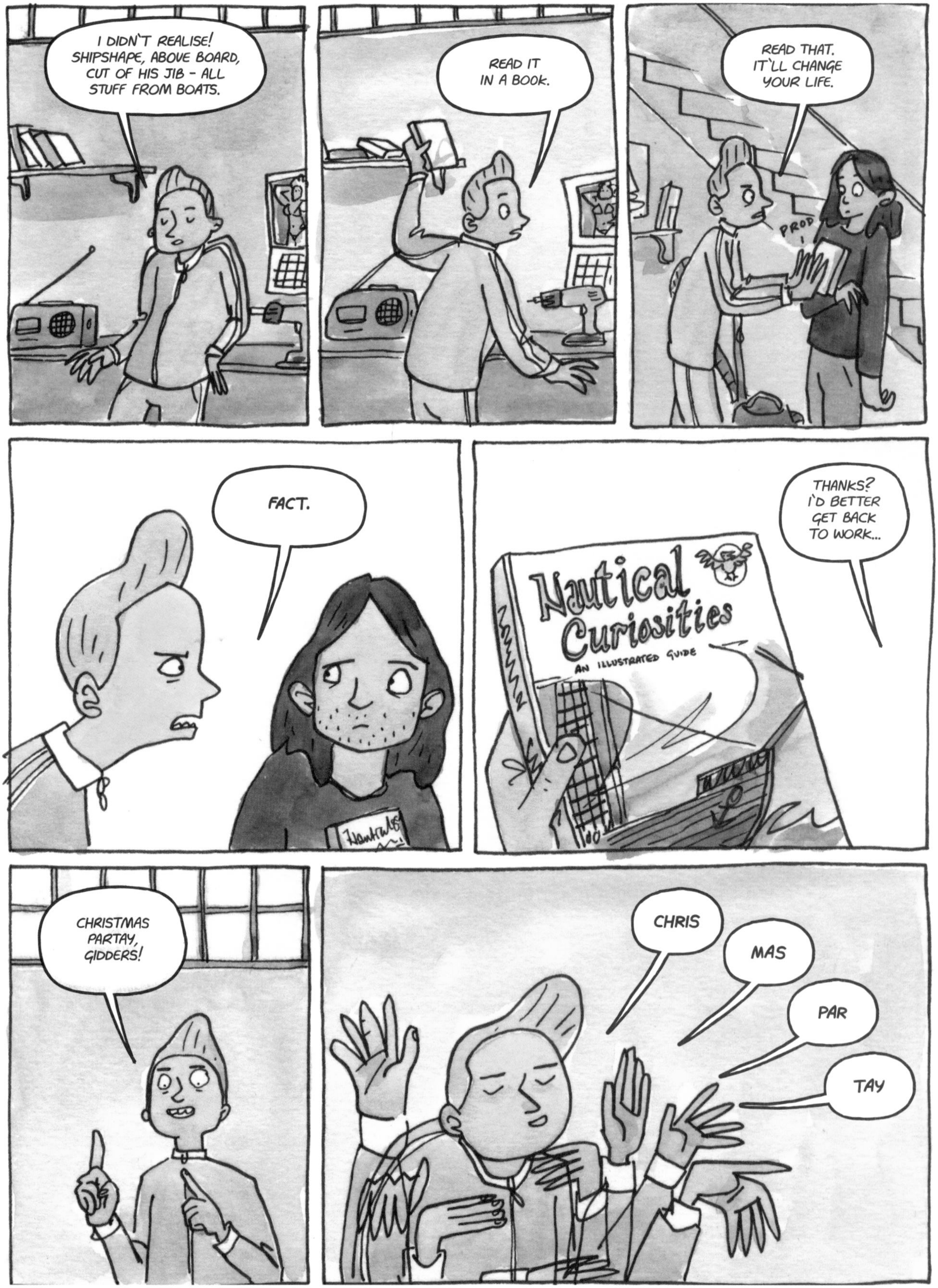
I DIDN'T REALISE! SHIPSHAPE, ABOVE BOARD, CUT OF HIS JIB - ALL STUFF FROM BOATS.
READ IT IN A BOOK.
READ THAT. IT'LL CHANGE YOUR LIFE.
PROD
FACT.
THANKS? I'D BETTER GET BACK TO WORK...
Nautical Curiosities
AN ILLUSTRATED GUIDE
CHRISTMAS PARTAY, GIDDERS!
CHRIS
MAS
PAR
TAY

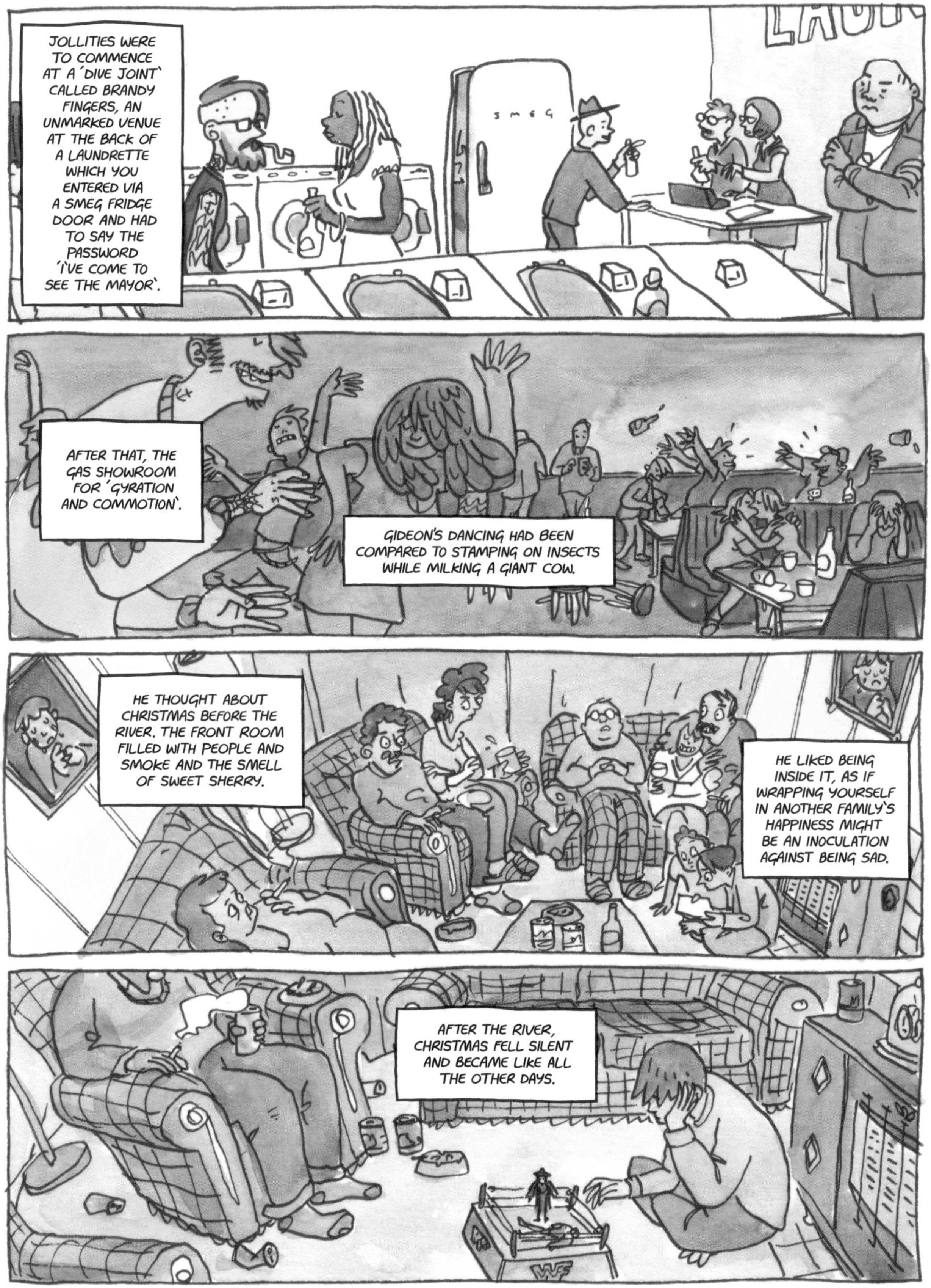
JOLLITIES WERE TO COMMENCE AT A 'DIVE JOINT' CALLED BRANDY FINGERS, AN UNMARKED VENUE AT THE BACK OF A LAUNDRETTE WHICH YOU ENTERED VIA A SMEG FRIDGE DOOR AND HAD TO SAY THE PASSWORD 'I'VE COME TO SEE THE MAYOR'.
SMEG
AFTER THAT, THE GAS SHOWROOM FOR 'GYRATION AND COMMOTION'.
GIDEON'S DANCING HAD BEEN COMPARED TO STAMPING ON INSECTS WHILE MILKING A GIANT COW.
HE THOUGHT ABOUT CHRISTMAS BEFORE THE RIVER. THE FRONT ROOM FILLED WITH PEOPLE AND SMOKE AND THE SMELL OF SWEET SHERRY.
HE LIKED BEING INSIDE IT, AS IF WRAPPING YOURSELF IN ANOTHER FAMILY'S HAPPINESS MIGHT BE AN INOCULATION AGAINST BEING SAD.
AFTER THE RIVER, CHRISTMAS FELL SILENT AND BECAME LIKE ALL THE OTHER DAYS.

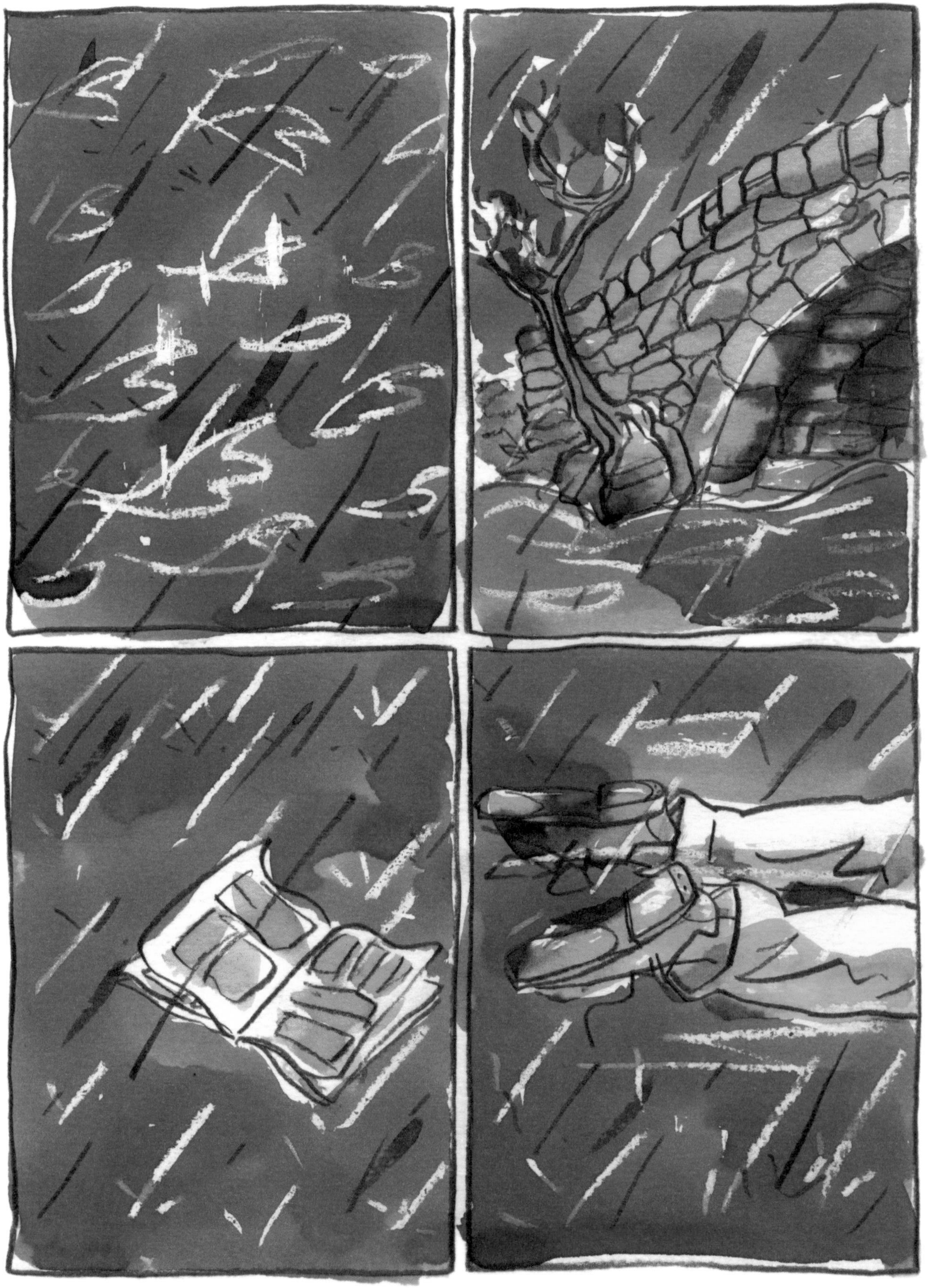

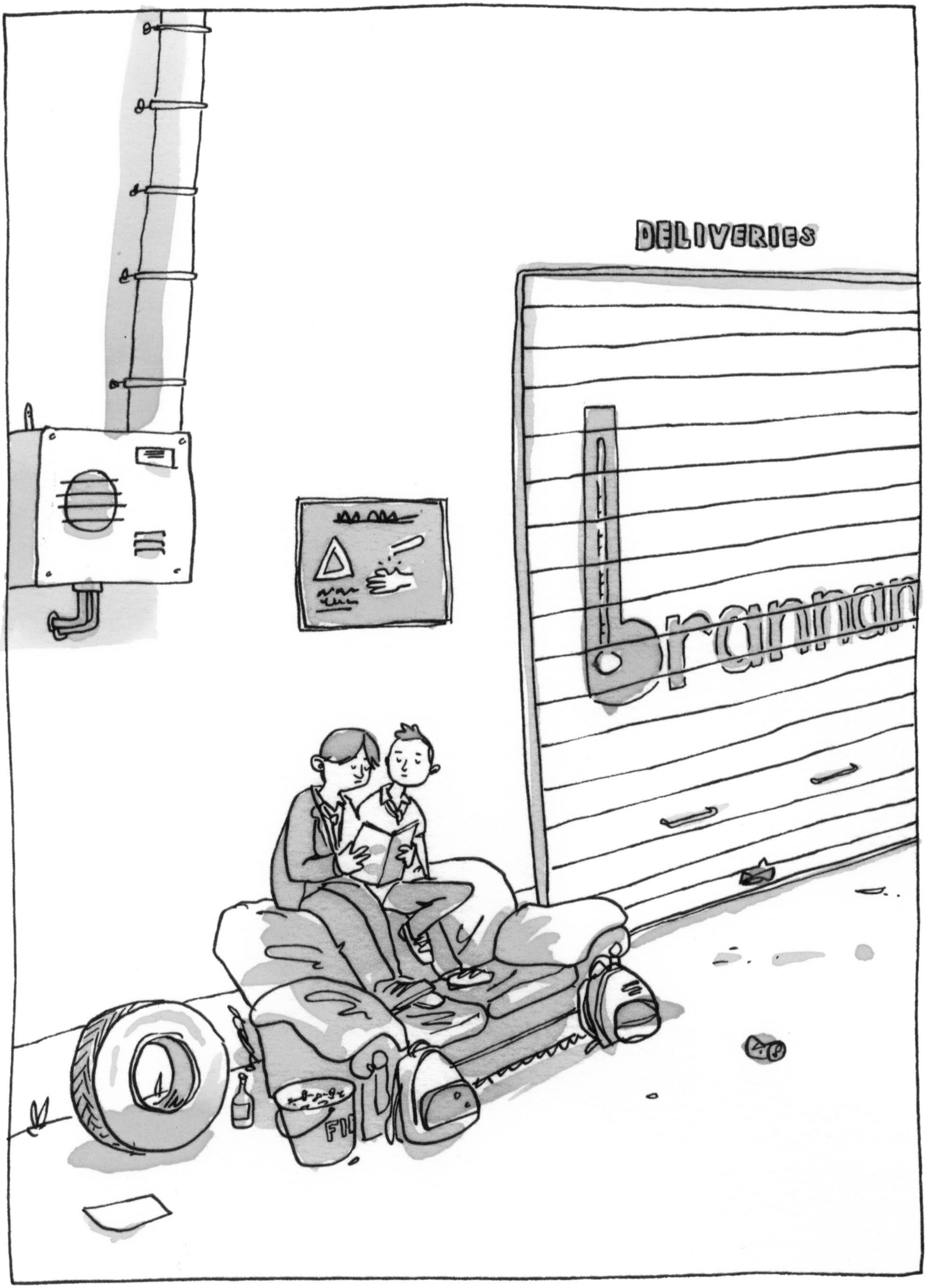
DELIVERIES

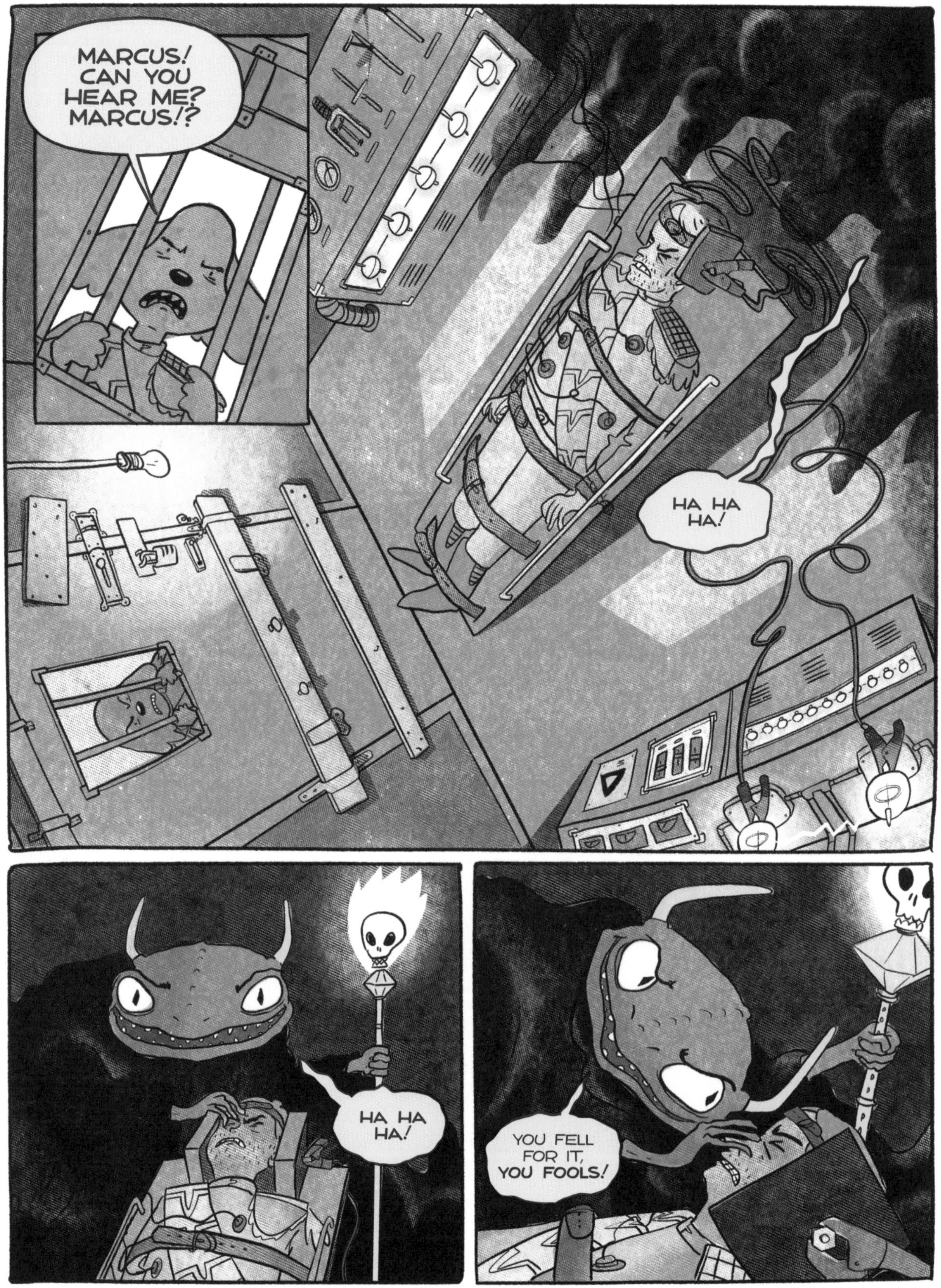
MARCUS! CAN YOU HEAR ME? MARCUS!?
HA HA HA!
HA HA HA!
YOU FELL FOR IT, **YOU FOOLS!**

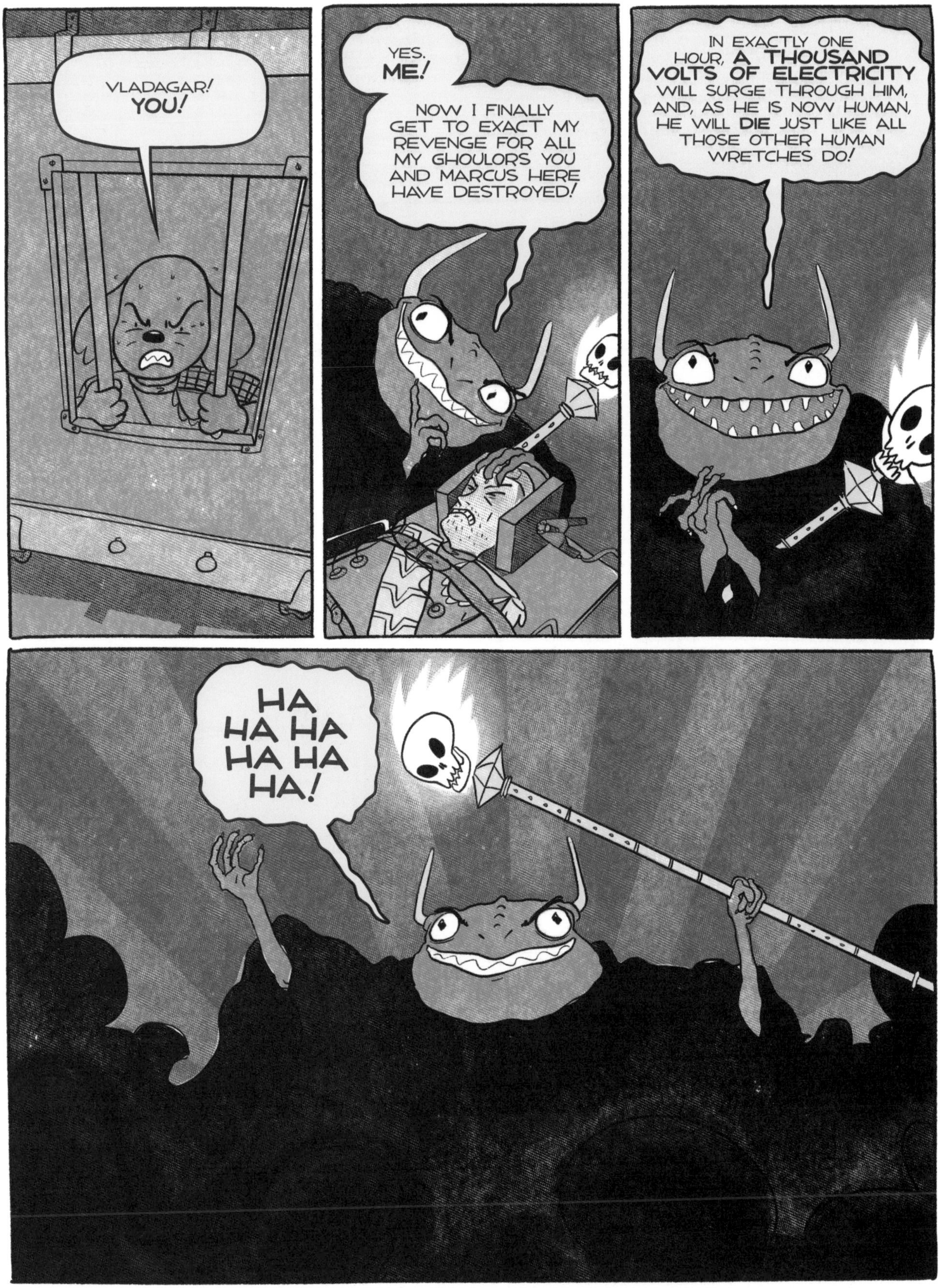
VLADAGAR! YOU!
YES. ME!
NOW I FINALLY GET TO EXACT MY REVENGE FOR ALL MY GHOULORS YOU AND MARCUS HERE HAVE DESTROYED!
IN EXACTLY ONE HOUR, A THOUSAND VOLTS OF ELECTRICITY WILL SURGE THROUGH HIM, AND, AS HE IS NOW HUMAN, HE WILL DIE JUST LIKE ALL THOSE OTHER HUMAN WRETCHES DO!
HA HA HA HA HA HA HA!

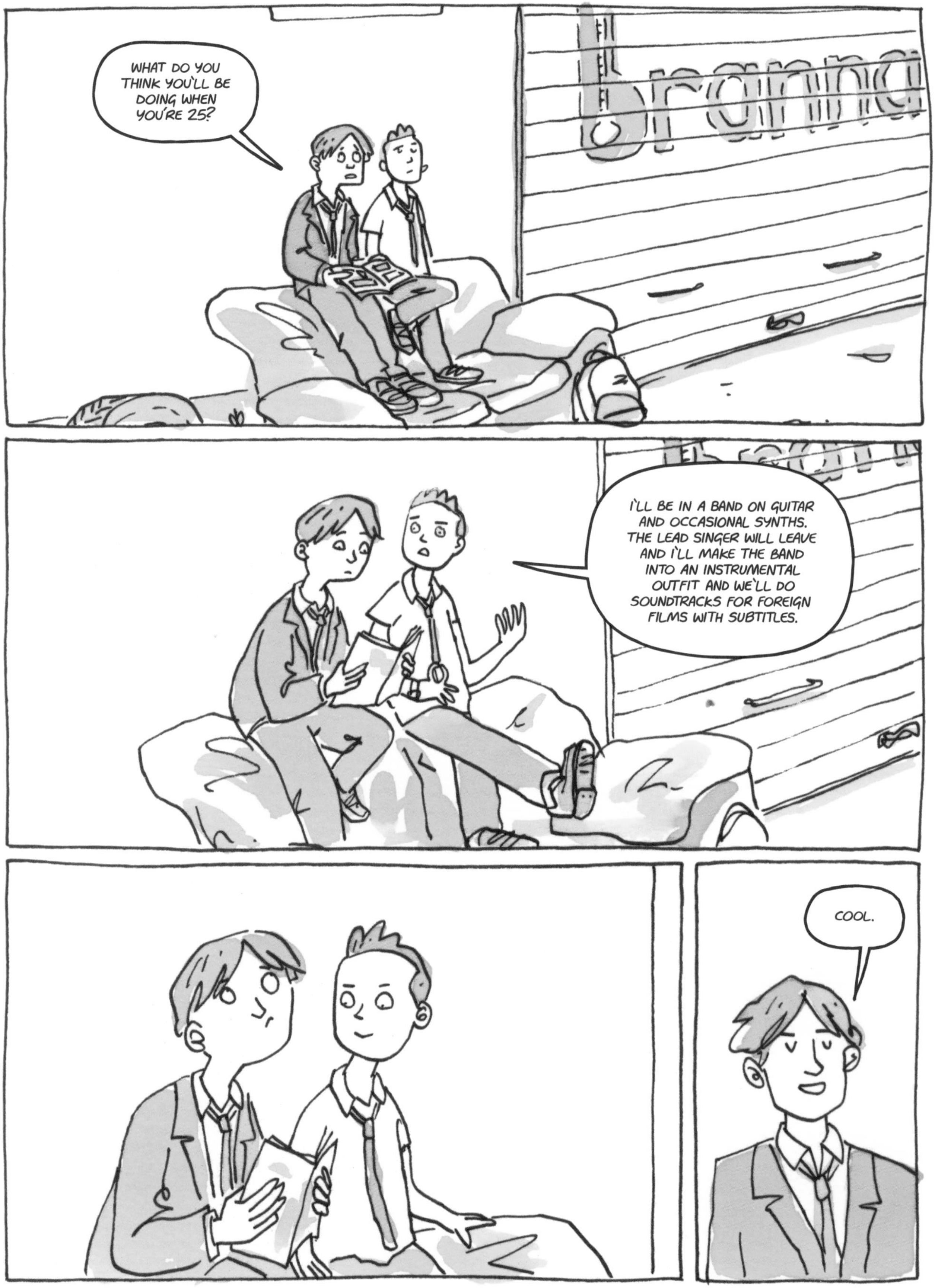
WHAT DO YOU THINK YOU'LL BE DOING WHEN YOU'RE 25?
I'LL BE IN A BAND ON GUITAR AND OCCASIONAL SYNTHS. THE LEAD SINGER WILL LEAVE AND I'LL MAKE THE BAND INTO AN INSTRUMENTAL OUTFIT AND WE'LL DO SOUNDTRACKS FOR FOREIGN FILMS WITH SUBTITLES.
COOL.

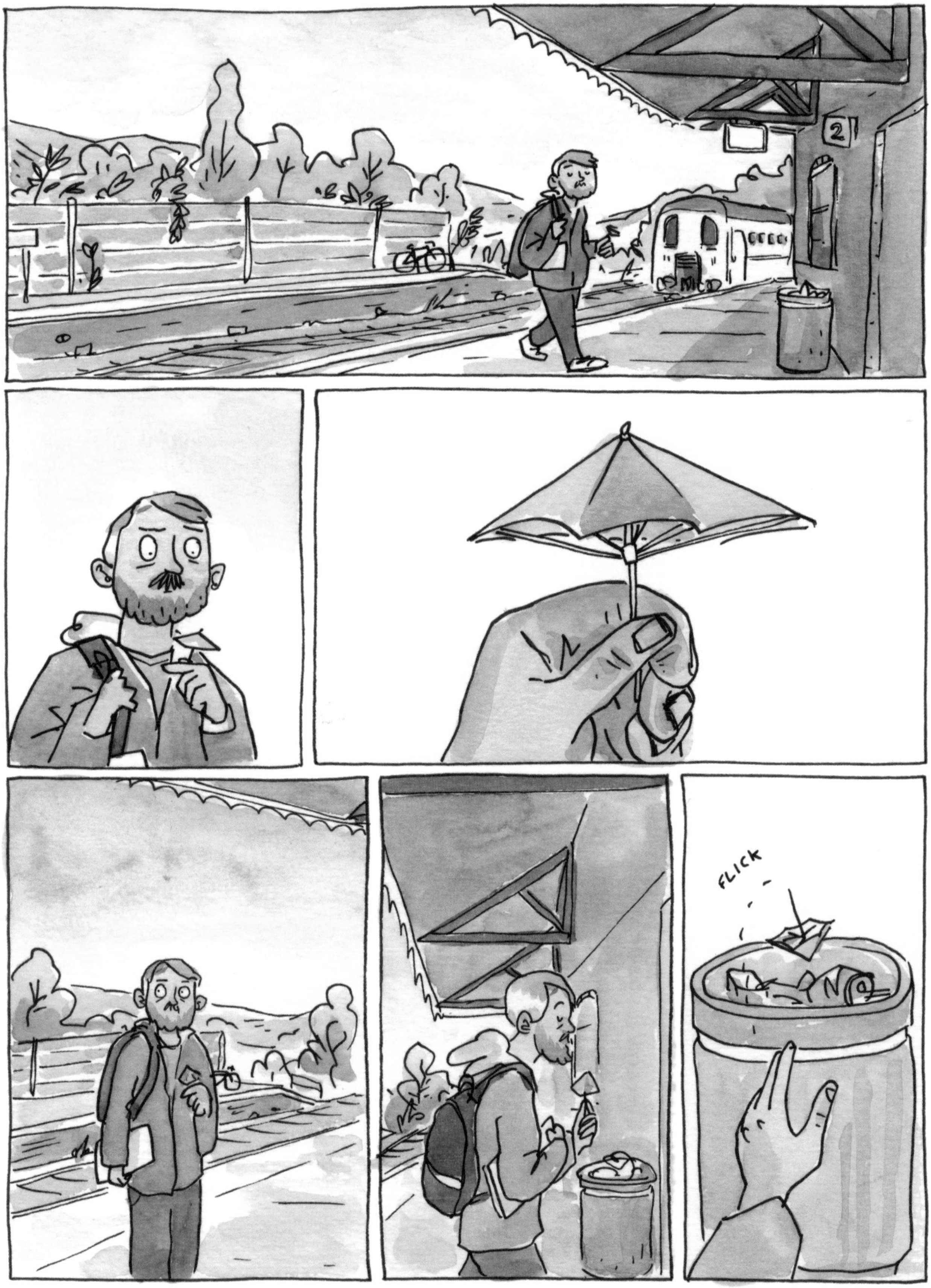
2
FLICK

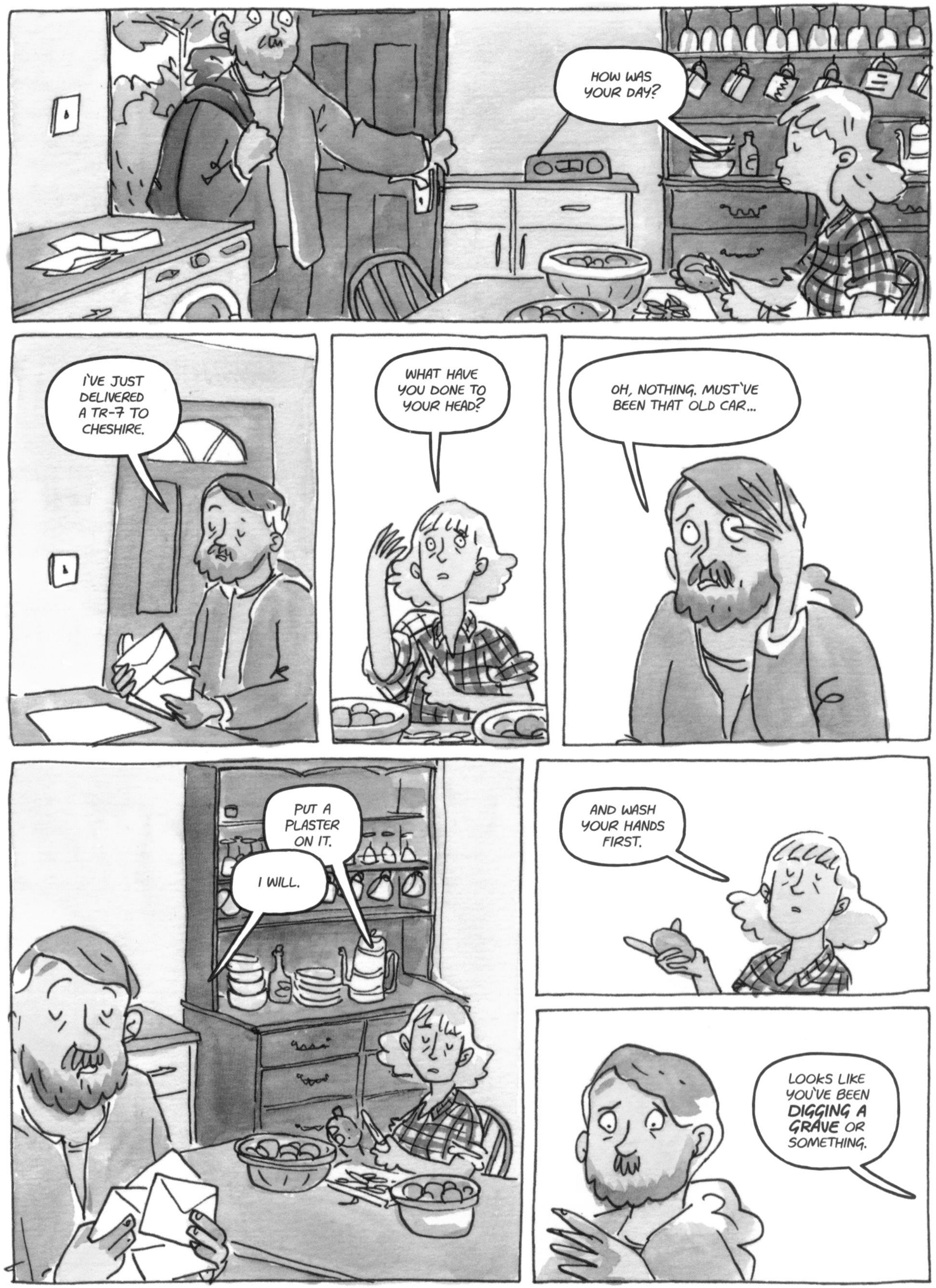

HOW WAS YOUR DAY?
I'VE JUST DELIVERED A TR-7 TO CHESHIRE.
WHAT HAVE YOU DONE TO YOUR HEAD?
OH, NOTHING. MUST'VE BEEN THAT OLD CAR...
PUT A PLASTER ON IT.
I WILL.
AND WASH YOUR HANDS FIRST.
LOOKS LIKE YOU'VE BEEN **DIGGING A GRAVE** OR SOMETHING.

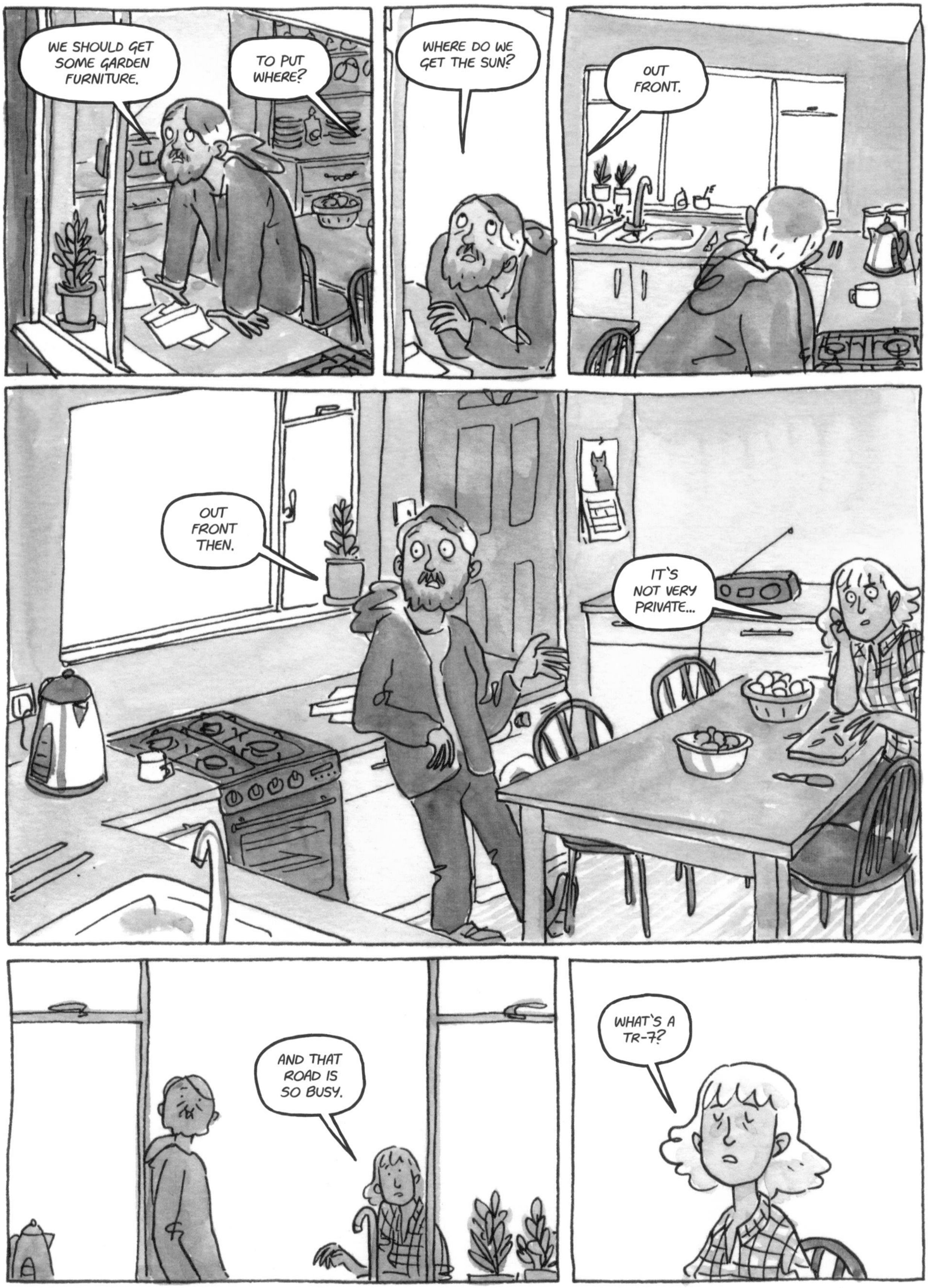
WE SHOULD GET SOME GARDEN FURNITURE.
TO PUT WHERE?
WHERE DO WE GET THE SUN?
OUT FRONT.
OUT FRONT THEN.
IT'S NOT VERY PRIVATE...
AND THAT ROAD IS SO BUSY.
WHAT'S A TR-7?

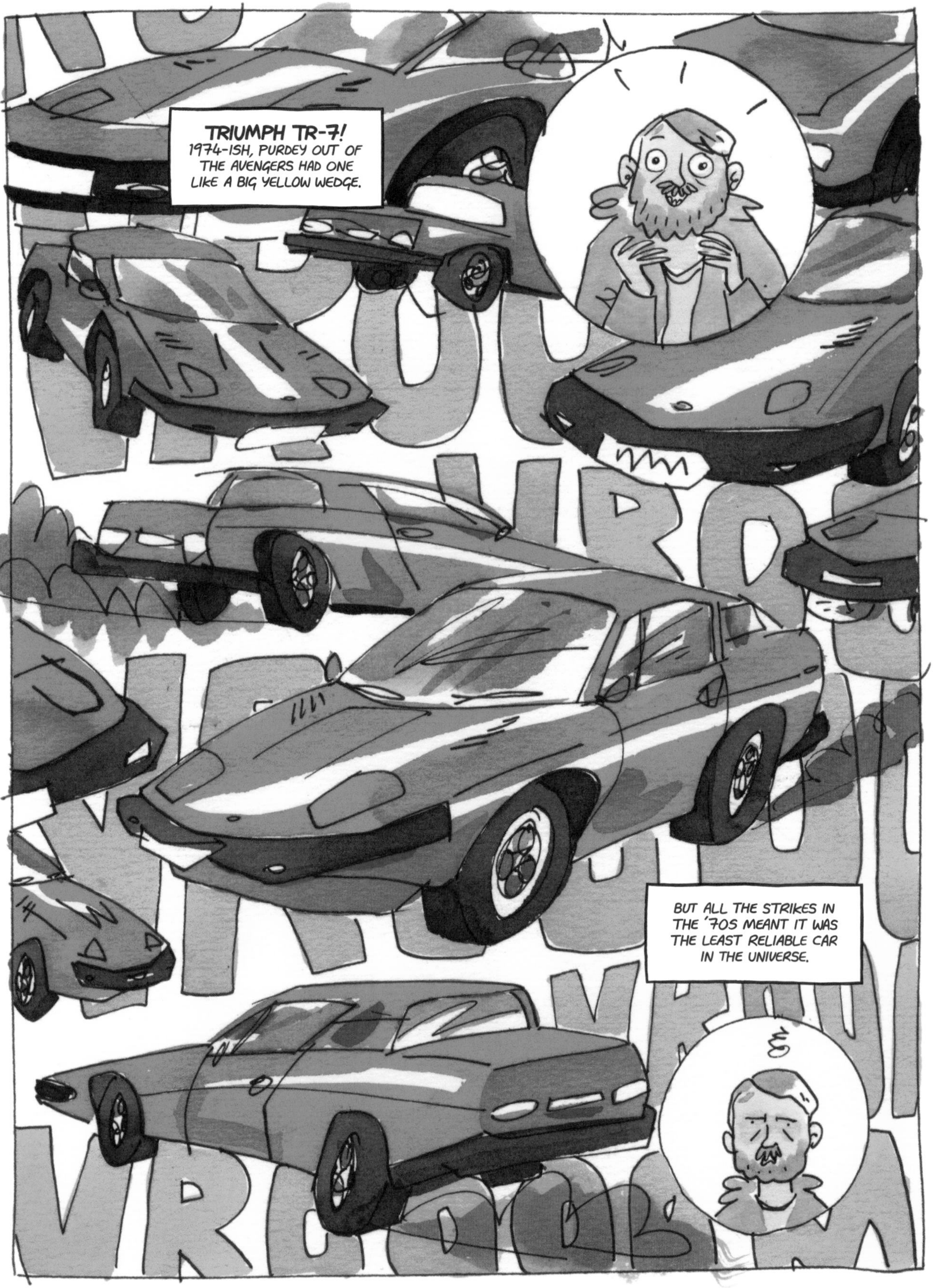
TRIUMPH TR-7!
1974-ISH, PURDEY OUT OF THE AVENGERS HAD ONE LIKE A BIG YELLOW WEDGE.
BUT ALL THE STRIKES IN THE '70S MEANT IT WAS THE LEAST RELIABLE CAR IN THE UNIVERSE.

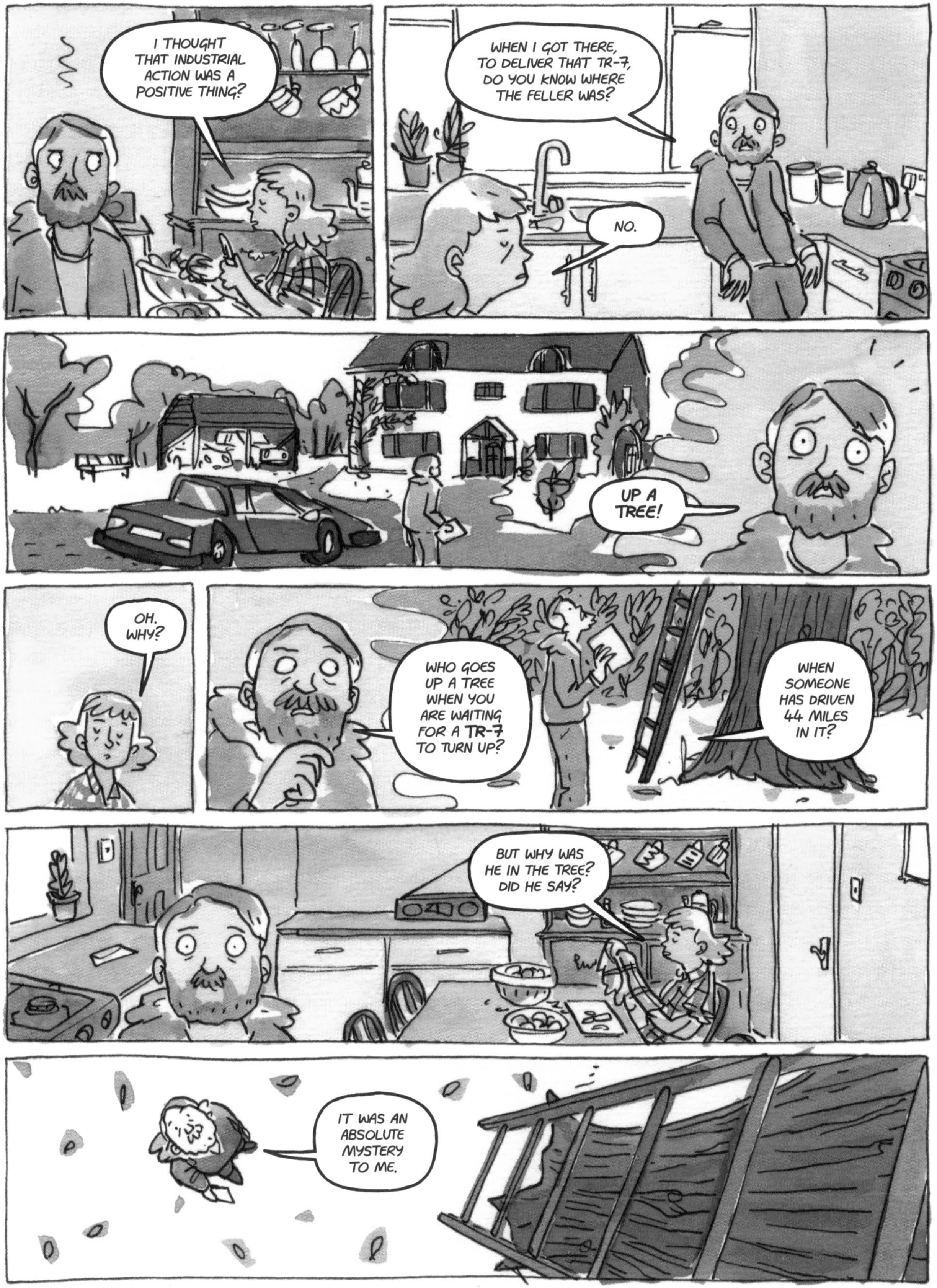
I THOUGHT THAT INDUSTRIAL ACTION WAS A POSITIVE THING?
WHEN I GOT THERE, TO DELIVER THAT TR-7, DO YOU KNOW WHERE THE FELLER WAS?
NO.
UP A TREE!
OH. WHY?
WHO GOES UP A TREE WHEN YOU ARE WAITING FOR A TR-7 TO TURN UP?
WHEN SOMEONE HAS DRIVEN 44 MILES IN IT?
BUT WHY WAS HE IN THE TREE? DID HE SAY?
IT WAS AN ABSOLUTE MYSTERY TO ME.

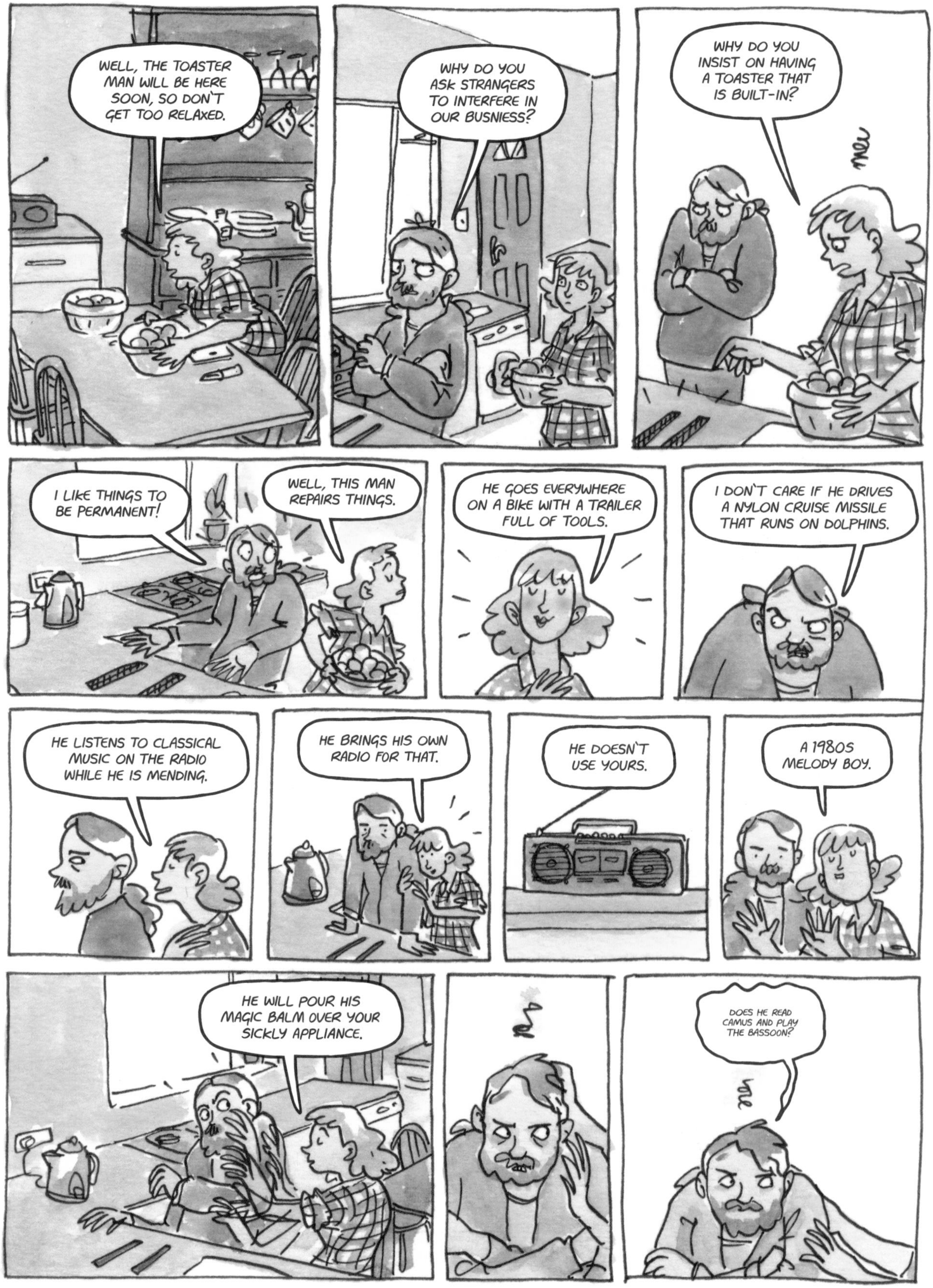
WELL, THE TOASTER MAN WILL BE HERE SOON, SO DON'T GET TOO RELAXED.
WHY DO YOU ASK STRANGERS TO INTERFERE IN OUR BUSNIESS?
WHY DO YOU INSIST ON HAVING A TOASTER THAT IS BUILT-IN?
I LIKE THINGS TO BE PERMANENT!
WELL, THIS MAN REPAIRS THINGS.
HE GOES EVERYWHERE ON A BIKE WITH A TRAILER FULL OF TOOLS.
I DON'T CARE IF HE DRIVES A NYLON CRUISE MISSILE THAT RUNS ON DOLPHINS.
HE LISTENS TO CLASSICAL MUSIC ON THE RADIO WHILE HE IS MENDING.
HE BRINGS HIS OWN RADIO FOR THAT.
HE DOESN'T USE YOURS.
A 1980S MELODY BOY.
HE WILL POUR HIS MAGIC BALM OVER YOUR SICKLY APPLIANCE.
DOES HE READ CAMUS AND PLAY THE BASSOON?

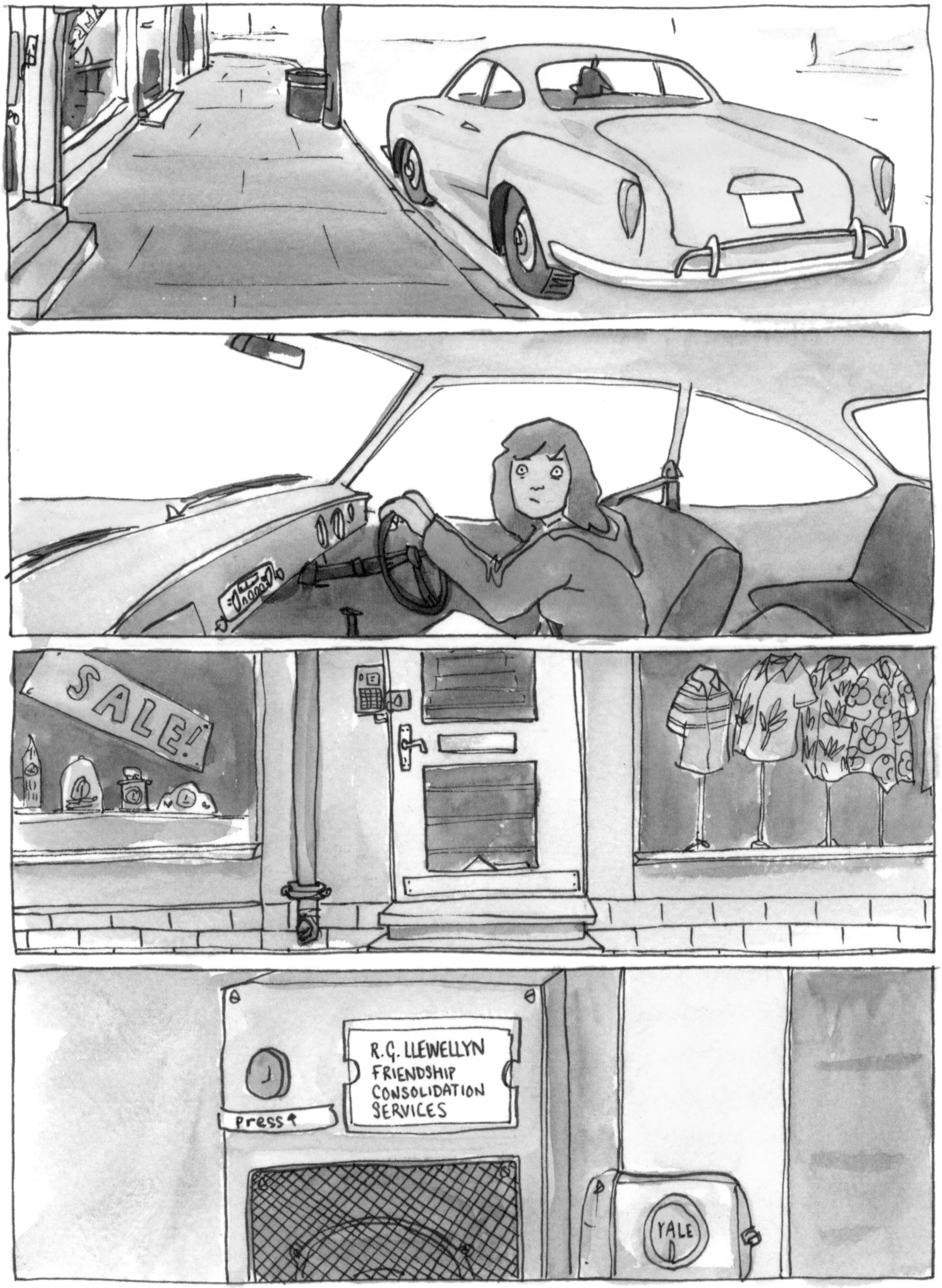
SALE!
R.G. LLEWELLYN
FRIENDSHIP
CONSOLIDATION
SERVICES
press
YALE

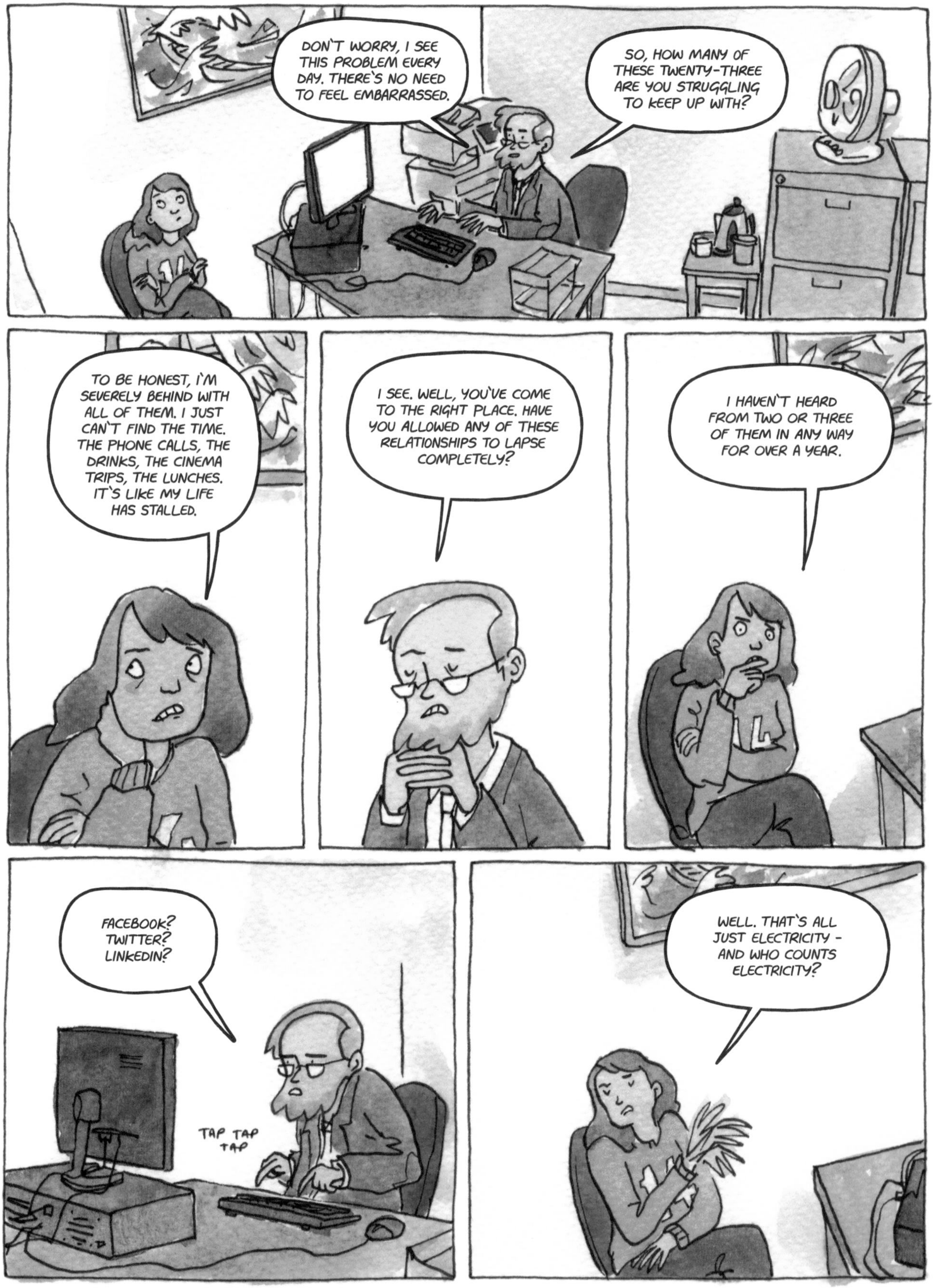
DON'T WORRY, I SEE THIS PROBLEM EVERY DAY. THERE'S NO NEED TO FEEL EMBARRASSED.
SO, HOW MANY OF THESE TWENTY-THREE ARE YOU STRUGGLING TO KEEP UP WITH?
TO BE HONEST, I'M SEVERELY BEHIND WITH ALL OF THEM. I JUST CAN'T FIND THE TIME. THE PHONE CALLS, THE DRINKS, THE CINEMA TRIPS, THE LUNCHES. IT'S LIKE MY LIFE HAS STALLED.
I SEE. WELL, YOU'VE COME TO THE RIGHT PLACE. HAVE YOU ALLOWED ANY OF THESE RELATIONSHIPS TO LAPSE COMPLETELY?
I HAVEN'T HEARD FROM TWO OR THREE OF THEM IN ANY WAY FOR OVER A YEAR.
FACEBOOK? TWITTER? LINKEDIN?
TAP TAP TAP
WELL. THAT'S ALL JUST ELECTRICITY - AND WHO COUNTS ELECTRICITY?

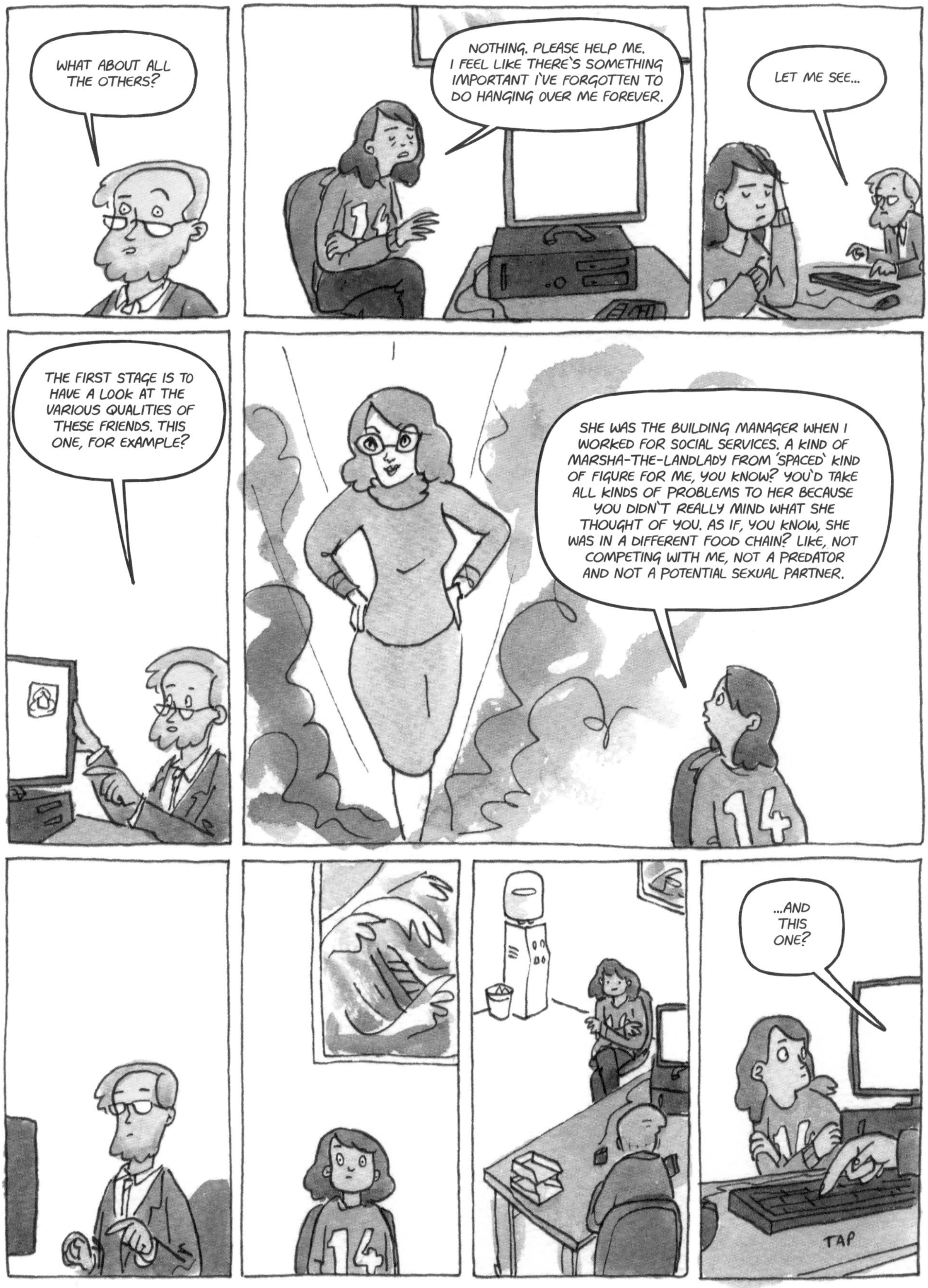

WHAT ABOUT ALL THE OTHERS?
NOTHING. PLEASE HELP ME. I FEEL LIKE THERE'S SOMETHING IMPORTANT I'VE FORGOTTEN TO DO HANGING OVER ME FOREVER.
LET ME SEE...
THE FIRST STAGE IS TO HAVE A LOOK AT THE VARIOUS QUALITIES OF THESE FRIENDS. THIS ONE, FOR EXAMPLE?
SHE WAS THE BUILDING MANAGER WHEN I WORKED FOR SOCIAL SERVICES. A KIND OF MARSHA-THE-LANDLADY FROM 'SPACED' KIND OF FIGURE FOR ME, YOU KNOW? YOU'D TAKE ALL KINDS OF PROBLEMS TO HER BECAUSE YOU DIDN'T REALLY MIND WHAT SHE THOUGHT OF YOU. AS IF, YOU KNOW, SHE WAS IN A DIFFERENT FOOD CHAIN? LIKE, NOT COMPETING WITH ME, NOT A PREDATOR AND NOT A POTENTIAL SEXUAL PARTNER.
...AND THIS ONE?
TAP

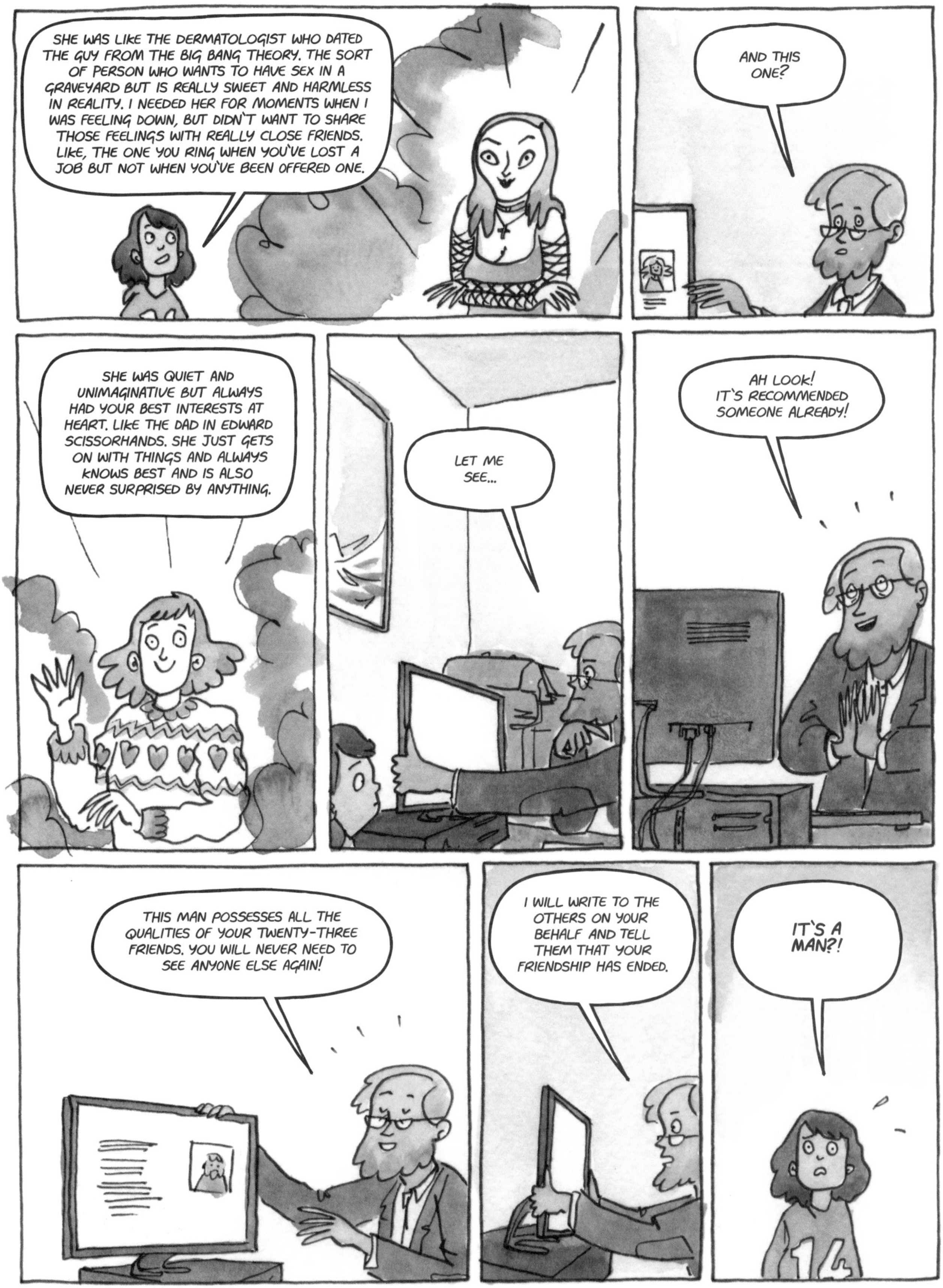
SHE WAS LIKE THE DERMATOLOGIST WHO DATED THE GUY FROM THE BIG BANG THEORY. THE SORT OF PERSON WHO WANTS TO HAVE SEX IN A GRAVEYARD BUT IS REALLY SWEET AND HARMLESS IN REALITY. I NEEDED HER FOR MOMENTS WHEN I WAS FEELING DOWN, BUT DIDN'T WANT TO SHARE THOSE FEELINGS WITH REALLY CLOSE FRIENDS. LIKE, THE ONE YOU RING WHEN YOU'VE LOST A JOB BUT NOT WHEN YOU'VE BEEN OFFERED ONE.
AND THIS ONE?
SHE WAS QUIET AND UNIMAGINATIVE BUT ALWAYS HAD YOUR BEST INTERESTS AT HEART. LIKE THE DAD IN EDWARD SCISSORHANDS. SHE JUST GETS ON WITH THINGS AND ALWAYS KNOWS BEST AND IS ALSO NEVER SURPRISED BY ANYTHING.
LET ME SEE...
AH LOOK! IT'S RECOMMENDED SOMEONE ALREADY!
THIS MAN POSSESSES ALL THE QUALITIES OF YOUR TWENTY-THREE FRIENDS. YOU WILL NEVER NEED TO SEE ANYONE ELSE AGAIN!
I WILL WRITE TO THE OTHERS ON YOUR BEHALF AND TELL THEM THAT YOUR FRIENDSHIP HAS ENDED.
IT'S A MAN?!
14

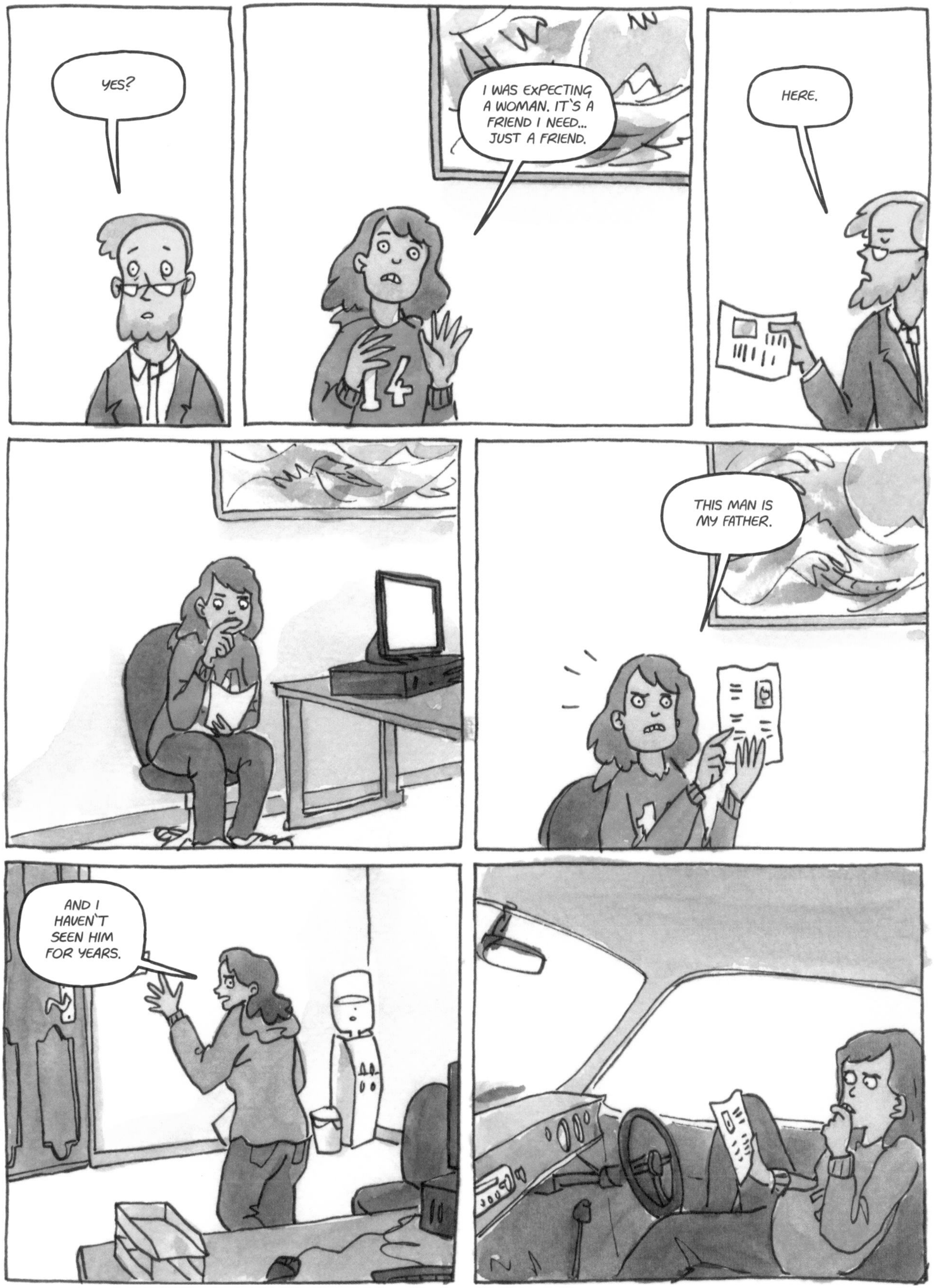
YES?
I WAS EXPECTING A WOMAN. IT`S A FRIEND I NEED... JUST A FRIEND.
HERE.
THIS MAN IS MY FATHER.
AND I HAVEN`T SEEN HIM FOR YEARS.

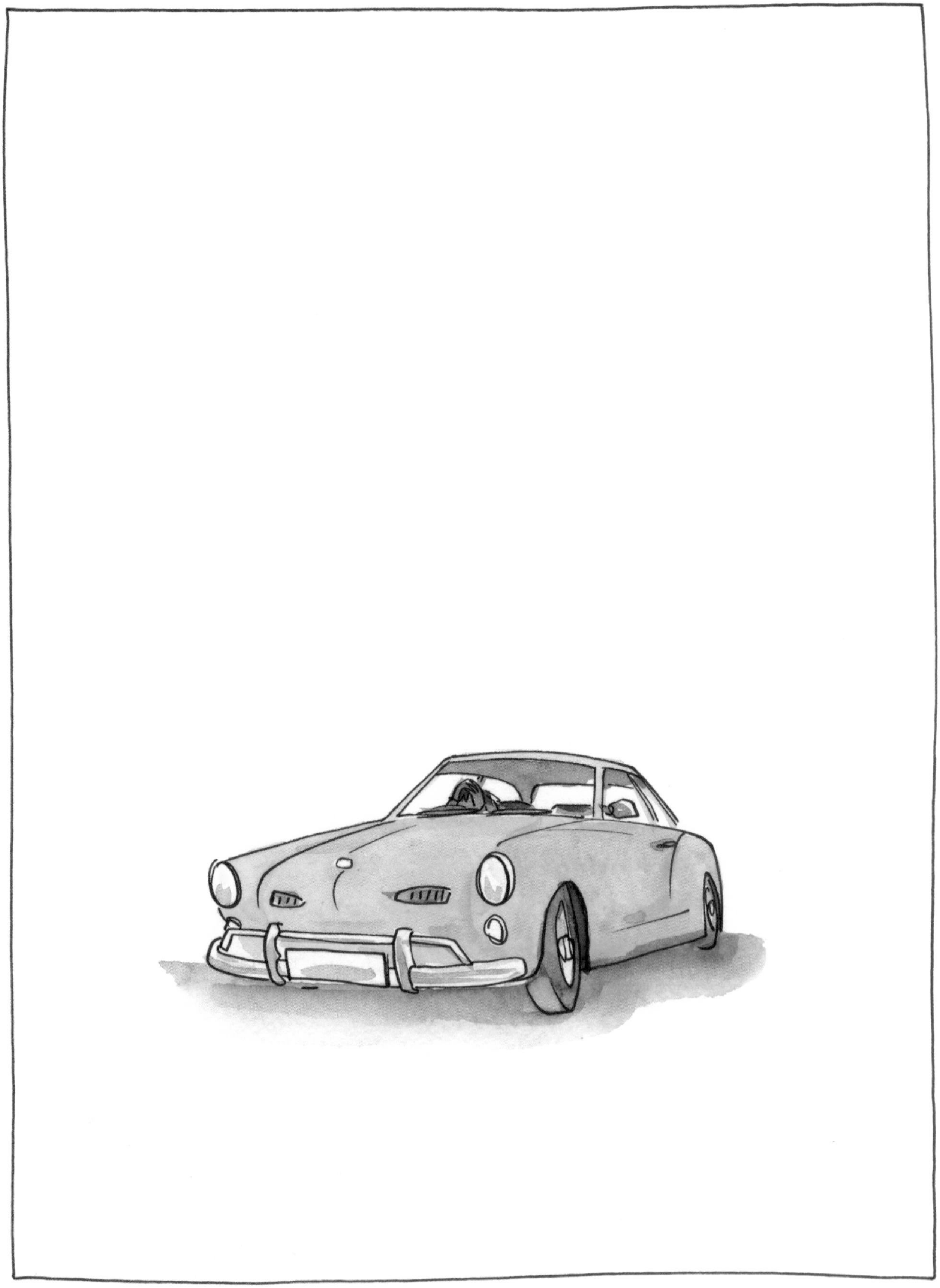

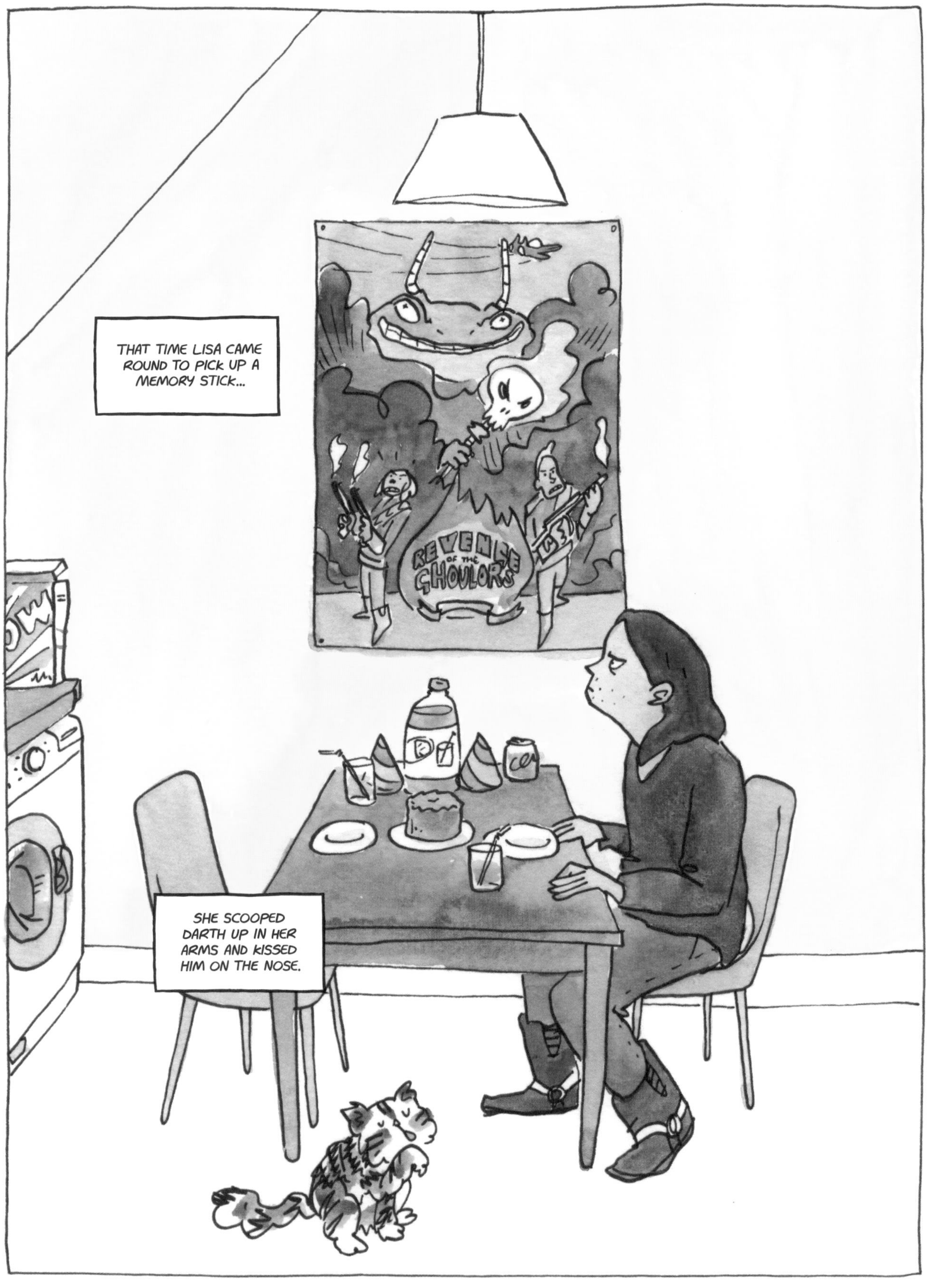
THAT TIME LISA CAME ROUND TO PICK UP A MEMORY STICK...
REVENGE OF THE GHOULORS
SHE SCOOPED DARTH UP IN HER ARMS AND KISSED HIM ON THE NOSE.

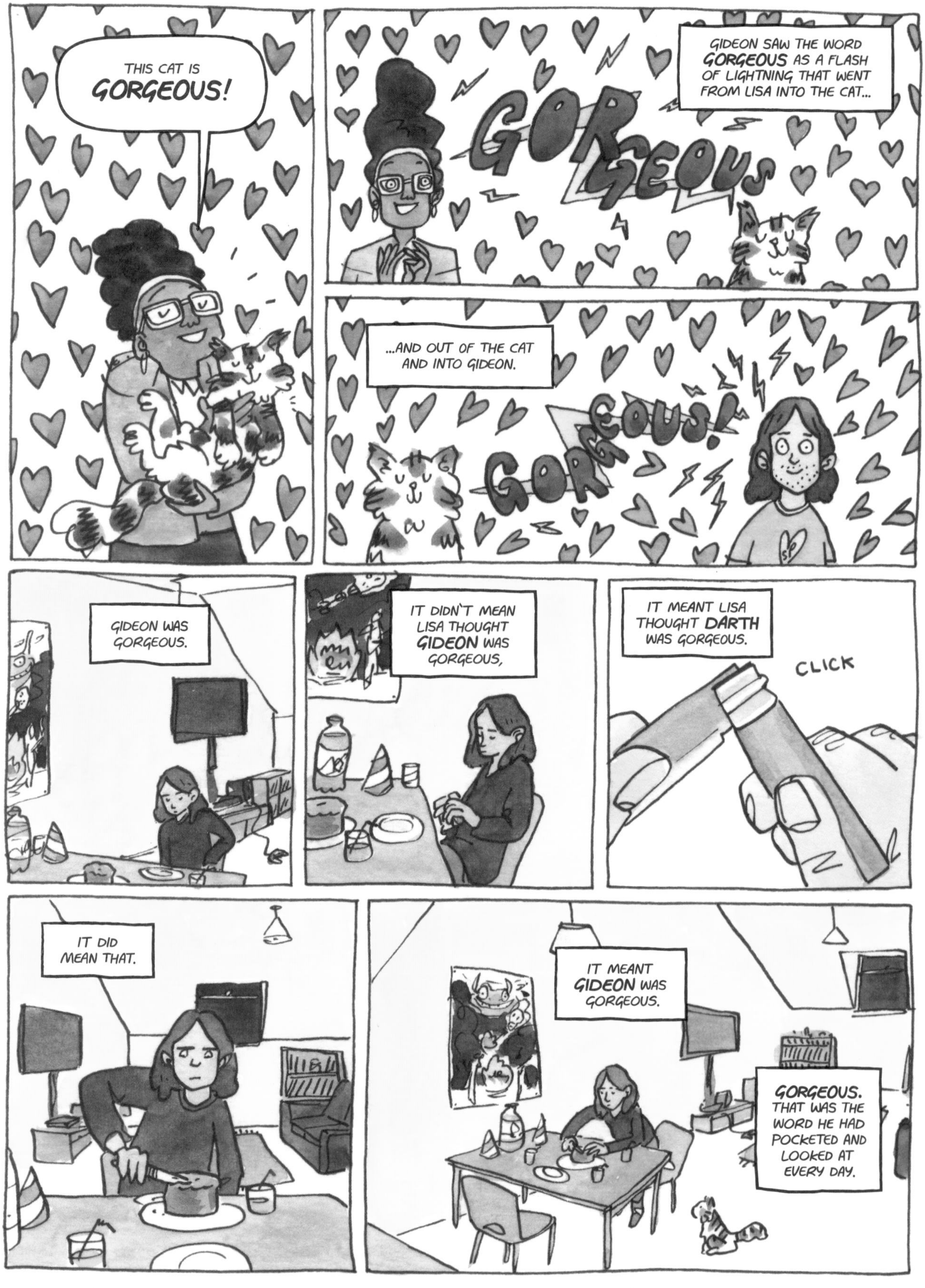
THIS CAT IS GORGEOUS!
GIDEON SAW THE WORD GORGEOUS AS A FLASH OF LIGHTNING THAT WENT FROM LISA INTO THE CAT...
GORGEOUS
...AND OUT OF THE CAT AND INTO GIDEON.
GORGEOUS!
GIDEON WAS GORGEOUS.
IT DIDN'T MEAN LISA THOUGHT GIDEON WAS GORGEOUS,
IT MEANT LISA THOUGHT DARTH WAS GORGEOUS.
CLICK
IT DID MEAN THAT.
IT MEANT GIDEON WAS GORGEOUS.
GORGEOUS. THAT WAS THE WORD HE HAD POCKETED AND LOOKED AT EVERY DAY.

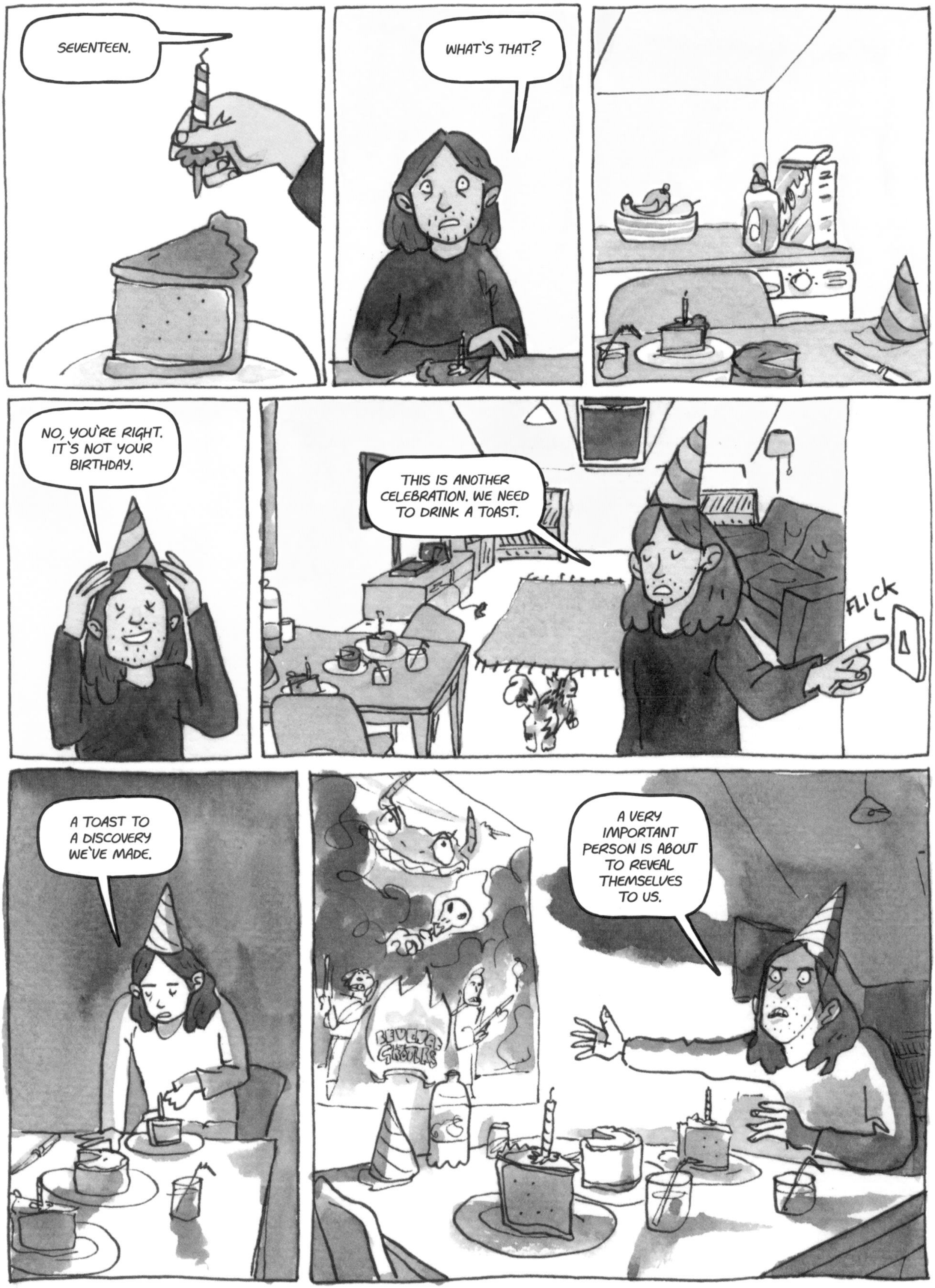
SEVENTEEN.
WHAT'S THAT?
NO, YOU'RE RIGHT. IT'S NOT YOUR BIRTHDAY.
THIS IS ANOTHER CELEBRATION. WE NEED TO DRINK A TOAST.
FLICK
A TOAST TO A DISCOVERY WE'VE MADE.
A VERY IMPORTANT PERSON IS ABOUT TO REVEAL THEMSELVES TO US.

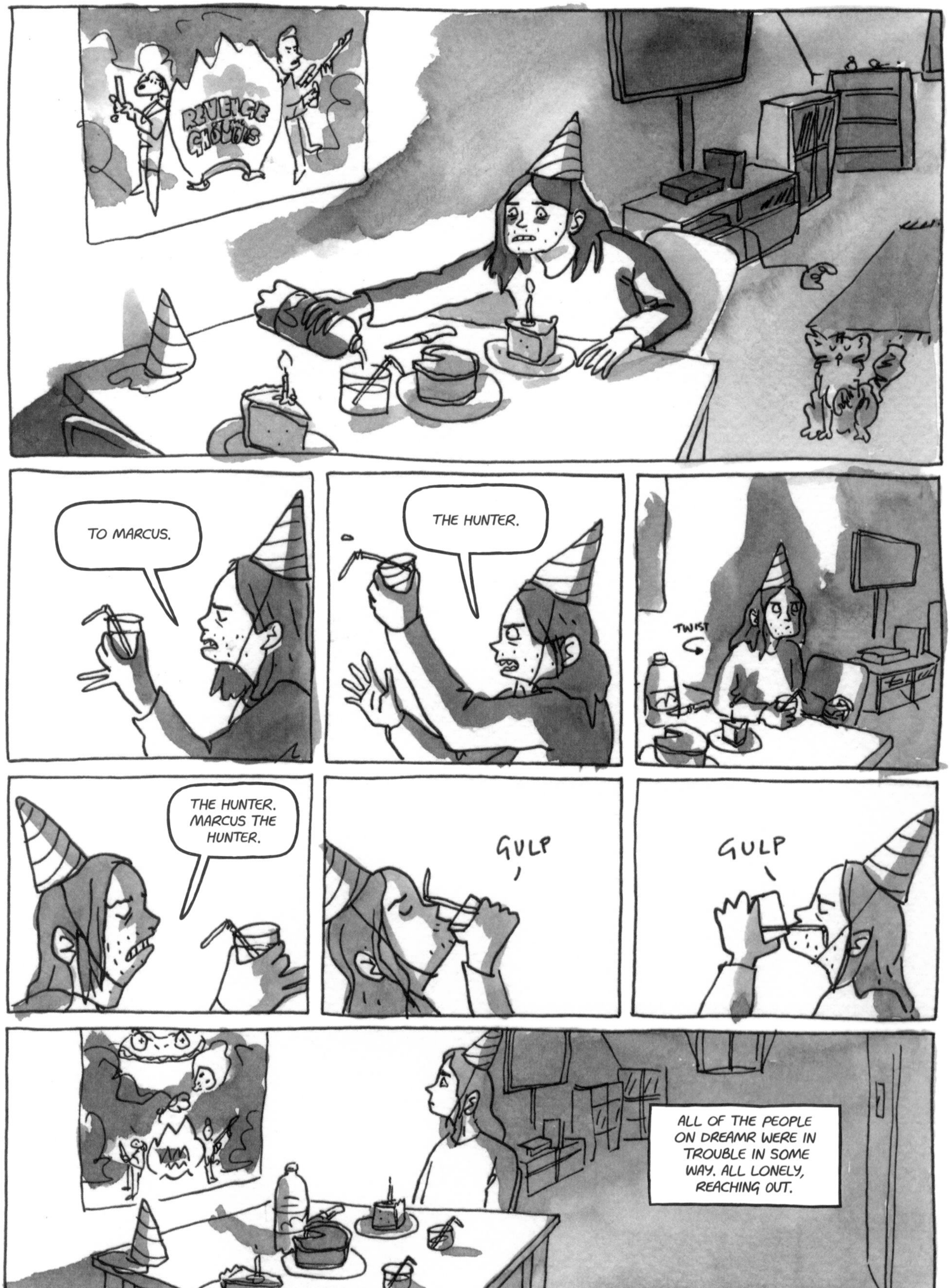
REVENGE OF THE GHOULS
TO MARCUS.
THE HUNTER.
TWIST
THE HUNTER. MARCUS THE HUNTER.
GULP
GULP
ALL OF THE PEOPLE ON DREAMR WERE IN TROUBLE IN SOME WAY. ALL LONELY, REACHING OUT.

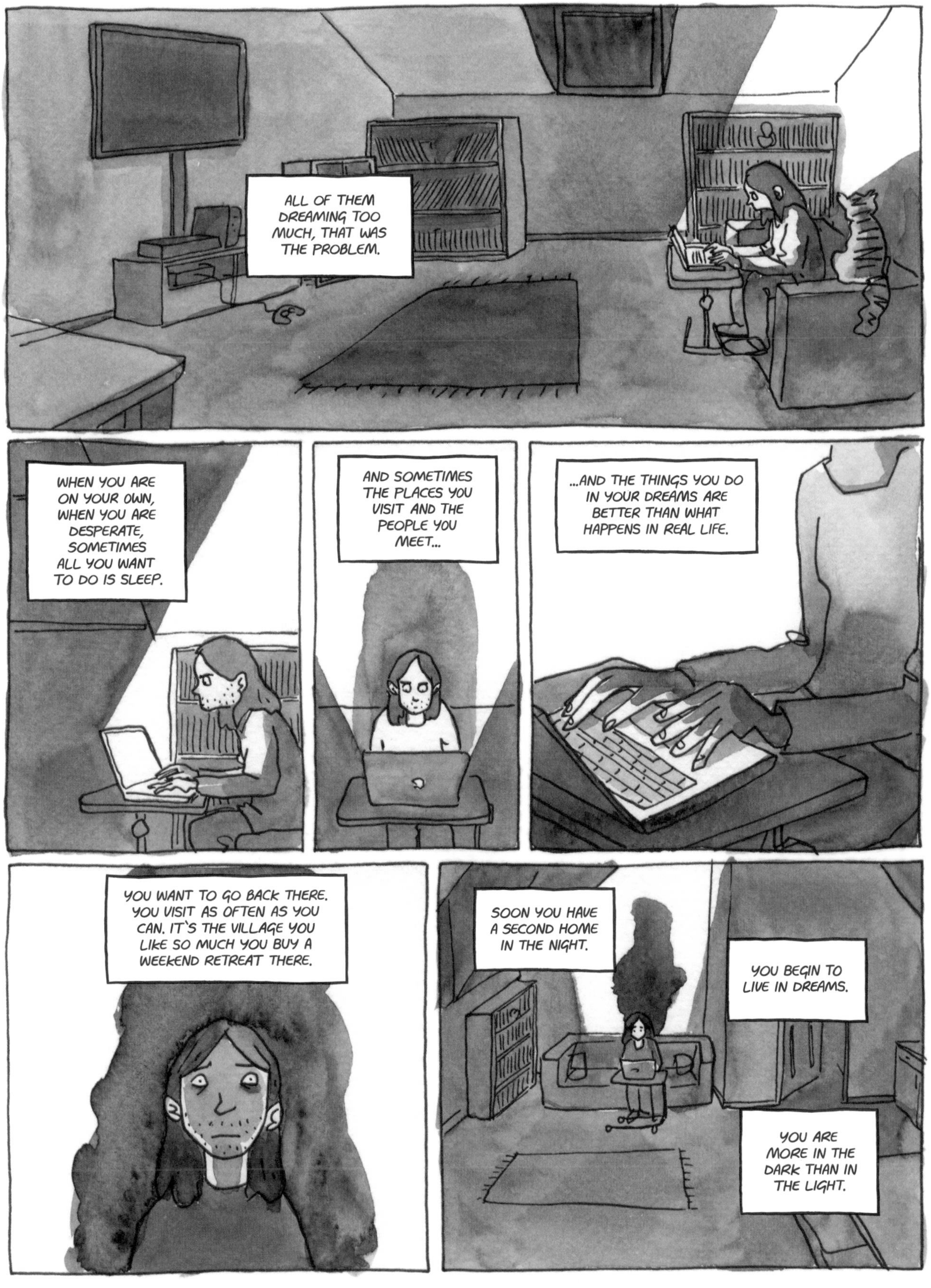
ALL OF THEM DREAMING TOO MUCH, THAT WAS THE PROBLEM.
WHEN YOU ARE ON YOUR OWN, WHEN YOU ARE DESPERATE, SOMETIMES ALL YOU WANT TO DO IS SLEEP.
AND SOMETIMES THE PLACES YOU VISIT AND THE PEOPLE YOU MEET...
...AND THE THINGS YOU DO IN YOUR DREAMS ARE BETTER THAN WHAT HAPPENS IN REAL LIFE.
YOU WANT TO GO BACK THERE. YOU VISIT AS OFTEN AS YOU CAN. IT'S THE VILLAGE YOU LIKE SO MUCH YOU BUY A WEEKEND RETREAT THERE.
SOON YOU HAVE A SECOND HOME IN THE NIGHT.
YOU BEGIN TO LIVE IN DREAMS.
YOU ARE MORE IN THE DARK THAN IN THE LIGHT.

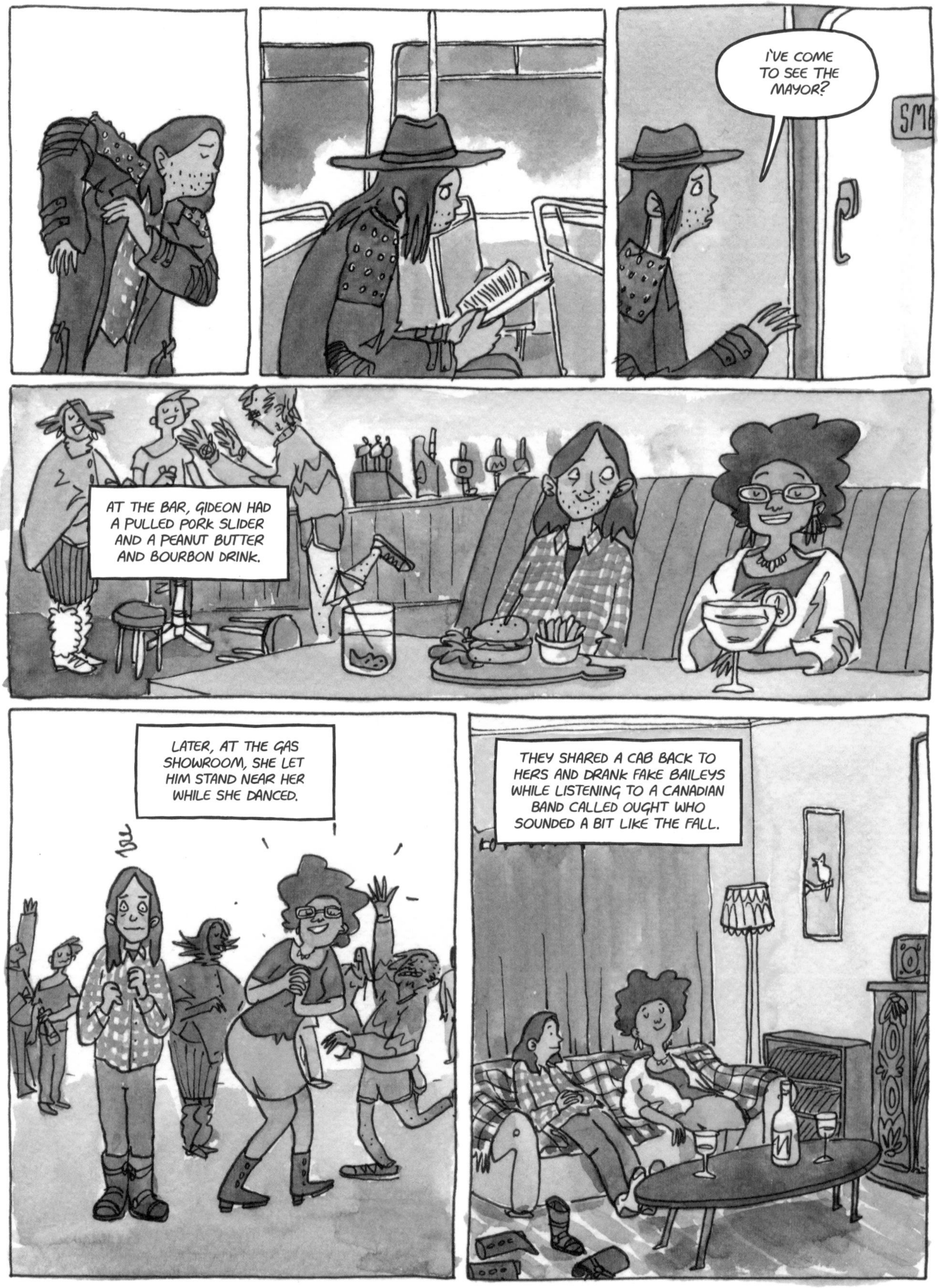
I'VE COME TO SEE THE MAYOR?
AT THE BAR, GIDEON HAD A PULLED PORK SLIDER AND A PEANUT BUTTER AND BOURBON DRINK.
LATER, AT THE GAS SHOWROOM, SHE LET HIM STAND NEAR HER WHILE SHE DANCED.
THEY SHARED A CAB BACK TO HERS AND DRANK FAKE BAILEYS WHILE LISTENING TO A CANADIAN BAND CALLED OUGHT WHO SOUNDED A BIT LIKE THE FALL.

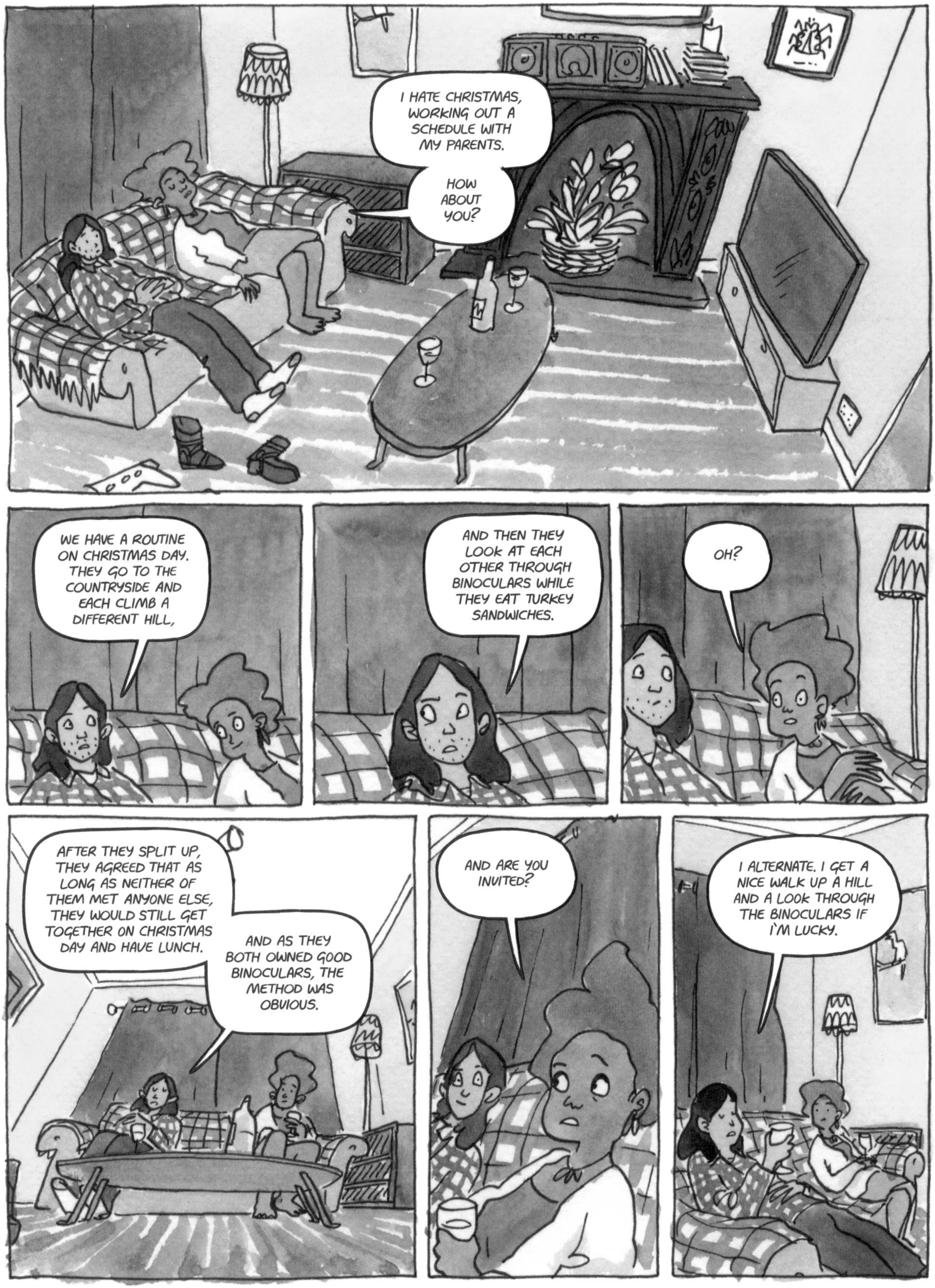
I HATE CHRISTMAS, WORKING OUT A SCHEDULE WITH MY PARENTS.
HOW ABOUT YOU?
WE HAVE A ROUTINE ON CHRISTMAS DAY. THEY GO TO THE COUNTRYSIDE AND EACH CLIMB A DIFFERENT HILL,
AND THEN THEY LOOK AT EACH OTHER THROUGH BINOCULARS WHILE THEY EAT TURKEY SANDWICHES.
OH?
AFTER THEY SPLIT UP, THEY AGREED THAT AS LONG AS NEITHER OF THEM MET ANYONE ELSE, THEY WOULD STILL GET TOGETHER ON CHRISTMAS DAY AND HAVE LUNCH.
AND AS THEY BOTH OWNED GOOD BINOCULARS, THE METHOD WAS OBVIOUS.
AND ARE YOU INVITED?
I ALTERNATE. I GET A NICE WALK UP A HILL AND A LOOK THROUGH THE BINOCULARS IF I'M LUCKY.

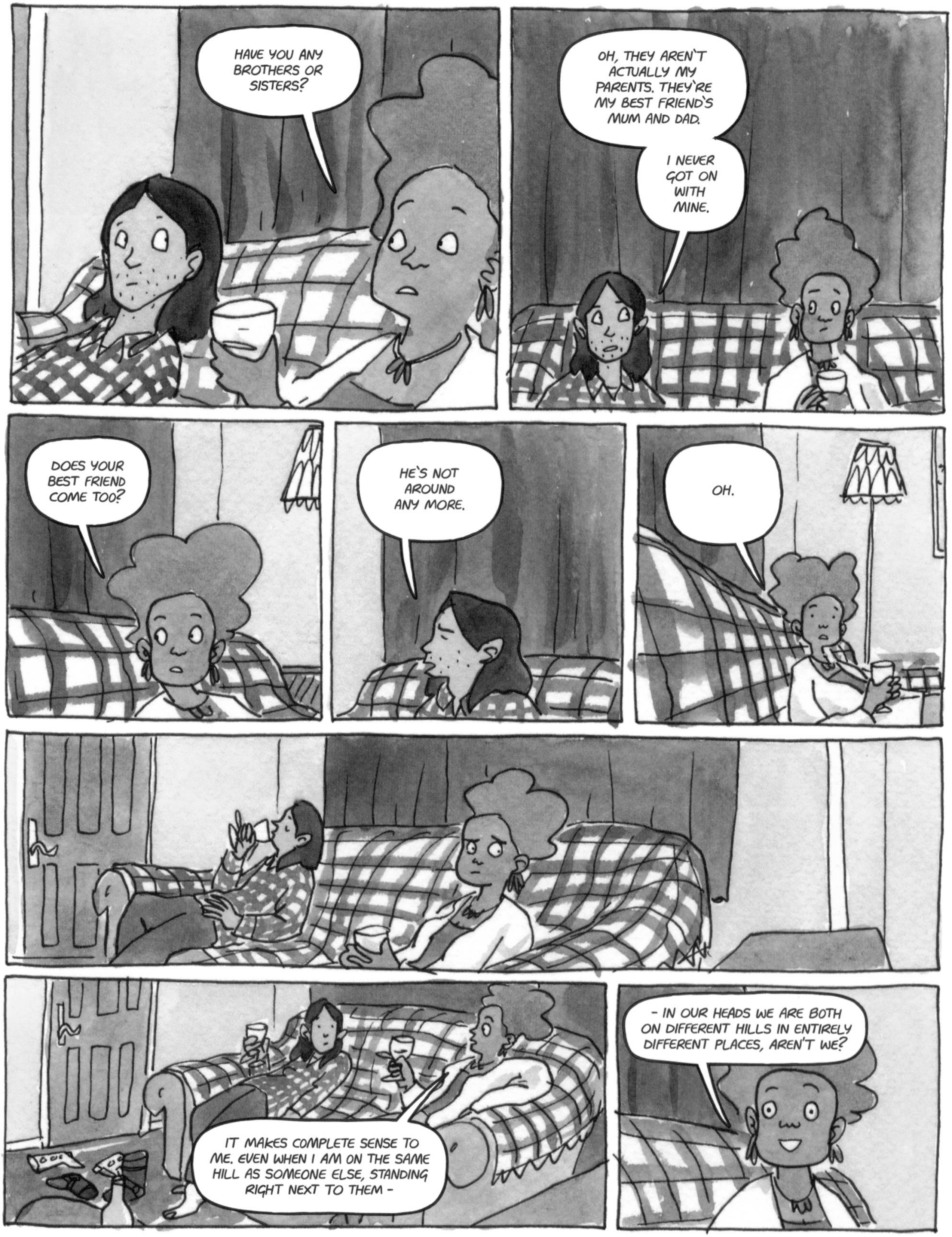
HAVE YOU ANY BROTHERS OR SISTERS?
OH, THEY AREN'T ACTUALLY MY PARENTS. THEY'RE MY BEST FRIEND'S MUM AND DAD.
I NEVER GOT ON WITH MINE.
DOES YOUR BEST FRIEND COME TOO?
HE'S NOT AROUND ANY MORE.
OH.
IT MAKES COMPLETE SENSE TO ME. EVEN WHEN I AM ON THE SAME HILL AS SOMEONE ELSE, STANDING RIGHT NEXT TO THEM -
- IN OUR HEADS WE ARE BOTH ON DIFFERENT HILLS IN ENTIRELY DIFFERENT PLACES, AREN'T WE?

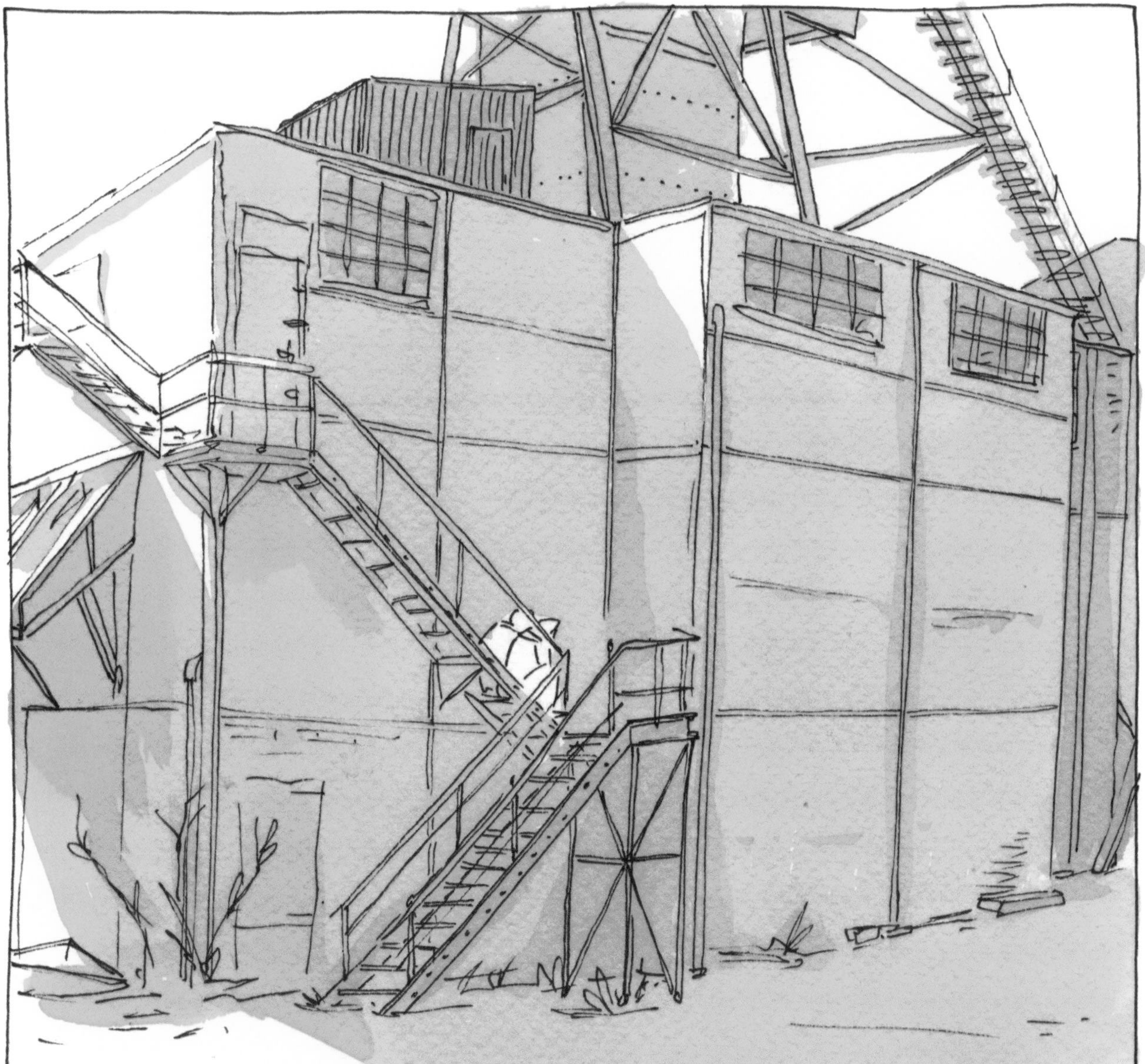

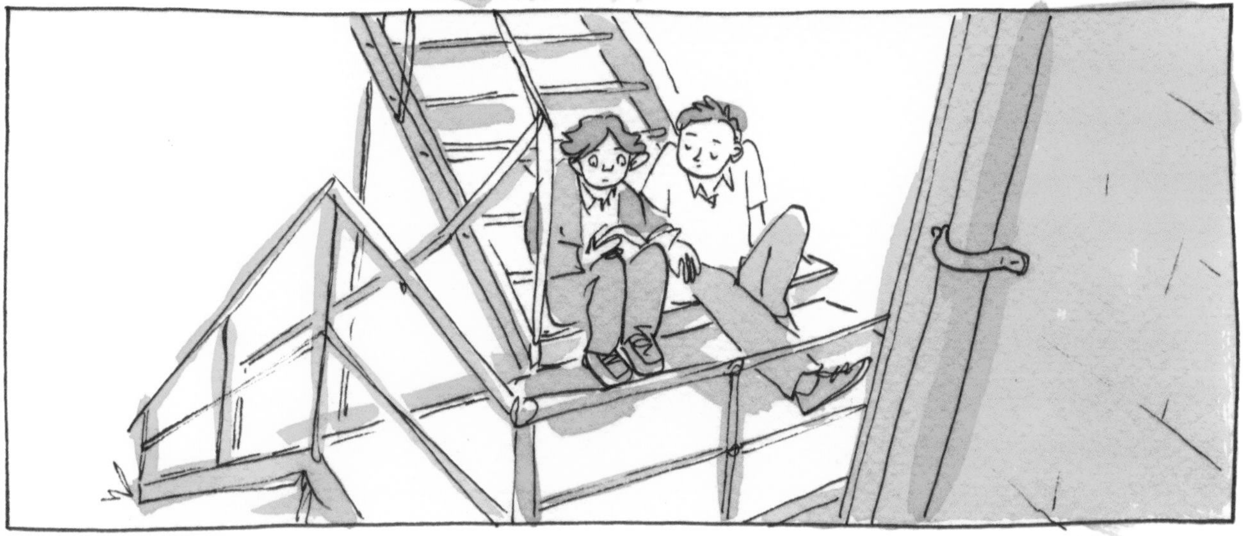

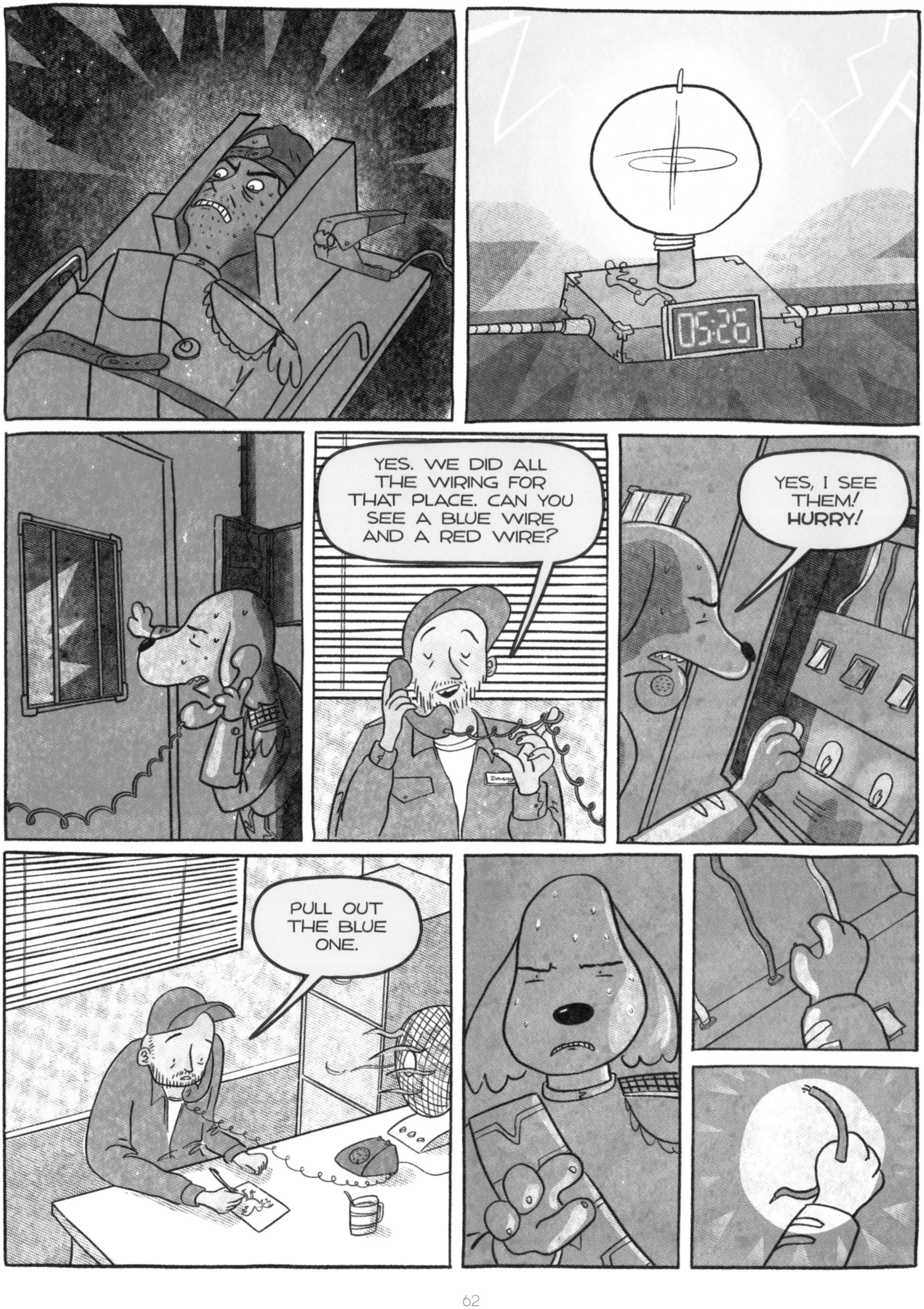
05:26
YES. WE DID ALL THE WIRING FOR THAT PLACE. CAN YOU SEE A BLUE WIRE AND A RED WIRE?
YES, I SEE THEM! **HURRY!**
PULL OUT THE BLUE ONE.

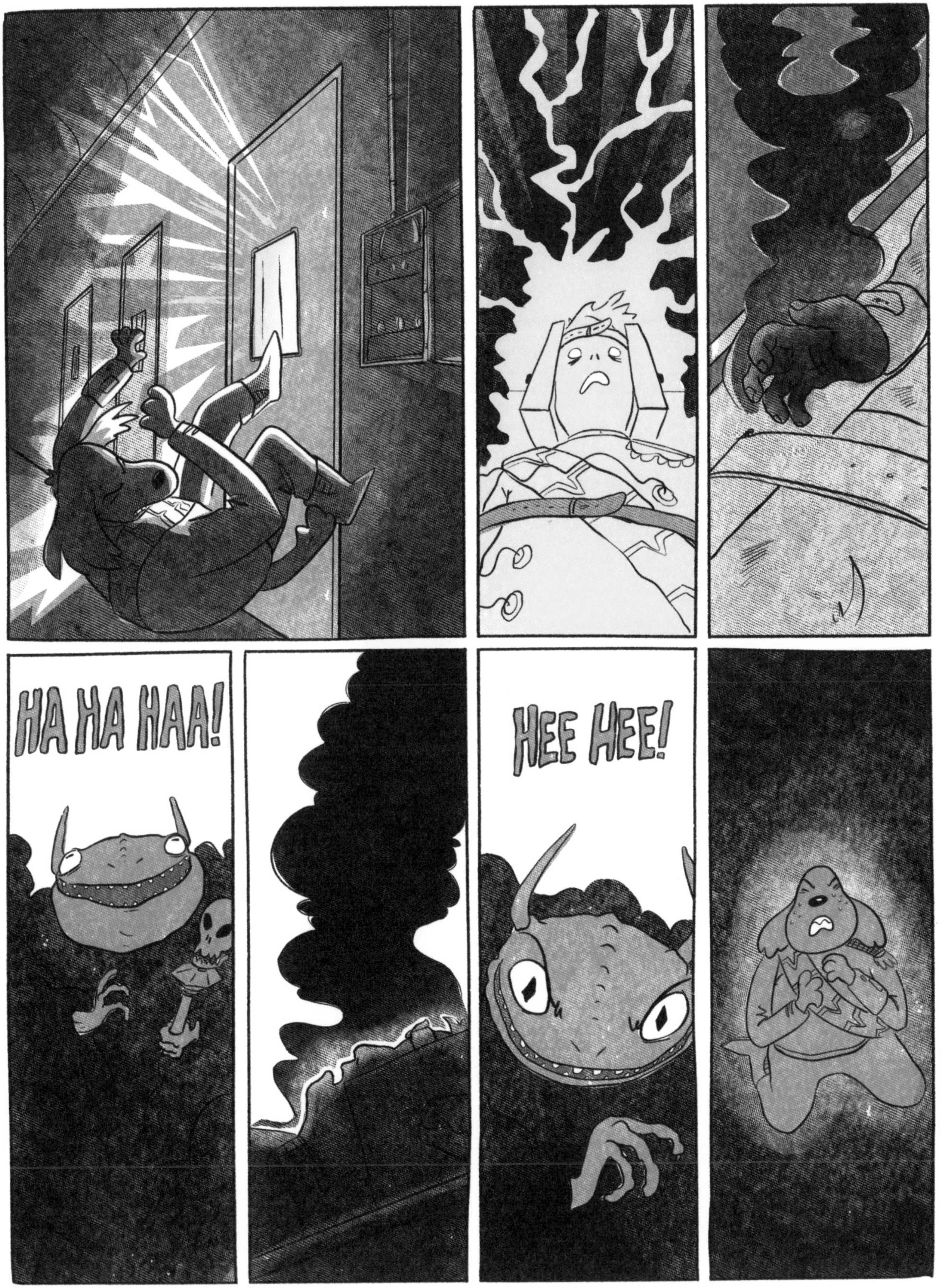
HA HA HAA!
HEE HEE!

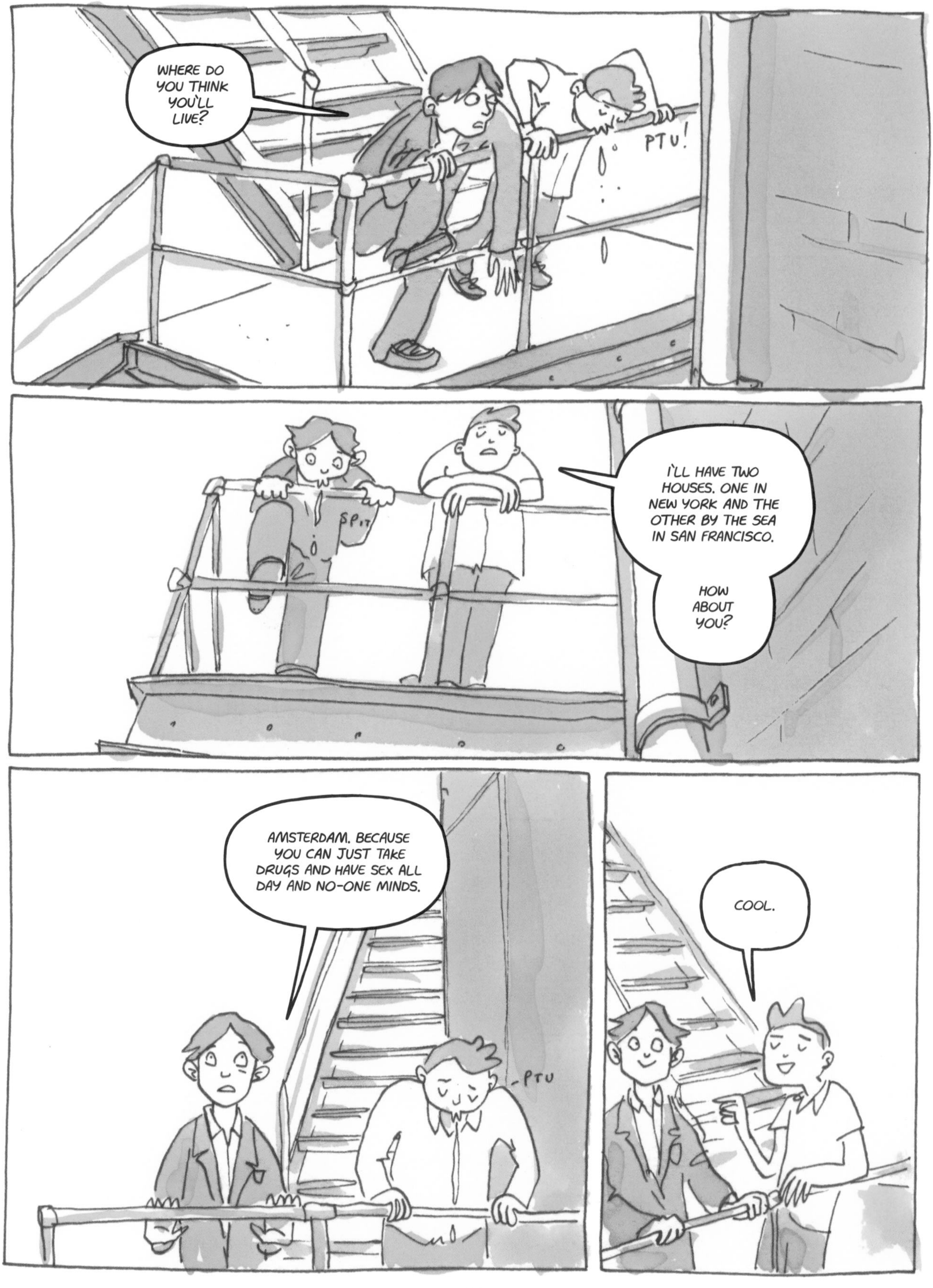
WHERE DO YOU THINK YOU'LL LIVE?
PTU!
SPIT
I'LL HAVE TWO HOUSES. ONE IN NEW YORK AND THE OTHER BY THE SEA IN SAN FRANCISCO.
HOW ABOUT YOU?
AMSTERDAM. BECAUSE YOU CAN JUST TAKE DRUGS AND HAVE SEX ALL DAY AND NO-ONE MINDS.
PTU
COOL.

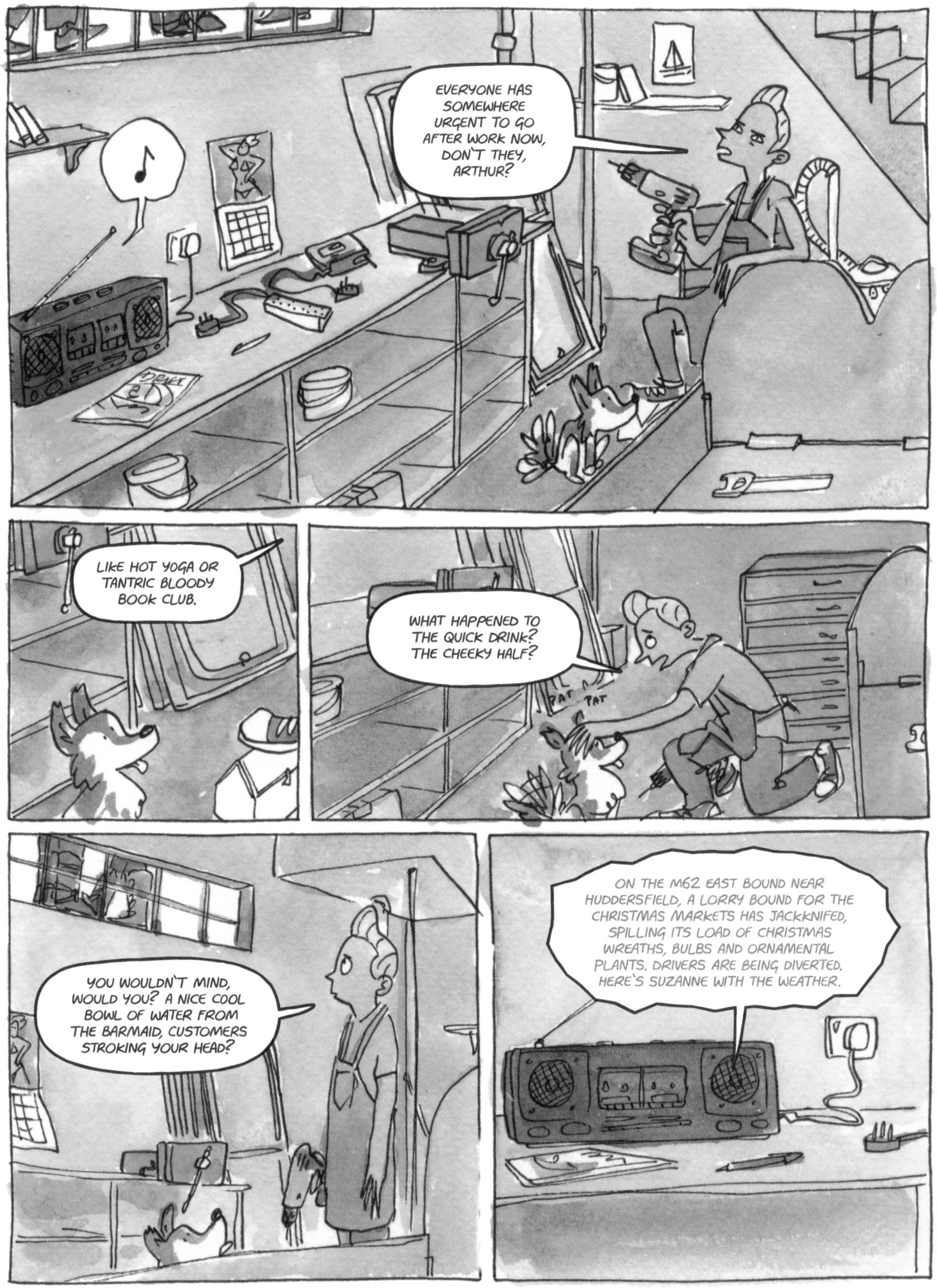
EVERYONE HAS SOMEWHERE URGENT TO GO AFTER WORK NOW, DON'T THEY, ARTHUR?
LIKE HOT YOGA OR TANTRIC BLOODY BOOK CLUB.
WHAT HAPPENED TO THE QUICK DRINK? THE CHEEKY HALF?
PAT PAT
YOU WOULDN'T MIND, WOULD YOU? A NICE COOL BOWL OF WATER FROM THE BARMAID, CUSTOMERS STROKING YOUR HEAD?
ON THE M62 EAST BOUND NEAR HUDDERSFIELD, A LORRY BOUND FOR THE CHRISTMAS MARKETS HAS JACKKNIFED, SPILLING ITS LOAD OF CHRISTMAS WREATHS, BULBS AND ORNAMENTAL PLANTS. DRIVERS ARE BEING DIVERTED. HERE'S SUZANNE WITH THE WEATHER.

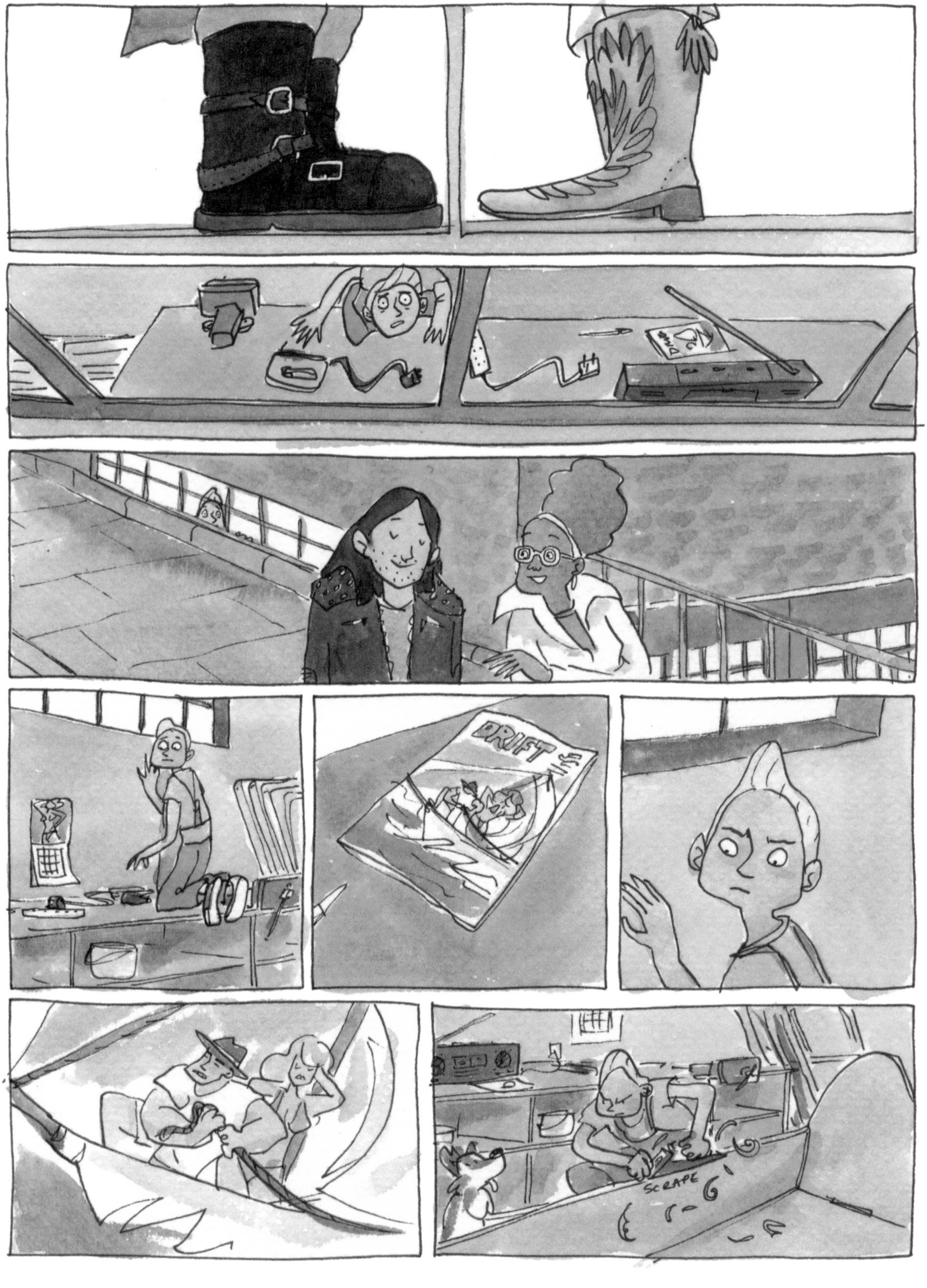
DRIFT
SCRAPE

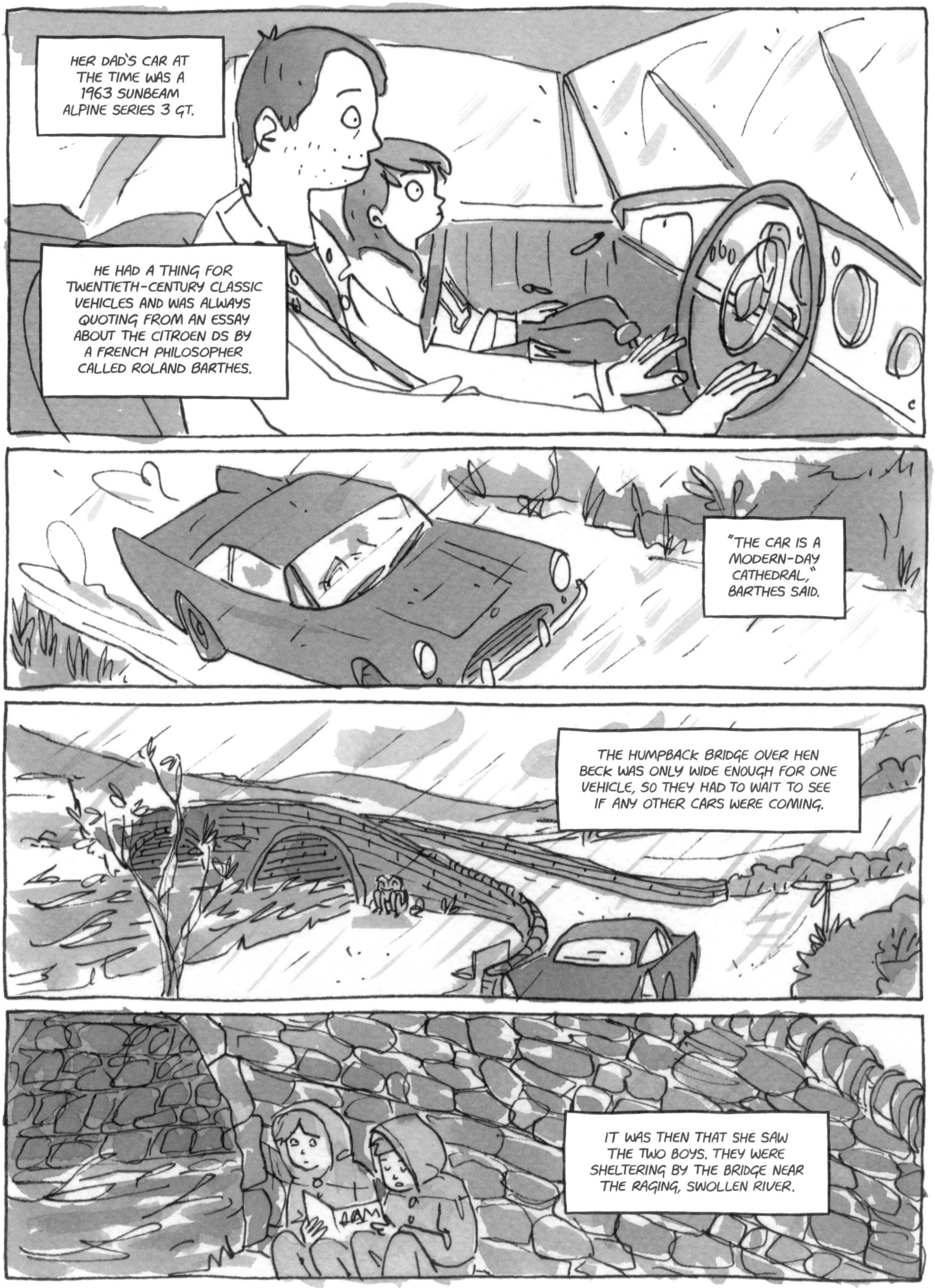
HER DAD'S CAR AT THE TIME WAS A 1963 SUNBEAM ALPINE SERIES 3 GT.
HE HAD A THING FOR TWENTIETH-CENTURY CLASSIC VEHICLES AND WAS ALWAYS QUOTING FROM AN ESSAY ABOUT THE CITROEN DS BY A FRENCH PHILOSOPHER CALLED ROLAND BARTHES.
"THE CAR IS A MODERN-DAY CATHEDRAL," BARTHES SAID.
THE HUMPBACK BRIDGE OVER HEN BECK WAS ONLY WIDE ENOUGH FOR ONE VEHICLE, SO THEY HAD TO WAIT TO SEE IF ANY OTHER CARS WERE COMING.
IT WAS THEN THAT SHE SAW THE TWO BOYS. THEY WERE SHELTERING BY THE BRIDGE NEAR THE RAGING, SWOLLEN RIVER.

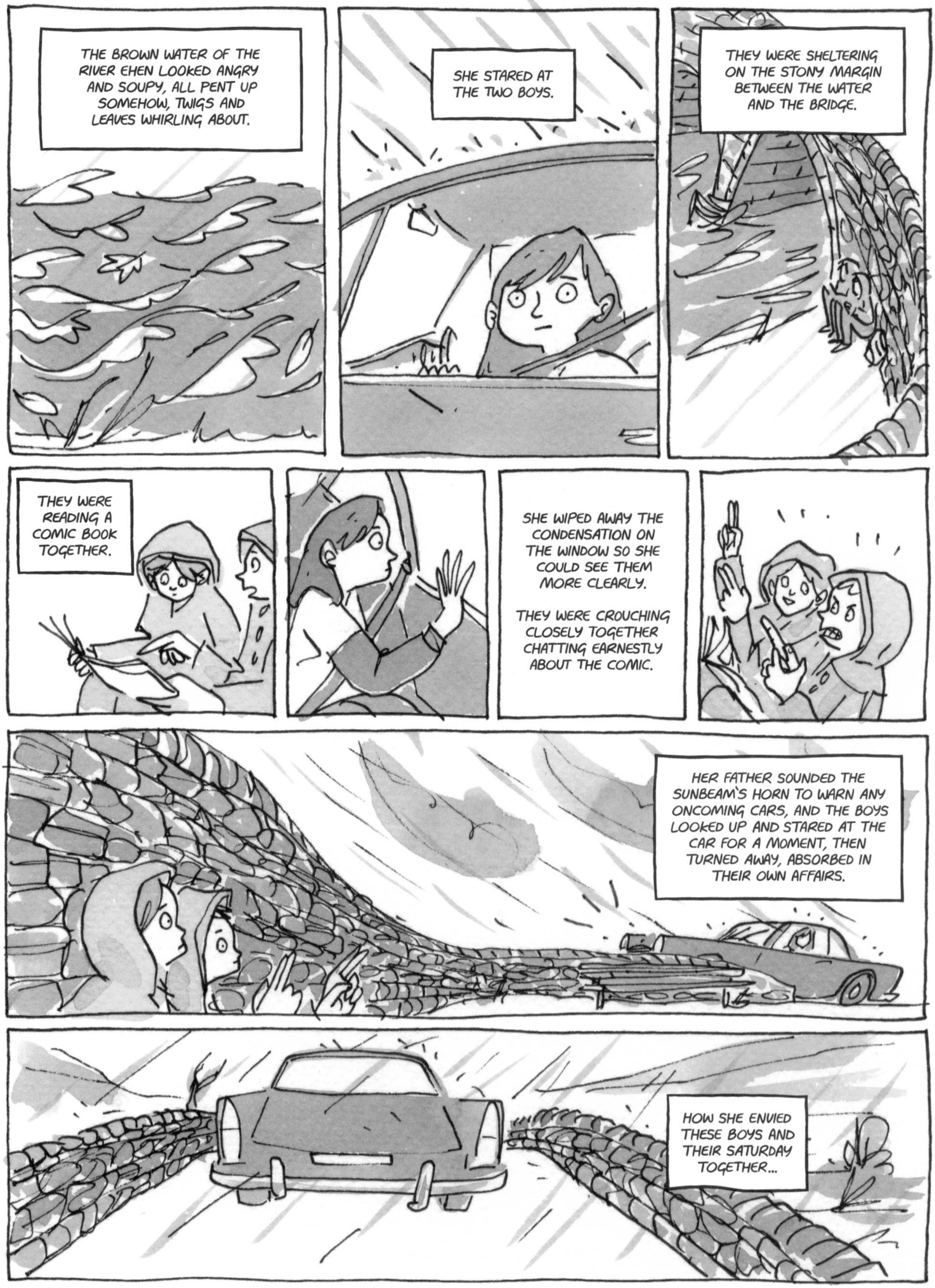
THE BROWN WATER OF THE RIVER EHEN LOOKED ANGRY AND SOUPY, ALL PENT UP SOMEHOW, TWIGS AND LEAVES WHIRLING ABOUT.
SHE STARED AT THE TWO BOYS.
THEY WERE SHELTERING ON THE STONY MARGIN BETWEEN THE WATER AND THE BRIDGE.
THEY WERE READING A COMIC BOOK TOGETHER.
SHE WIPED AWAY THE CONDENSATION ON THE WINDOW SO SHE COULD SEE THEM MORE CLEARLY.
THEY WERE CROUCHING CLOSELY TOGETHER CHATTING EARNESTLY ABOUT THE COMIC.
HER FATHER SOUNDED THE SUNBEAM'S HORN TO WARN ANY ONCOMING CARS, AND THE BOYS LOOKED UP AND STARED AT THE CAR FOR A MOMENT, THEN TURNED AWAY, ABSORBED IN THEIR OWN AFFAIRS.
HOW SHE ENVIED THESE BOYS AND THEIR SATURDAY TOGETHER...

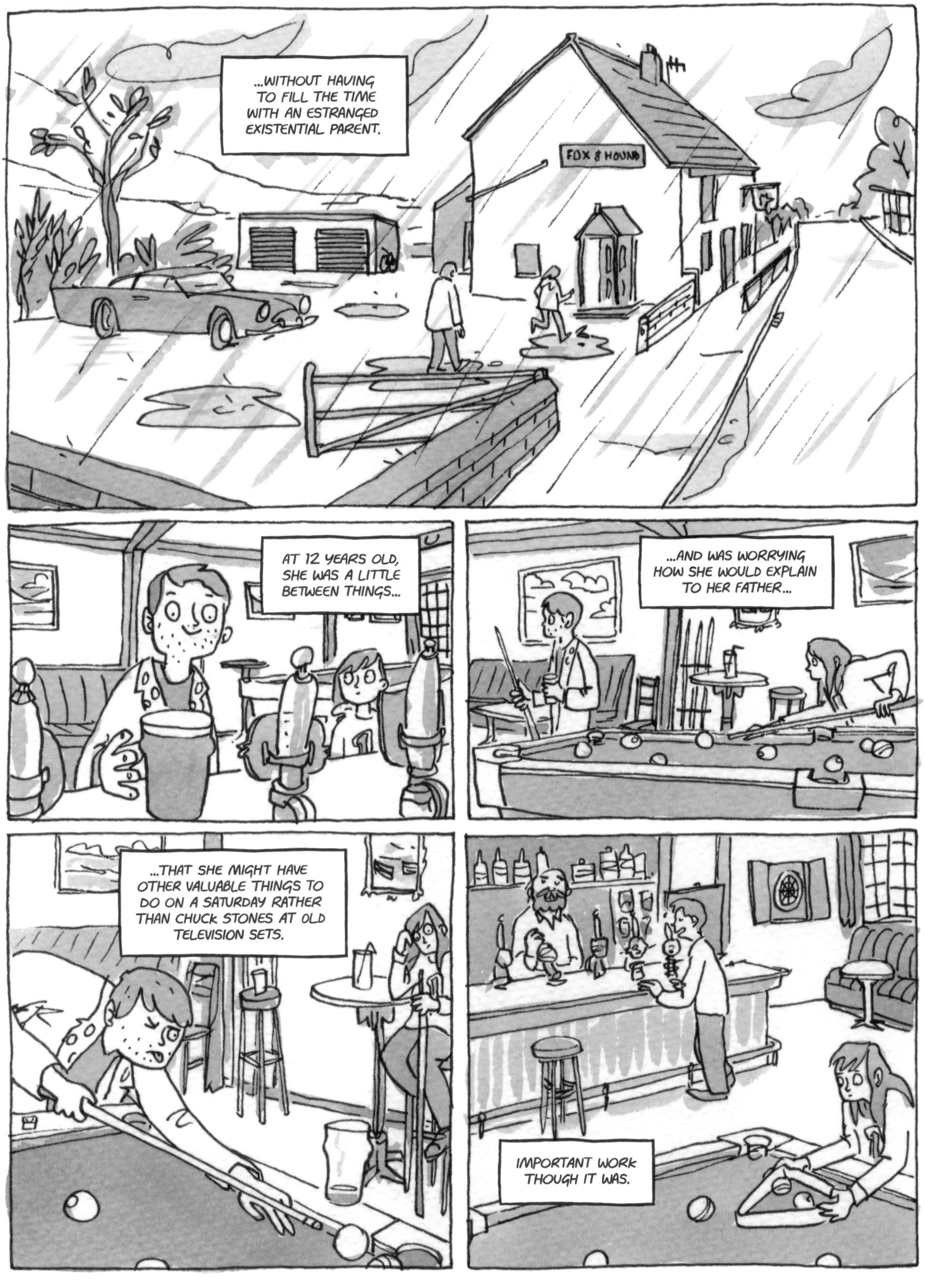
...WITHOUT HAVING TO FILL THE TIME WITH AN ESTRANGED EXISTENTIAL PARENT.
FOX & HOUND
AT 12 YEARS OLD, SHE WAS A LITTLE BETWEEN THINGS...
...AND WAS WORRYING HOW SHE WOULD EXPLAIN TO HER FATHER...
...THAT SHE MIGHT HAVE OTHER VALUABLE THINGS TO DO ON A SATURDAY RATHER THAN CHUCK STONES AT OLD TELEVISION SETS.
IMPORTANT WORK THOUGH IT WAS.

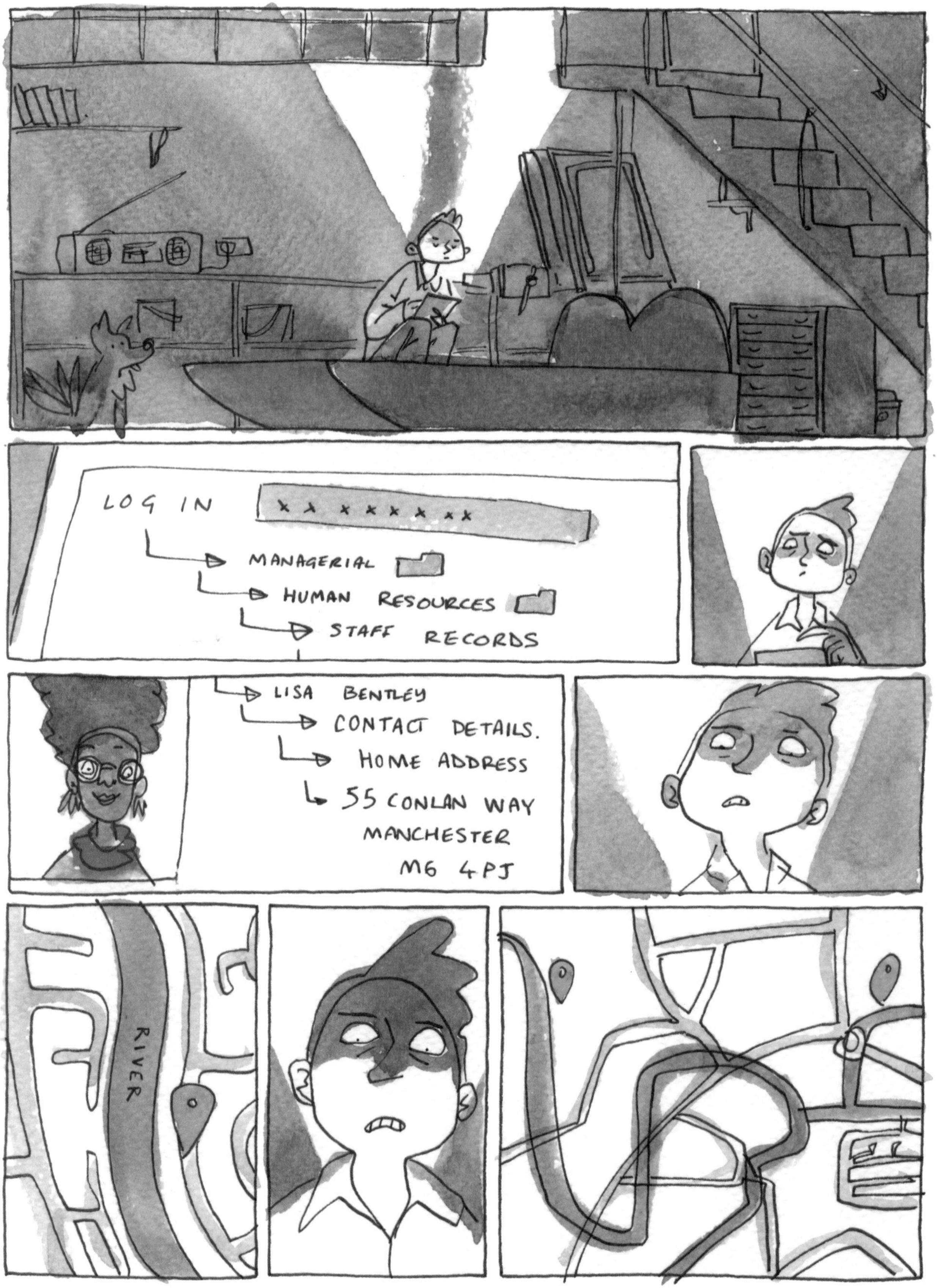
LOG IN
MANAGERIAL
HUMAN RESOURCES
STAFF RECORDS
LISA BENTLEY
CONTACT DETAILS.
HOME ADDRESS
55 CONLAN WAY
MANCHESTER
M6 4PJ
RIVER

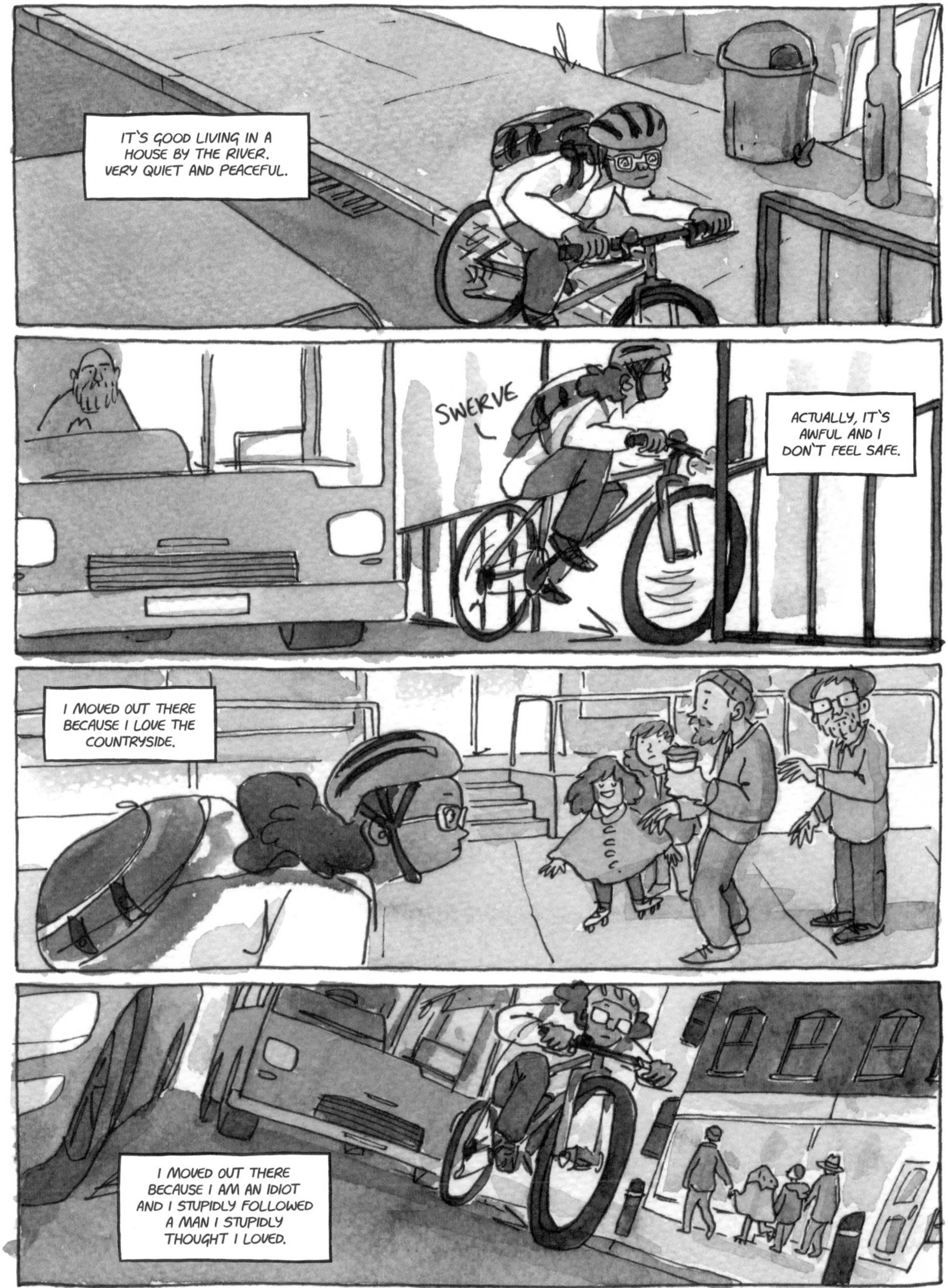
IT'S GOOD LIVING IN A HOUSE BY THE RIVER. VERY QUIET AND PEACEFUL.
SWERVE
ACTUALLY, IT'S AWFUL AND I DON'T FEEL SAFE.
I MOVED OUT THERE BECAUSE I LOVE THE COUNTRYSIDE.
I MOVED OUT THERE BECAUSE I AM AN IDIOT AND I STUPIDLY FOLLOWED A MAN I STUPIDLY THOUGHT I LOVED.

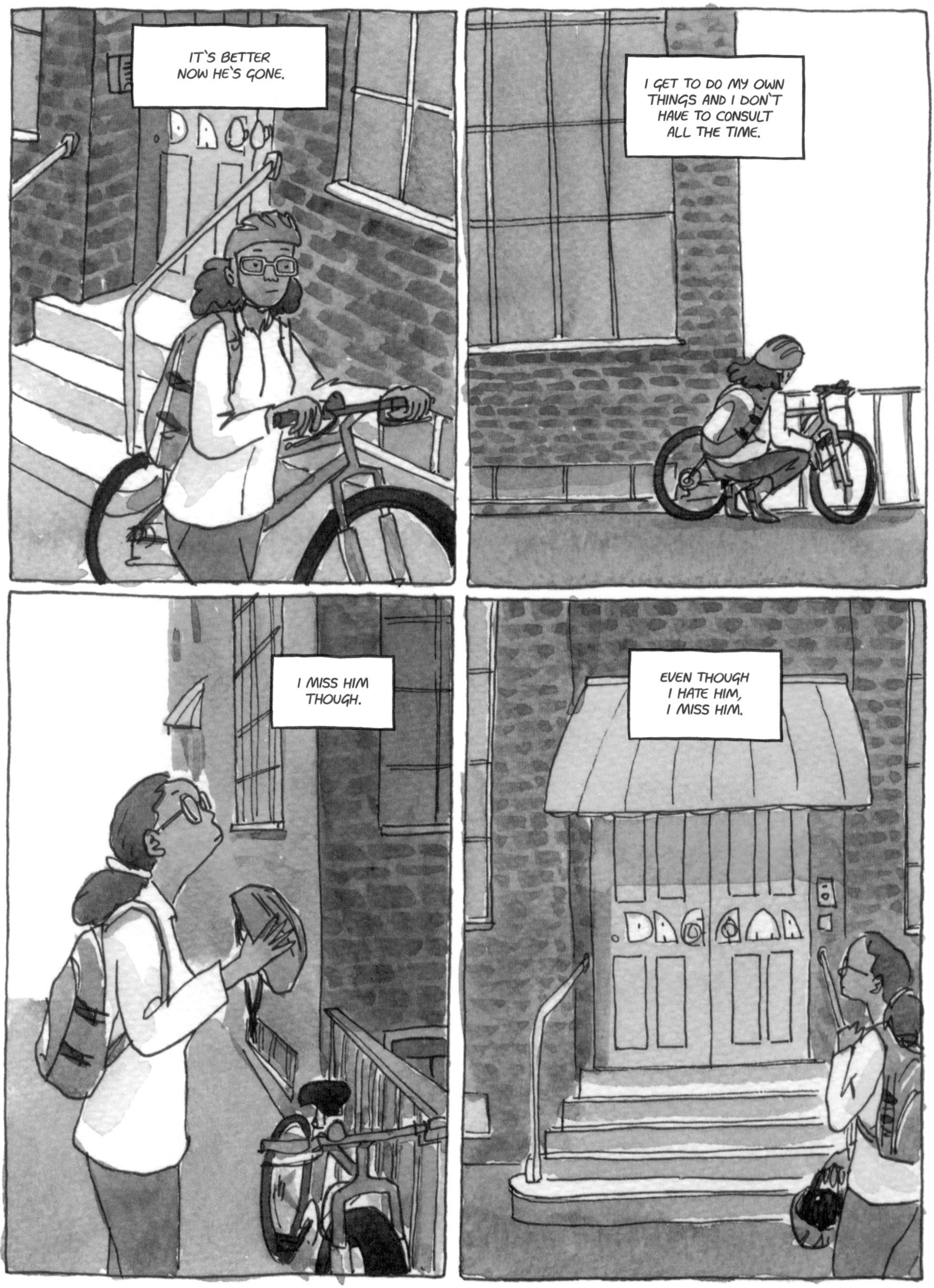
IT'S BETTER
NOW HE'S GONE.
I GET TO DO MY OWN
THINGS AND I DON'T
HAVE TO CONSULT
ALL THE TIME.
I MISS HIM
THOUGH.
EVEN THOUGH
I HATE HIM,
I MISS HIM.

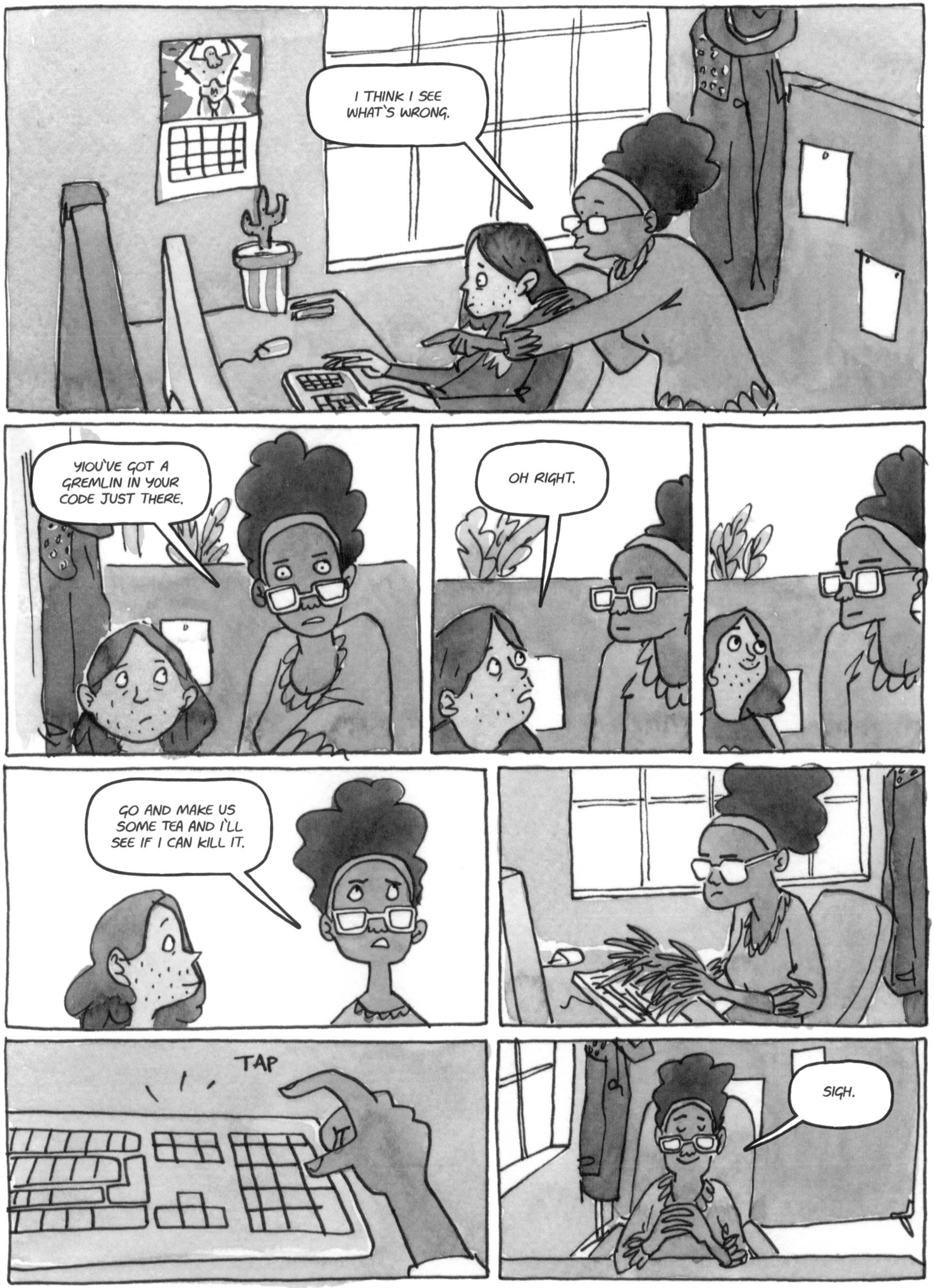
I THINK I SEE WHAT`S WRONG.
YIOU`VE GOT A GREMLIN IN YOUR CODE JUST THERE.
OH RIGHT.
GO AND MAKE US SOME TEA AND I`LL SEE IF I CAN KILL IT.
TAP
SIGH.

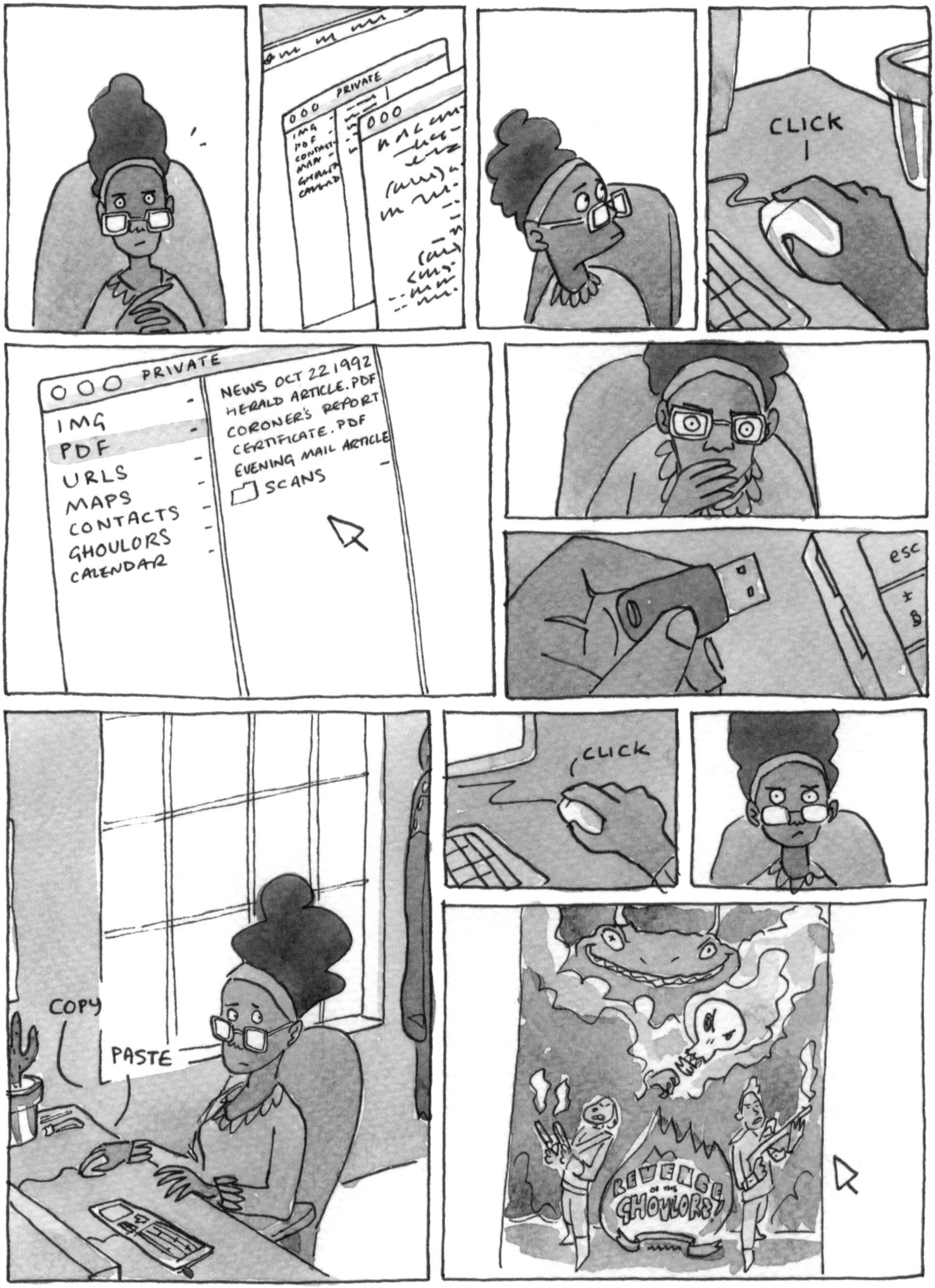
PRIVATE
CLICK
PRIVATE
IMG
PDF
URLS
MAPS
CONTACTS
GHOULORS
CALENDAR
NEWS OCT 22 1992
HERALD ARTICLE.PDF
CORONER'S REPORT
CERTIFICATE.PDF
EVENING MAIL ARTICLE
SCANS
esc
COPY
PASTE
CLICK
REVENGE

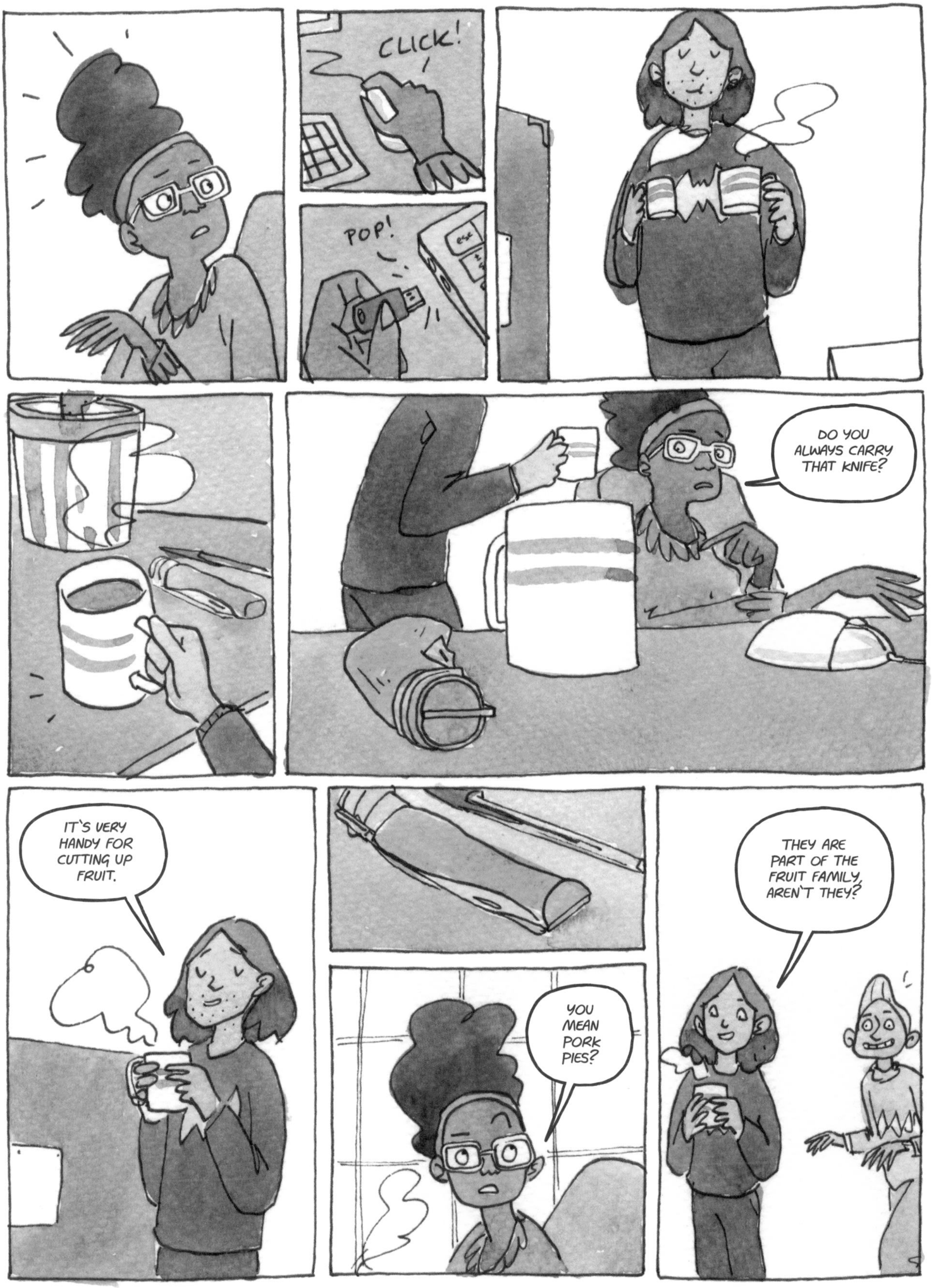
CLICK!
POP!
DO YOU ALWAYS CARRY THAT KNIFE?
IT'S VERY HANDY FOR CUTTING UP FRUIT.
YOU MEAN PORK PIES?
THEY ARE PART OF THE FRUIT FAMILY, AREN'T THEY?

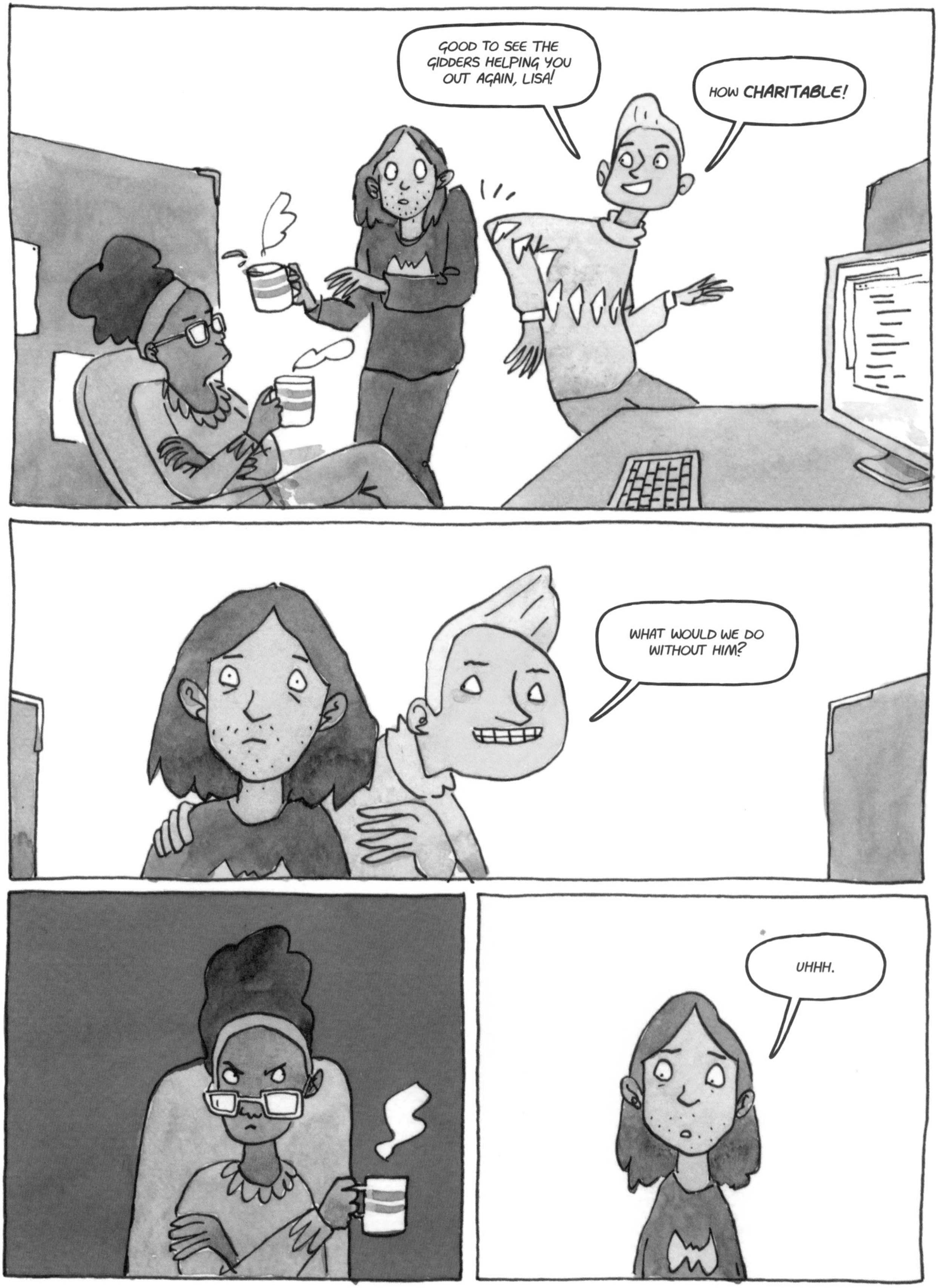
GOOD TO SEE THE GIDDERS HELPING YOU OUT AGAIN, LISA!
HOW CHARITABLE!
WHAT WOULD WE DO WITHOUT HIM?
UHHH.

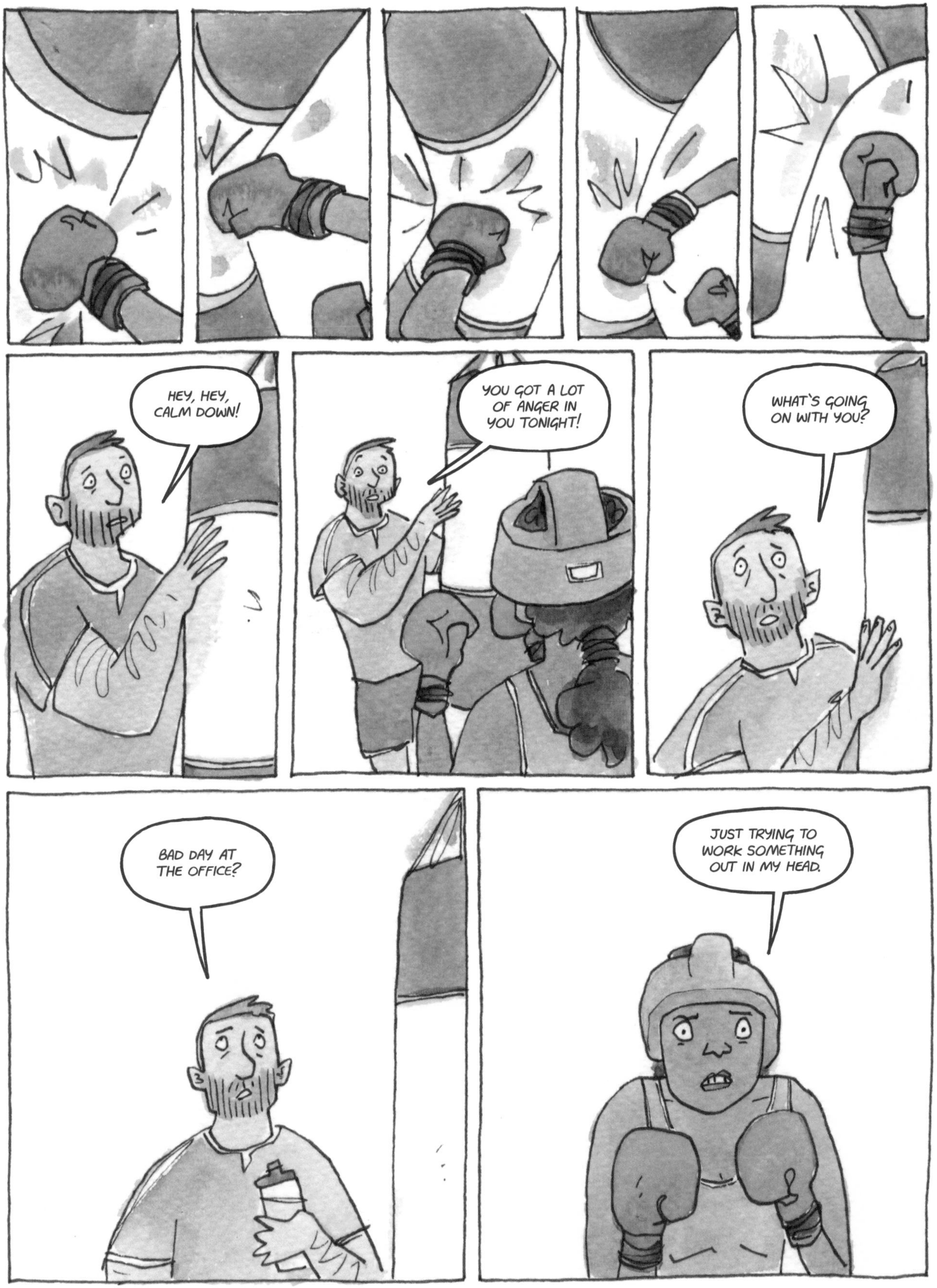
HEY, HEY, CALM DOWN!
YOU GOT A LOT OF ANGER IN YOU TONIGHT!
WHAT'S GOING ON WITH YOU?
BAD DAY AT THE OFFICE?
JUST TRYING TO WORK SOMETHING OUT IN MY HEAD.

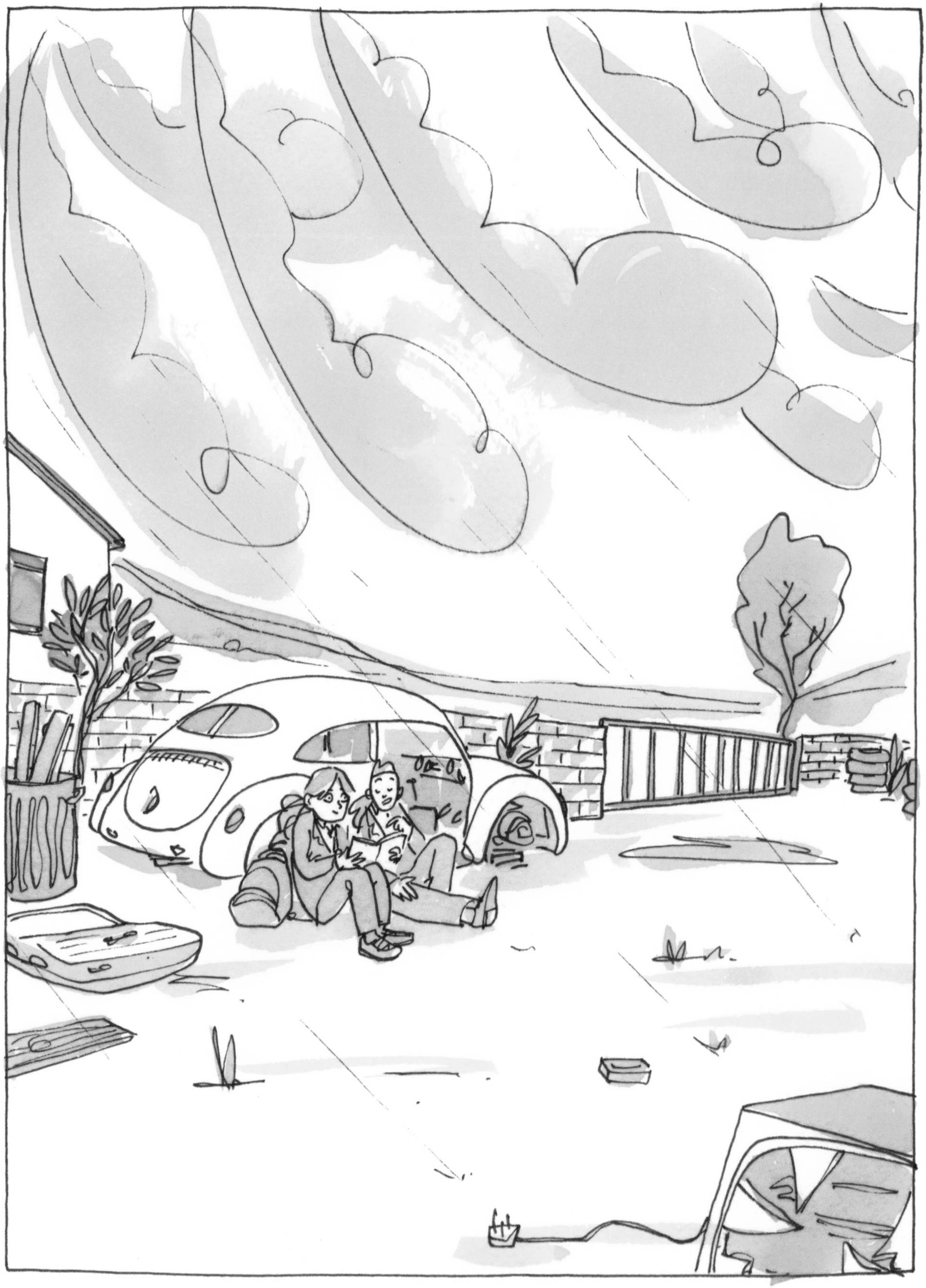

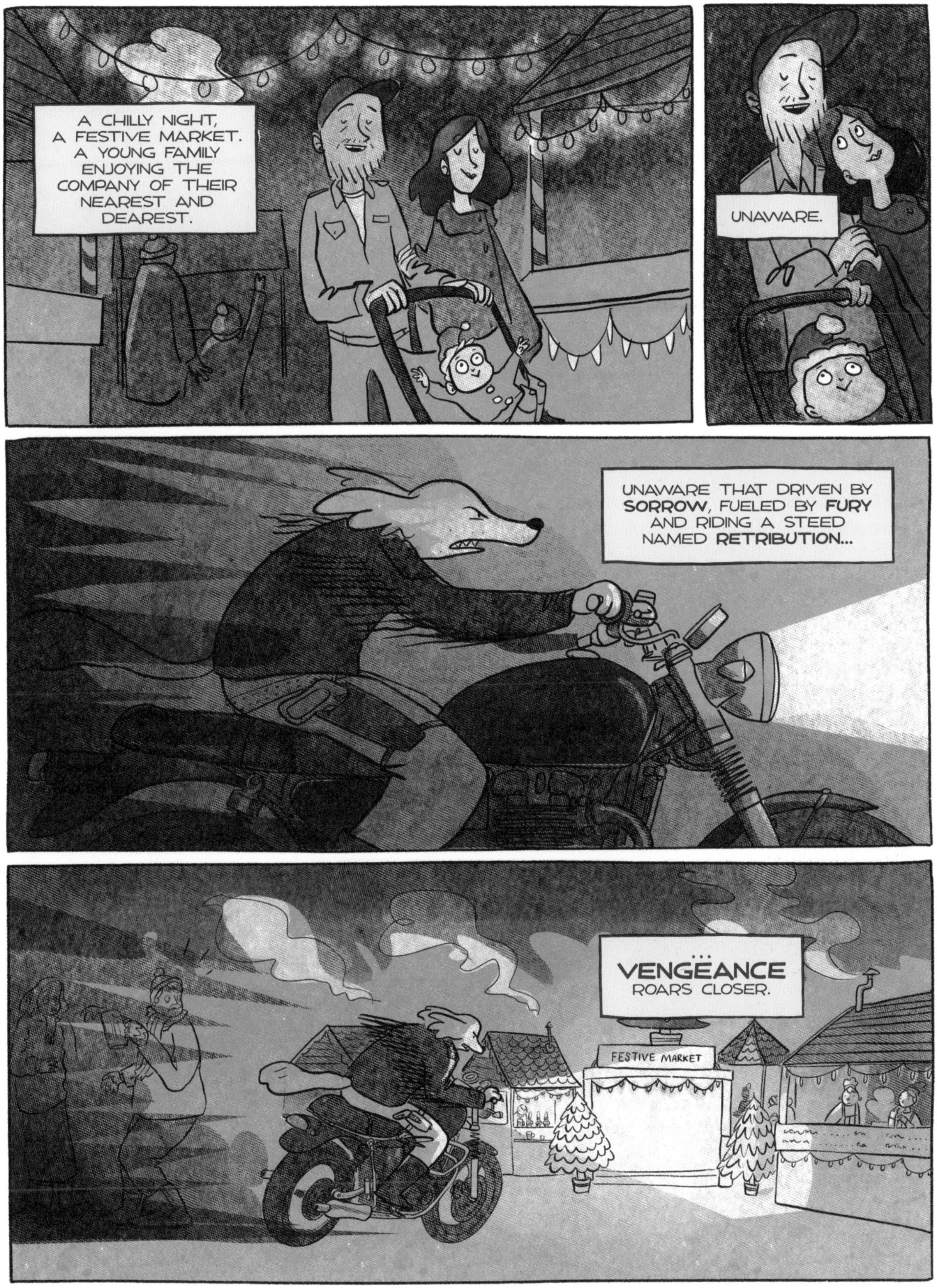
A CHILLY NIGHT, A FESTIVE MARKET. A YOUNG FAMILY ENJOYING THE COMPANY OF THEIR NEAREST AND DEAREST.
UNAWARE.
UNAWARE THAT DRIVEN BY **SORROW**, FUELED BY **FURY** AND RIDING A STEED NAMED **RETRIBUTION...**
... **VENGEANCE** ROARS CLOSER.
FESTIVE MARKET

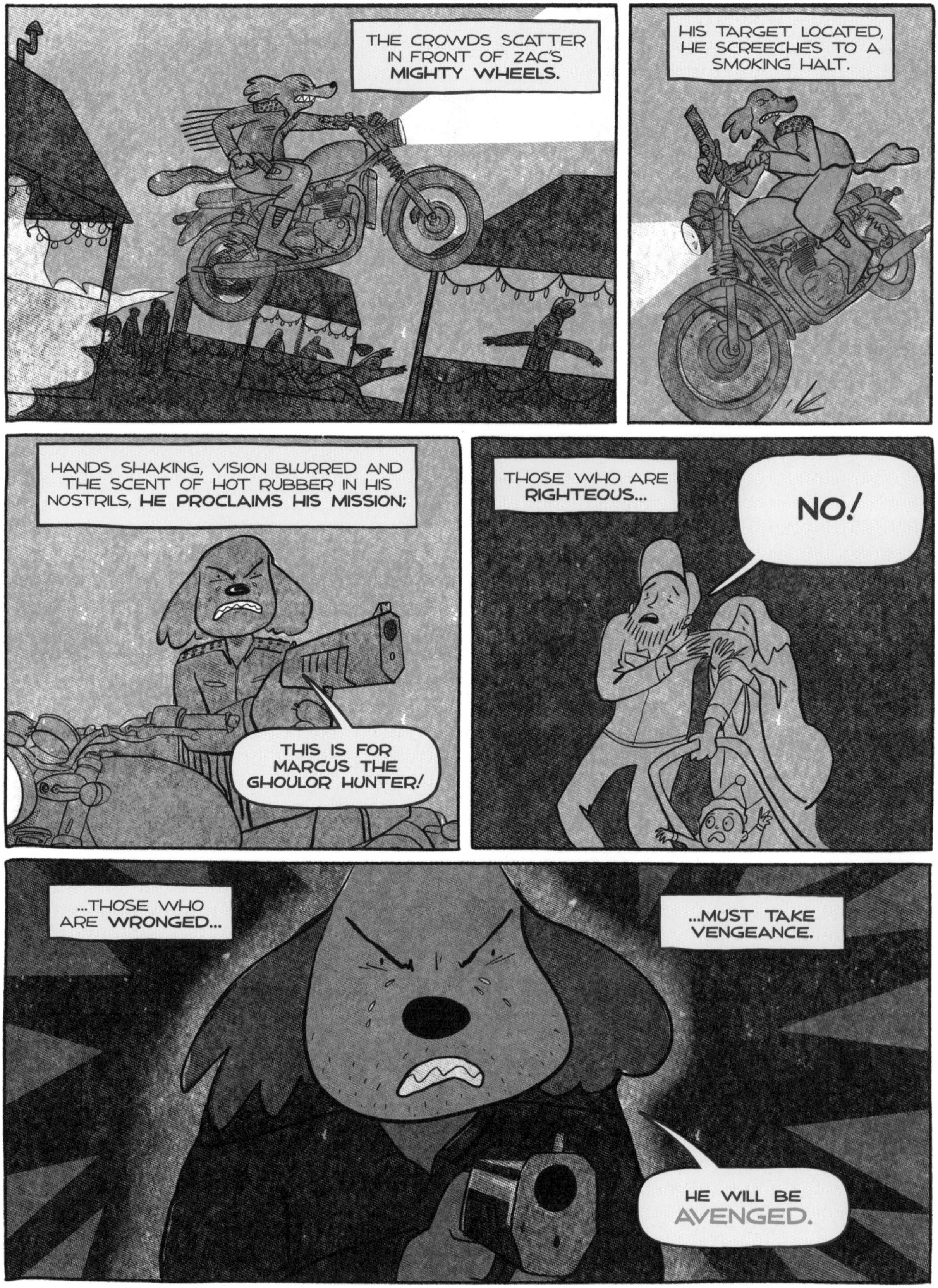
THE CROWDS SCATTER IN FRONT OF ZAC'S **MIGHTY WHEELS.**
HIS TARGET LOCATED, HE SCREECHES TO A SMOKING HALT.
HANDS SHAKING, VISION BLURRED AND THE SCENT OF HOT RUBBER IN HIS NOSTRILS, **HE PROCLAIMS HIS MISSION;**
THIS IS FOR MARCUS THE GHOULOR HUNTER!
THOSE WHO ARE **RIGHTEOUS...**
NO!
...THOSE WHO ARE **WRONGED...**
...MUST TAKE VENGEANCE.
HE WILL BE AVENGED.

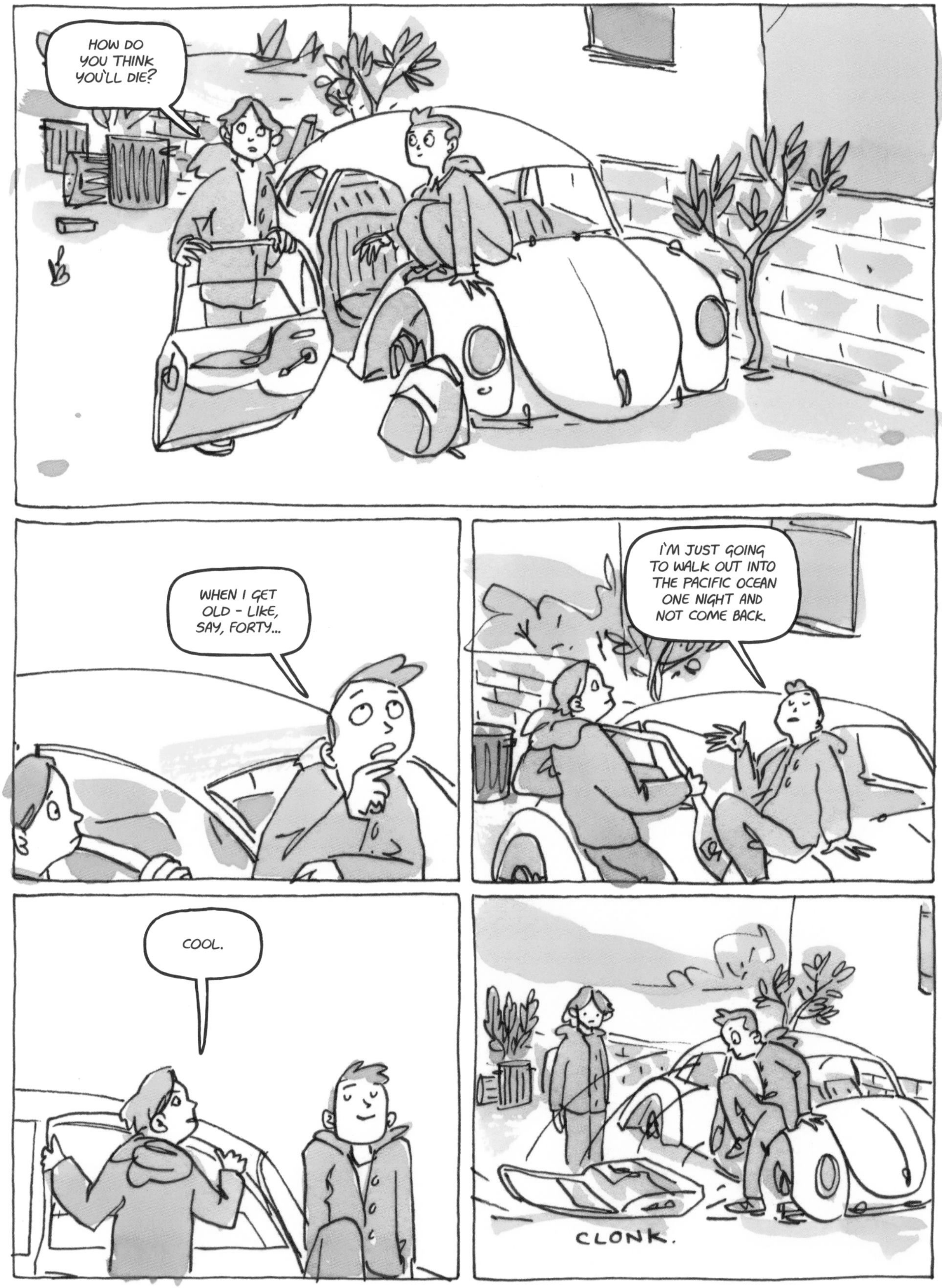
HOW DO YOU THINK YOU'LL DIE?
WHEN I GET OLD - LIKE, SAY, FORTY...
I'M JUST GOING TO WALK OUT INTO THE PACIFIC OCEAN ONE NIGHT AND NOT COME BACK.
COOL.
CLONK.

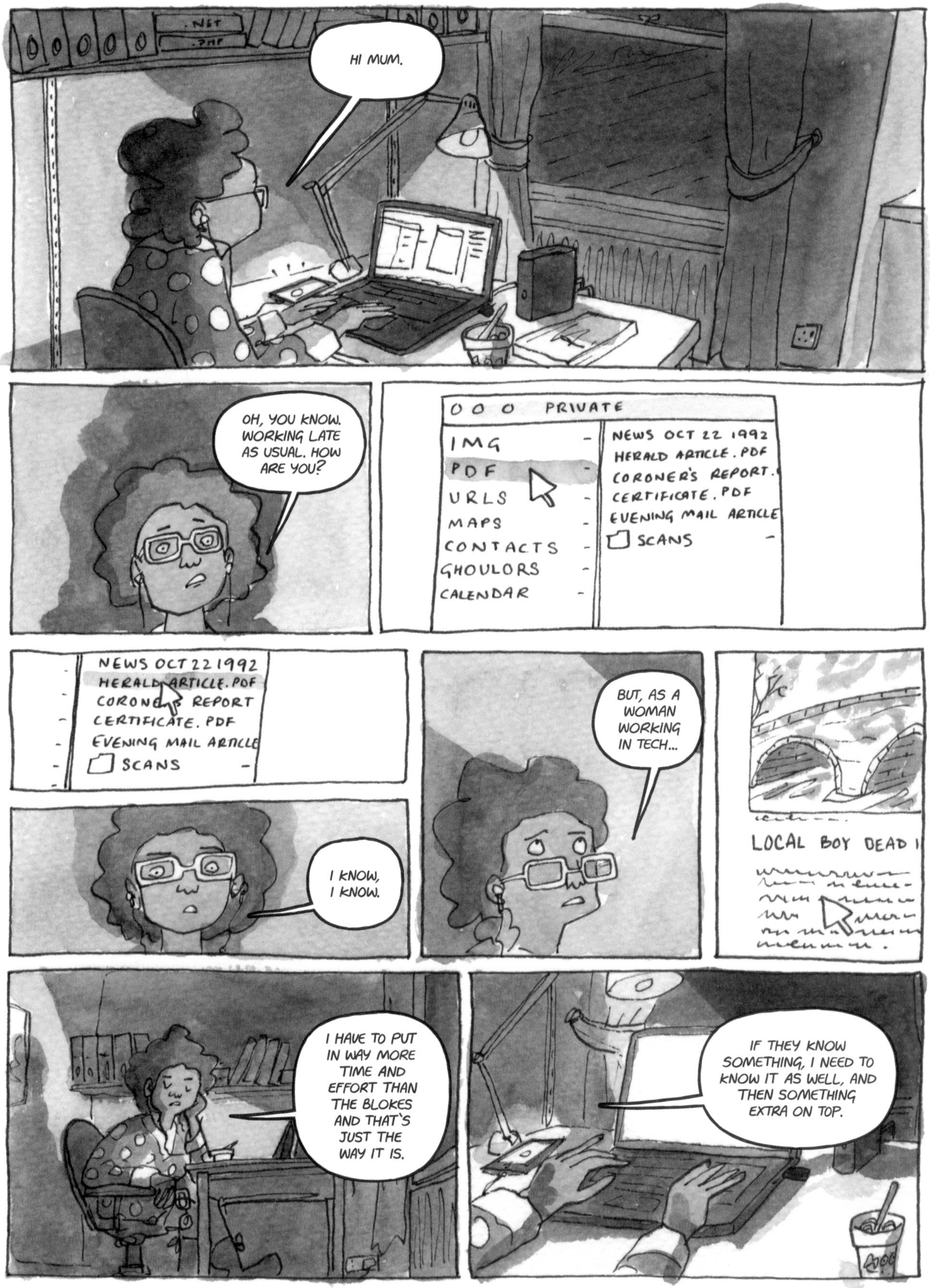

.NET
.PHP
HI MUM.
OH, YOU KNOW. WORKING LATE AS USUAL. HOW ARE YOU?
O O O PRIVATE
IMG
PDF
URLS
MAPS
CONTACTS
GHOULORS
CALENDAR
NEWS OCT 22 1992
HERALD ARTICLE.PDF
CORONER'S REPORT.
CERTIFICATE.PDF
EVENING MAIL ARTICLE
SCANS
NEWS OCT 22 1992
HERALD ARTICLE.PDF
CERTIFICATE.PDF
EVENING MAIL ARTICLE
SCANS
I KNOW, I KNOW.
BUT, AS A WOMAN WORKING IN TECH...
LOCAL BOY DEAD
I HAVE TO PUT IN WAY MORE TIME AND EFFORT THAN THE BLOKES AND THAT'S JUST THE WAY IT IS.
IF THEY KNOW SOMETHING, I NEED TO KNOW IT AS WELL, AND THEN SOMETHING EXTRA ON TOP.

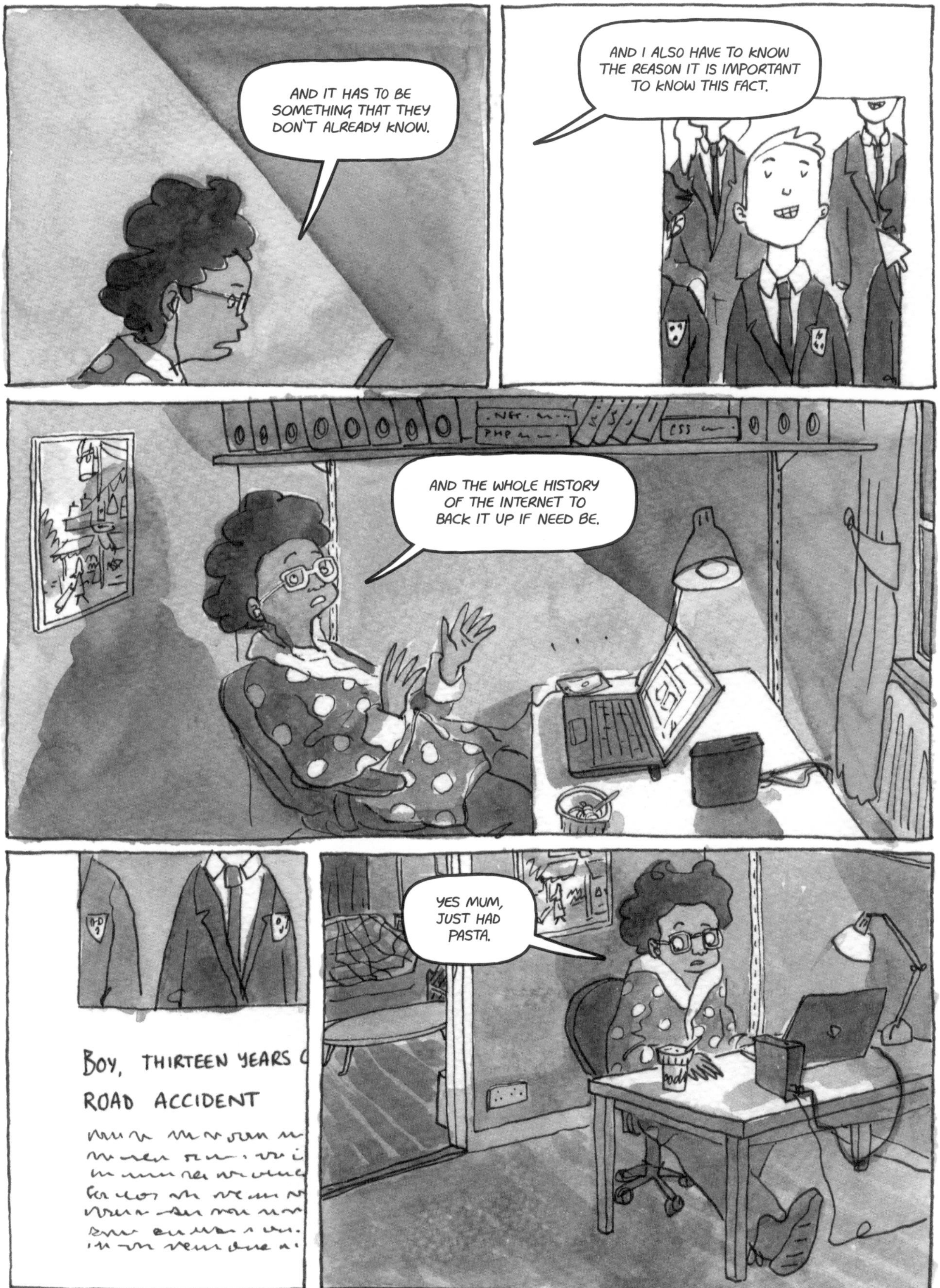
AND IT HAS TO BE SOMETHING THAT THEY DON'T ALREADY KNOW.
AND I ALSO HAVE TO KNOW THE REASON IT IS IMPORTANT TO KNOW THIS FACT.
AND THE WHOLE HISTORY OF THE INTERNET TO BACK IT UP IF NEED BE.
BOY, THIRTEEN YEARS
ROAD ACCIDENT
YES MUM, JUST HAD PASTA.

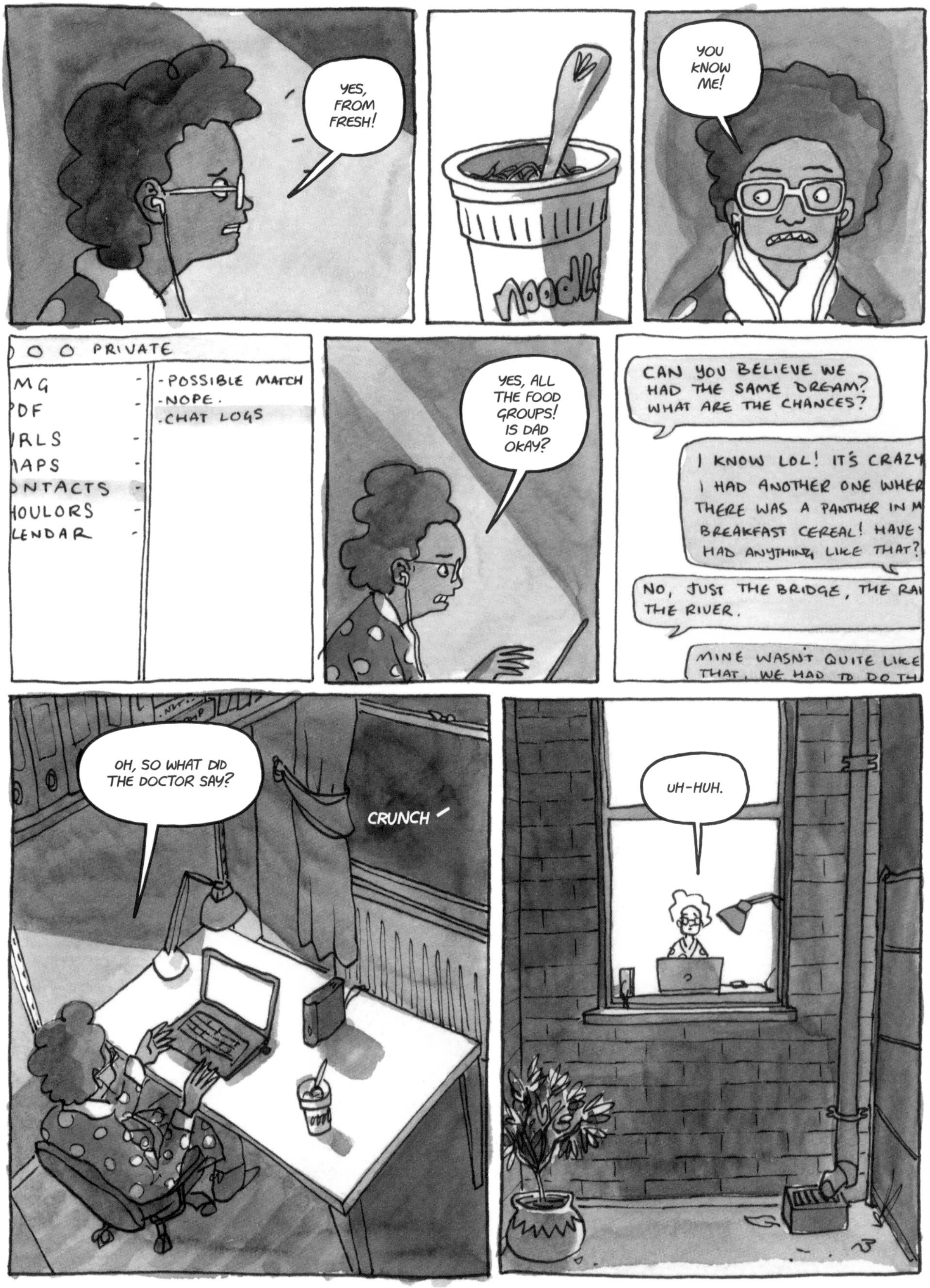
YES, FROM FRESH!
YOU KNOW ME!
O O O PRIVATE
MG
PDF
RLS
APS
NTACTS
OULORS
LENDAR
-POSSIBLE MATCH
-NOPE.
-CHAT LOGS
YES, ALL THE FOOD GROUPS! IS DAD OKAY?
CAN YOU BELIEVE WE HAD THE SAME DREAM? WHAT ARE THE CHANCES?
I KNOW LOL! IT'S CRAZY I HAD ANOTHER ONE WHER THERE WAS A PANTHER IN M BREAKFAST CEREAL! HAVE HAD ANYTHING LIKE THAT?
NO, JUST THE BRIDGE, THE RA THE RIVER.
MINE WASN'T QUITE LIKE
OH, SO WHAT DID THE DOCTOR SAY?
CRUNCH
UH-HUH.

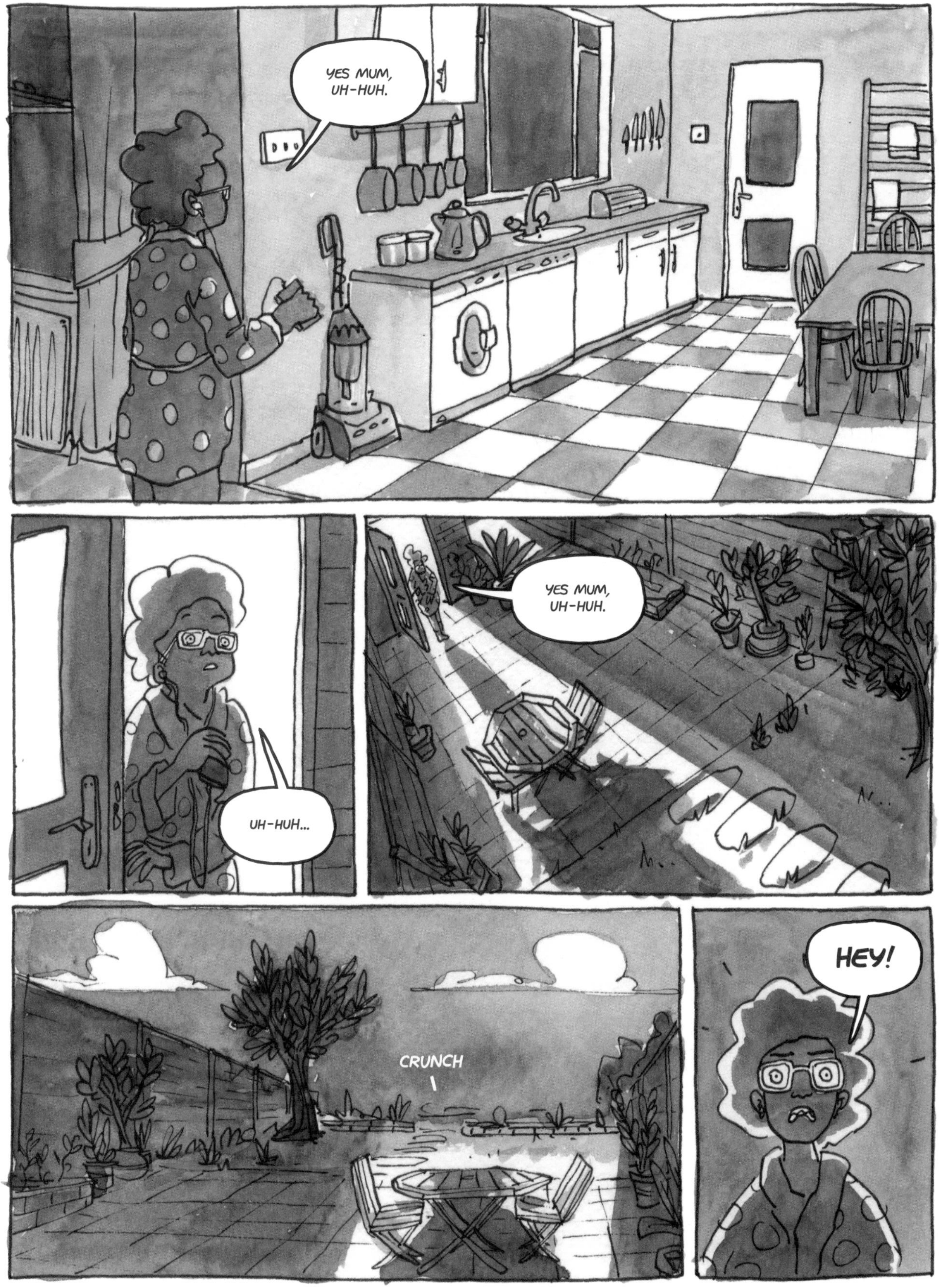
YES MUM, UH-HUH.
UH-HUH...
YES MUM, UH-HUH.
CRUNCH
HEY!

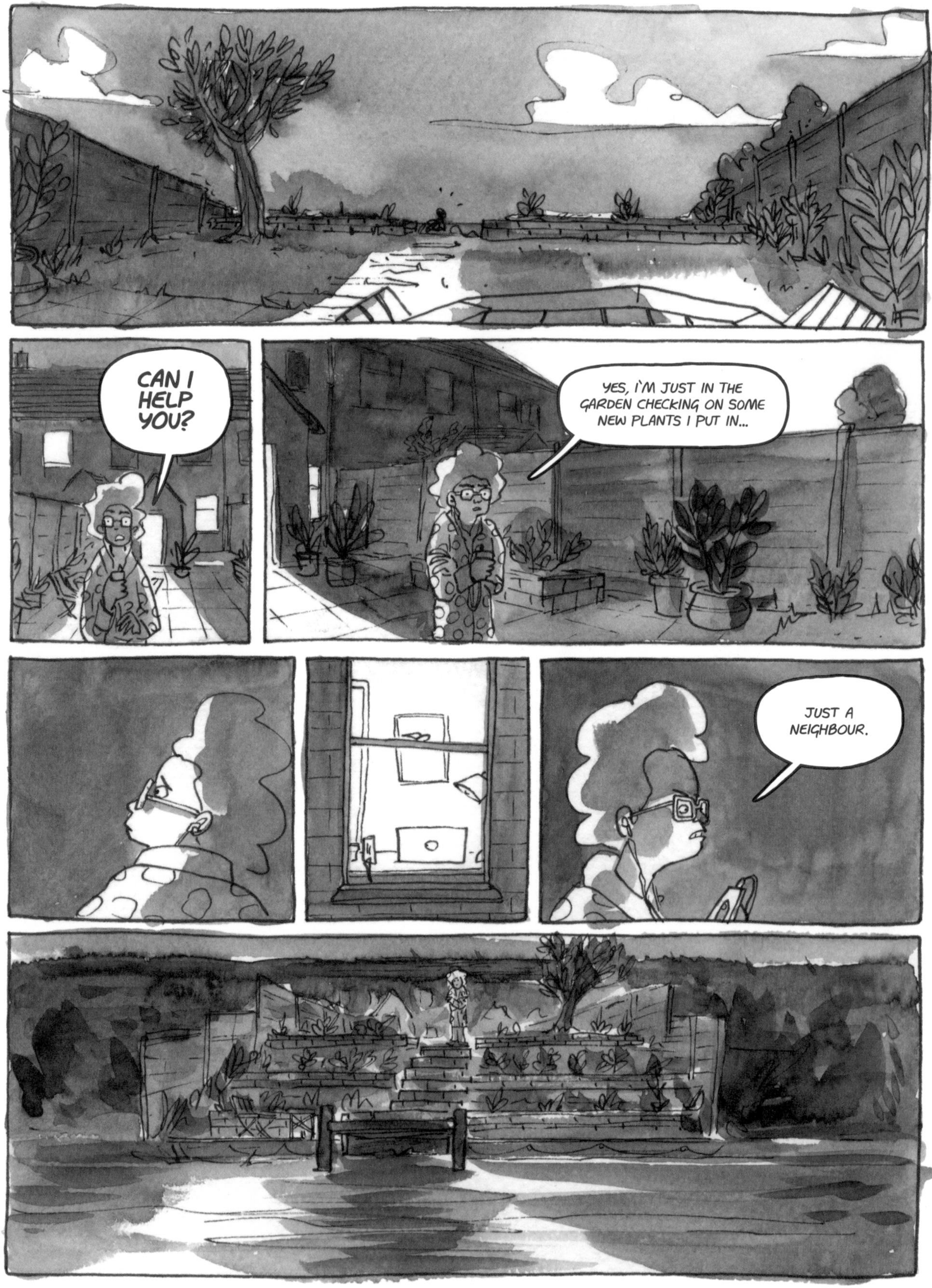
CAN I HELP YOU?
YES, I'M JUST IN THE GARDEN CHECKING ON SOME NEW PLANTS I PUT IN...
JUST A NEIGHBOUR.

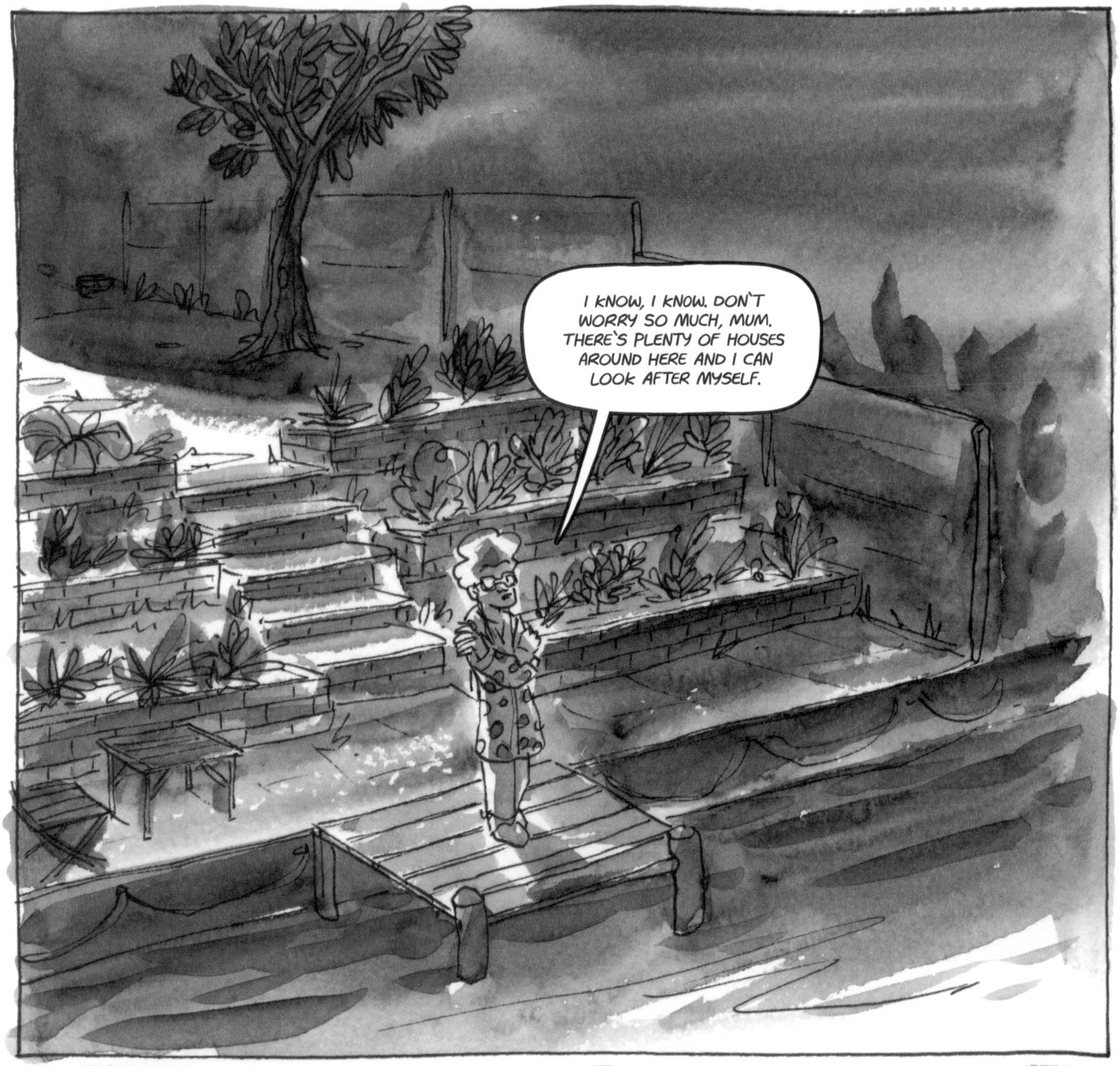
I KNOW, I KNOW. DON'T WORRY SO MUCH, MUM. THERE'S PLENTY OF HOUSES AROUND HERE AND I CAN LOOK AFTER MYSELF.

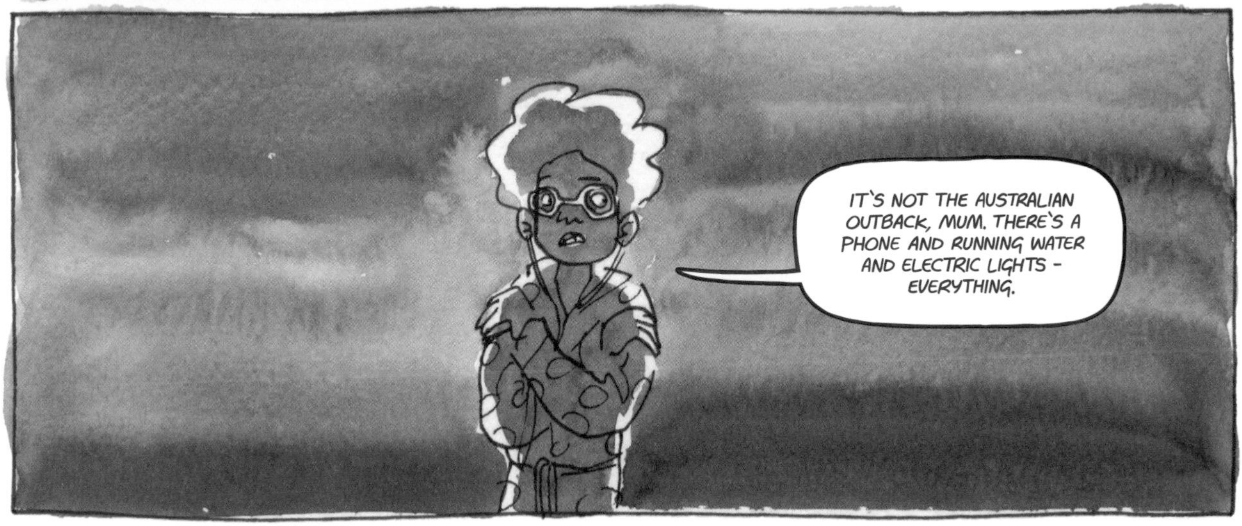
IT'S NOT THE AUSTRALIAN OUTBACK, MUM. THERE'S A PHONE AND RUNNING WATER AND ELECTRIC LIGHTS - EVERYTHING.

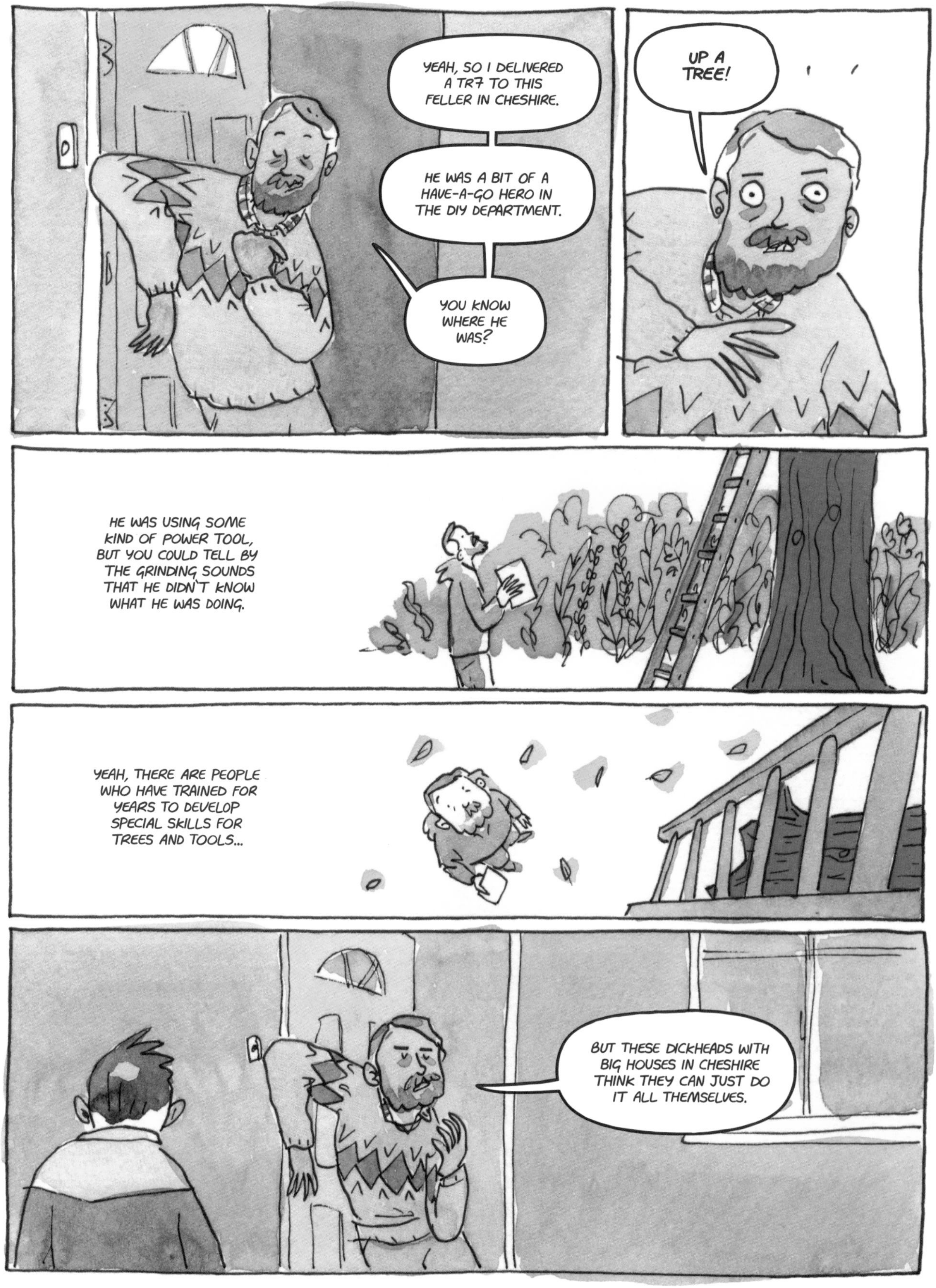
YEAH, SO I DELIVERED A TR7 TO THIS FELLER IN CHESHIRE.
HE WAS A BIT OF A HAVE-A-GO HERO IN THE DIY DEPARTMENT.
YOU KNOW WHERE HE WAS?
UP A TREE!
HE WAS USING SOME KIND OF POWER TOOL, BUT YOU COULD TELL BY THE GRINDING SOUNDS THAT HE DIDN'T KNOW WHAT HE WAS DOING.
YEAH, THERE ARE PEOPLE WHO HAVE TRAINED FOR YEARS TO DEVELOP SPECIAL SKILLS FOR TREES AND TOOLS...
BUT THESE DICKHEADS WITH BIG HOUSES IN CHESHIRE THINK THEY CAN JUST DO IT ALL THEMSELVES.

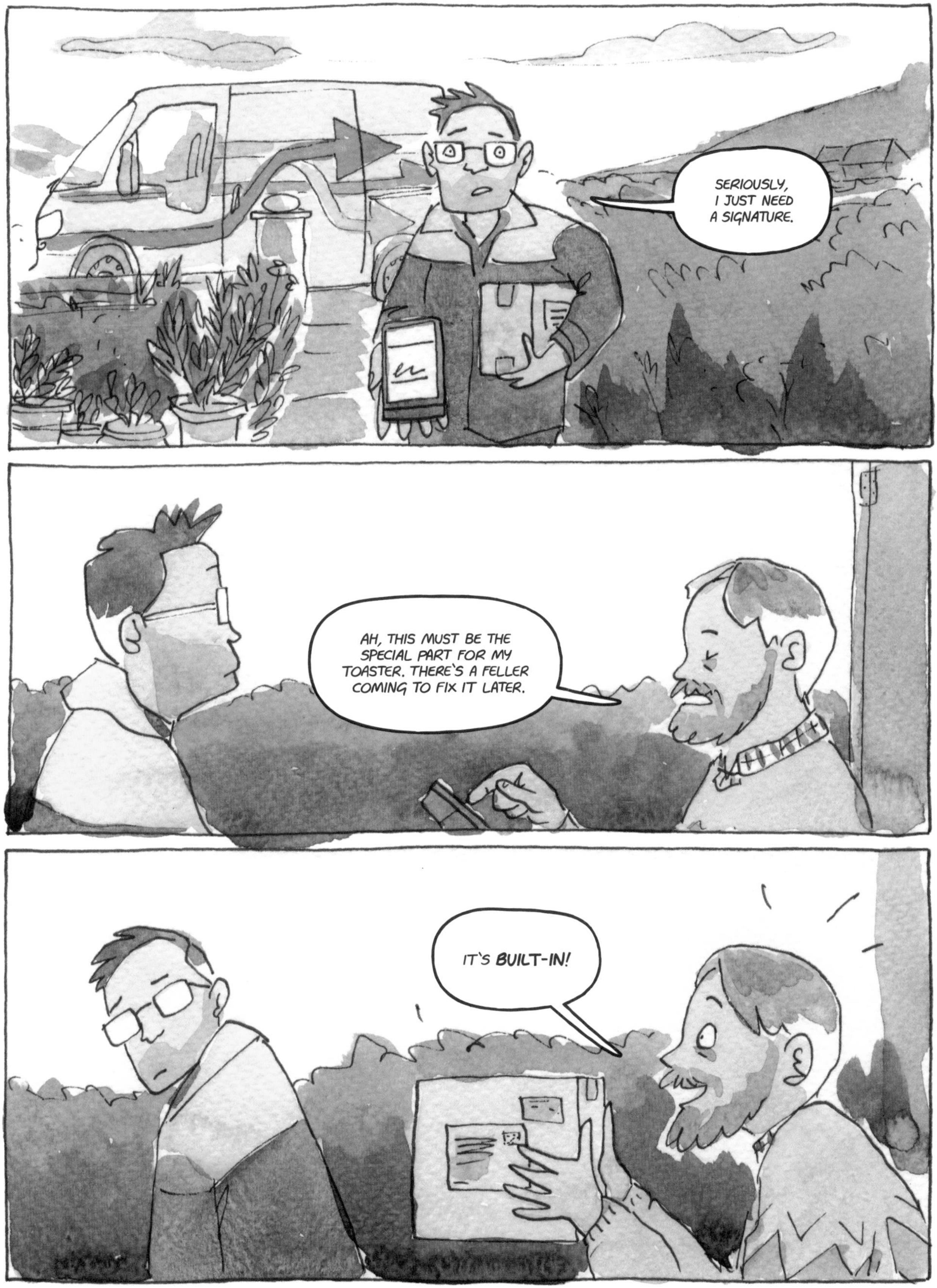
SERIOUSLY, I JUST NEED A SIGNATURE.
AH, THIS MUST BE THE SPECIAL PART FOR MY TOASTER. THERE'S A FELLER COMING TO FIX IT LATER.
IT'S **BUILT-IN**!

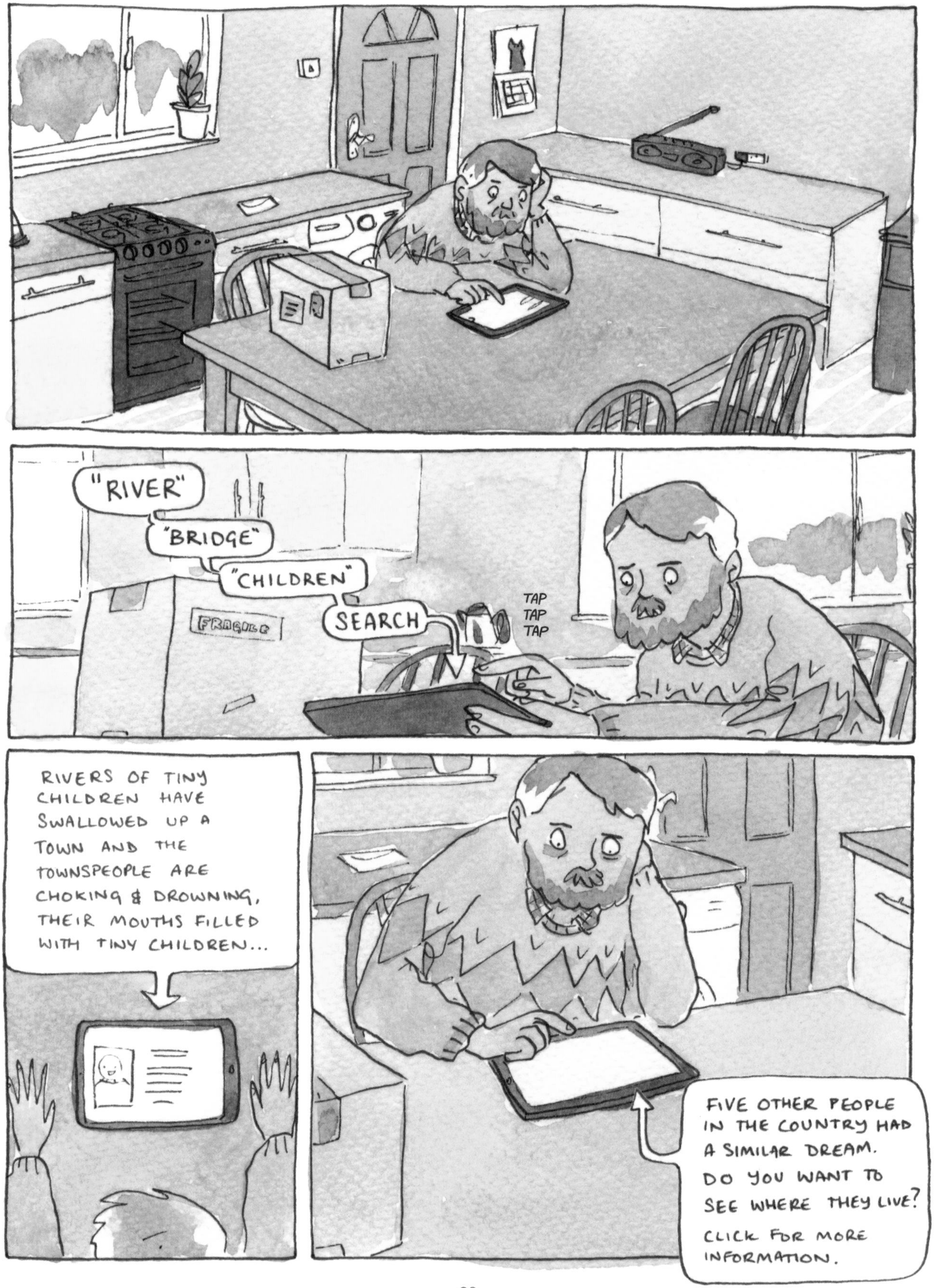

"RIVER"
"BRIDGE"
"CHILDREN"
SEARCH
TAP TAP TAP
FRAGILE
RIVERS OF TINY CHILDREN HAVE SWALLOWED UP A TOWN AND THE TOWNSPEOPLE ARE CHOKING & DROWNING, THEIR MOUTHS FILLED WITH TINY CHILDREN...
FIVE OTHER PEOPLE IN THE COUNTRY HAD A SIMILAR DREAM. DO YOU WANT TO SEE WHERE THEY LIVE? CLICK FOR MORE INFORMATION.

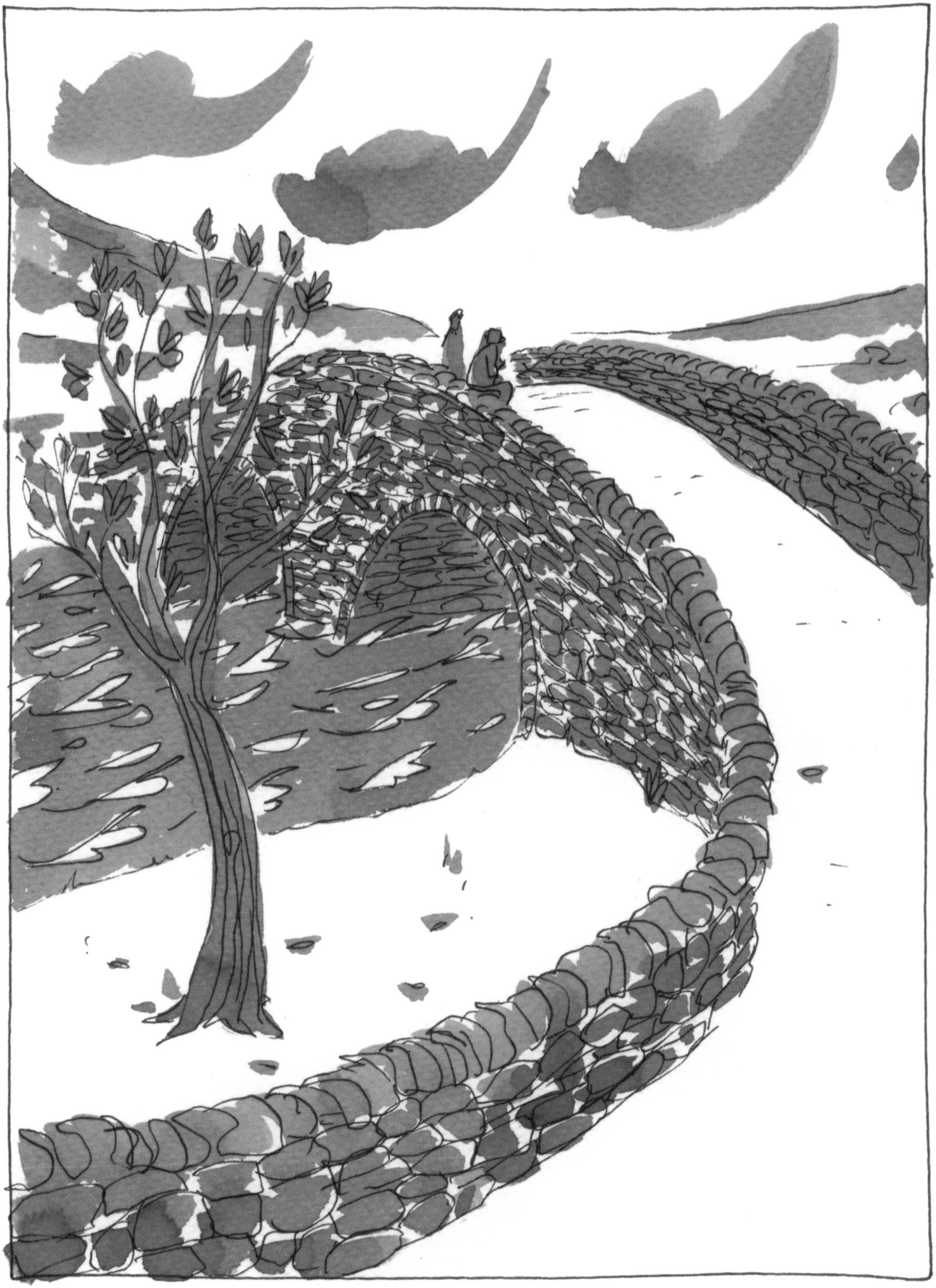

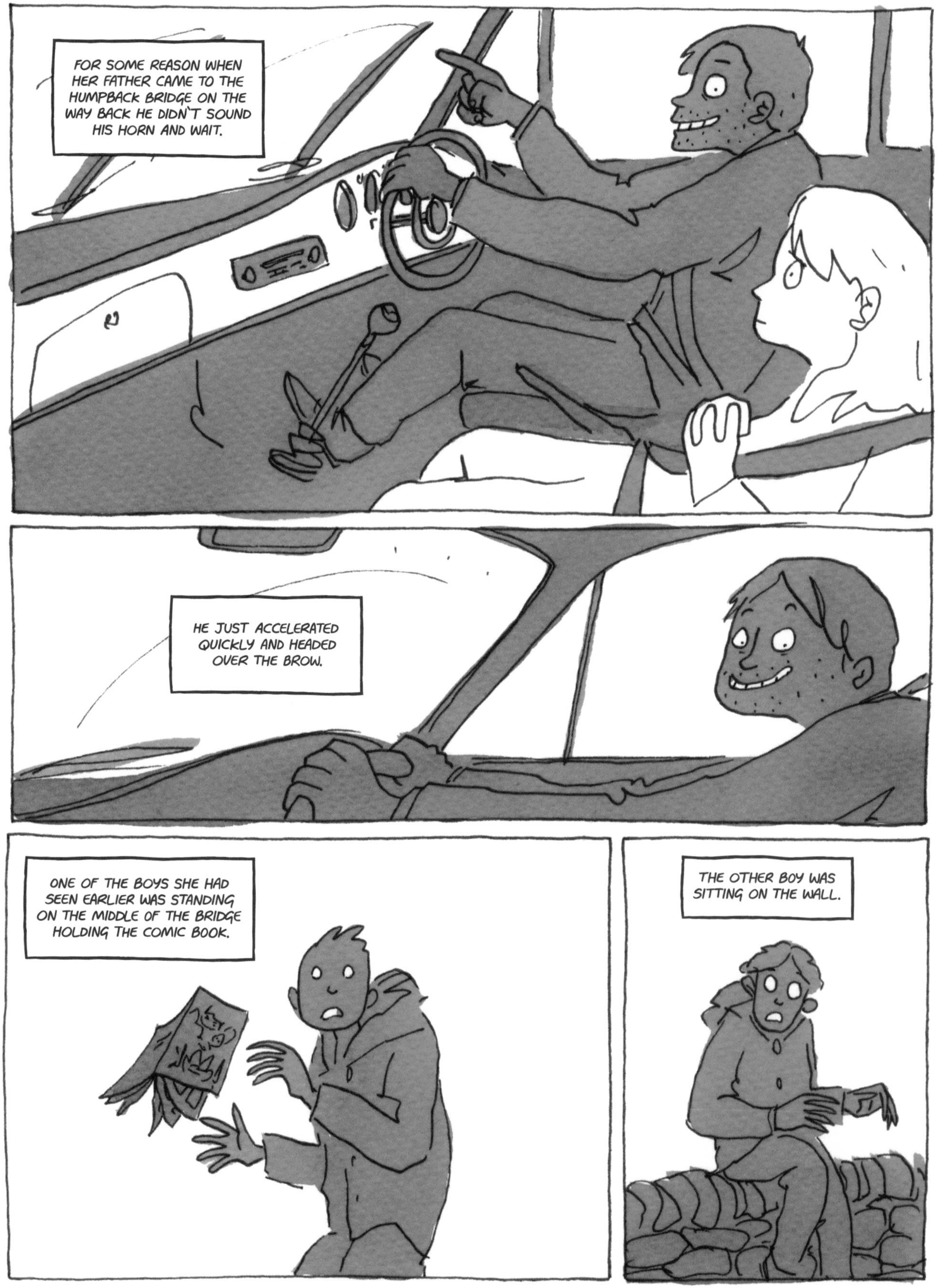
FOR SOME REASON WHEN HER FATHER CAME TO THE HUMPBACK BRIDGE ON THE WAY BACK HE DIDN'T SOUND HIS HORN AND WAIT.
HE JUST ACCELERATED QUICKLY AND HEADED OVER THE BROW.
ONE OF THE BOYS SHE HAD SEEN EARLIER WAS STANDING ON THE MIDDLE OF THE BRIDGE HOLDING THE COMIC BOOK.
THE OTHER BOY WAS SITTING ON THE WALL.

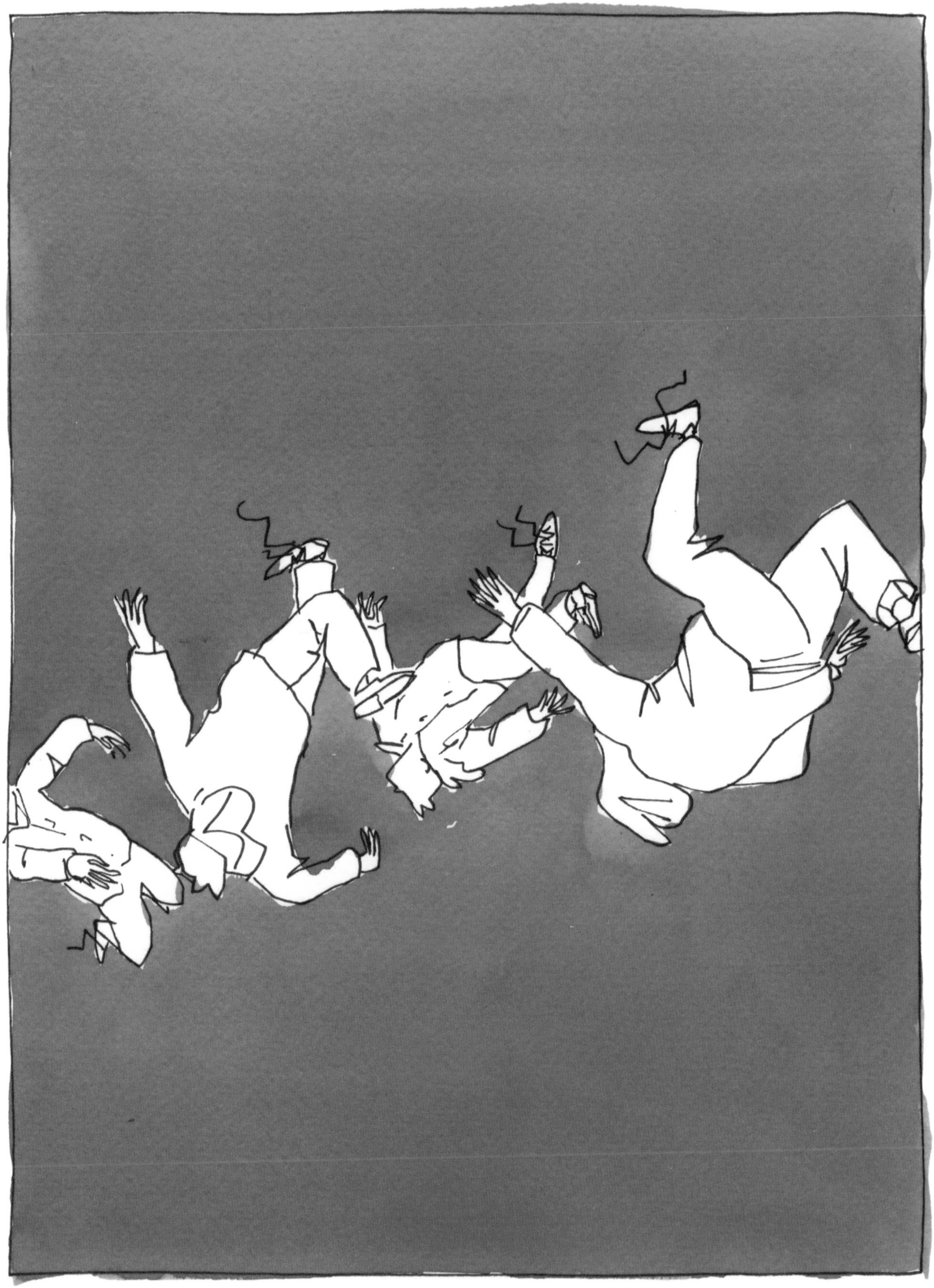

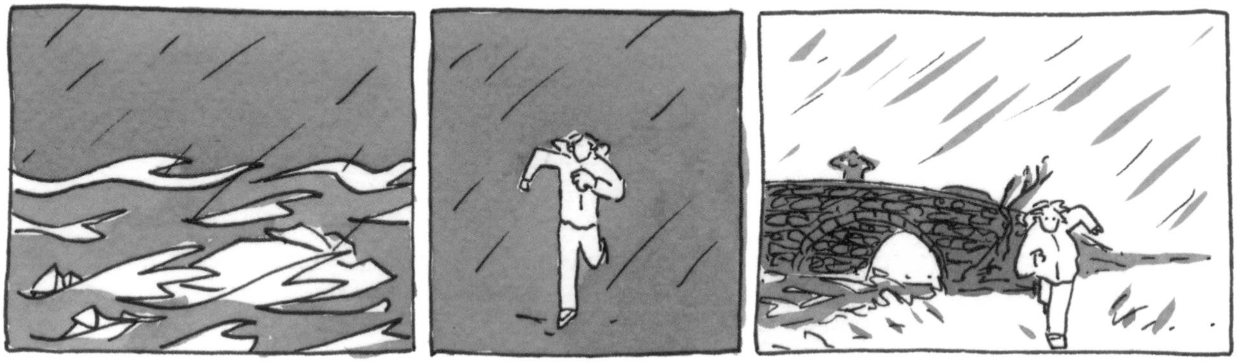

THE BOY WAS RUSHED AWAY ON THE CURRENT AND HIS FRIEND JUMPED OFF THE WALL AND RAN ALONG THE BANK OF THE RIVER AS IF HE COULD CATCH UP AND SAVE HIM.

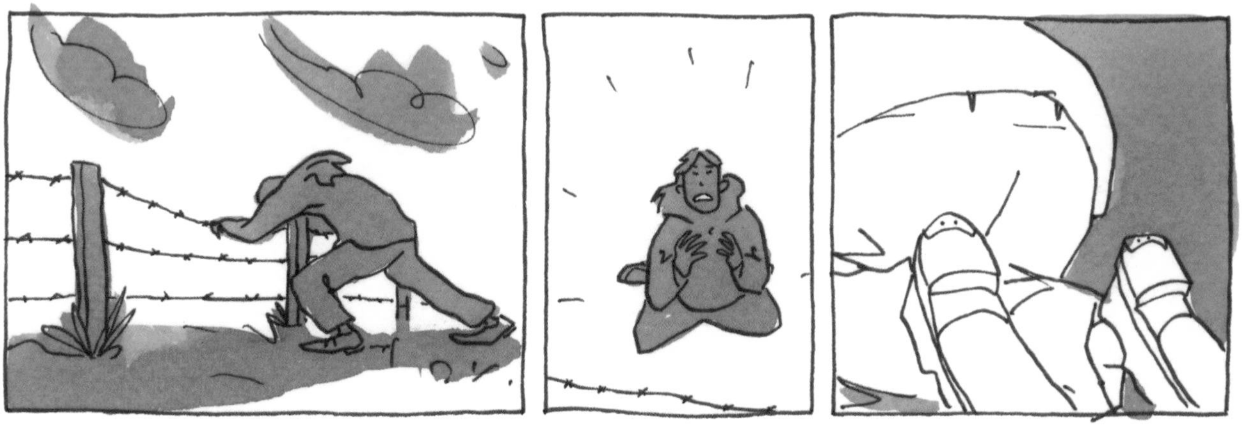

BUT SUDDENLY A BARBED-WIRE FENCE WAS BLOCKING HIS WAY, AND THE BOY THREW HIMSELF ONTO THE GRASS AND BEGAN TO BEAT THE EARTH WITH HIS FISTS.

THE SOLES OF HIS SHOES POINTED UP TOWARDS THE SKY LIKE TWO LONG FACES.

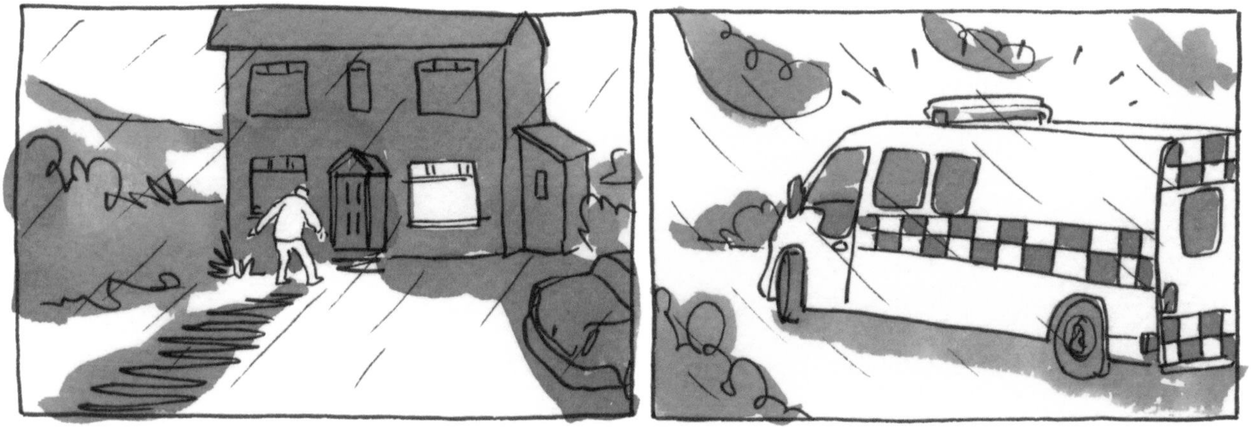

HER DAD RAN TO A NEARBY HOUSE WHERE A FARMER LIVED AND AFTER WHAT SEEMED LIKE AGES, BUT WAS NAMED AT THE INQUEST AS FOURTEEN AND A HALF MINUTES, AN AMBULANCE TURNED UP.

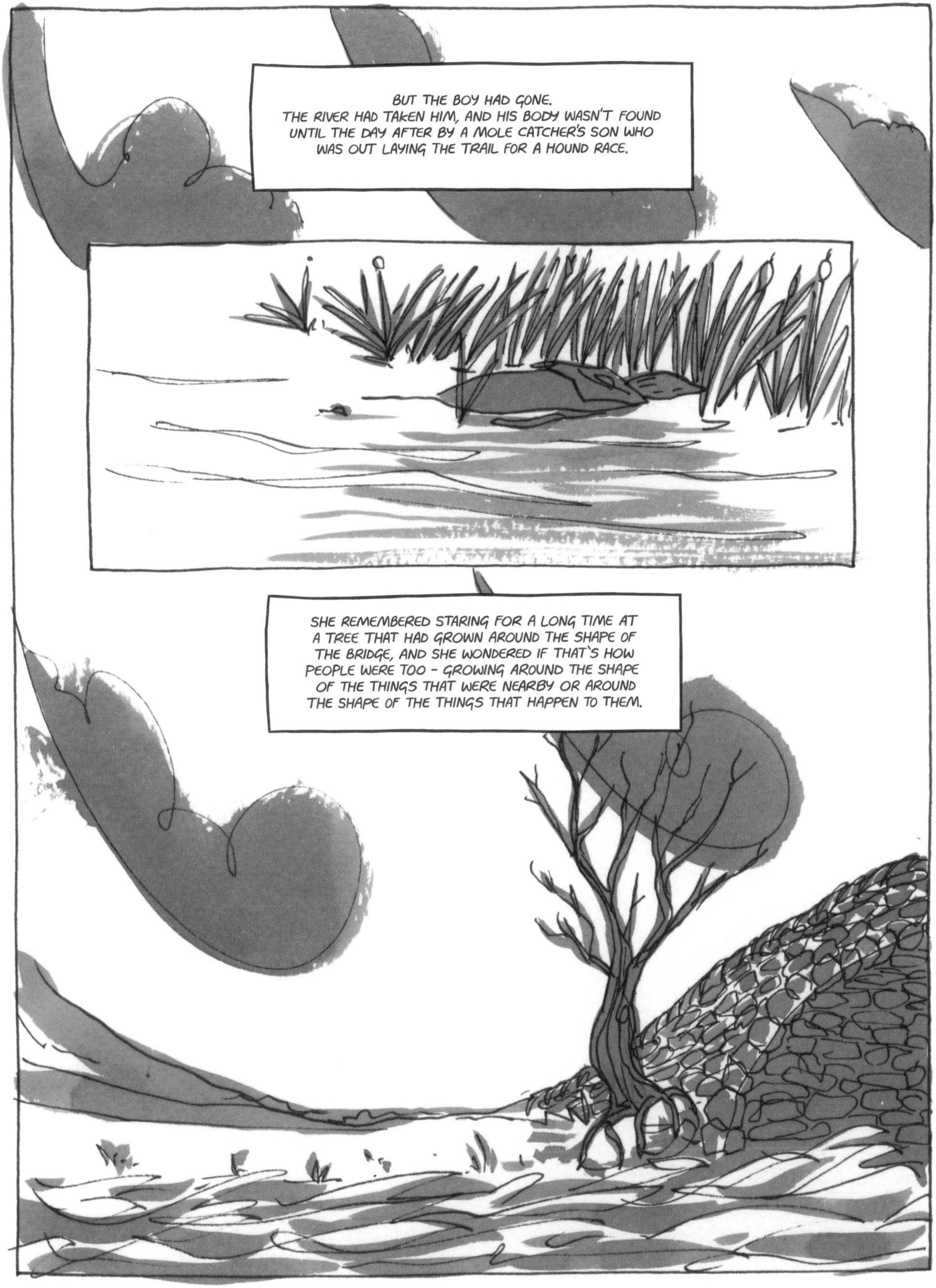
BUT THE BOY HAD GONE. THE RIVER HAD TAKEN HIM, AND HIS BODY WASN'T FOUND UNTIL THE DAY AFTER BY A MOLE CATCHER'S SON WHO WAS OUT LAYING THE TRAIL FOR A HOUND RACE.
SHE REMEMBERED STARING FOR A LONG TIME AT A TREE THAT HAD GROWN AROUND THE SHAPE OF THE BRIDGE, AND SHE WONDERED IF THAT'S HOW PEOPLE WERE TOO - GROWING AROUND THE SHAPE OF THE THINGS THAT WERE NEARBY OR AROUND THE SHAPE OF THE THINGS THAT HAPPEN TO THEM.

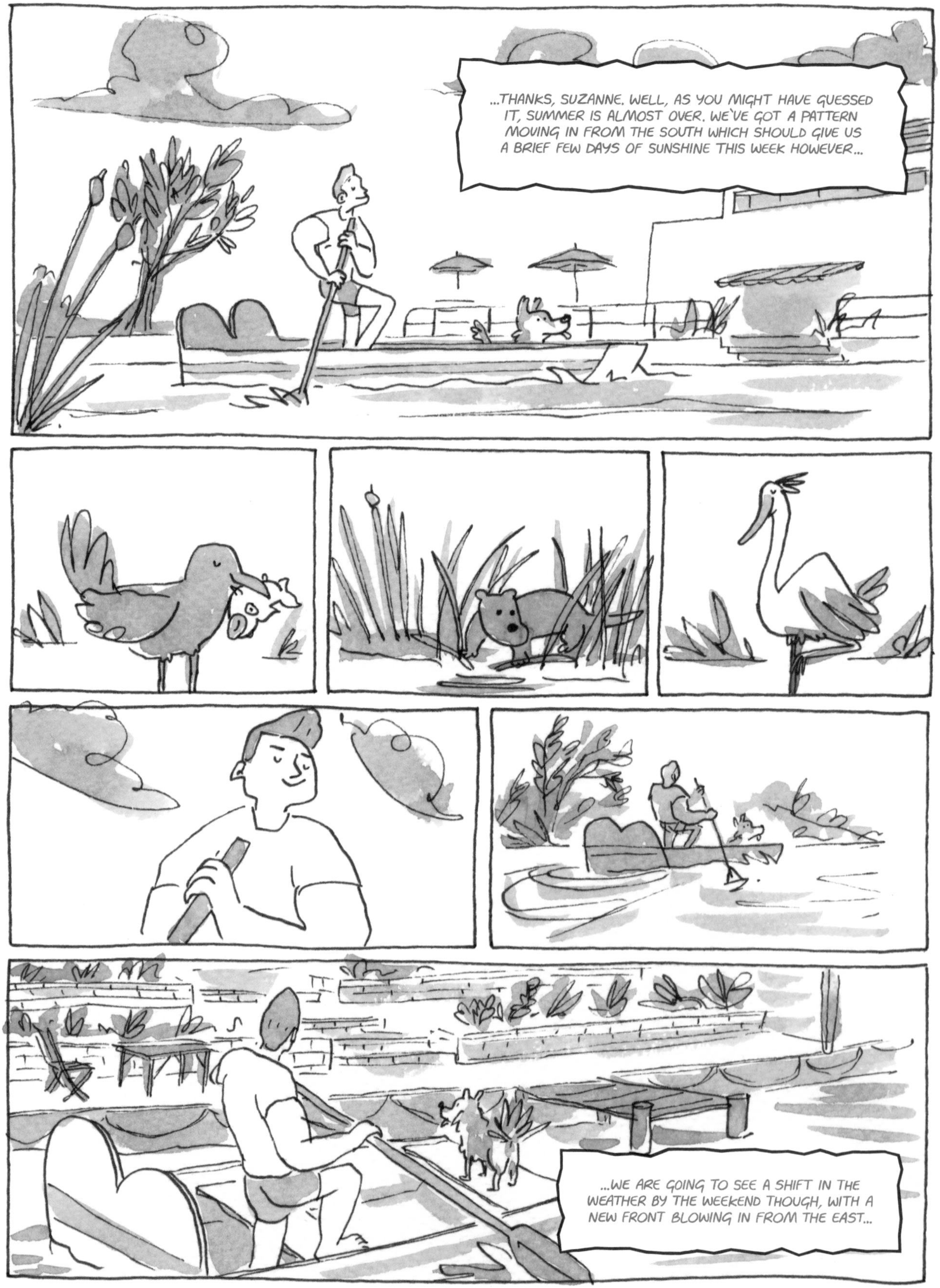
...THANKS, SUZANNE. WELL, AS YOU MIGHT HAVE GUESSED IT, SUMMER IS ALMOST OVER. WE'VE GOT A PATTERN MOVING IN FROM THE SOUTH WHICH SHOULD GIVE US A BRIEF FEW DAYS OF SUNSHINE THIS WEEK HOWEVER...
...WE ARE GOING TO SEE A SHIFT IN THE WEATHER BY THE WEEKEND THOUGH, WITH A NEW FRONT BLOWING IN FROM THE EAST...

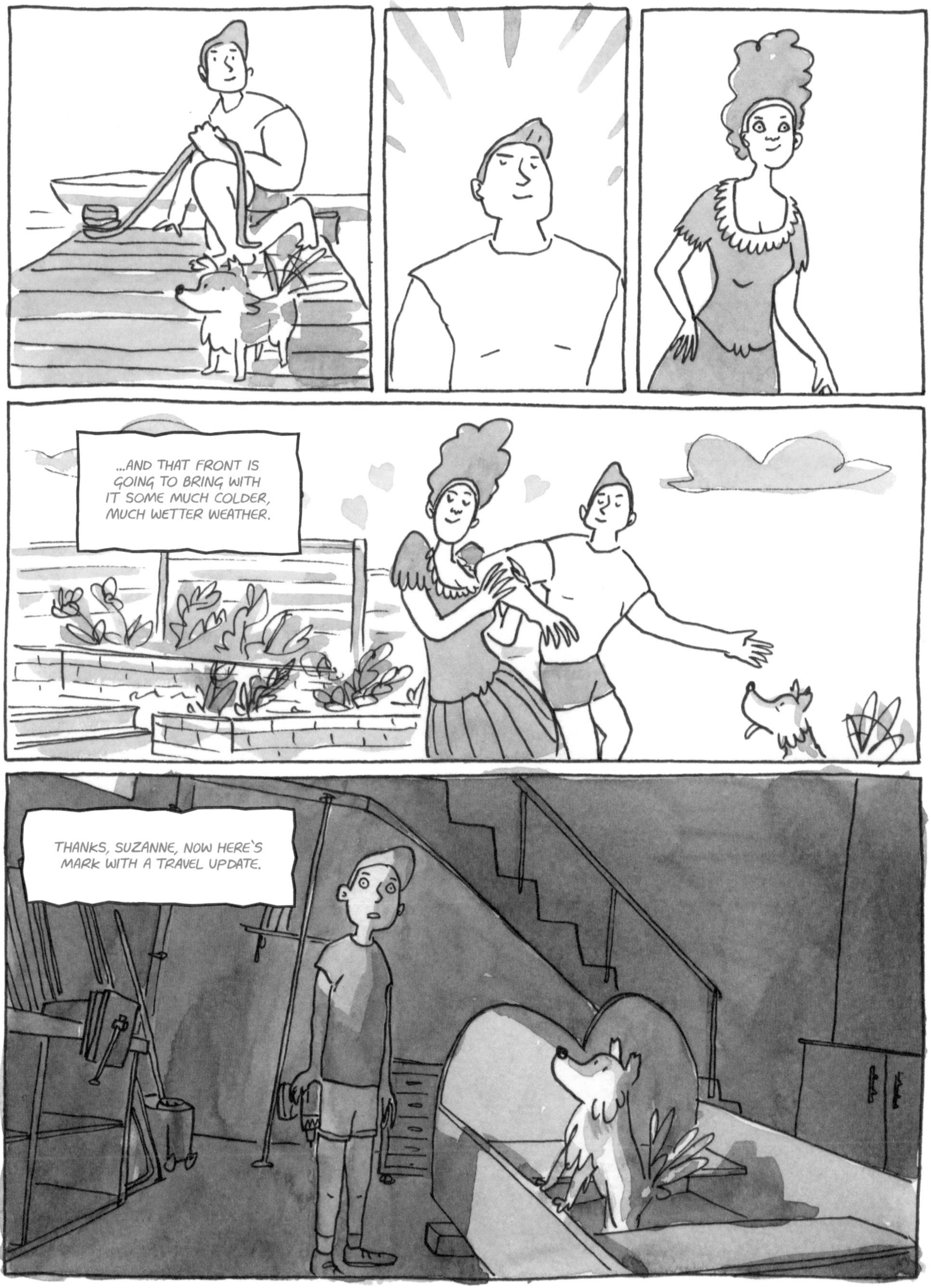

...AND THAT FRONT IS GOING TO BRING WITH IT SOME MUCH COLDER, MUCH WETTER WEATHER.
THANKS, SUZANNE, NOW HERE'S MARK WITH A TRAVEL UPDATE.

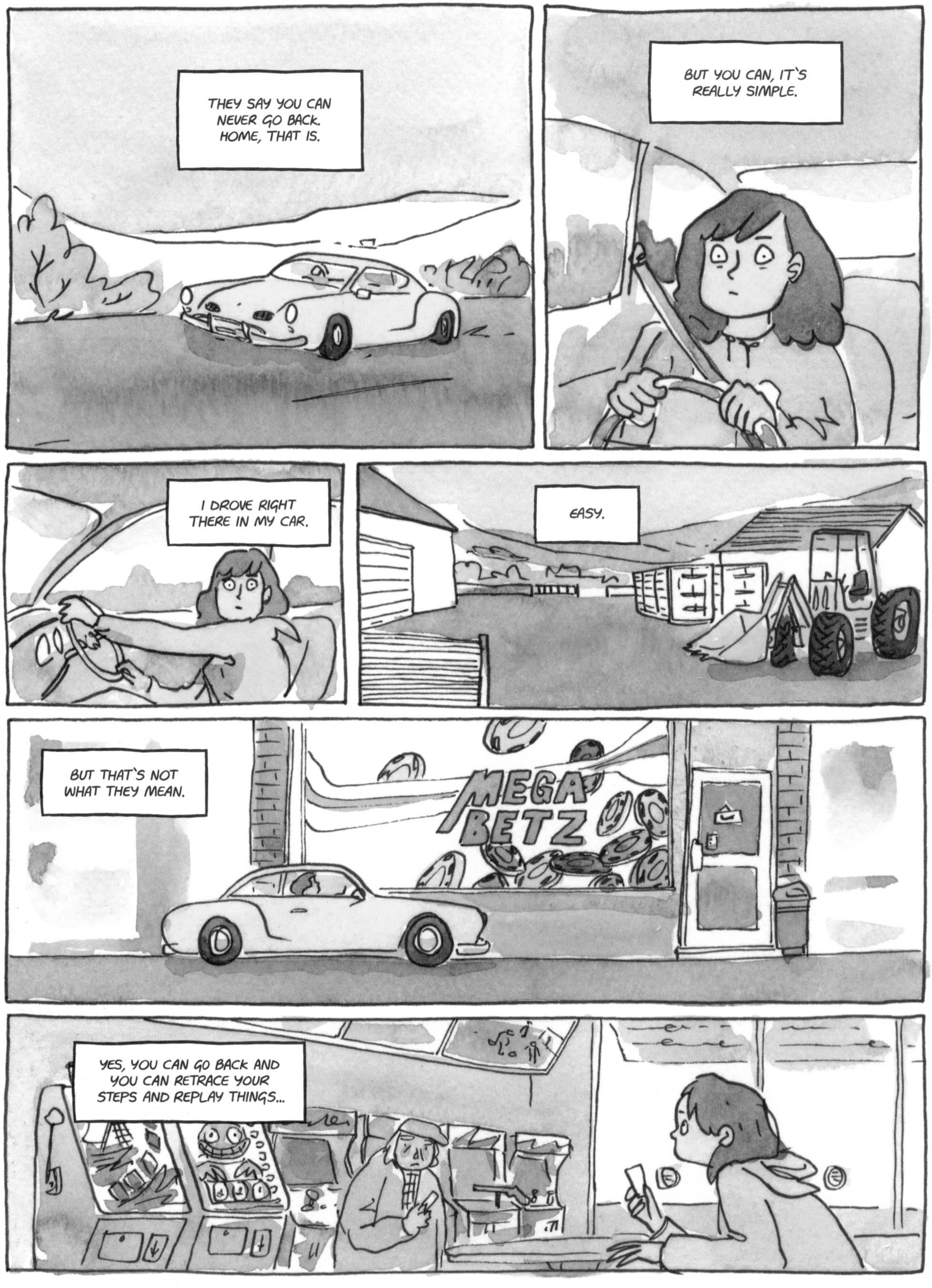
THEY SAY YOU CAN NEVER GO BACK. HOME, THAT IS.
BUT YOU CAN, IT`S REALLY SIMPLE.
I DROVE RIGHT THERE IN MY CAR.
EASY.
BUT THAT`S NOT WHAT THEY MEAN.
MEGA BETZ
YES, YOU CAN GO BACK AND YOU CAN RETRACE YOUR STEPS AND REPLAY THINGS...

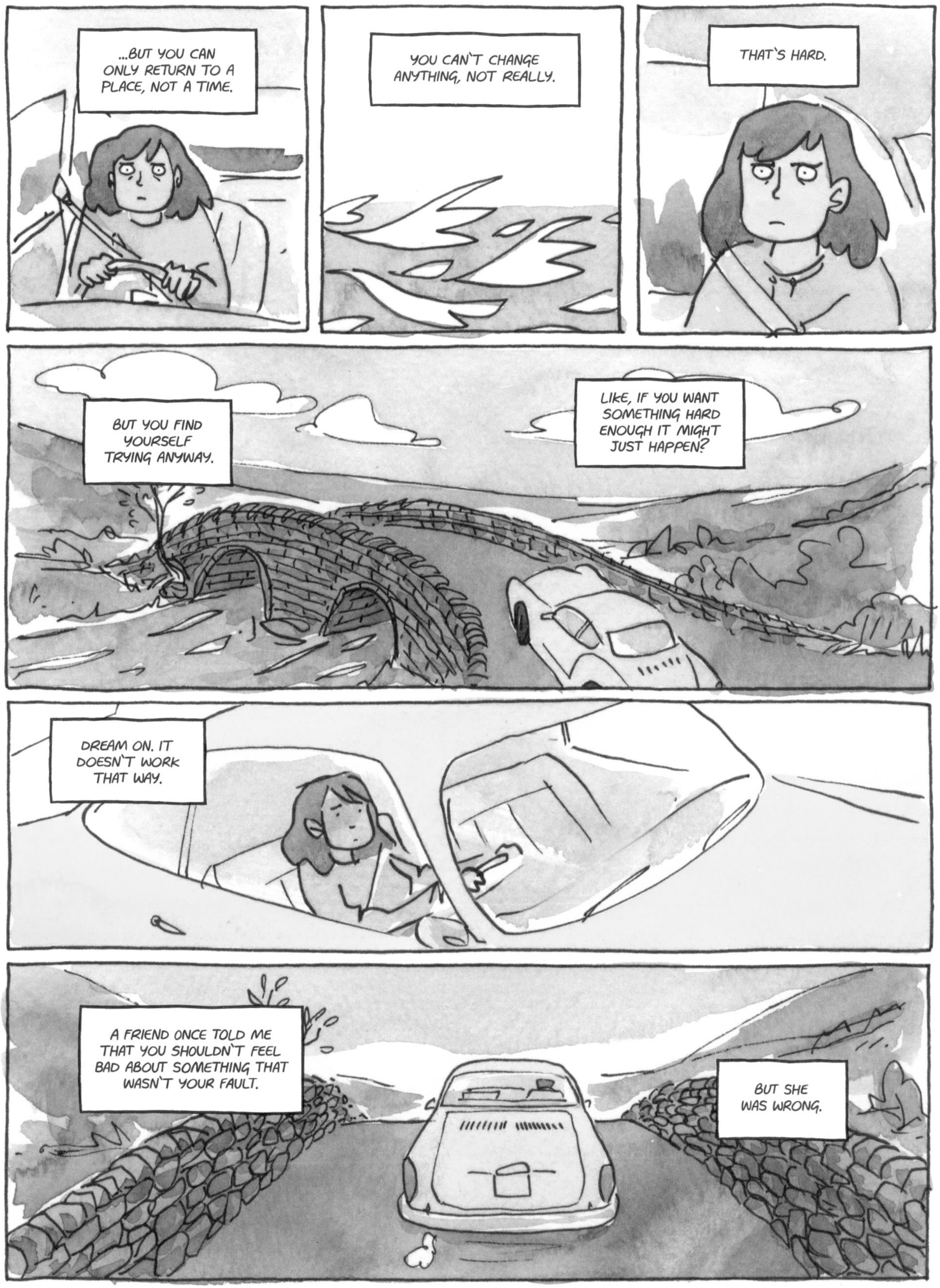
...BUT YOU CAN ONLY RETURN TO A PLACE, NOT A TIME.
YOU CAN'T CHANGE ANYTHING, NOT REALLY.
THAT'S HARD.
BUT YOU FIND YOURSELF TRYING ANYWAY.
LIKE, IF YOU WANT SOMETHING HARD ENOUGH IT MIGHT JUST HAPPEN?
DREAM ON. IT DOESN'T WORK THAT WAY.
A FRIEND ONCE TOLD ME THAT YOU SHOULDN'T FEEL BAD ABOUT SOMETHING THAT WASN'T YOUR FAULT.
BUT SHE WAS WRONG.

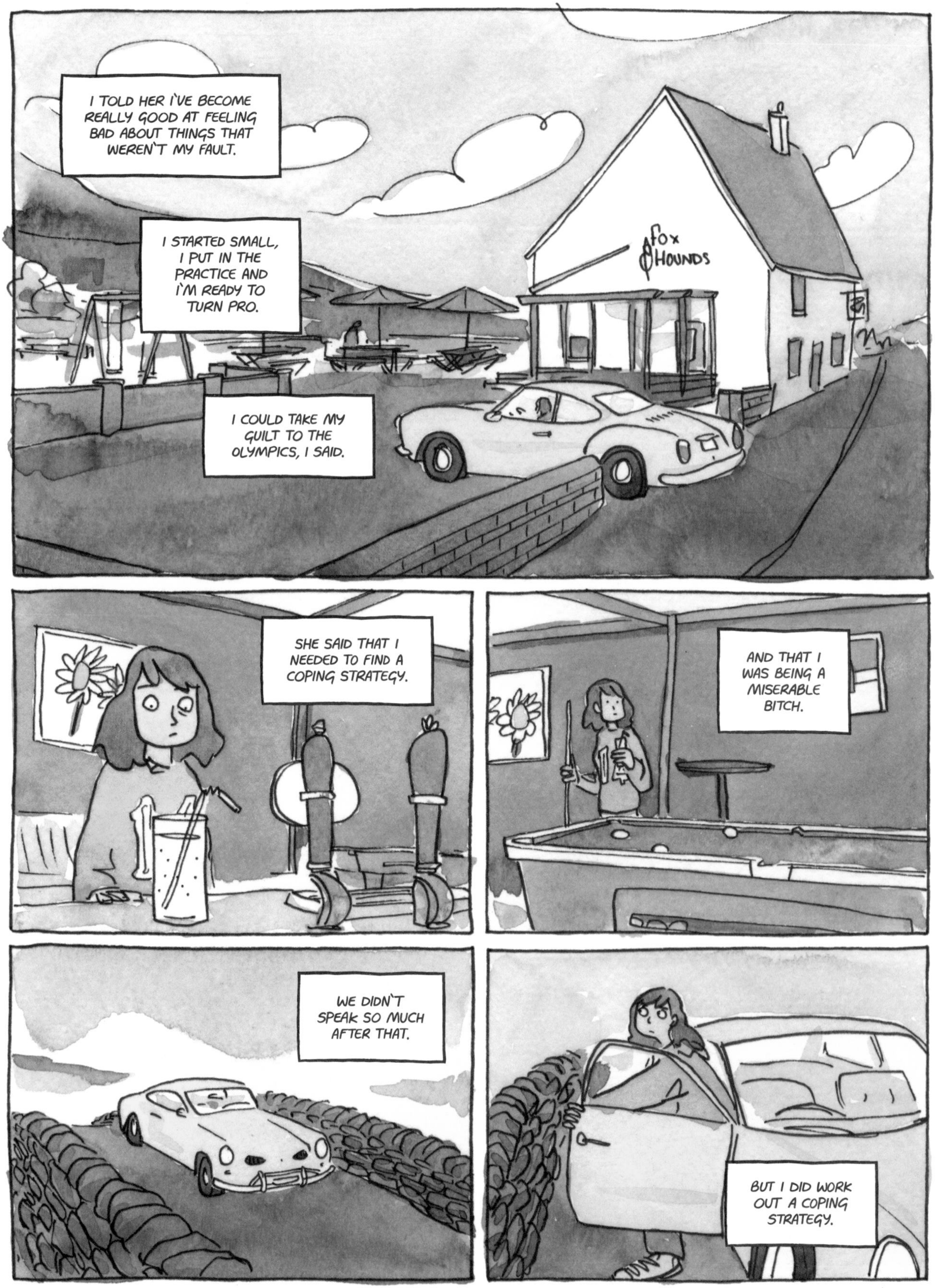
I TOLD HER I'VE BECOME REALLY GOOD AT FEELING BAD ABOUT THINGS THAT WEREN'T MY FAULT.
FOX HOUNDS
I STARTED SMALL, I PUT IN THE PRACTICE AND I'M READY TO TURN PRO.
I COULD TAKE MY GUILT TO THE OLYMPICS, I SAID.
SHE SAID THAT I NEEDED TO FIND A COPING STRATEGY.
AND THAT I WAS BEING A MISERABLE BITCH.
WE DIDN'T SPEAK SO MUCH AFTER THAT.
BUT I DID WORK OUT A COPING STRATEGY.

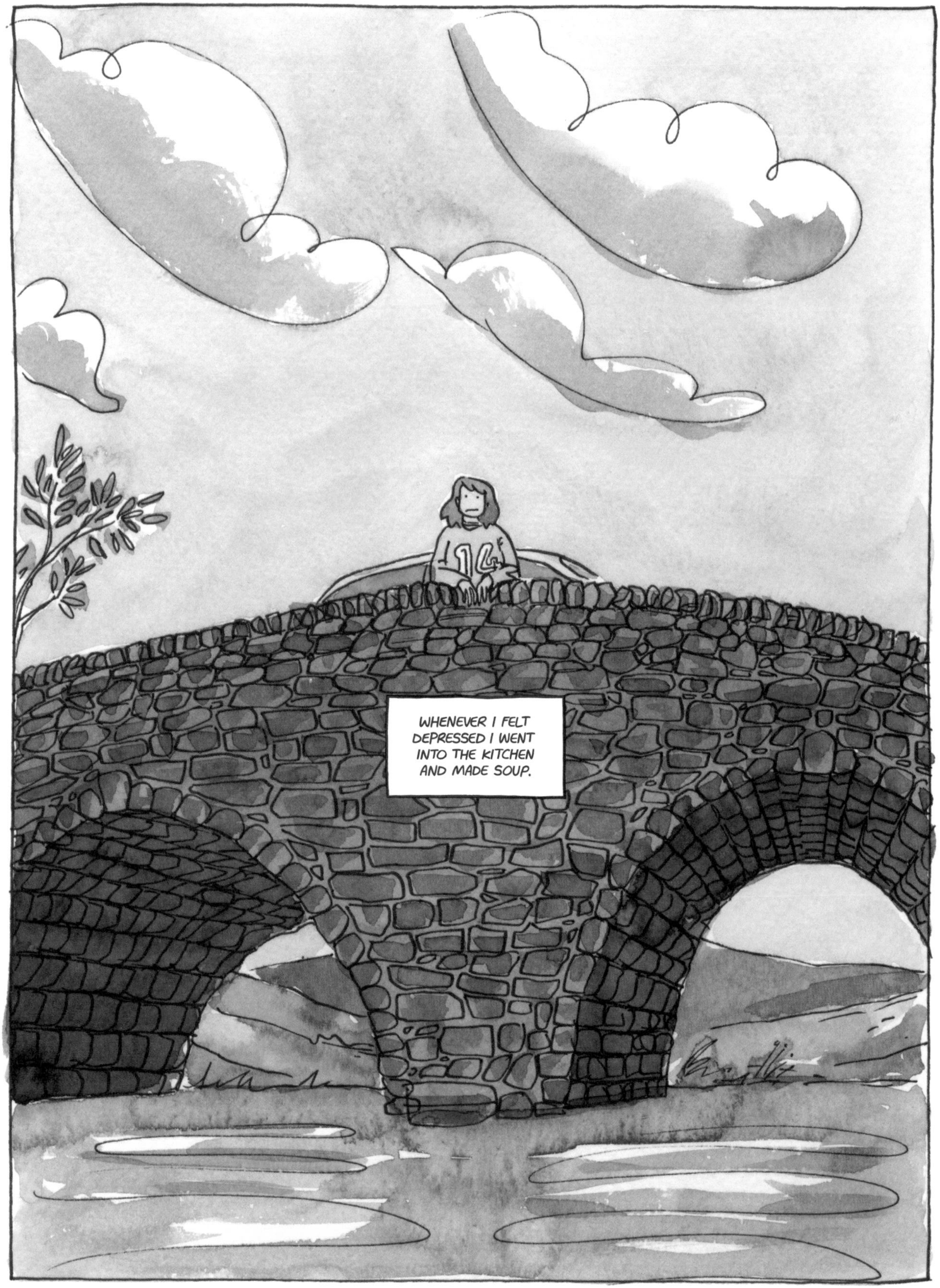
WHENEVER I FELT DEPRESSED I WENT INTO THE KITCHEN AND MADE SOUP.

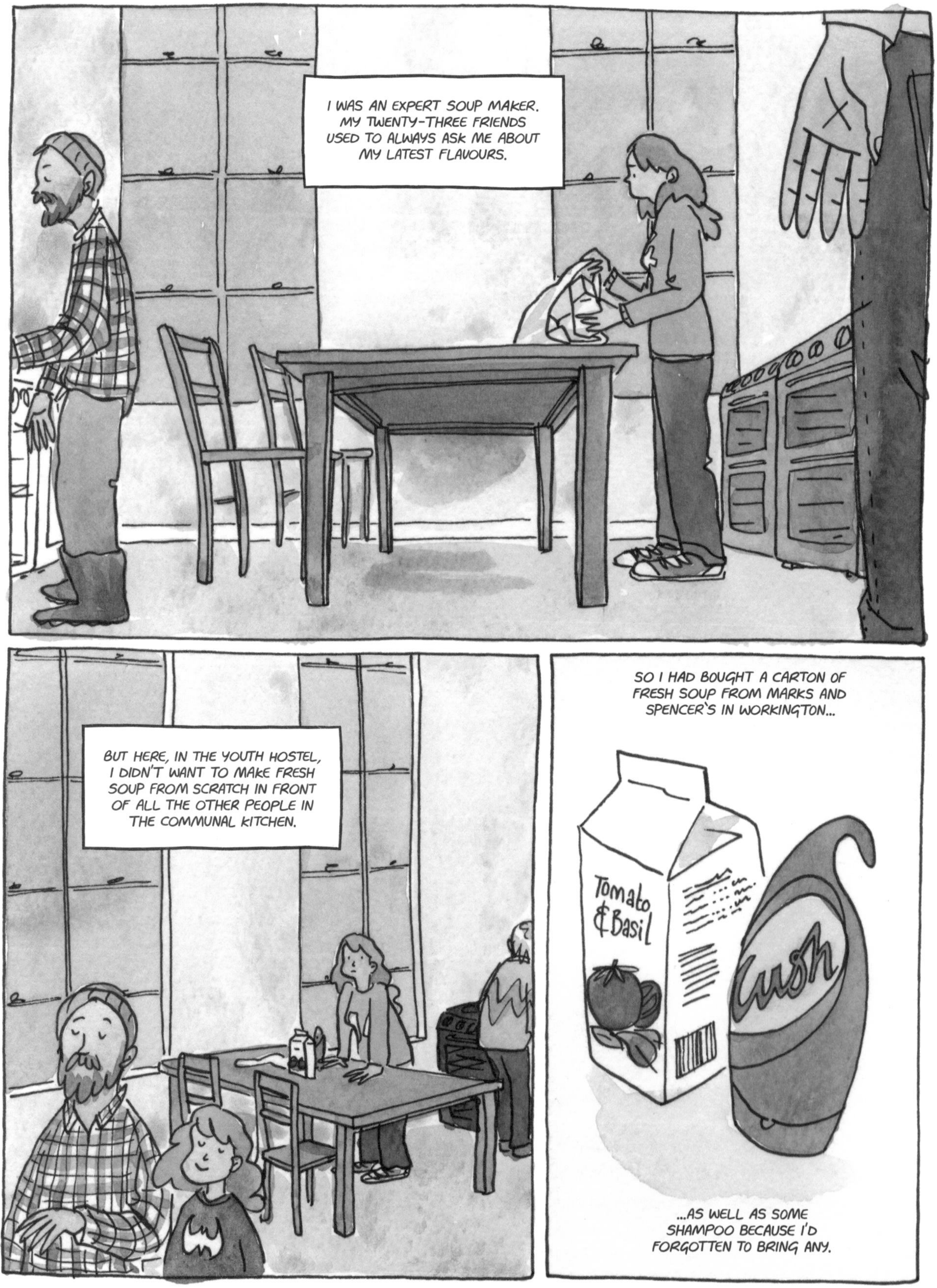
I WAS AN EXPERT SOUP MAKER. MY TWENTY-THREE FRIENDS USED TO ALWAYS ASK ME ABOUT MY LATEST FLAVOURS.
BUT HERE, IN THE YOUTH HOSTEL, I DIDN'T WANT TO MAKE FRESH SOUP FROM SCRATCH IN FRONT OF ALL THE OTHER PEOPLE IN THE COMMUNAL KITCHEN.
SO I HAD BOUGHT A CARTON OF FRESH SOUP FROM MARKS AND SPENCER'S IN WORKINGTON...
Tomato & Basil
...AS WELL AS SOME SHAMPOO BECAUSE I'D FORGOTTEN TO BRING ANY.

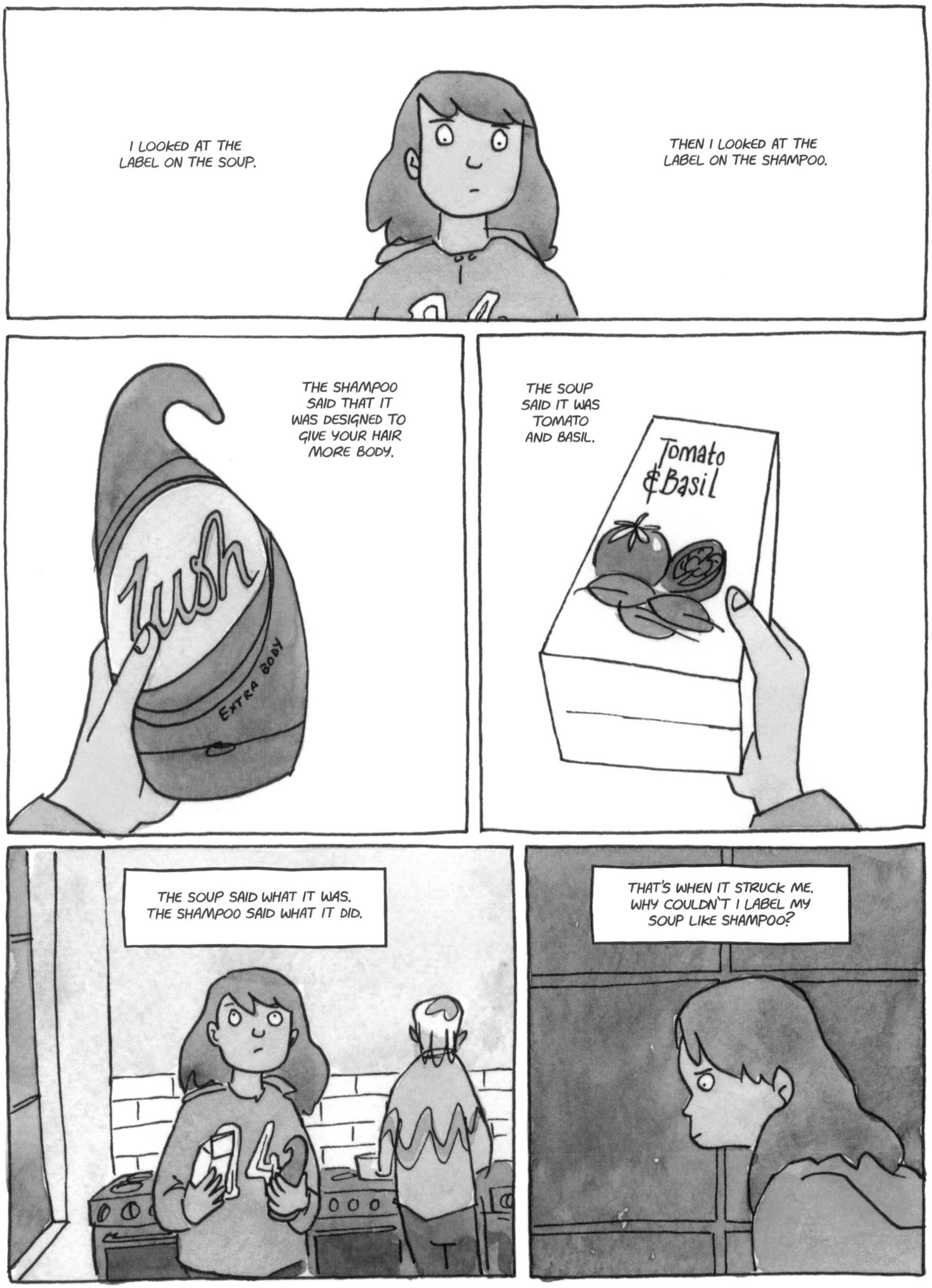
I LOOKED AT THE LABEL ON THE SOUP.
THEN I LOOKED AT THE LABEL ON THE SHAMPOO.
THE SHAMPOO SAID THAT IT WAS DESIGNED TO GIVE YOUR HAIR MORE BODY.
lush
EXTRA BODY
THE SOUP SAID IT WAS TOMATO AND BASIL.
Tomato &Basil
THE SOUP SAID WHAT IT WAS. THE SHAMPOO SAID WHAT IT DID.
THAT'S WHEN IT STRUCK ME. WHY COULDN'T I LABEL MY SOUP LIKE SHAMPOO?

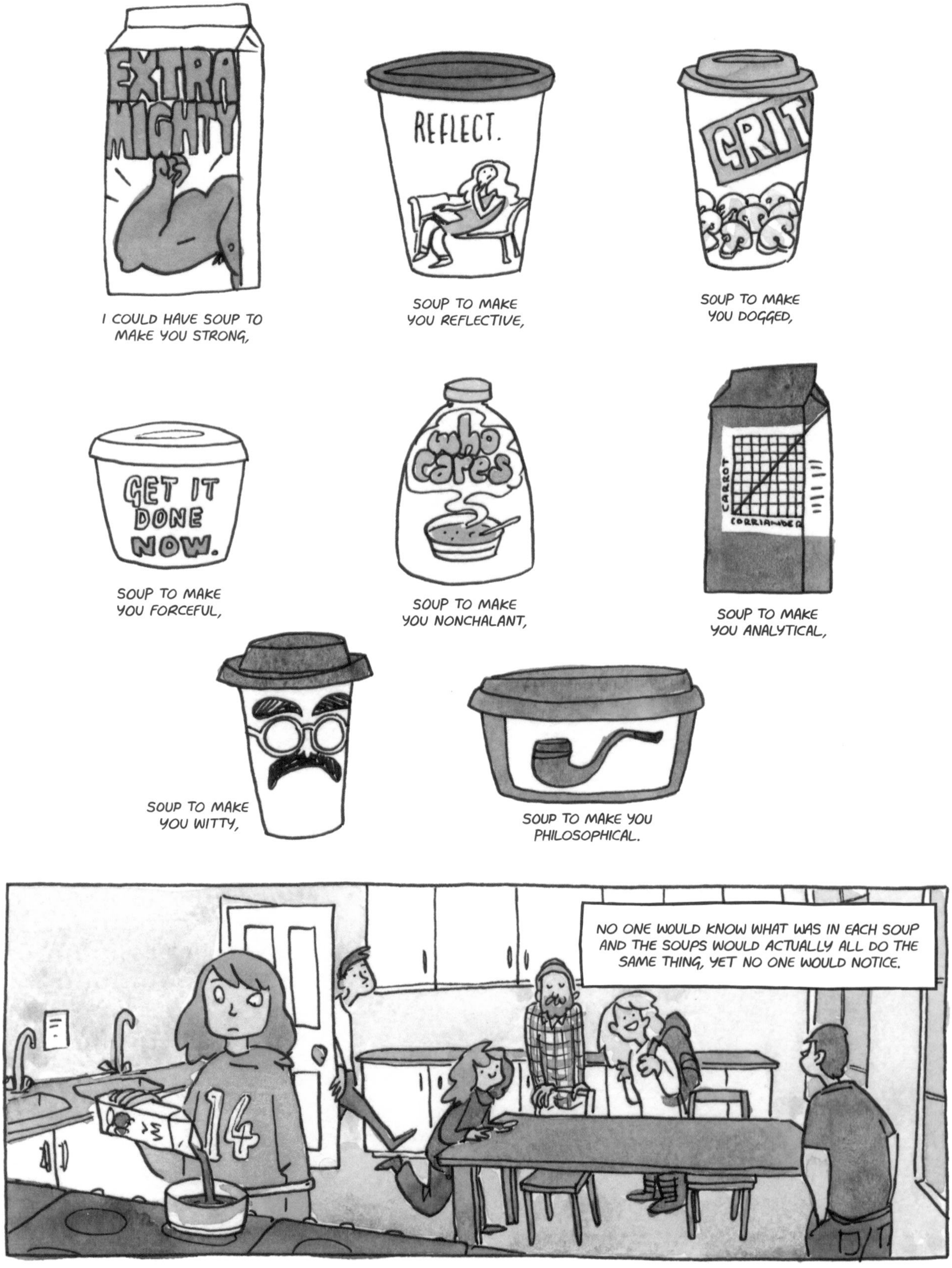
EXTRA MIGHTY
I COULD HAVE SOUP TO MAKE YOU STRONG,
REFLECT.
SOUP TO MAKE YOU REFLECTIVE,
GRIT
SOUP TO MAKE YOU DOGGED,
GET IT DONE NOW.
SOUP TO MAKE YOU FORCEFUL,
who cares
SOUP TO MAKE YOU NONCHALANT,
CARROT
CORRIANDER
SOUP TO MAKE YOU ANALYTICAL,
SOUP TO MAKE YOU WITTY,
SOUP TO MAKE YOU PHILOSOPHICAL.
NO ONE WOULD KNOW WHAT WAS IN EACH SOUP AND THE SOUPS WOULD ACTUALLY ALL DO THE SAME THING, YET NO ONE WOULD NOTICE.
14

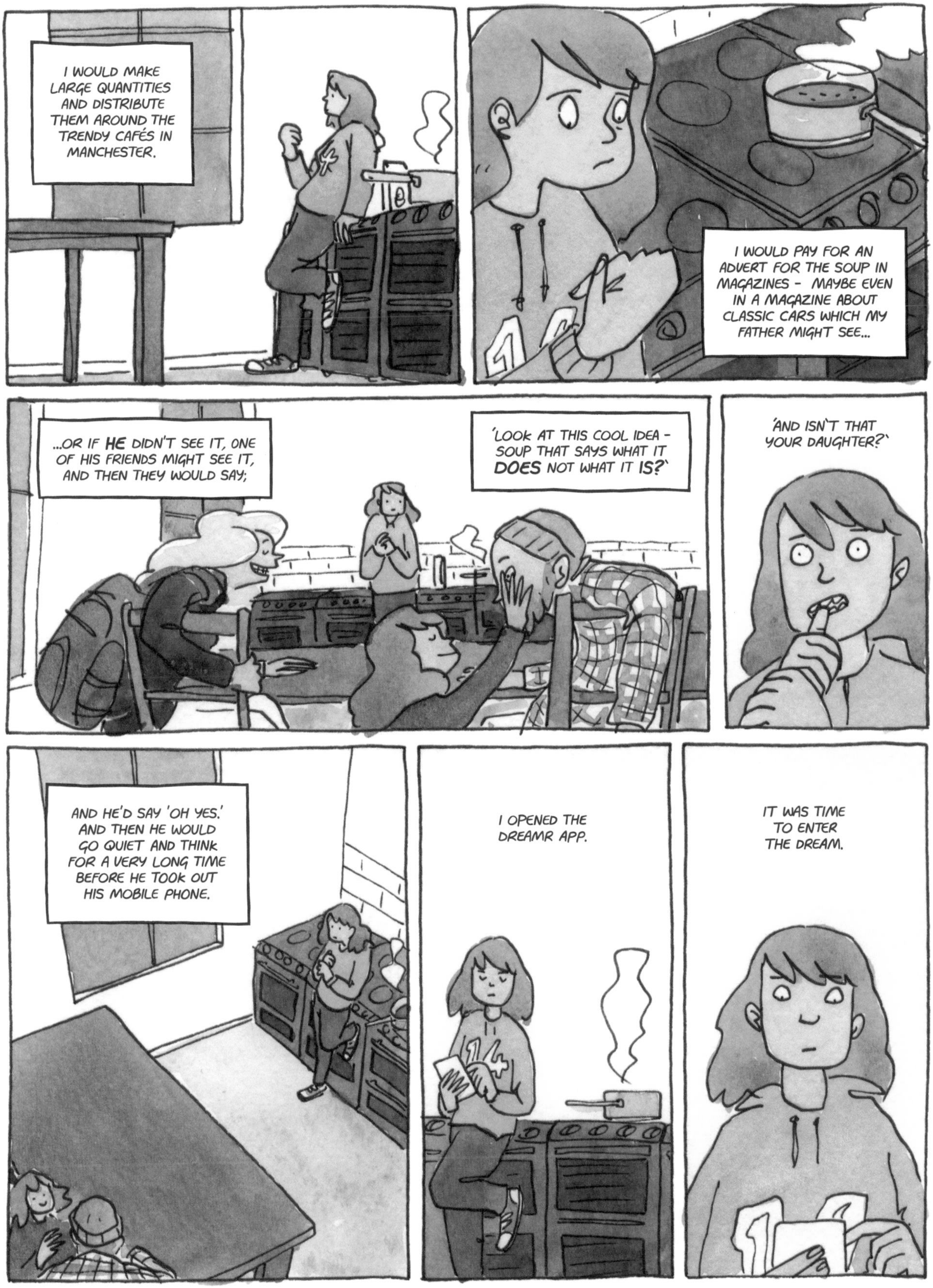
I WOULD MAKE LARGE QUANTITIES AND DISTRIBUTE THEM AROUND THE TRENDY CAFÉS IN MANCHESTER.
I WOULD PAY FOR AN ADVERT FOR THE SOUP IN MAGAZINES - MAYBE EVEN IN A MAGAZINE ABOUT CLASSIC CARS WHICH MY FATHER MIGHT SEE...
...OR IF **HE** DIDN'T SEE IT, ONE OF HIS FRIENDS MIGHT SEE IT, AND THEN THEY WOULD SAY;
'LOOK AT THIS COOL IDEA - SOUP THAT SAYS WHAT IT **DOES** NOT WHAT IT **IS?**'
'AND ISN'T THAT YOUR DAUGHTER?'
AND HE'D SAY 'OH YES.' AND THEN HE WOULD GO QUIET AND THINK FOR A VERY LONG TIME BEFORE HE TOOK OUT HIS MOBILE PHONE.
I OPENED THE DREAMR APP.
IT WAS TIME TO ENTER THE DREAM.

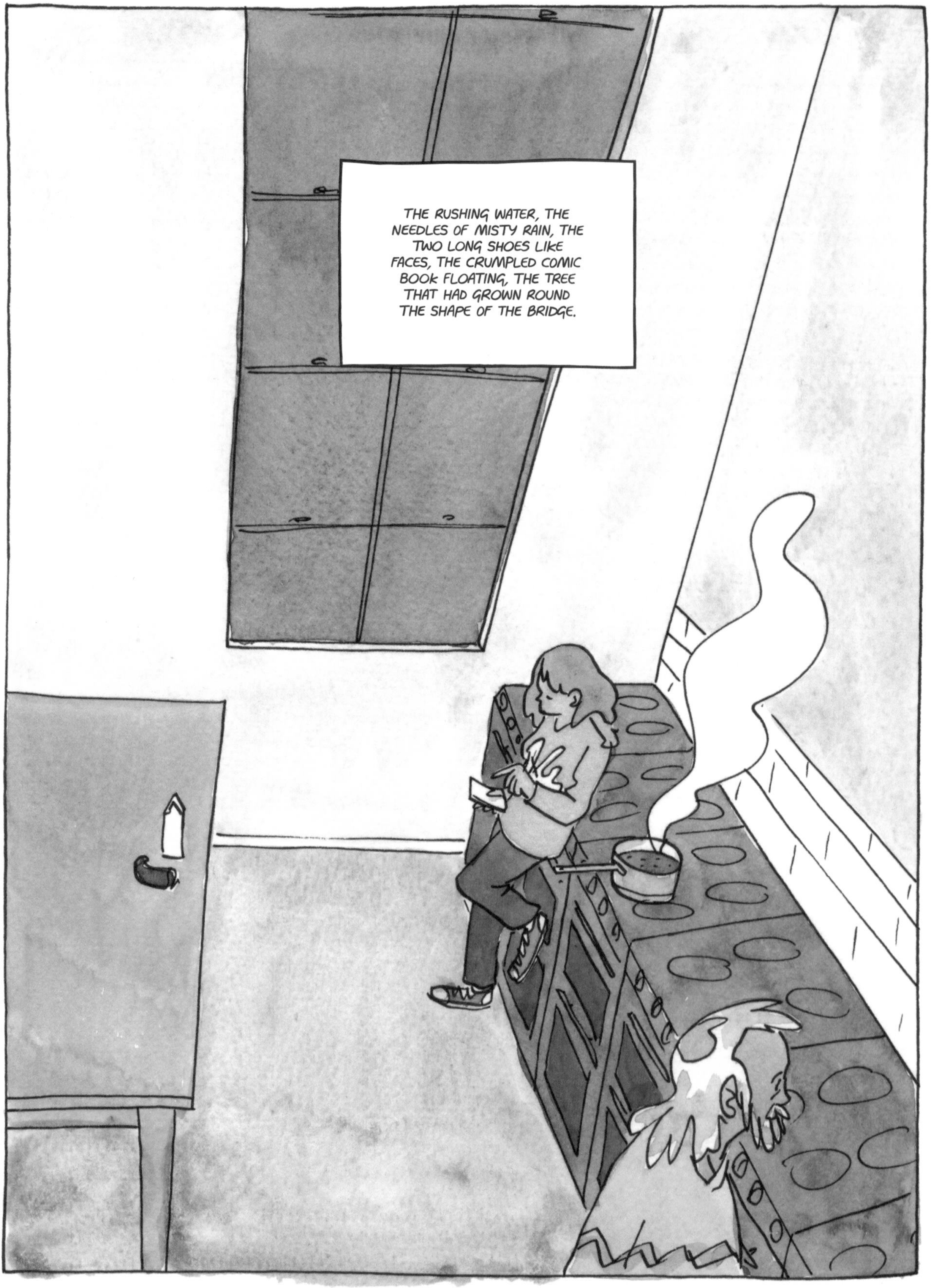
THE RUSHING WATER, THE NEEDLES OF MISTY RAIN, THE TWO LONG SHOES LIKE FACES, THE CRUMPLED COMIC BOOK FLOATING, THE TREE THAT HAD GROWN ROUND THE SHAPE OF THE BRIDGE.

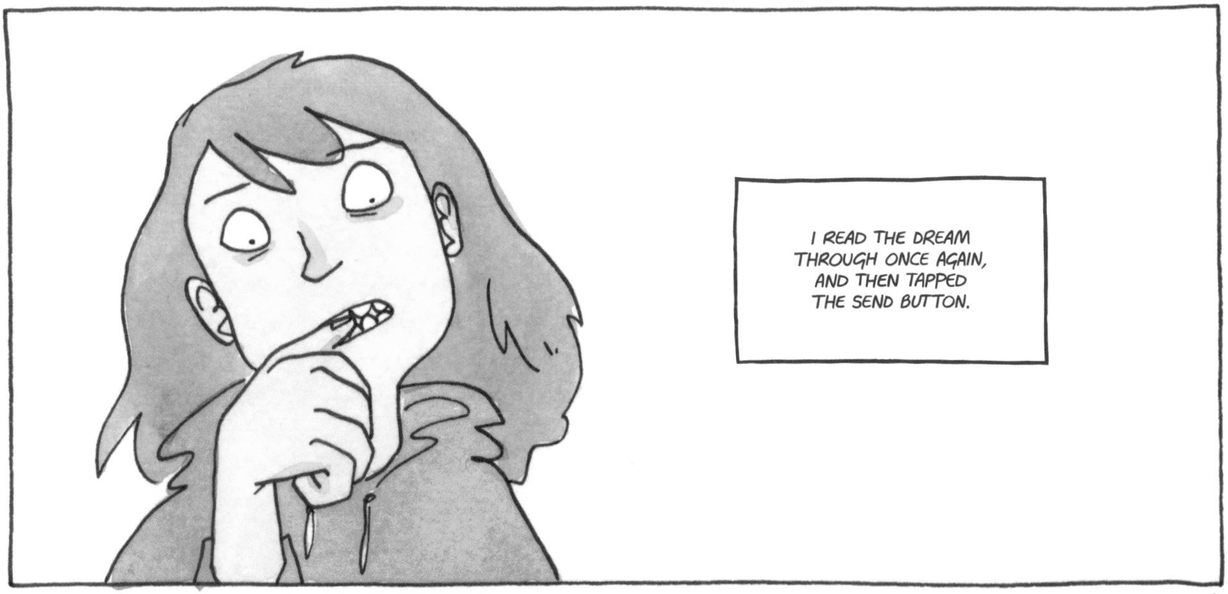
I READ THE DREAM THROUGH ONCE AGAIN, AND THEN TAPPED THE SEND BUTTON.

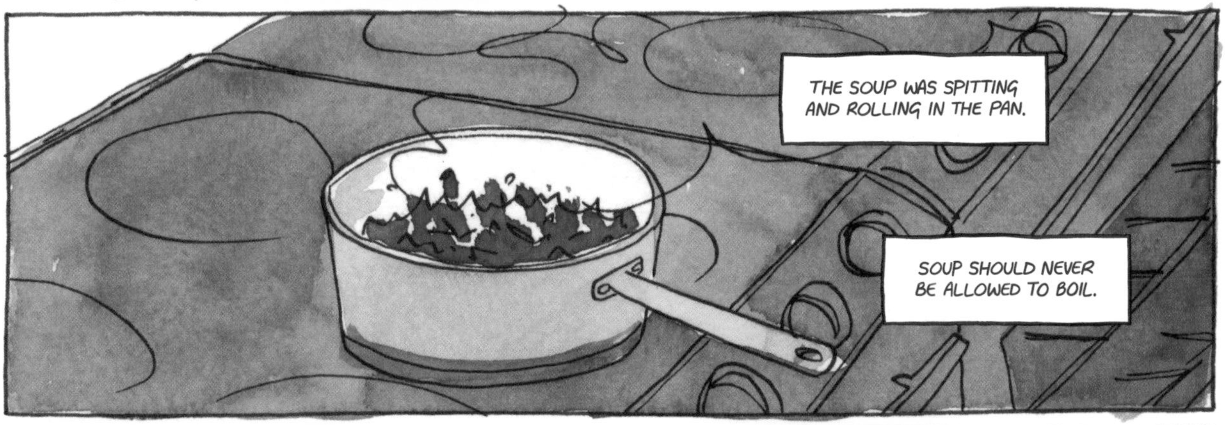
THE SOUP WAS SPITTING AND ROLLING IN THE PAN.
SOUP SHOULD NEVER BE ALLOWED TO BOIL.

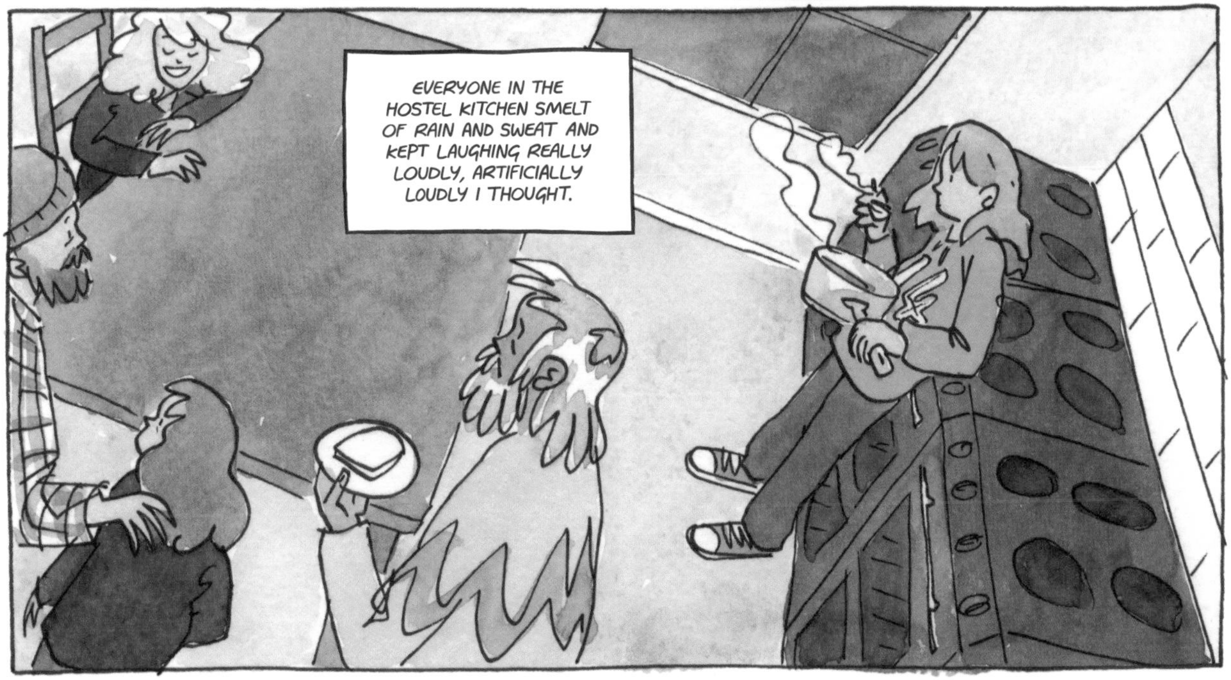
EVERYONE IN THE HOSTEL KITCHEN SMELT OF RAIN AND SWEAT AND KEPT LAUGHING REALLY LOUDLY, ARTIFICIALLY LOUDLY I THOUGHT.

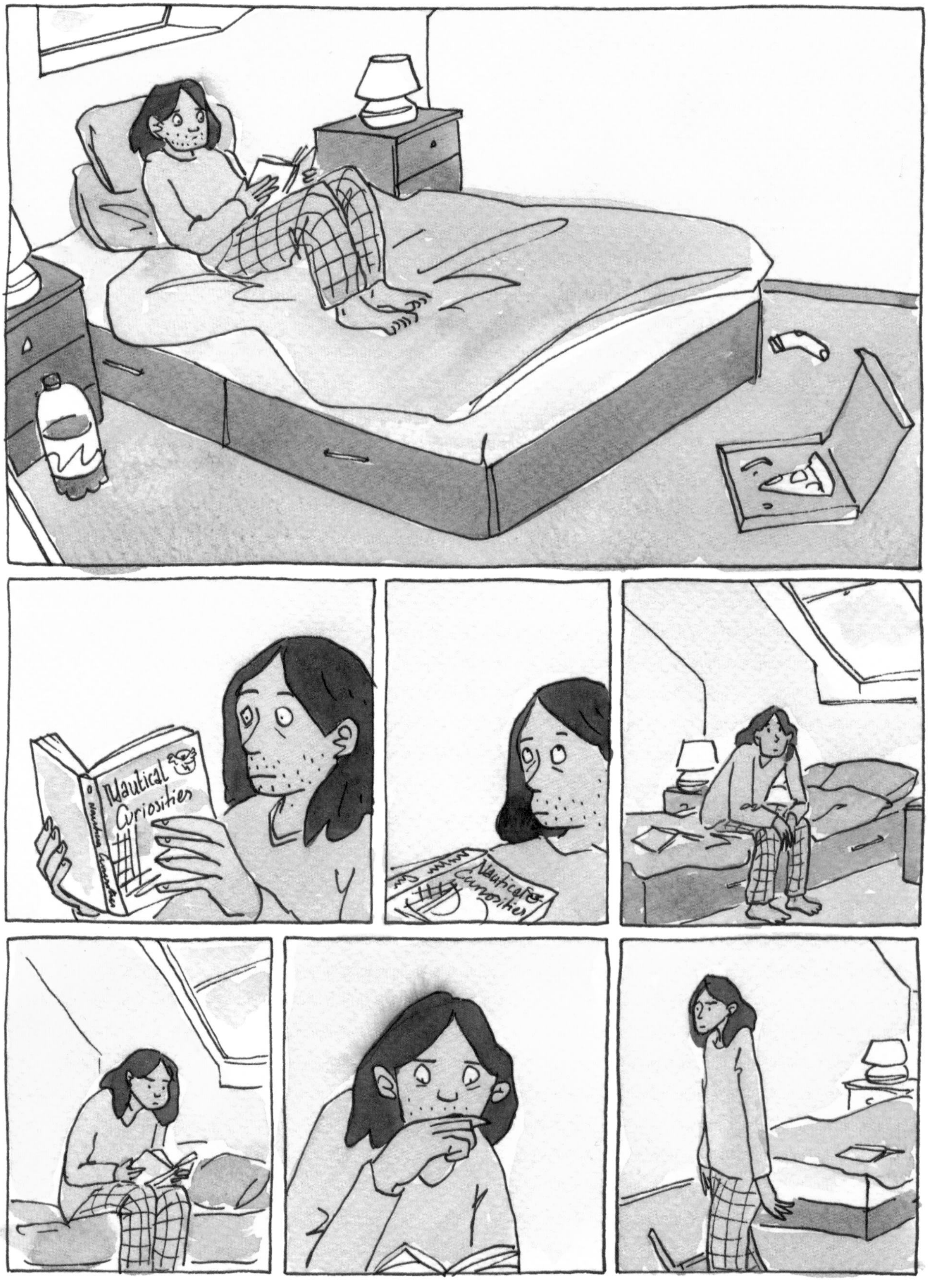
Nautical Curiosities

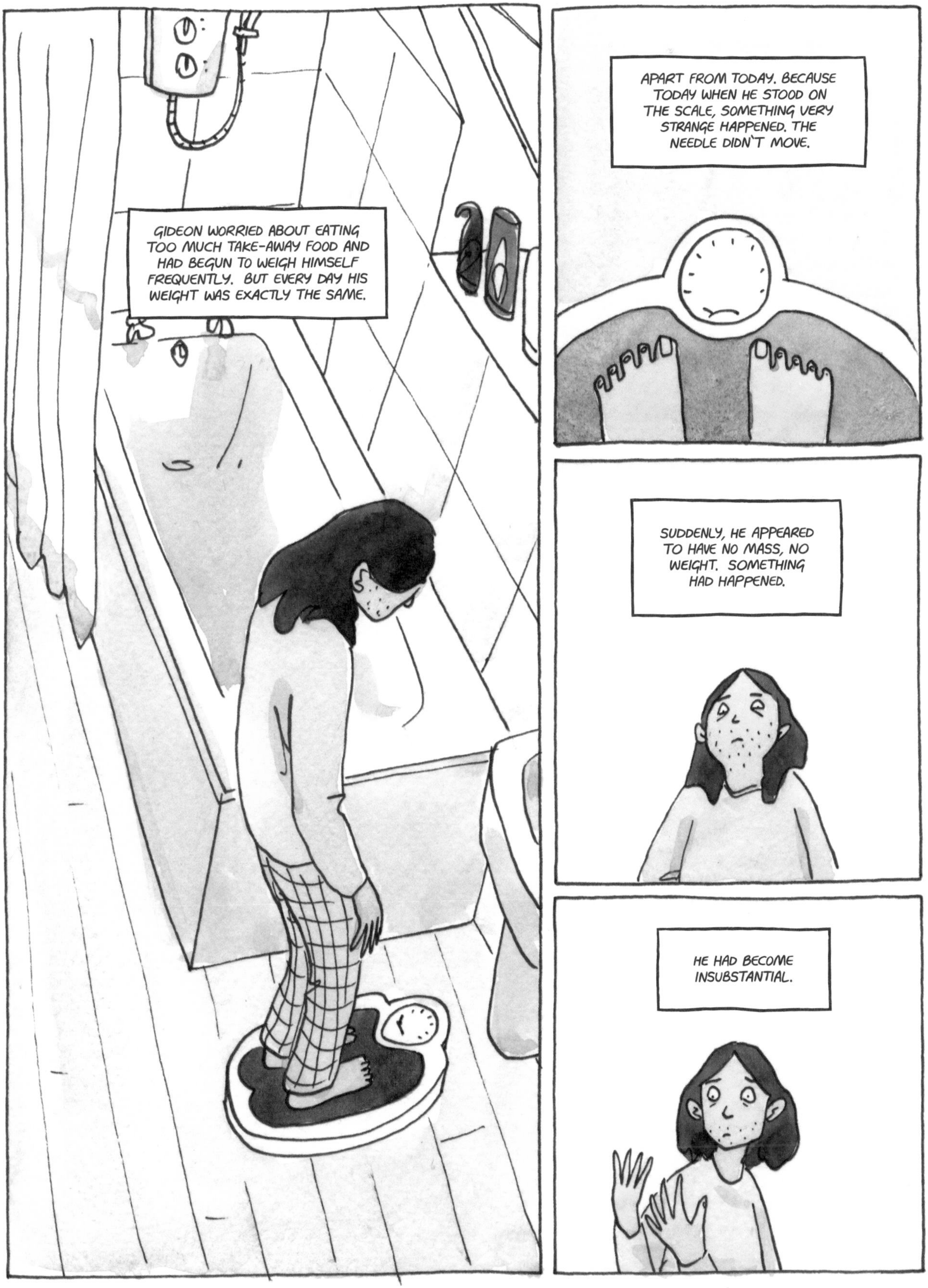
GIDEON WORRIED ABOUT EATING TOO MUCH TAKE-AWAY FOOD AND HAD BEGUN TO WEIGH HIMSELF FREQUENTLY. BUT EVERY DAY HIS WEIGHT WAS EXACTLY THE SAME.
APART FROM TODAY. BECAUSE TODAY WHEN HE STOOD ON THE SCALE, SOMETHING VERY STRANGE HAPPENED. THE NEEDLE DIDN'T MOVE.
SUDDENLY, HE APPEARED TO HAVE NO MASS, NO WEIGHT. SOMETHING HAD HAPPENED.
HE HAD BECOME INSUBSTANTIAL.

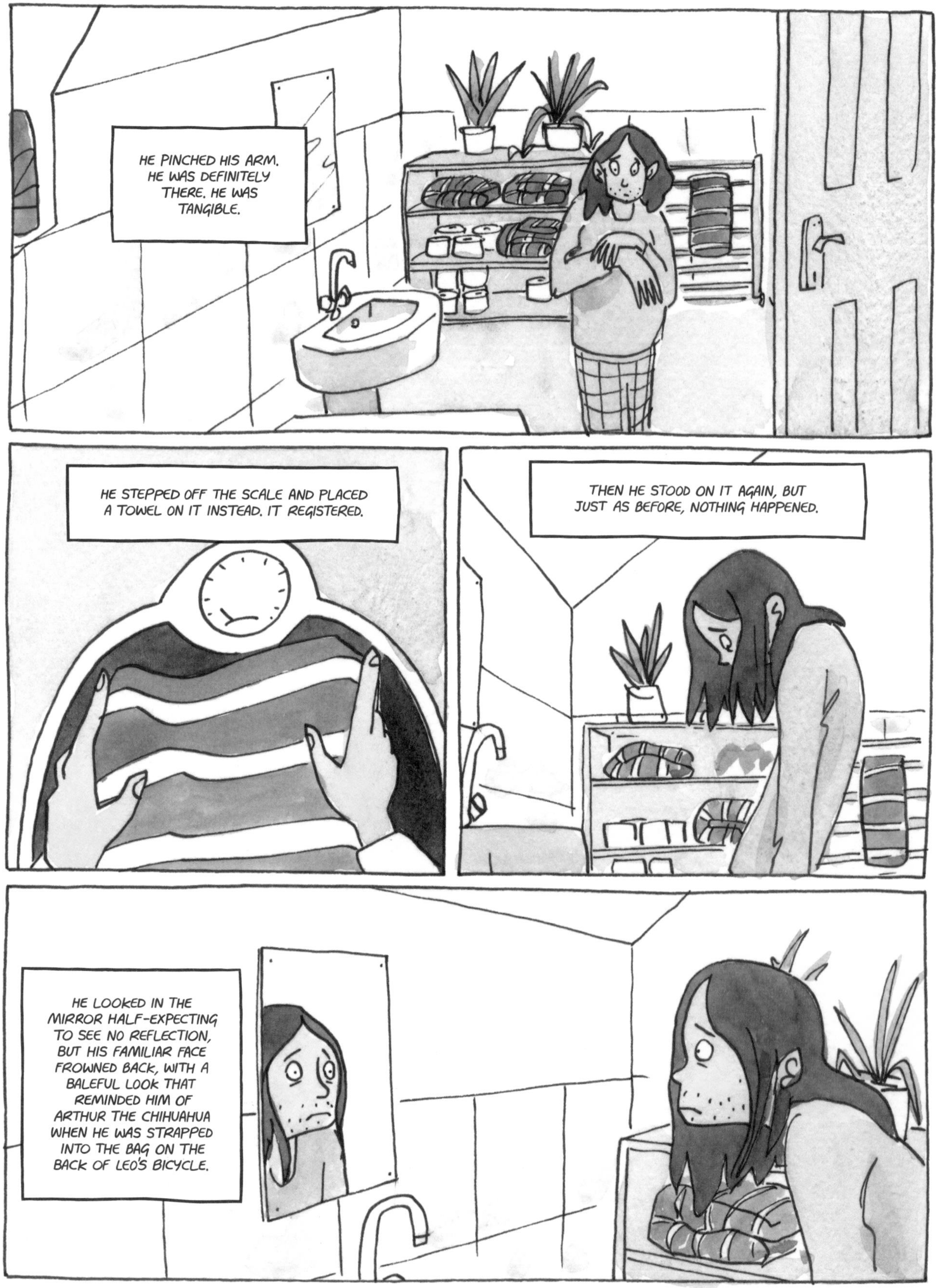
HE PINCHED HIS ARM. HE WAS DEFINITELY THERE. HE WAS TANGIBLE.
HE STEPPED OFF THE SCALE AND PLACED A TOWEL ON IT INSTEAD. IT REGISTERED.
THEN HE STOOD ON IT AGAIN, BUT JUST AS BEFORE, NOTHING HAPPENED.
HE LOOKED IN THE MIRROR HALF-EXPECTING TO SEE NO REFLECTION, BUT HIS FAMILIAR FACE FROWNED BACK, WITH A BALEFUL LOOK THAT REMINDED HIM OF ARTHUR THE CHIHUAHUA WHEN HE WAS STRAPPED INTO THE BAG ON THE BACK OF LEO'S BICYCLE.

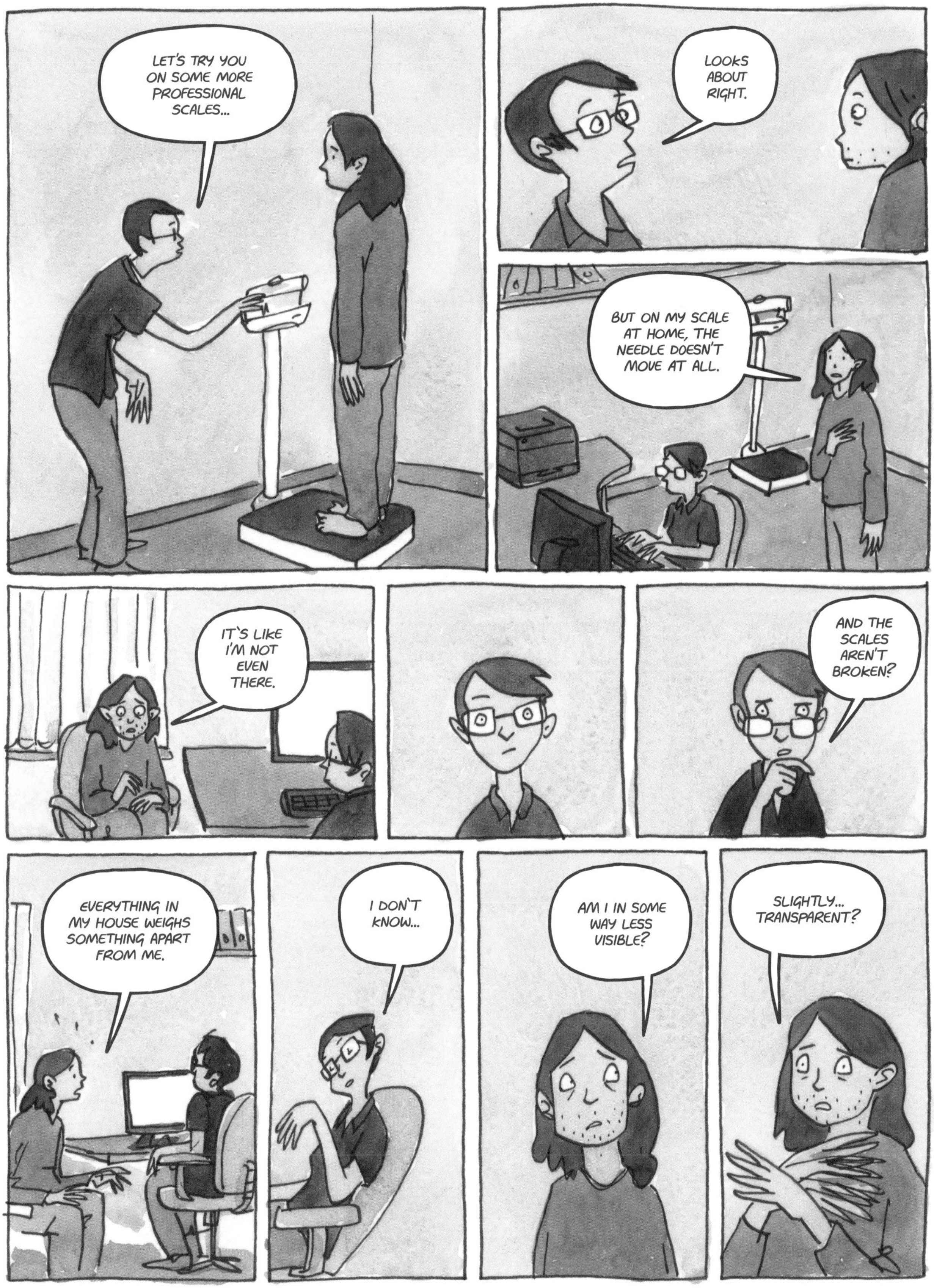
LET'S TRY YOU ON SOME MORE PROFESSIONAL SCALES...
LOOKS ABOUT RIGHT.
BUT ON MY SCALE AT HOME, THE NEEDLE DOESN'T MOVE AT ALL.
IT'S LIKE I'M NOT EVEN THERE.
AND THE SCALES AREN'T BROKEN?
EVERYTHING IN MY HOUSE WEIGHS SOMETHING APART FROM ME.
I DON'T KNOW...
AM I IN SOME WAY LESS VISIBLE?
SLIGHTLY... TRANSPARENT?

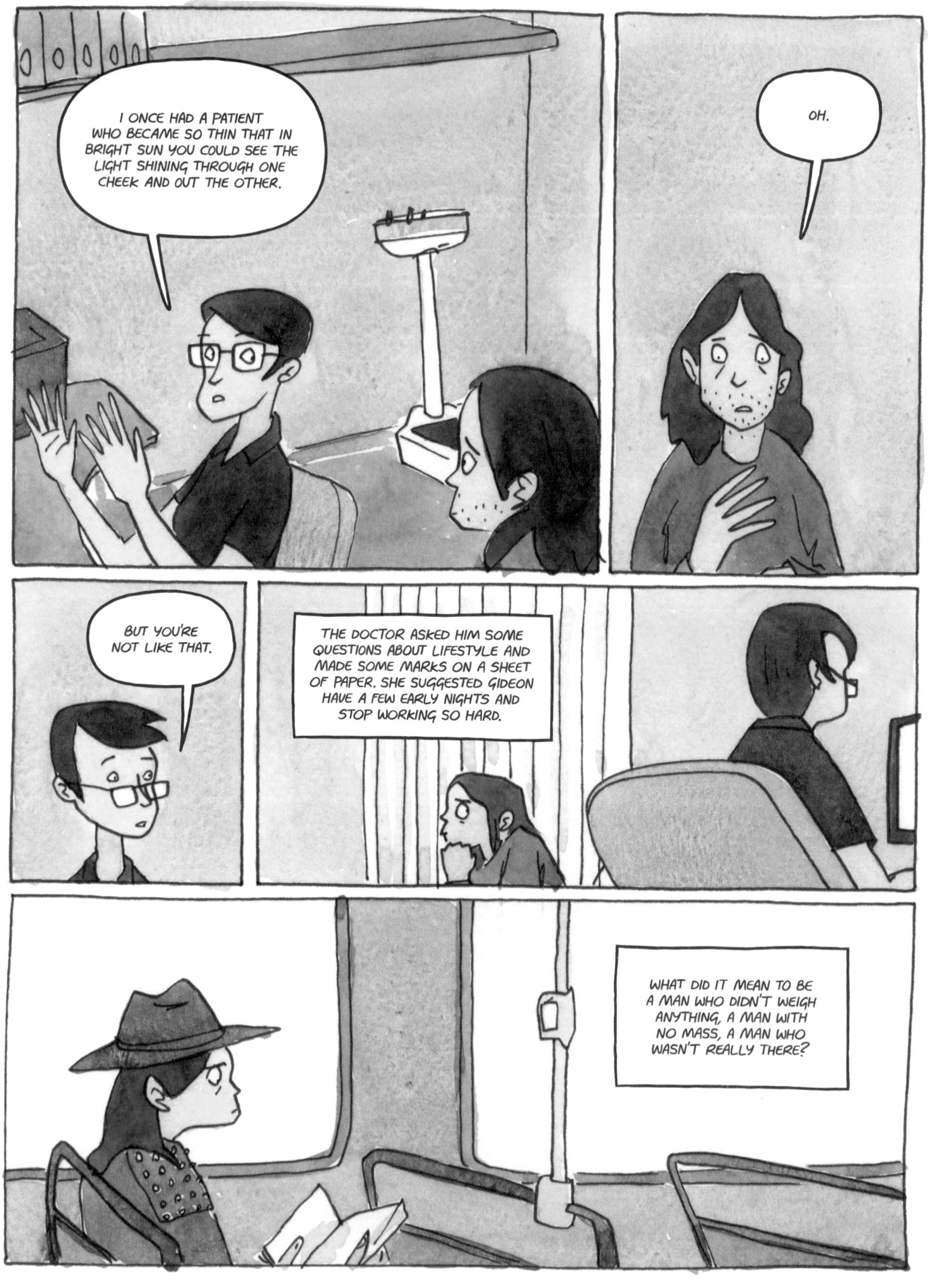
I ONCE HAD A PATIENT WHO BECAME SO THIN THAT IN BRIGHT SUN YOU COULD SEE THE LIGHT SHINING THROUGH ONE CHEEK AND OUT THE OTHER.
OH.
BUT YOU'RE NOT LIKE THAT.
THE DOCTOR ASKED HIM SOME QUESTIONS ABOUT LIFESTYLE AND MADE SOME MARKS ON A SHEET OF PAPER. SHE SUGGESTED GIDEON HAVE A FEW EARLY NIGHTS AND STOP WORKING SO HARD.
WHAT DID IT MEAN TO BE A MAN WHO DIDN'T WEIGH ANYTHING, A MAN WITH NO MASS, A MAN WHO WASN'T REALLY THERE?

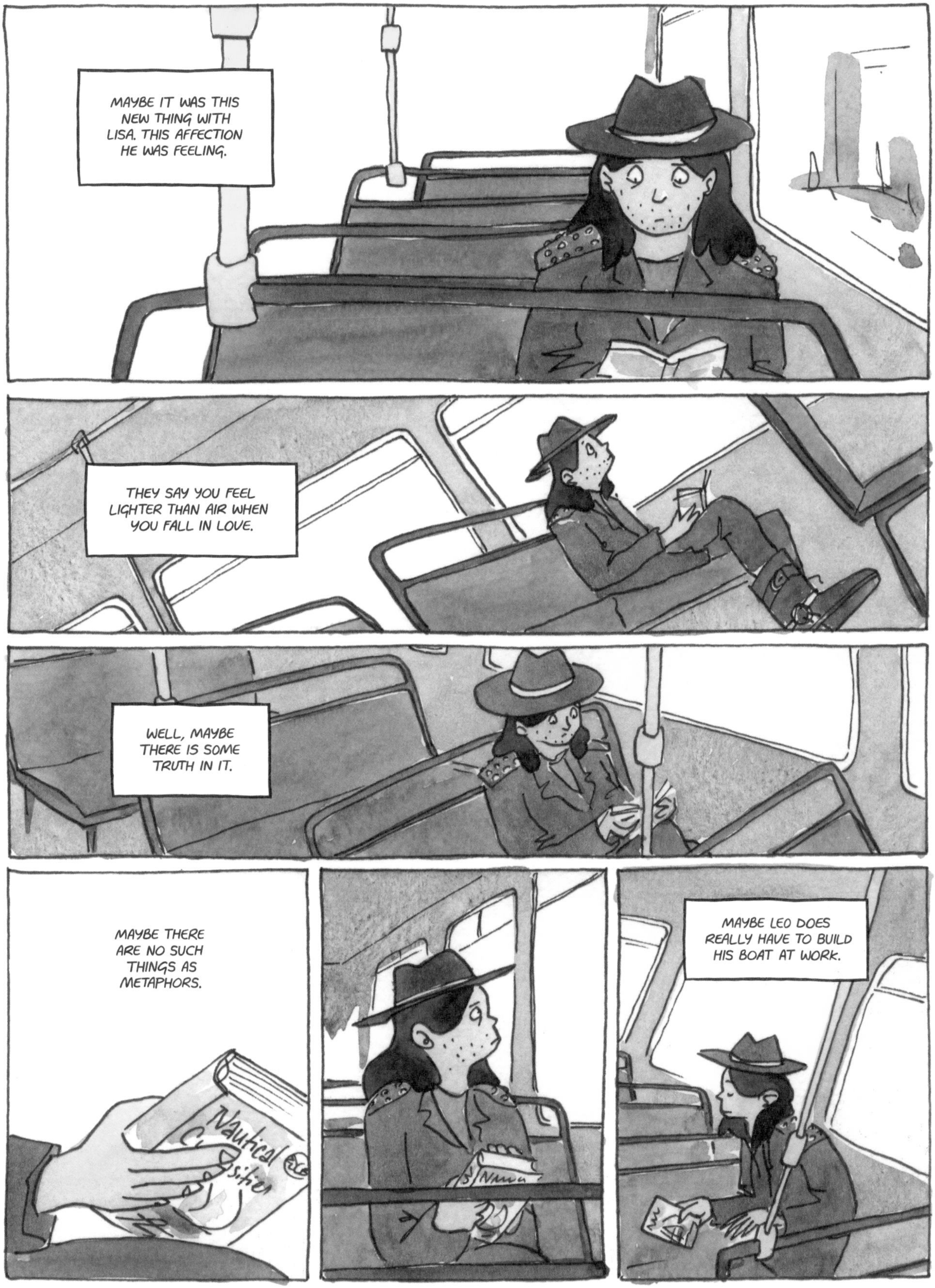
MAYBE IT WAS THIS NEW THING WITH LISA. THIS AFFECTION HE WAS FEELING.
THEY SAY YOU FEEL LIGHTER THAN AIR WHEN YOU FALL IN LOVE.
WELL, MAYBE THERE IS SOME TRUTH IN IT.
MAYBE THERE ARE NO SUCH THINGS AS METAPHORS.
Nautical
MAYBE LEO DOES REALLY HAVE TO BUILD HIS BOAT AT WORK.

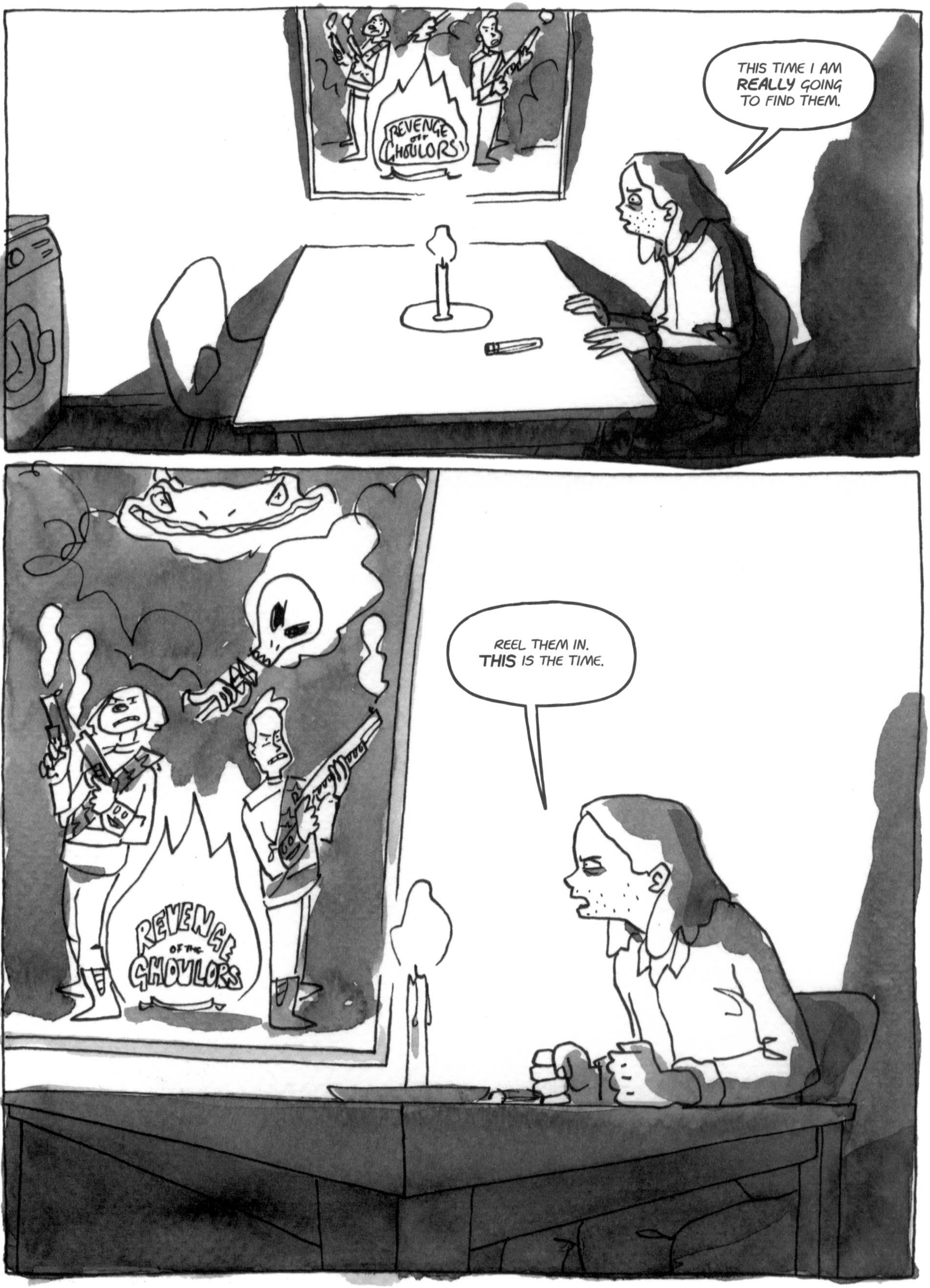
REVENGE OF THE GHOULORS!
THIS TIME I AM REALLY GOING TO FIND THEM.
REVENGE OF THE GHOULORS
REEL THEM IN. THIS IS THE TIME.

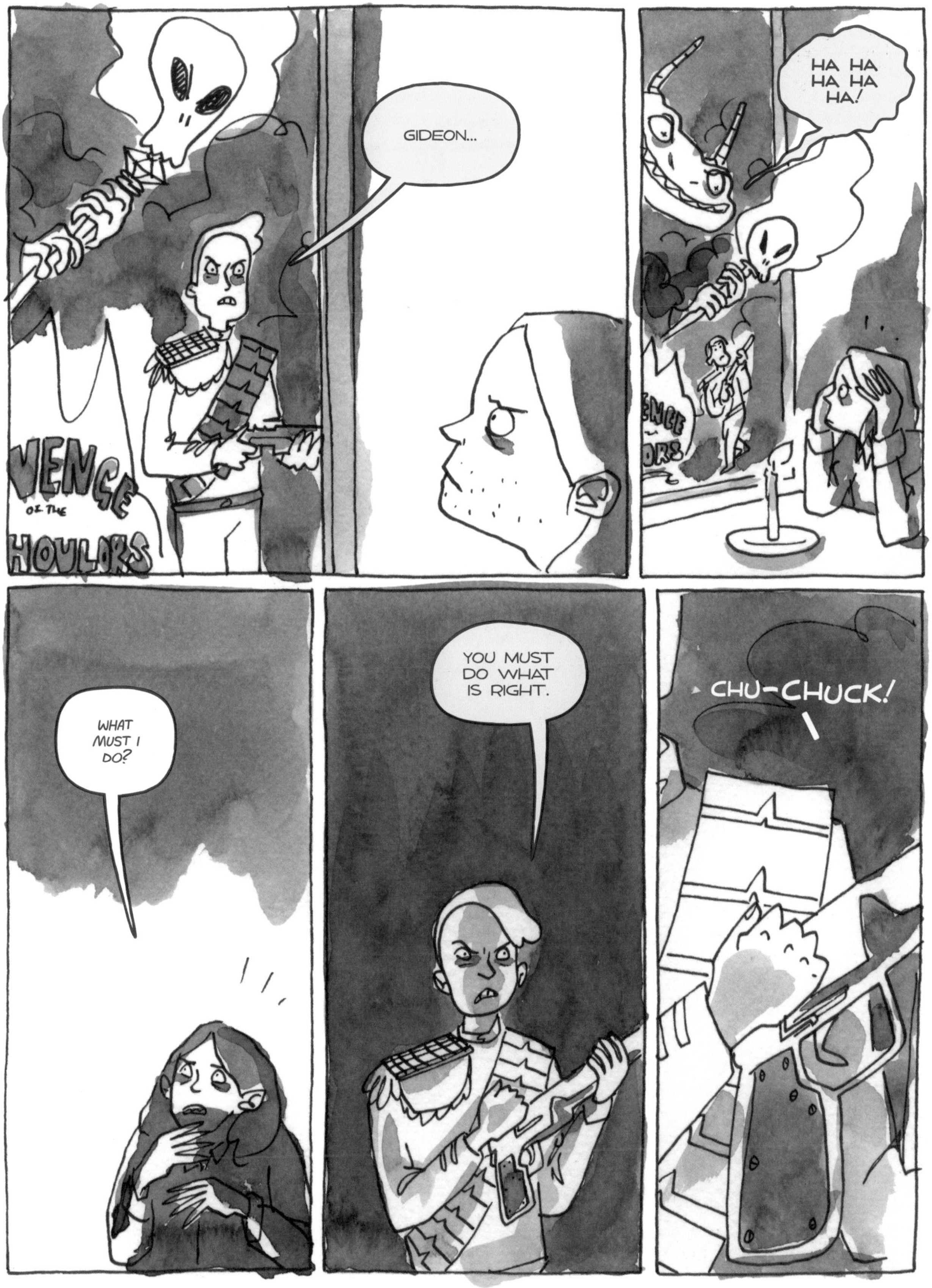
VENGE
OF THE
HOULORS
GIDEON...
HA HA
HA HA
HA!
WHAT
MUST I
DO?
YOU MUST
DO WHAT
IS RIGHT.
CHU-CHUCK!

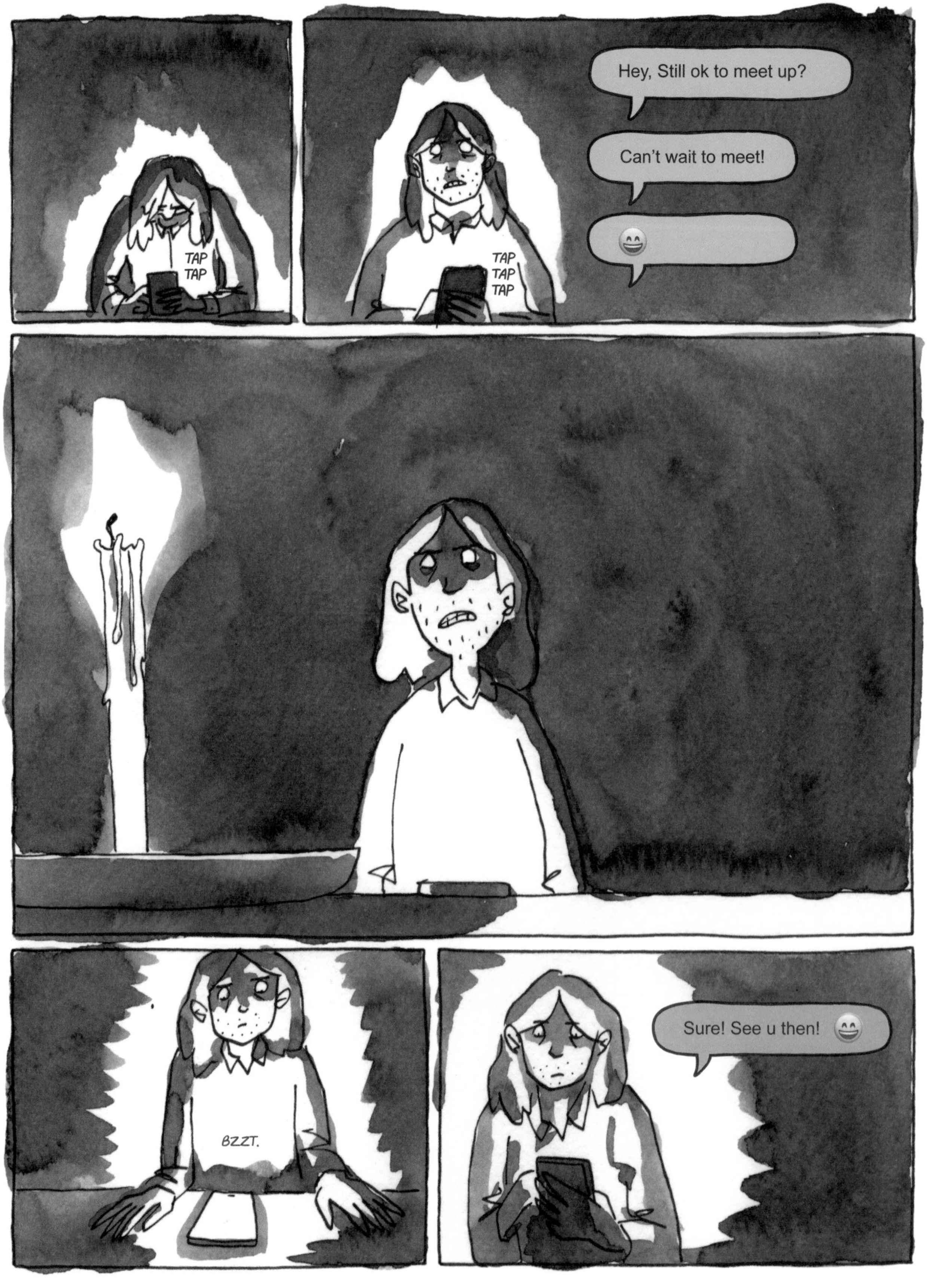
TAP
TAP
TAP
TAP
TAP
Hey, Still ok to meet up?
Can't wait to meet!
BZZT.
Sure! See u then!

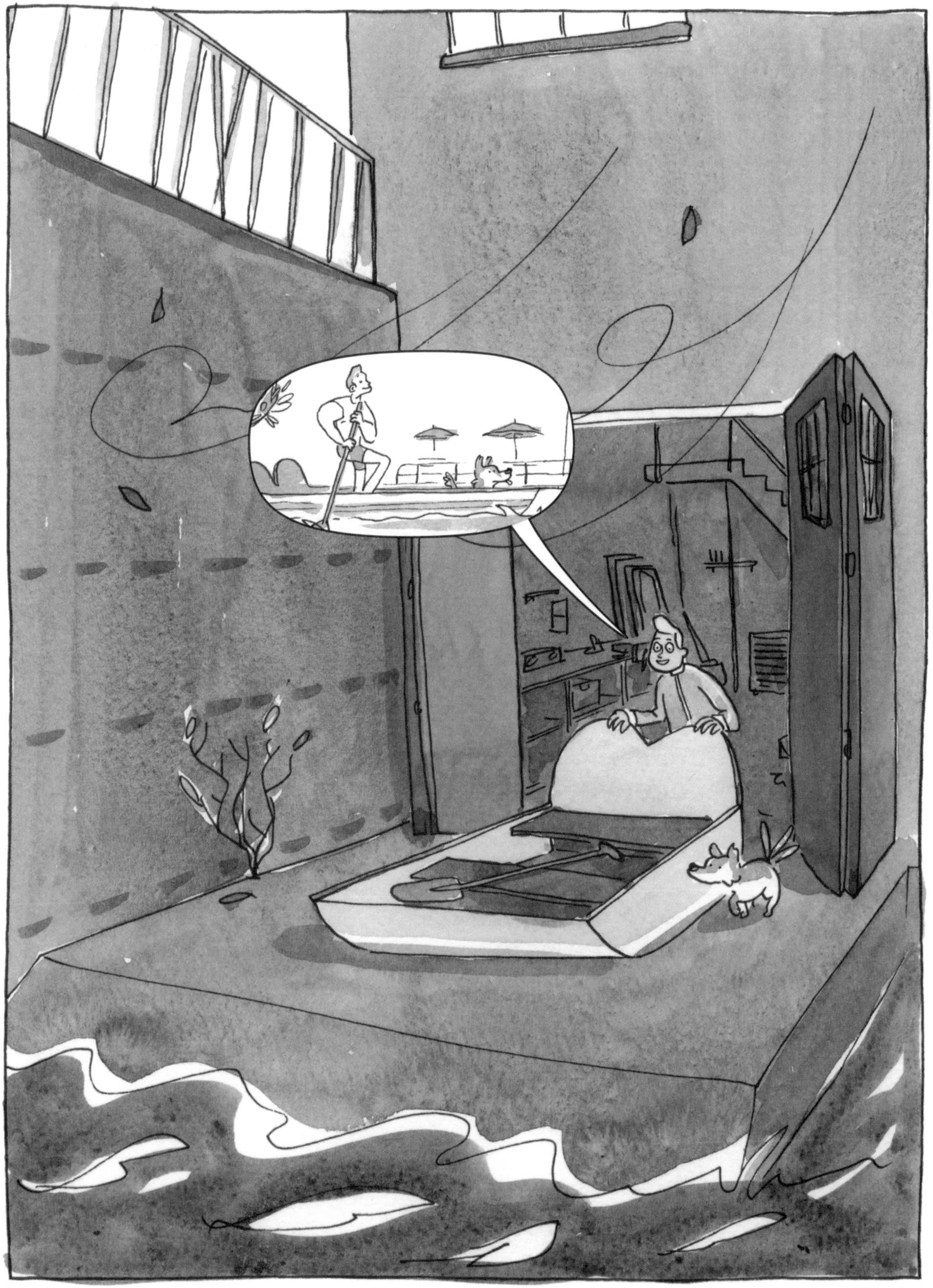

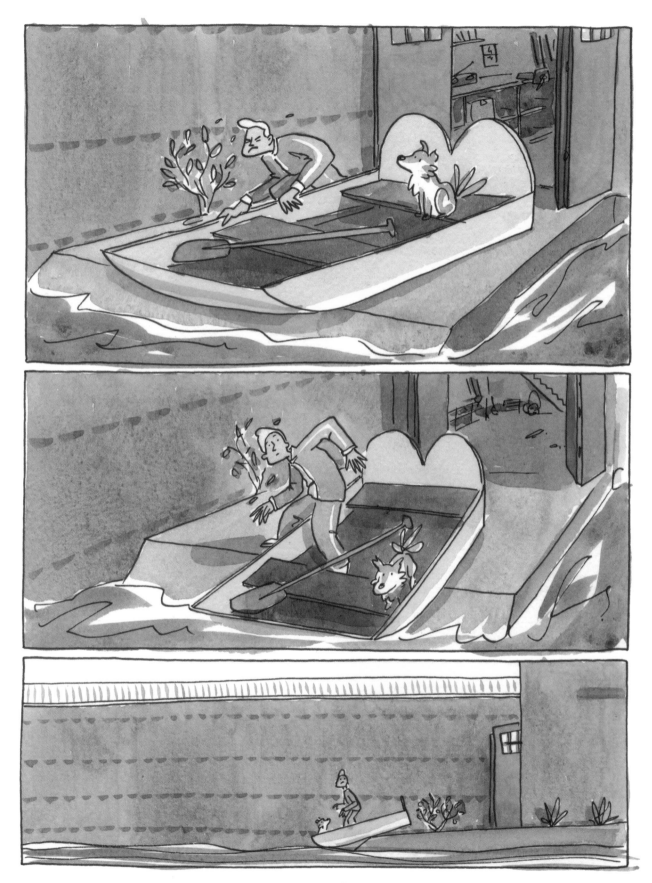

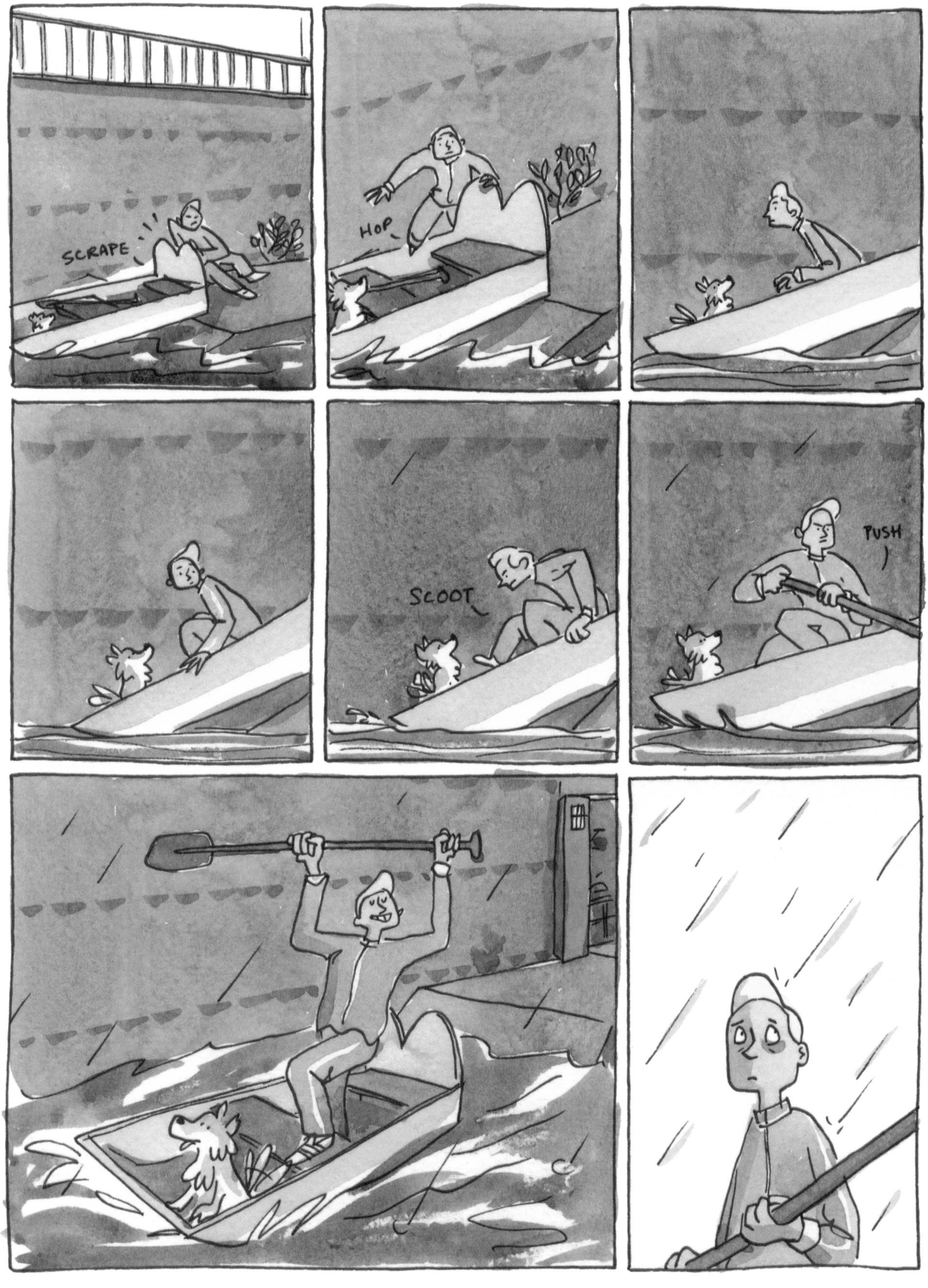

SCRAPE
HOP
SCOOT
PUSH

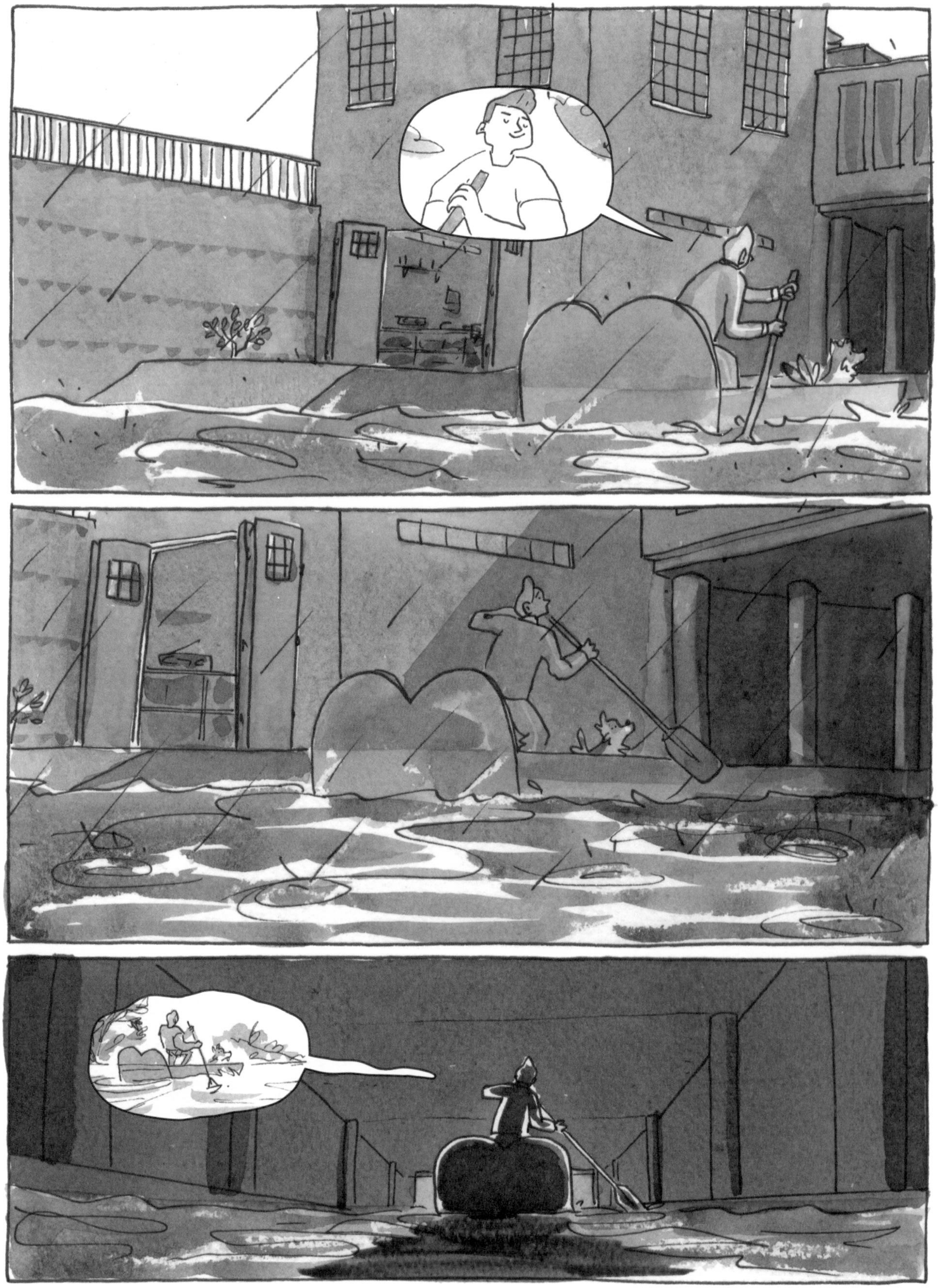

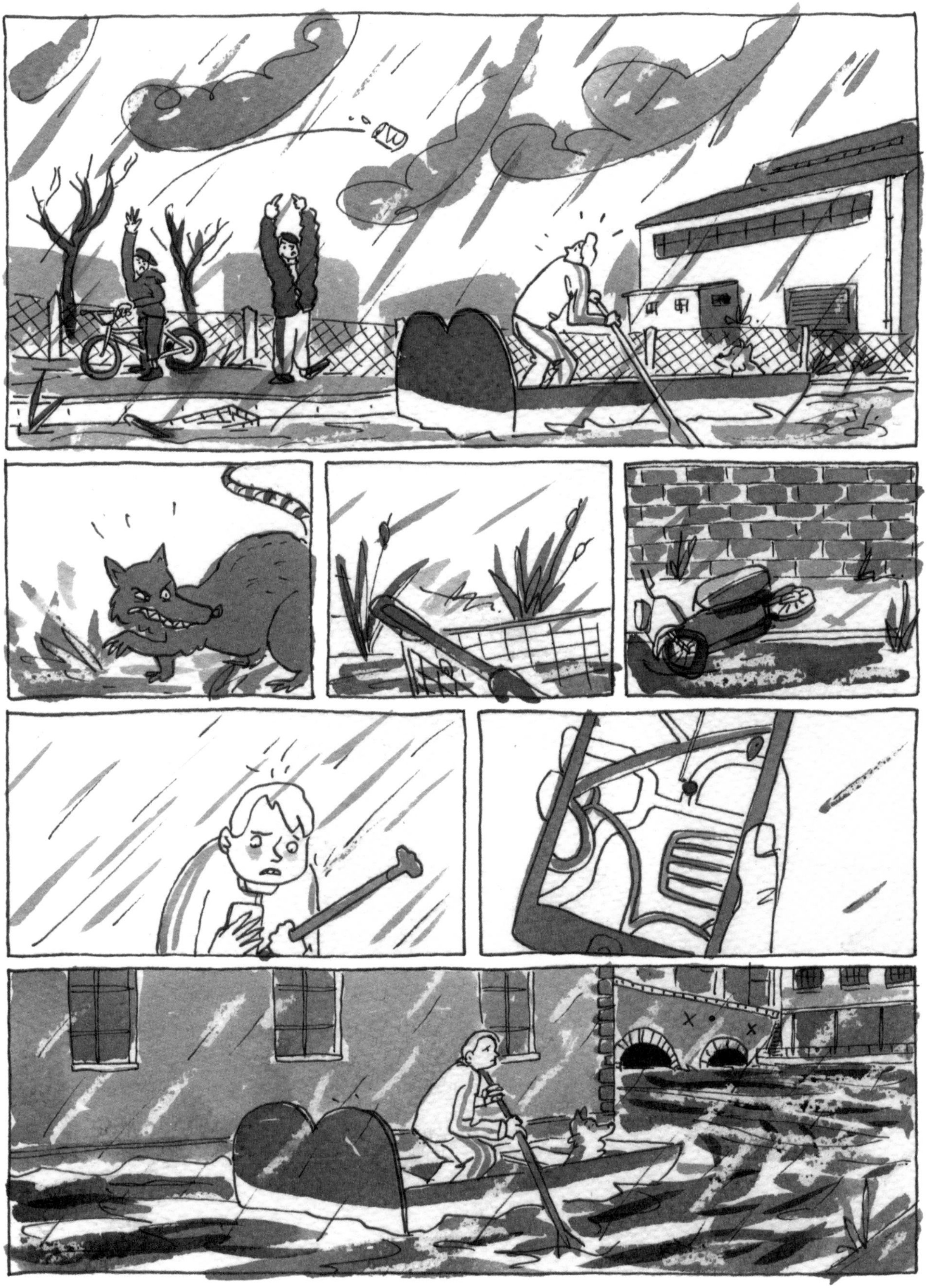

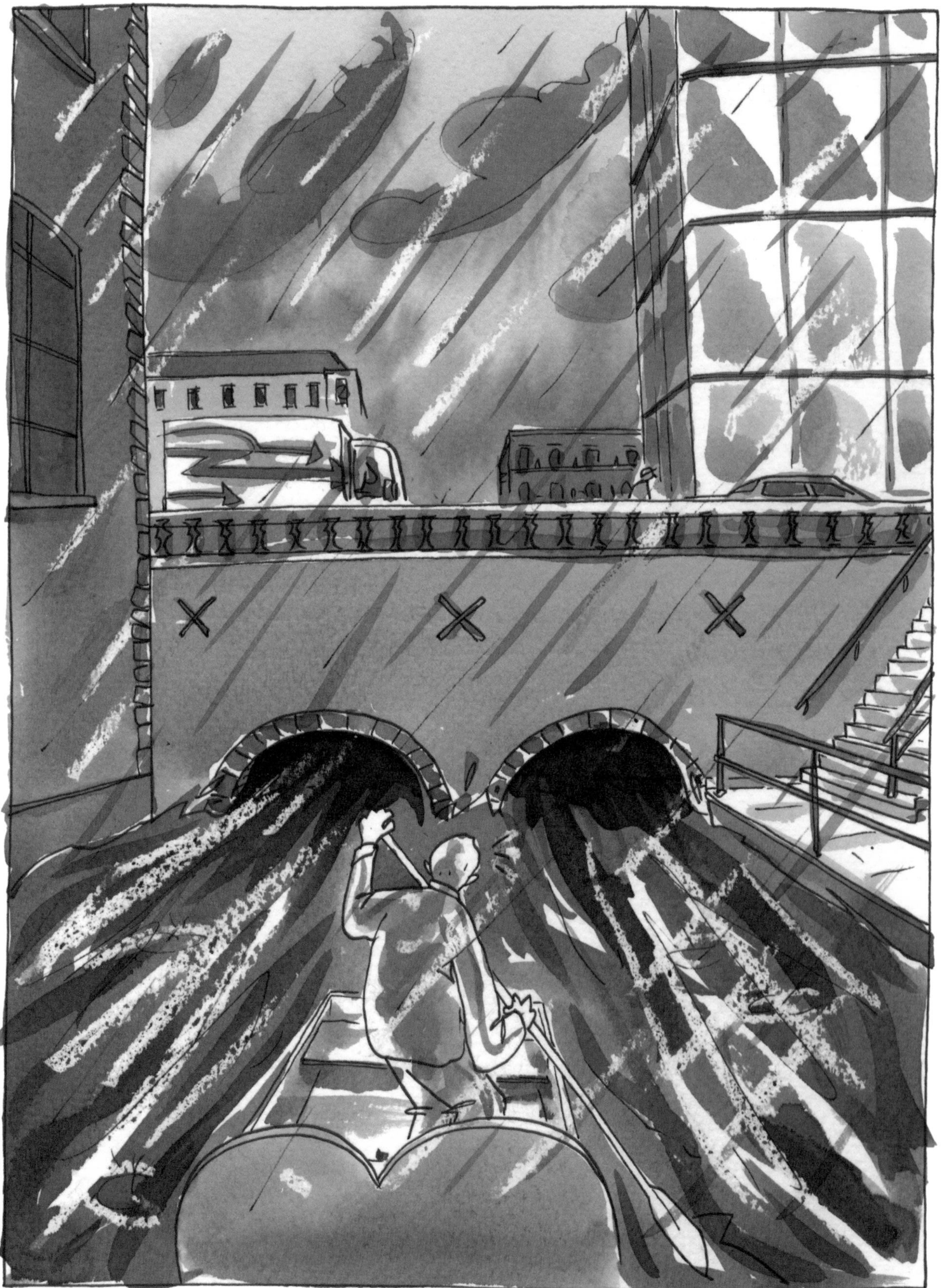

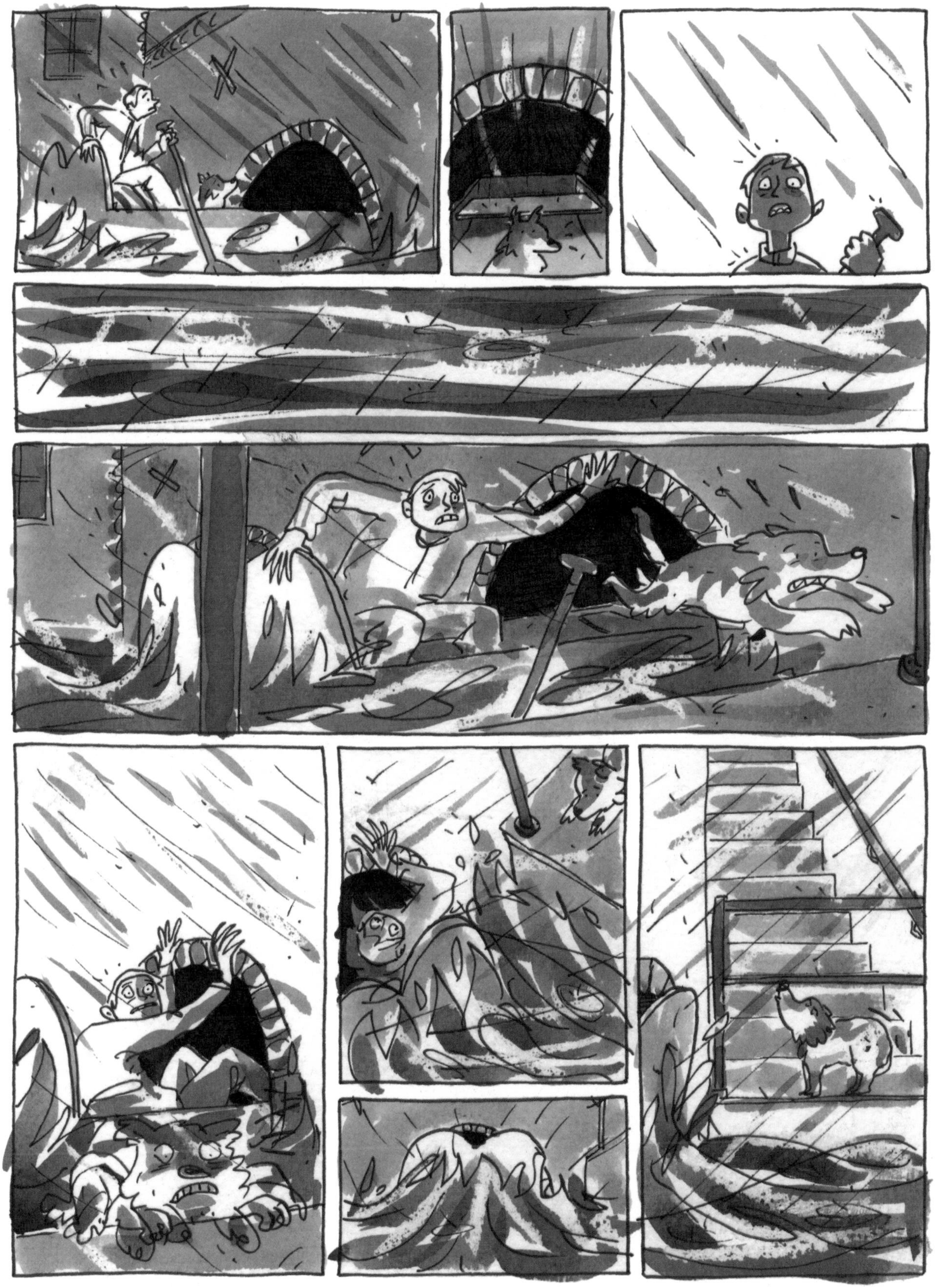

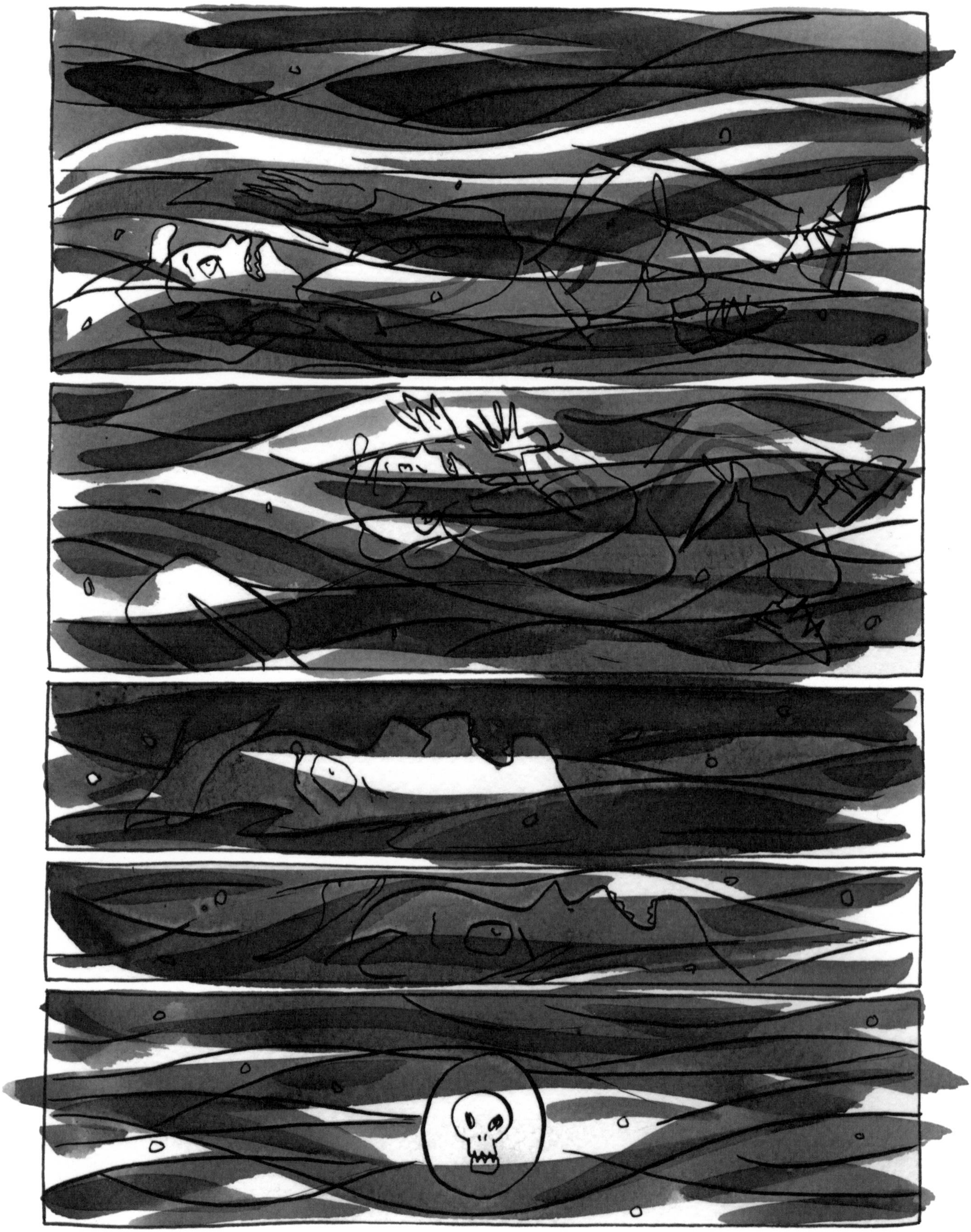

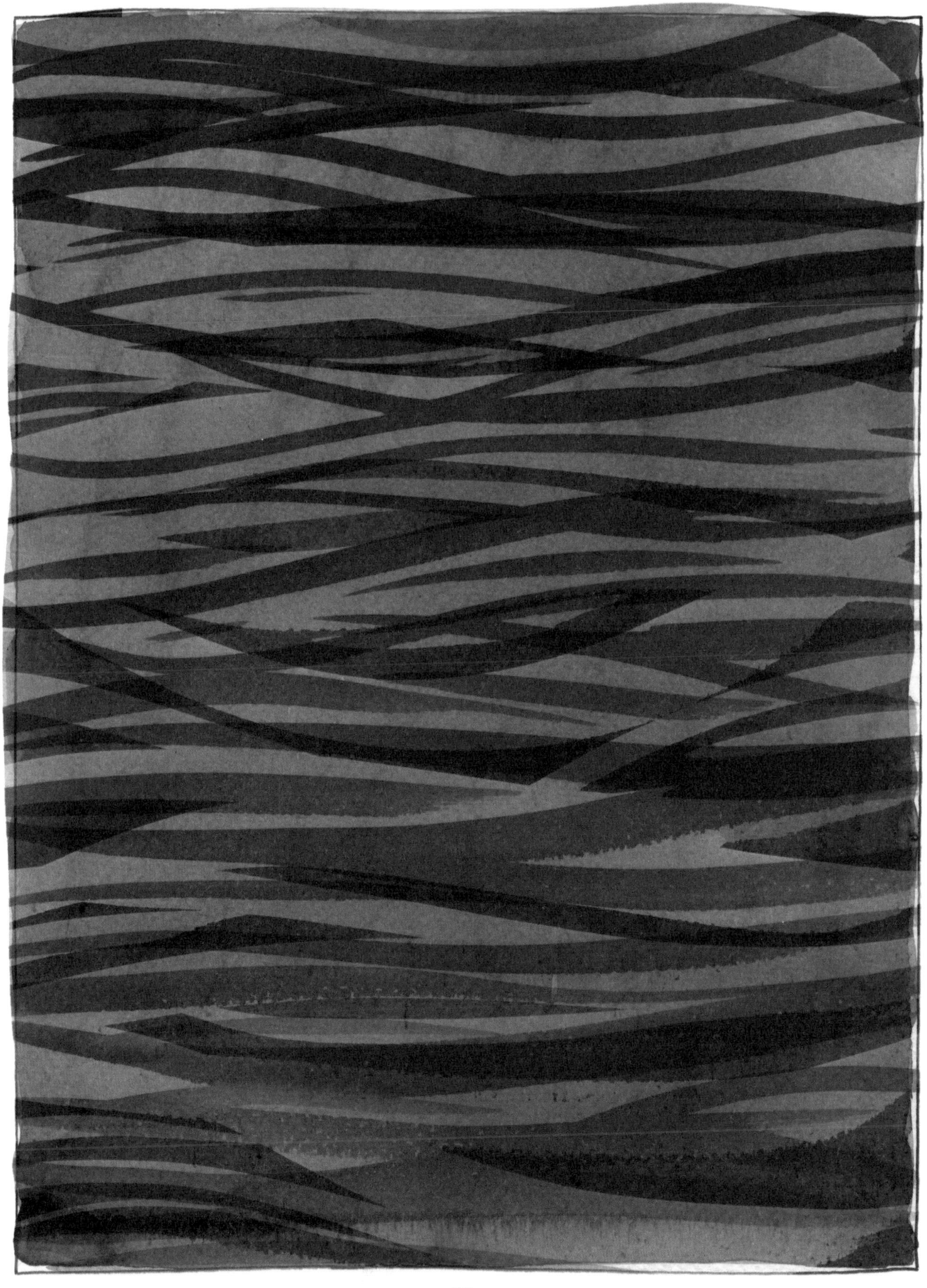

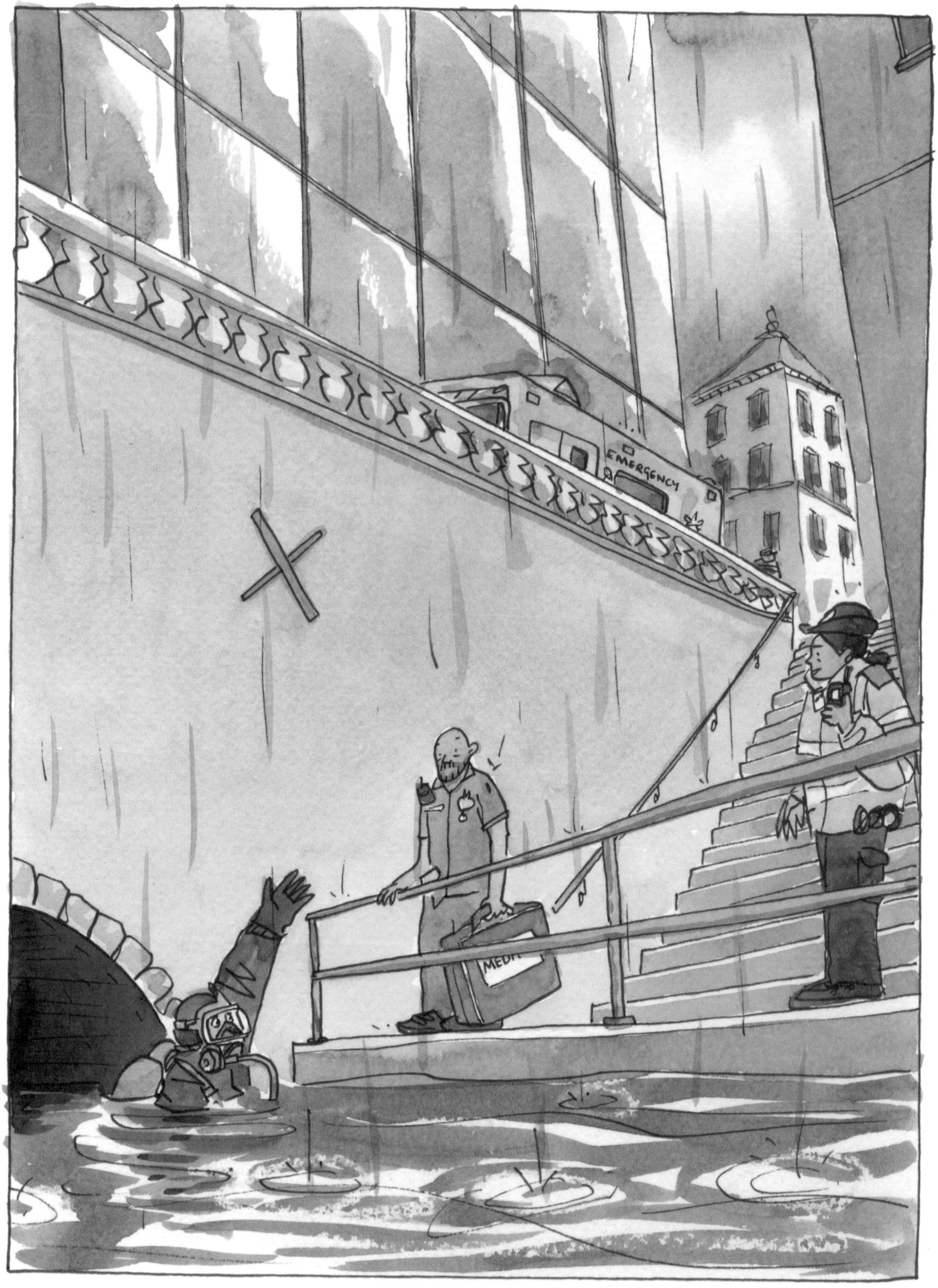
EMERGENCY

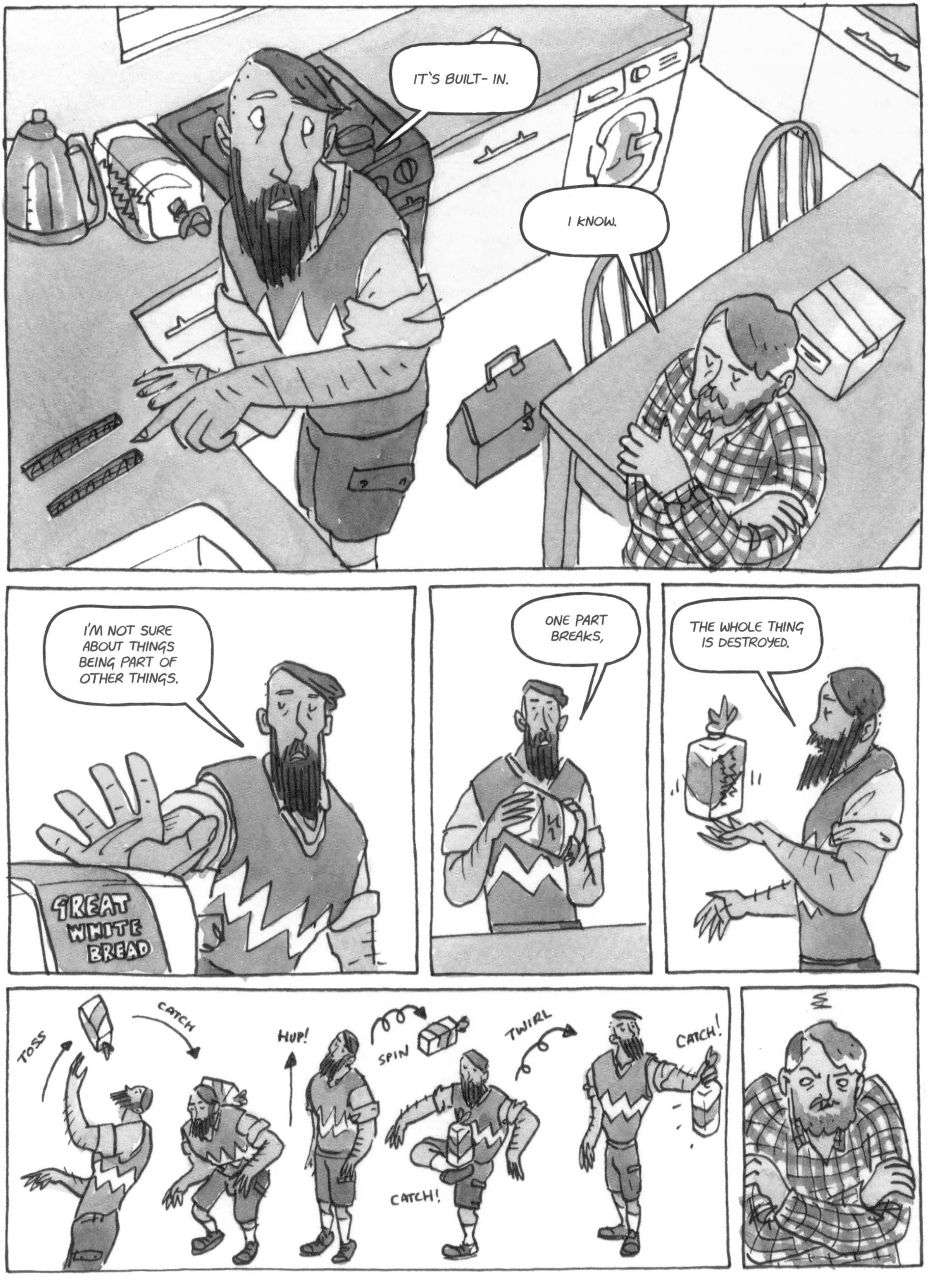
IT'S BUILT- IN.
I KNOW.
I'M NOT SURE ABOUT THINGS BEING PART OF OTHER THINGS.
GREAT WHITE BREAD
ONE PART BREAKS,
THE WHOLE THING IS DESTROYED.
TOSS
CATCH
HUP!
SPIN
CATCH!
TWIRL
CATCH!

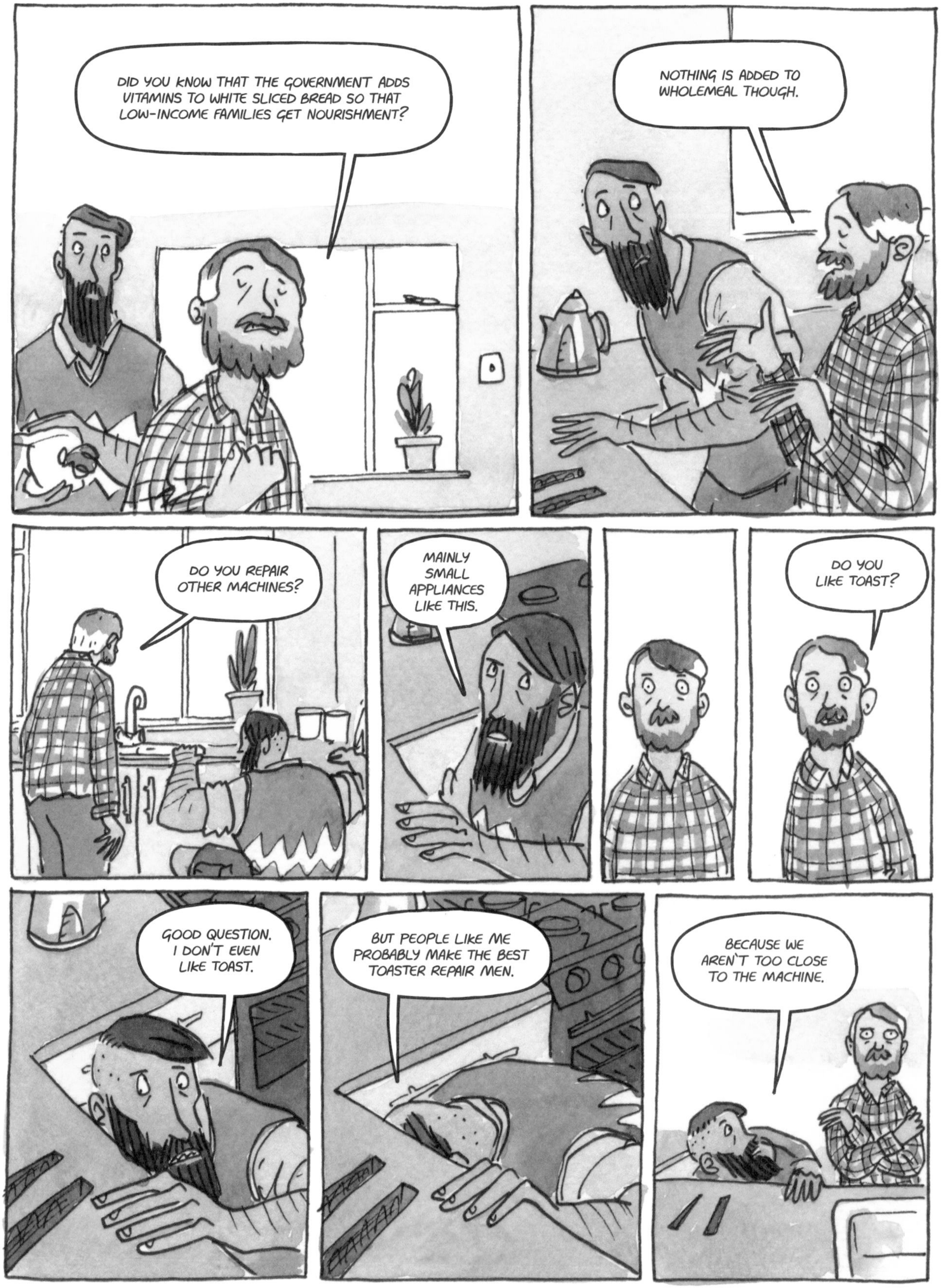
DID YOU KNOW THAT THE GOVERNMENT ADDS VITAMINS TO WHITE SLICED BREAD SO THAT LOW-INCOME FAMILIES GET NOURISHMENT?
NOTHING IS ADDED TO WHOLEMEAL THOUGH.
DO YOU REPAIR OTHER MACHINES?
MAINLY SMALL APPLIANCES LIKE THIS.
DO YOU LIKE TOAST?
GOOD QUESTION. I DON'T EVEN LIKE TOAST.
BUT PEOPLE LIKE ME PROBABLY MAKE THE BEST TOASTER REPAIR MEN.
BECAUSE WE AREN'T TOO CLOSE TO THE MACHINE.

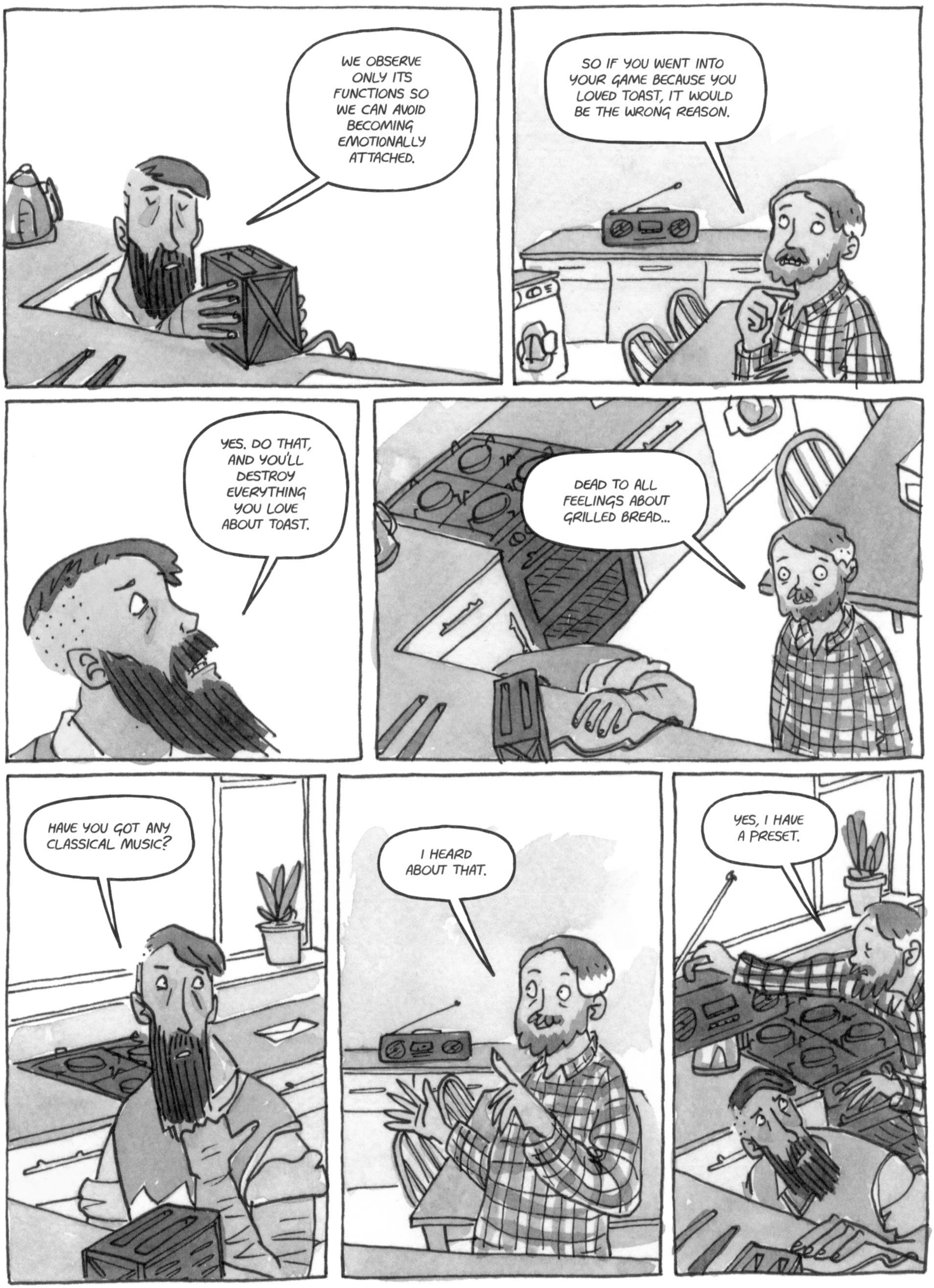
WE OBSERVE ONLY ITS FUNCTIONS SO WE CAN AVOID BECOMING EMOTIONALLY ATTACHED.
SO IF YOU WENT INTO YOUR GAME BECAUSE YOU LOVED TOAST, IT WOULD BE THE WRONG REASON.
YES. DO THAT, AND YOU'LL DESTROY EVERYTHING YOU LOVE ABOUT TOAST.
DEAD TO ALL FEELINGS ABOUT GRILLED BREAD...
HAVE YOU GOT ANY CLASSICAL MUSIC?
I HEARD ABOUT THAT.
YES, I HAVE A PRESET.

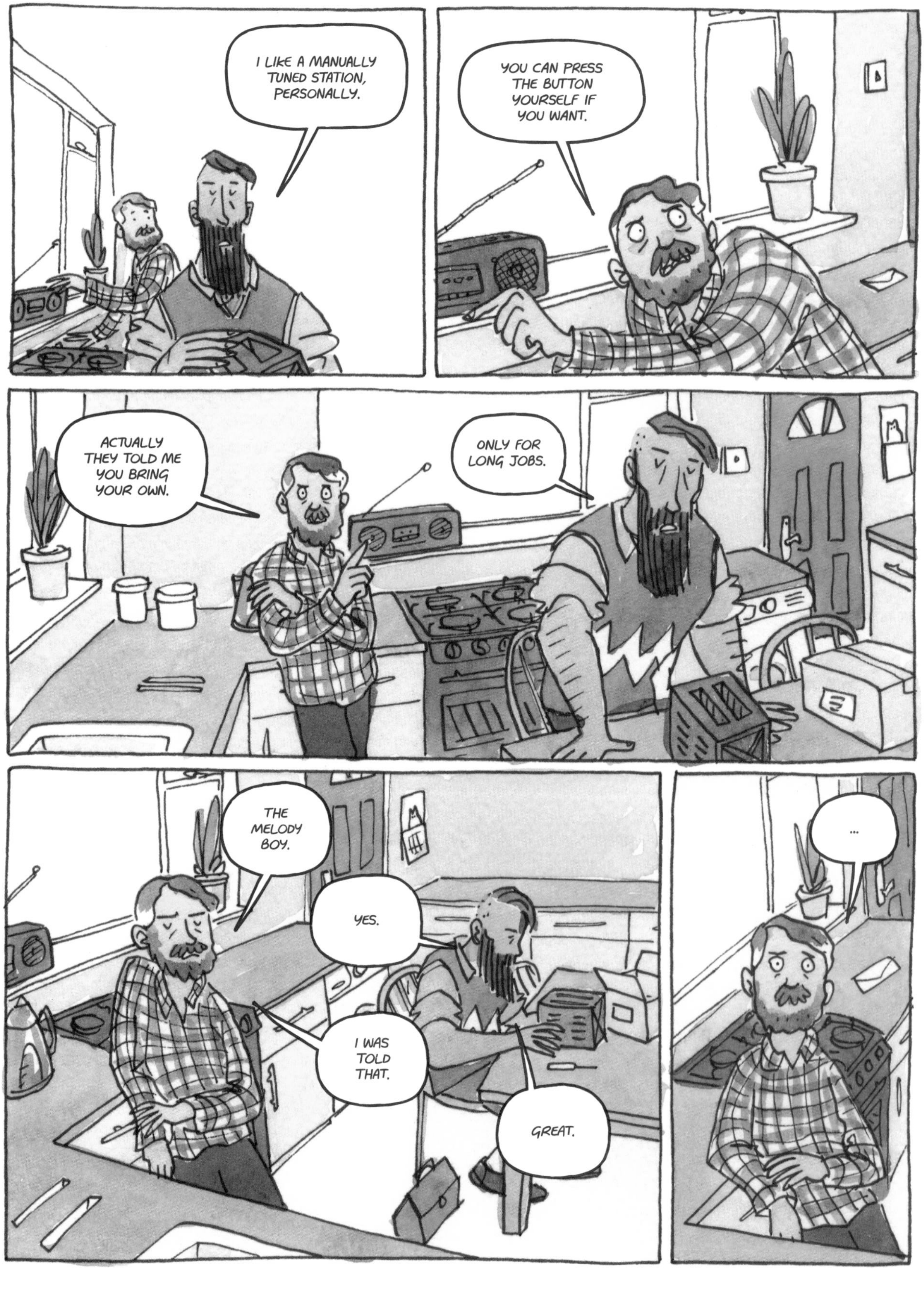
I LIKE A MANUALLY TUNED STATION, PERSONALLY.
YOU CAN PRESS THE BUTTON YOURSELF IF YOU WANT.
ACTUALLY THEY TOLD ME YOU BRING YOUR OWN.
ONLY FOR LONG JOBS.
THE MELODY BOY.
YES.
I WAS TOLD THAT.
GREAT.
...

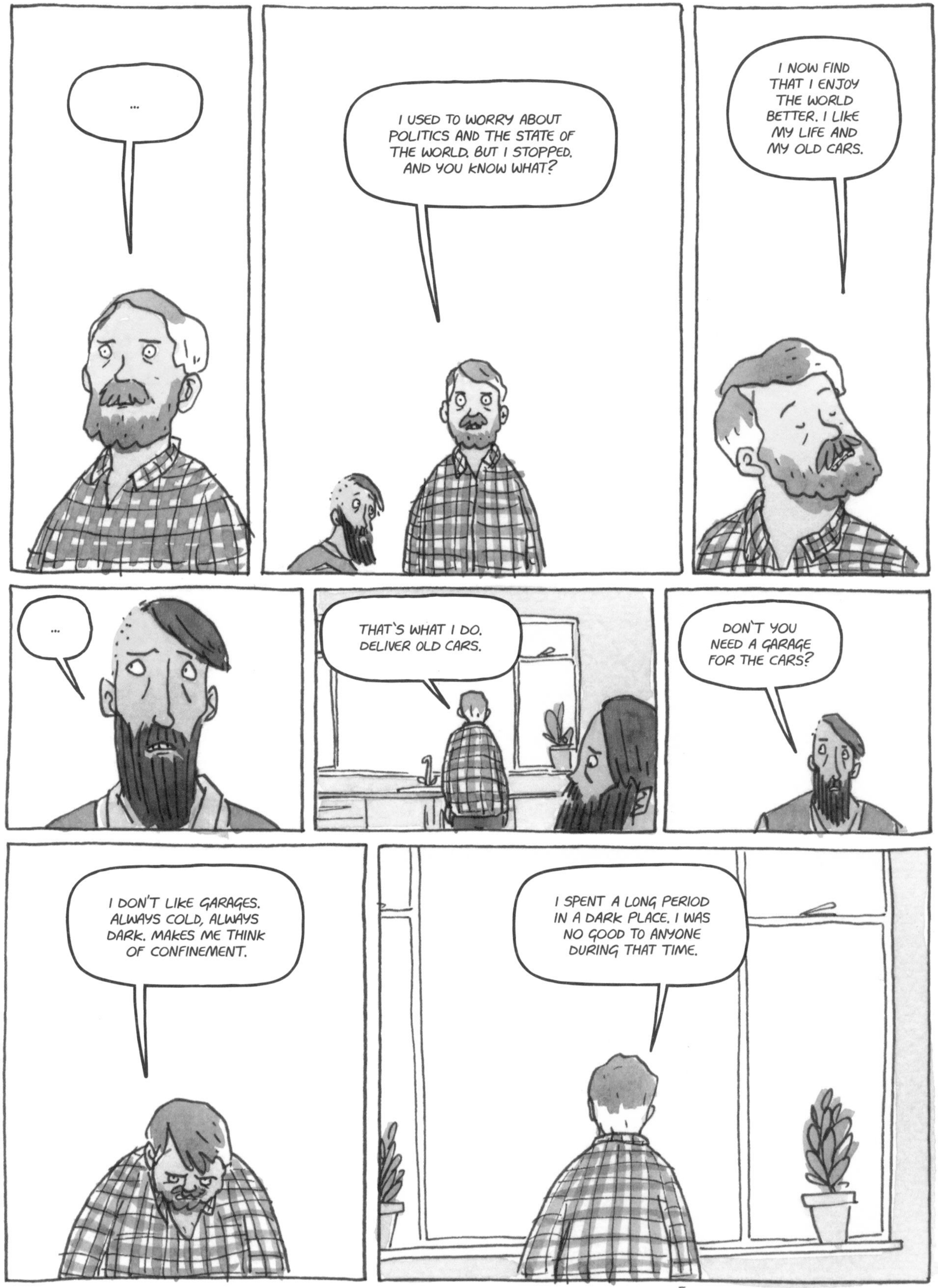
...
I USED TO WORRY ABOUT POLITICS AND THE STATE OF THE WORLD. BUT I STOPPED. AND YOU KNOW WHAT?
I NOW FIND THAT I ENJOY THE WORLD BETTER. I LIKE MY LIFE AND MY OLD CARS.
...
THAT'S WHAT I DO. DELIVER OLD CARS.
DON'T YOU NEED A GARAGE FOR THE CARS?
I DON'T LIKE GARAGES. ALWAYS COLD, ALWAYS DARK. MAKES ME THINK OF CONFINEMENT.
I SPENT A LONG PERIOD IN A DARK PLACE. I WAS NO GOOD TO ANYONE DURING THAT TIME.

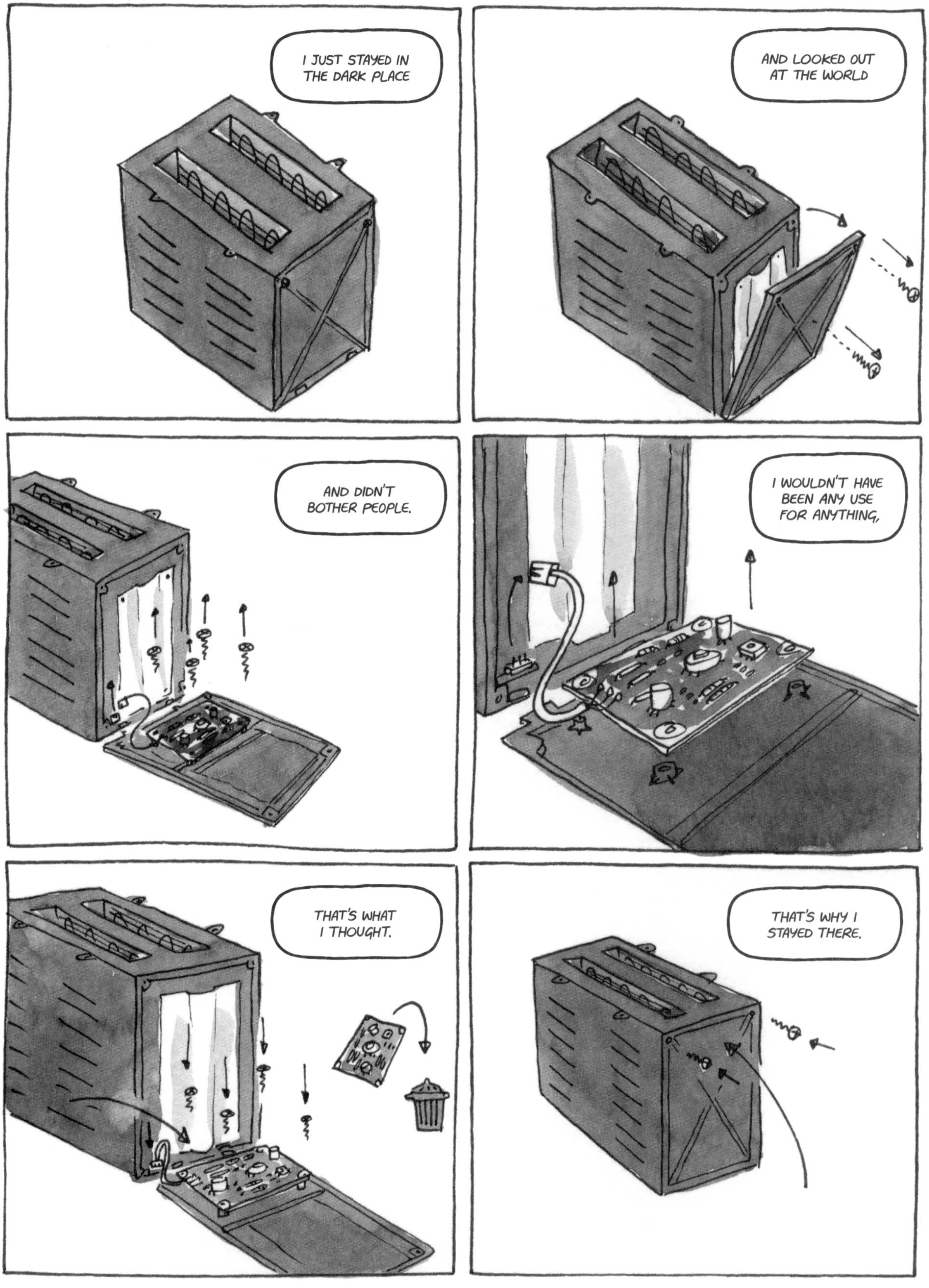
I JUST STAYED IN THE DARK PLACE
AND LOOKED OUT AT THE WORLD
AND DIDN'T BOTHER PEOPLE.
I WOULDN'T HAVE BEEN ANY USE FOR ANYTHING,
THAT'S WHAT I THOUGHT.
THAT'S WHY I STAYED THERE.

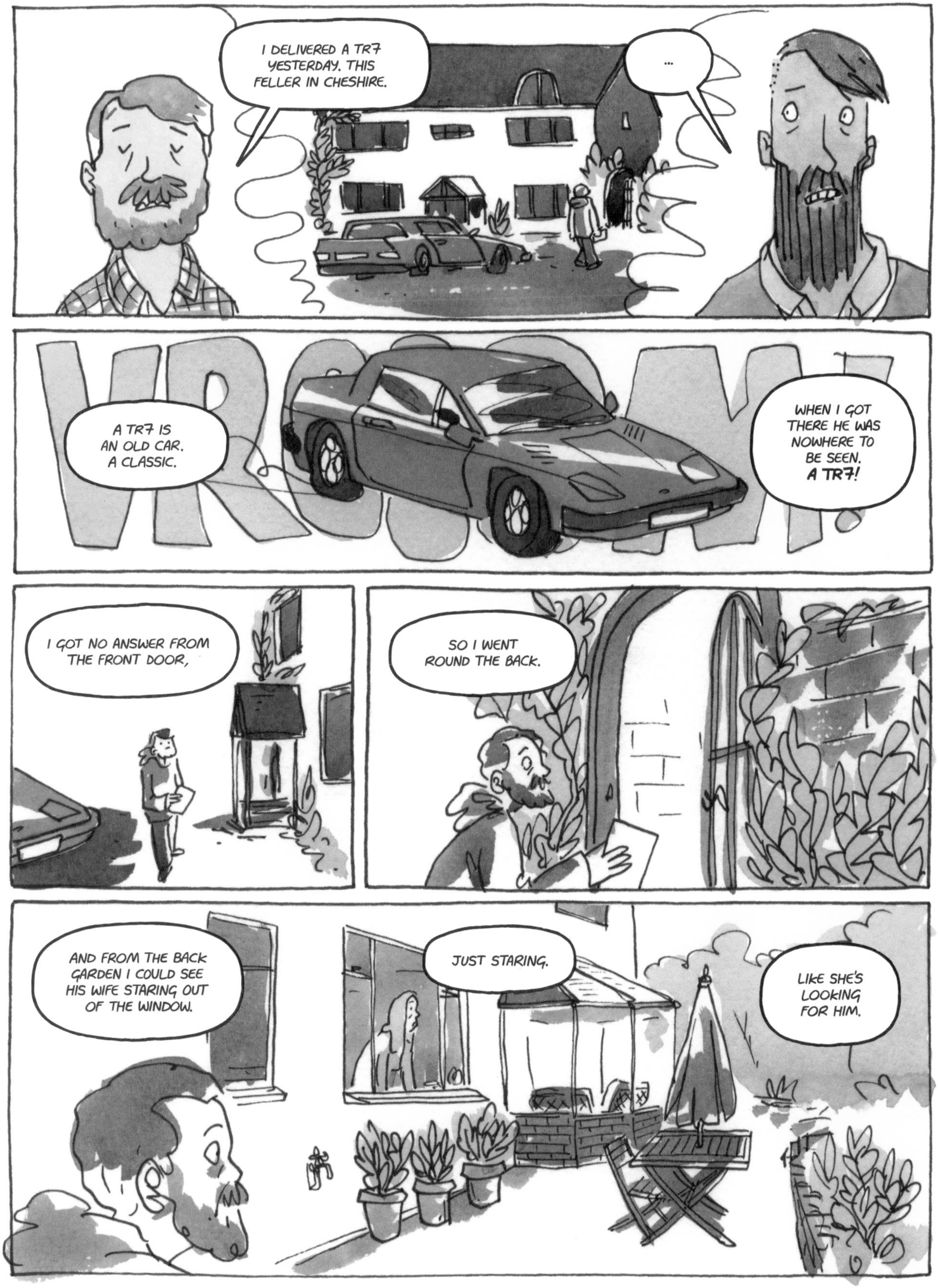
I DELIVERED A TR7 YESTERDAY. THIS FELLER IN CHESHIRE.
...
A TR7 IS AN OLD CAR. A CLASSIC.
WHEN I GOT THERE HE WAS NOWHERE TO BE SEEN. A TR7!
I GOT NO ANSWER FROM THE FRONT DOOR,
SO I WENT ROUND THE BACK.
AND FROM THE BACK GARDEN I COULD SEE HIS WIFE STARING OUT OF THE WINDOW.
JUST STARING.
LIKE SHE'S LOOKING FOR HIM.

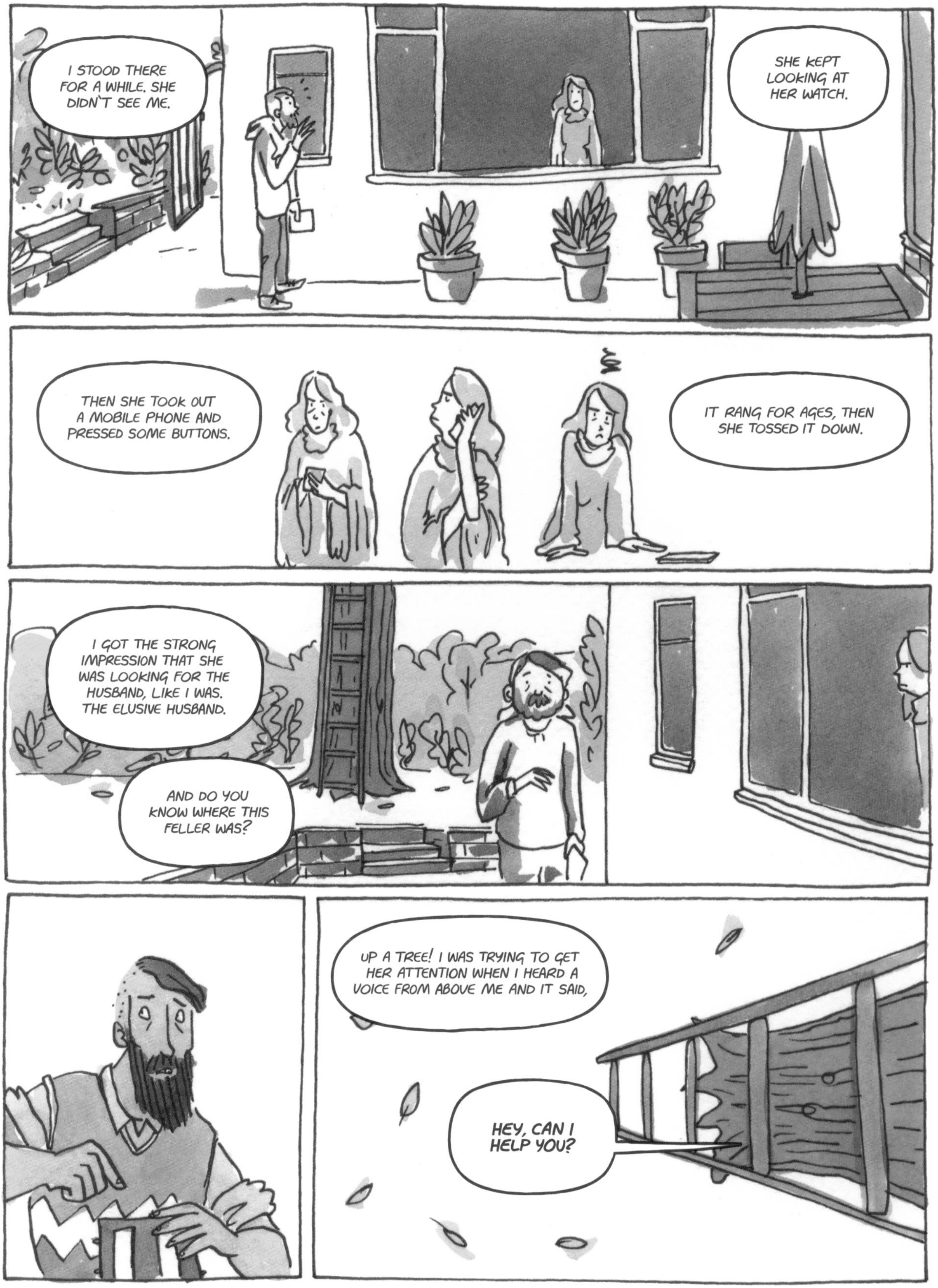
I STOOD THERE FOR A WHILE. SHE DIDN'T SEE ME.
SHE KEPT LOOKING AT HER WATCH.
THEN SHE TOOK OUT A MOBILE PHONE AND PRESSED SOME BUTTONS.
IT RANG FOR AGES, THEN SHE TOSSED IT DOWN.
I GOT THE STRONG IMPRESSION THAT SHE WAS LOOKING FOR THE HUSBAND, LIKE I WAS. THE ELUSIVE HUSBAND.
AND DO YOU KNOW WHERE THIS FELLER WAS?
UP A TREE! I WAS TRYING TO GET HER ATTENTION WHEN I HEARD A VOICE FROM ABOVE ME AND IT SAID,
HEY, CAN I HELP YOU?

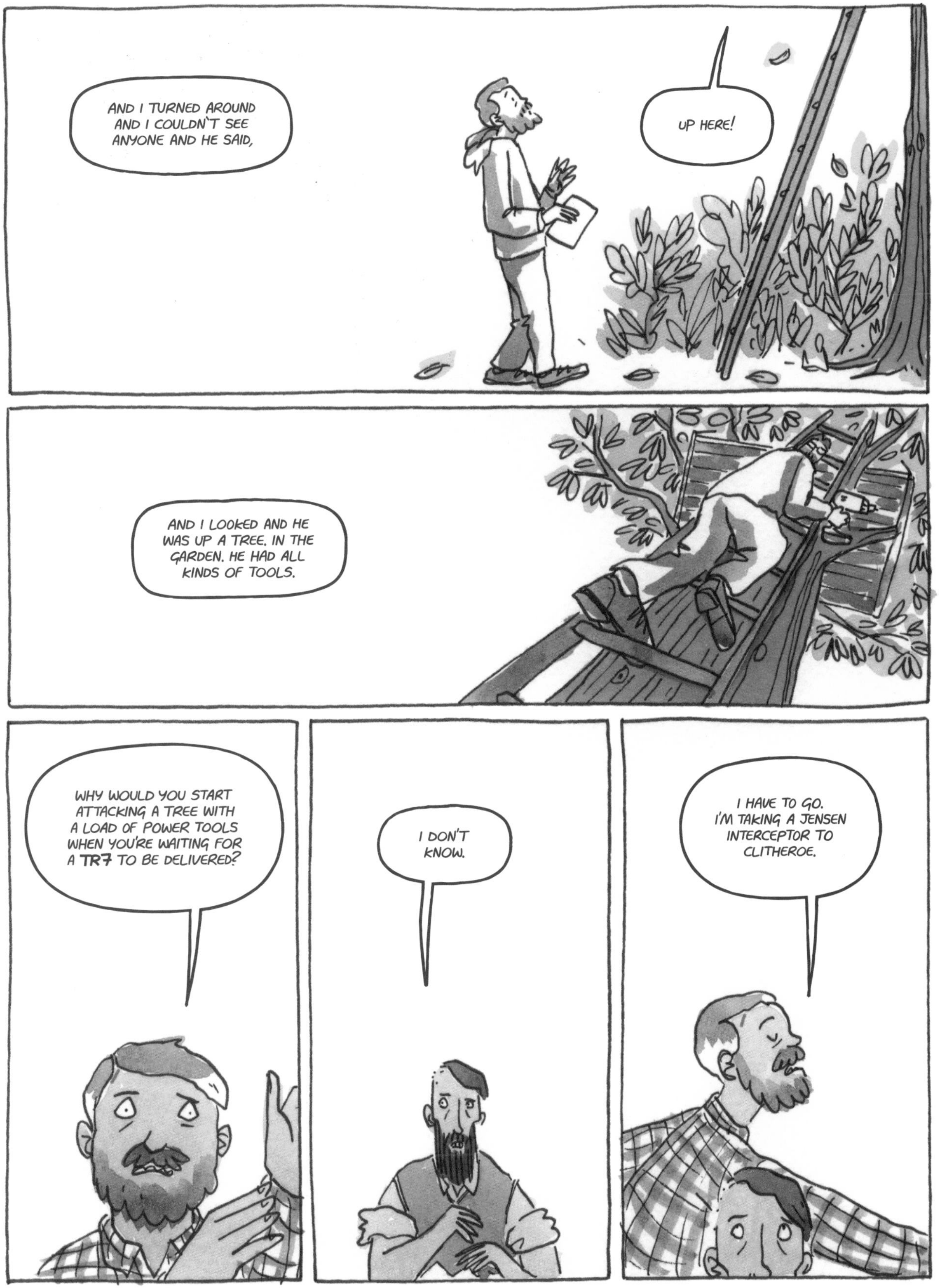
AND I TURNED AROUND AND I COULDN'T SEE ANYONE AND HE SAID,
UP HERE!
AND I LOOKED AND HE WAS UP A TREE. IN THE GARDEN. HE HAD ALL KINDS OF TOOLS.
WHY WOULD YOU START ATTACKING A TREE WITH A LOAD OF POWER TOOLS WHEN YOU'RE WAITING FOR A TR7 TO BE DELIVERED?
I DON'T KNOW.
I HAVE TO GO. I'M TAKING A JENSEN INTERCEPTOR TO CLITHEROE.

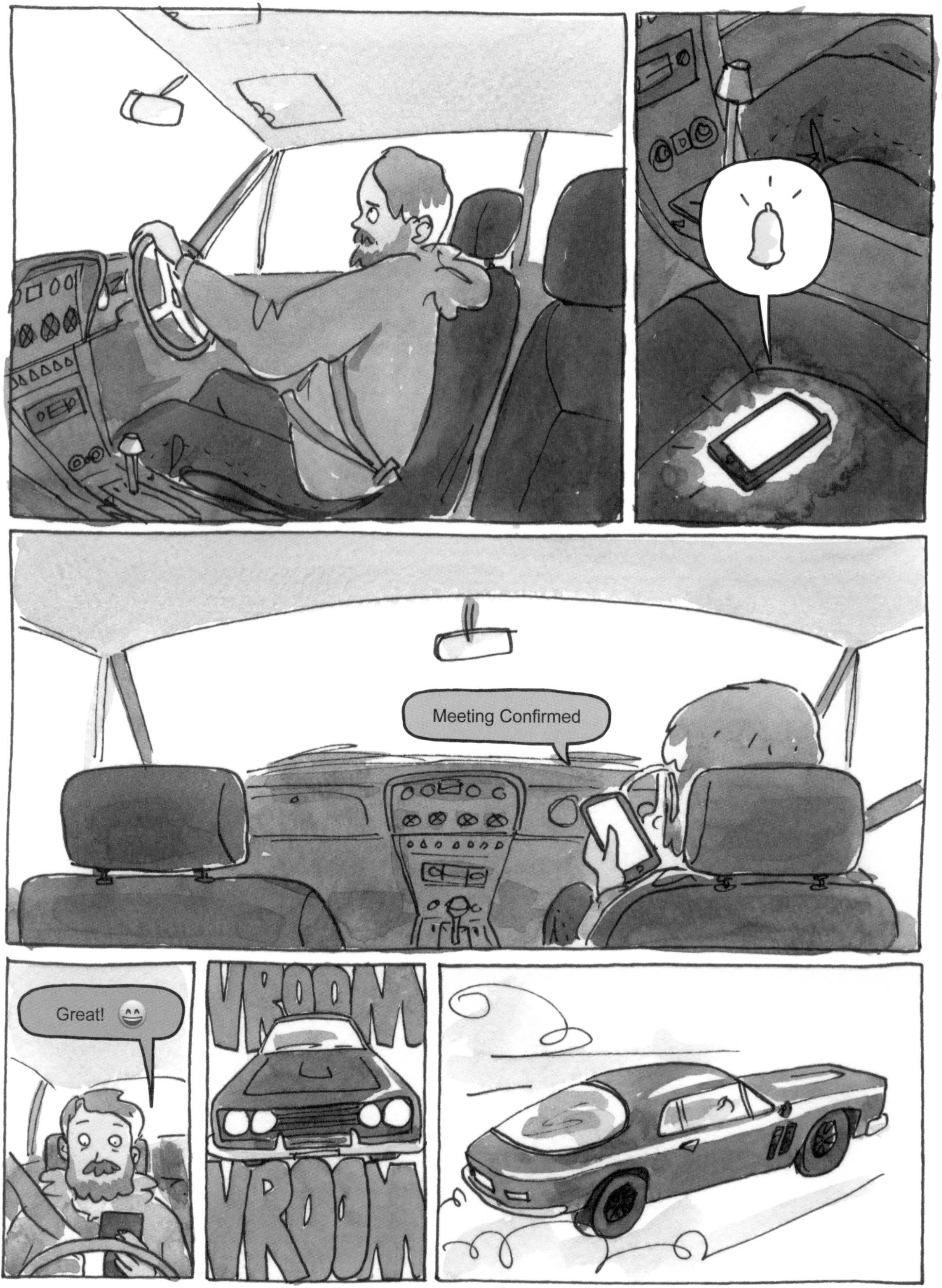
Meeting Confirmed
Great!
VROOM
VROOM

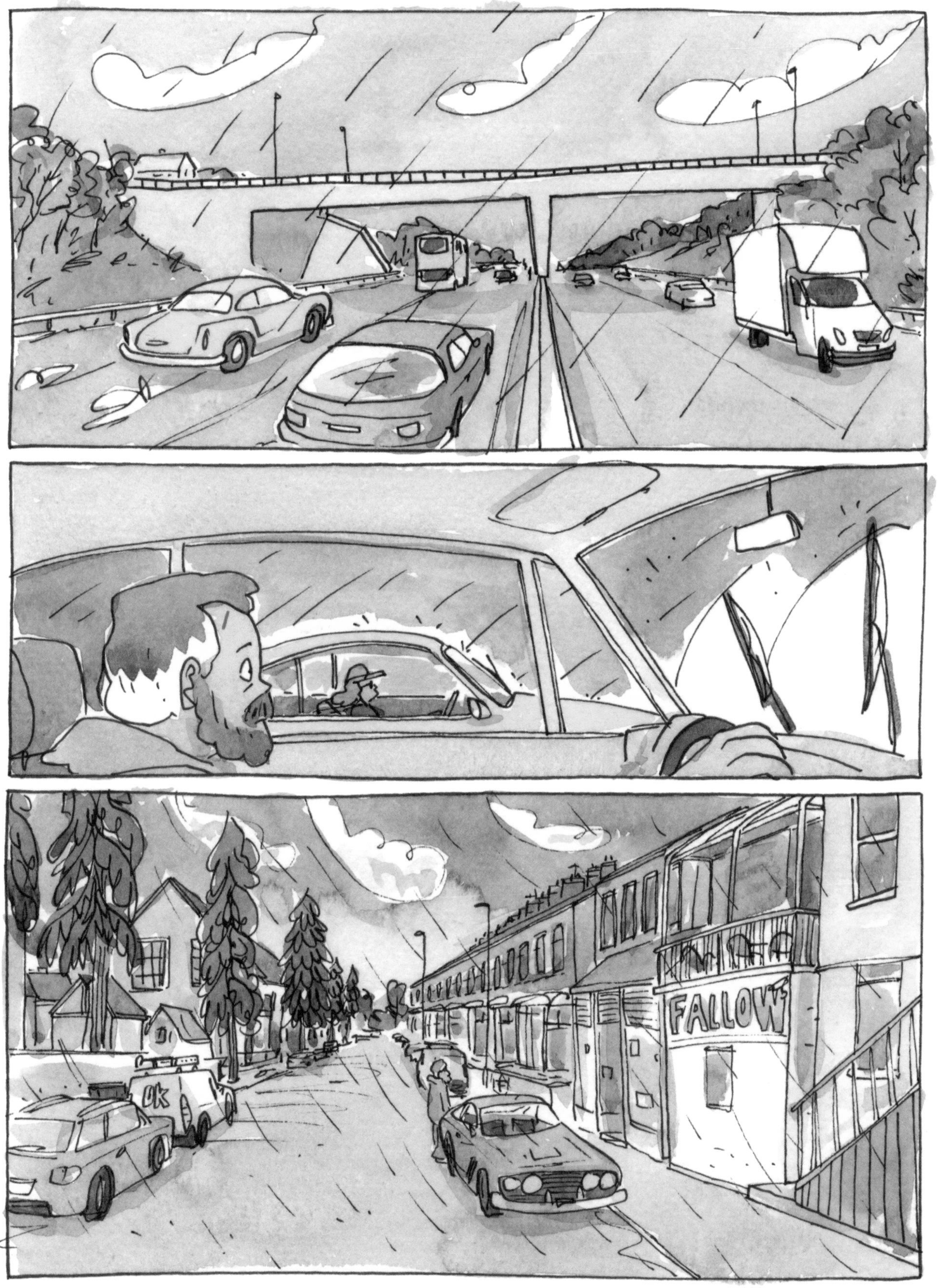
OK
FALLOWS

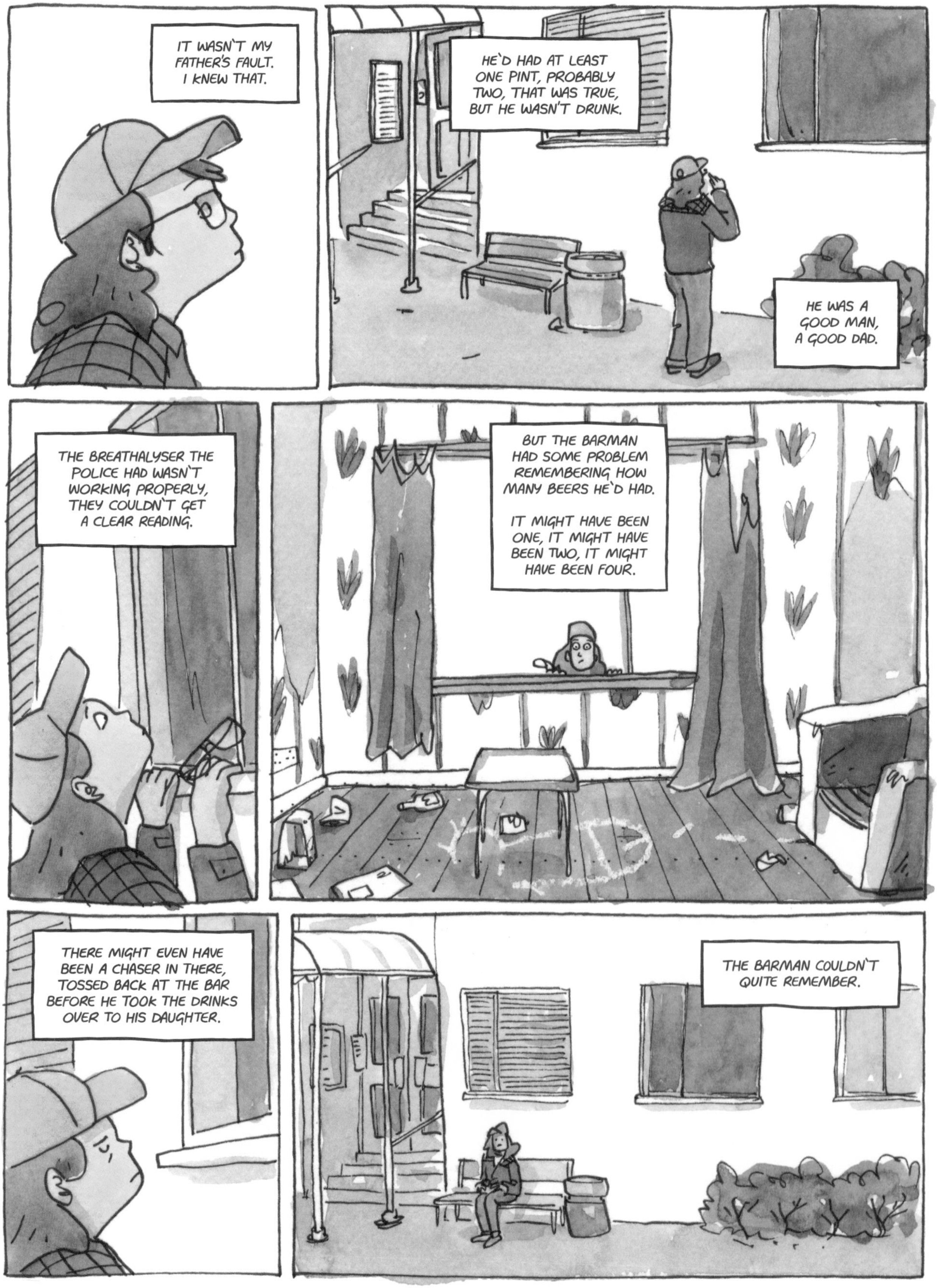
IT WASN'T MY FATHER'S FAULT. I KNEW THAT.
HE'D HAD AT LEAST ONE PINT, PROBABLY TWO, THAT WAS TRUE, BUT HE WASN'T DRUNK.
HE WAS A GOOD MAN, A GOOD DAD.
THE BREATHALYSER THE POLICE HAD WASN'T WORKING PROPERLY, THEY COULDN'T GET A CLEAR READING.
BUT THE BARMAN HAD SOME PROBLEM REMEMBERING HOW MANY BEERS HE'D HAD.
IT MIGHT HAVE BEEN ONE, IT MIGHT HAVE BEEN TWO, IT MIGHT HAVE BEEN FOUR.
THERE MIGHT EVEN HAVE BEEN A CHASER IN THERE, TOSSED BACK AT THE BAR BEFORE HE TOOK THE DRINKS OVER TO HIS DAUGHTER.
THE BARMAN COULDN'T QUITE REMEMBER.

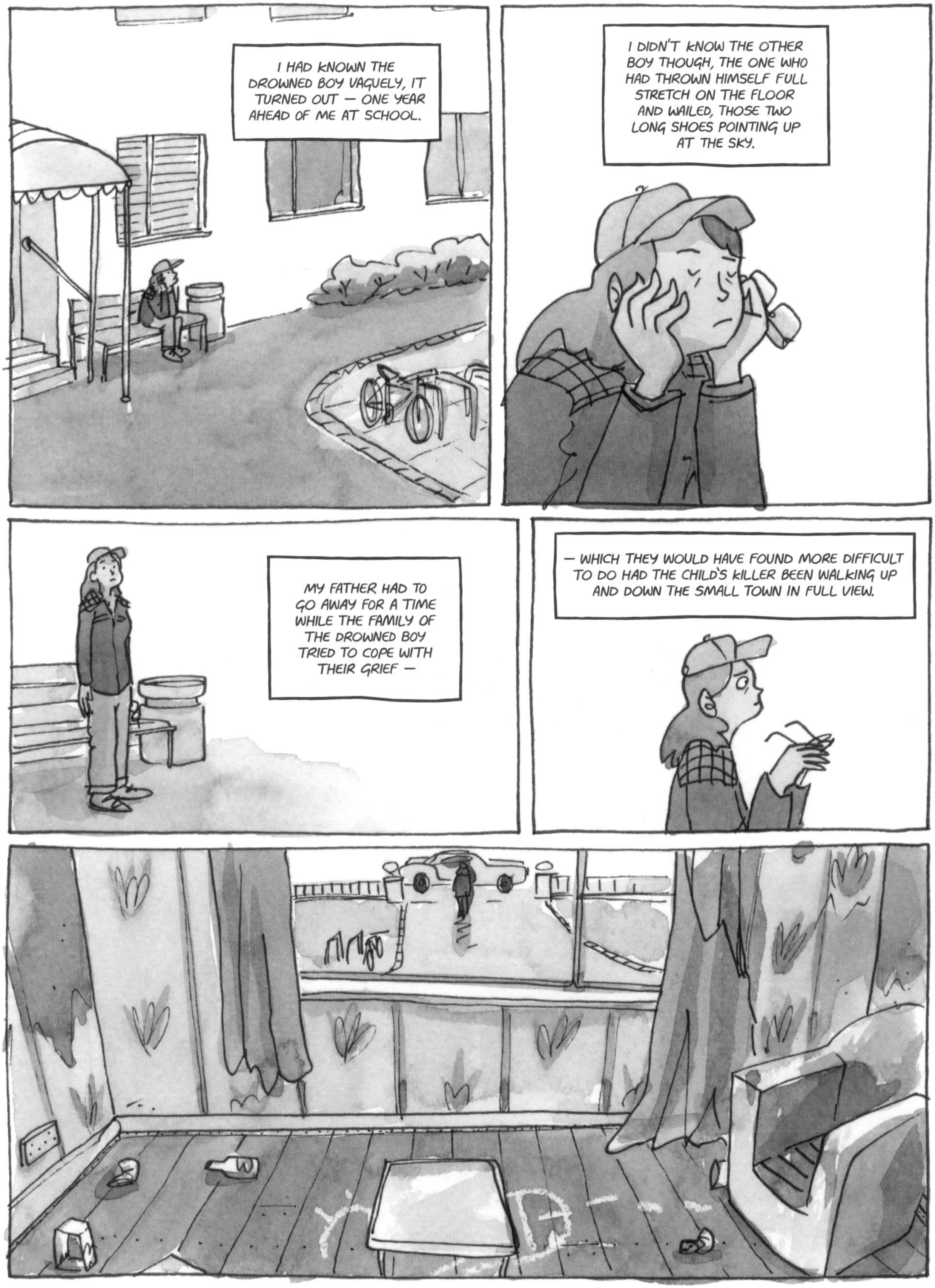
I HAD KNOWN THE DROWNED BOY VAGUELY, IT TURNED OUT — ONE YEAR AHEAD OF ME AT SCHOOL.
I DIDN'T KNOW THE OTHER BOY THOUGH, THE ONE WHO HAD THROWN HIMSELF FULL STRETCH ON THE FLOOR AND WAILED, THOSE TWO LONG SHOES POINTING UP AT THE SKY.
MY FATHER HAD TO GO AWAY FOR A TIME WHILE THE FAMILY OF THE DROWNED BOY TRIED TO COPE WITH THEIR GRIEF —
— WHICH THEY WOULD HAVE FOUND MORE DIFFICULT TO DO HAD THE CHILD'S KILLER BEEN WALKING UP AND DOWN THE SMALL TOWN IN FULL VIEW.

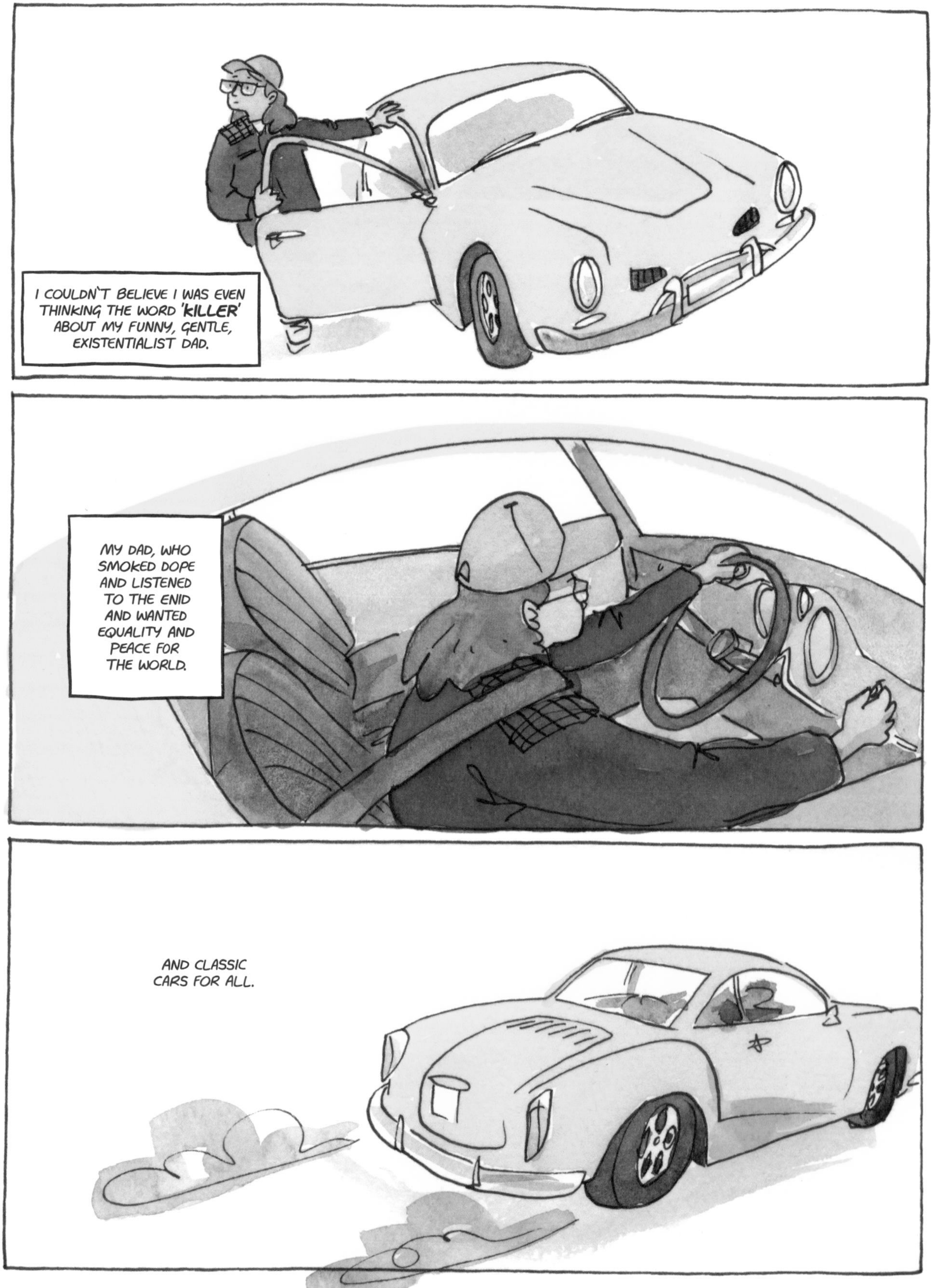
I COULDN'T BELIEVE I WAS EVEN THINKING THE WORD '**KILLER**' ABOUT MY FUNNY, GENTLE, EXISTENTIALIST DAD.
MY DAD, WHO SMOKED DOPE AND LISTENED TO THE ENID AND WANTED EQUALITY AND PEACE FOR THE WORLD.
AND CLASSIC CARS FOR ALL.

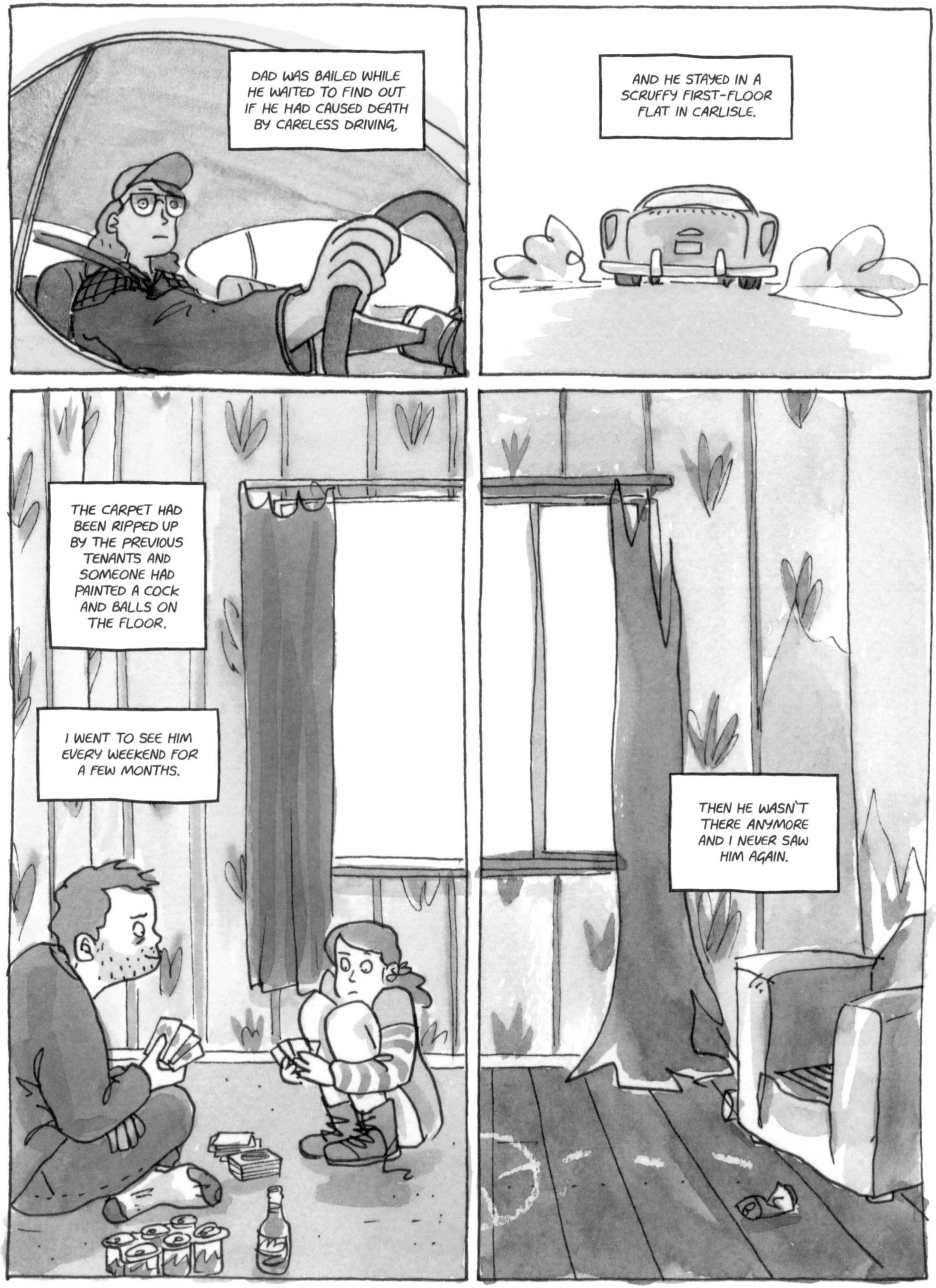
DAD WAS BAILED WHILE HE WAITED TO FIND OUT IF HE HAD CAUSED DEATH BY CARELESS DRIVING,
AND HE STAYED IN A SCRUFFY FIRST-FLOOR FLAT IN CARLISLE.
THE CARPET HAD BEEN RIPPED UP BY THE PREVIOUS TENANTS AND SOMEONE HAD PAINTED A COCK AND BALLS ON THE FLOOR.
I WENT TO SEE HIM EVERY WEEKEND FOR A FEW MONTHS.
THEN HE WASN'T THERE ANYMORE AND I NEVER SAW HIM AGAIN.

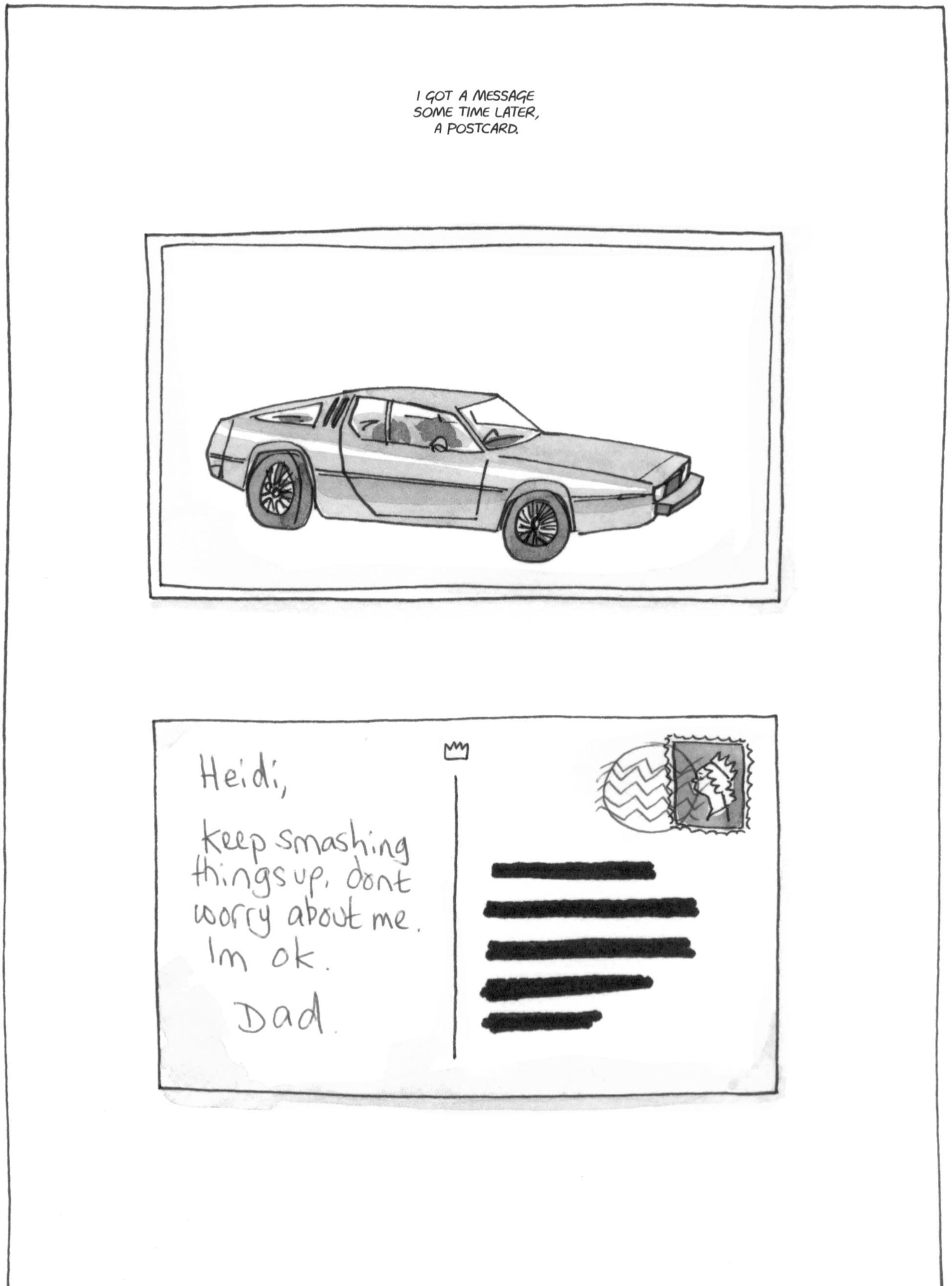
I GOT A MESSAGE SOME TIME LATER, A POSTCARD.
Heidi,
keep smashing things up, dont worry about me. Im ok.
Dad
[redacted]

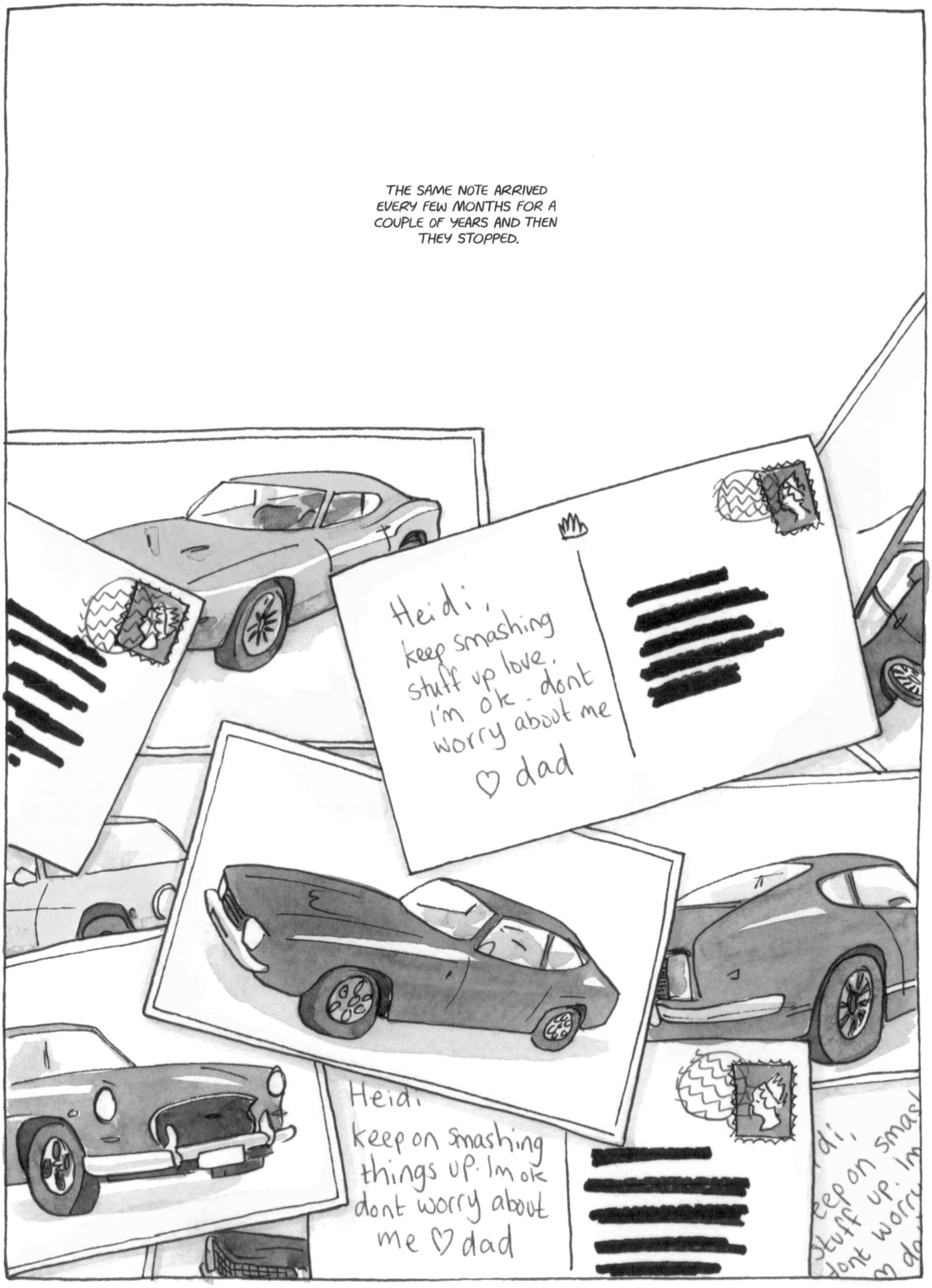
THE SAME NOTE ARRIVED EVERY FEW MONTHS FOR A COUPLE OF YEARS AND THEN THEY STOPPED.
Heidi, keep smashing stuff up love. i'm ok. dont worry about me ♡ dad
[redacted]
Heidi keep on smashing things up. Im ok dont worry about me ♡ dad
[redacted]

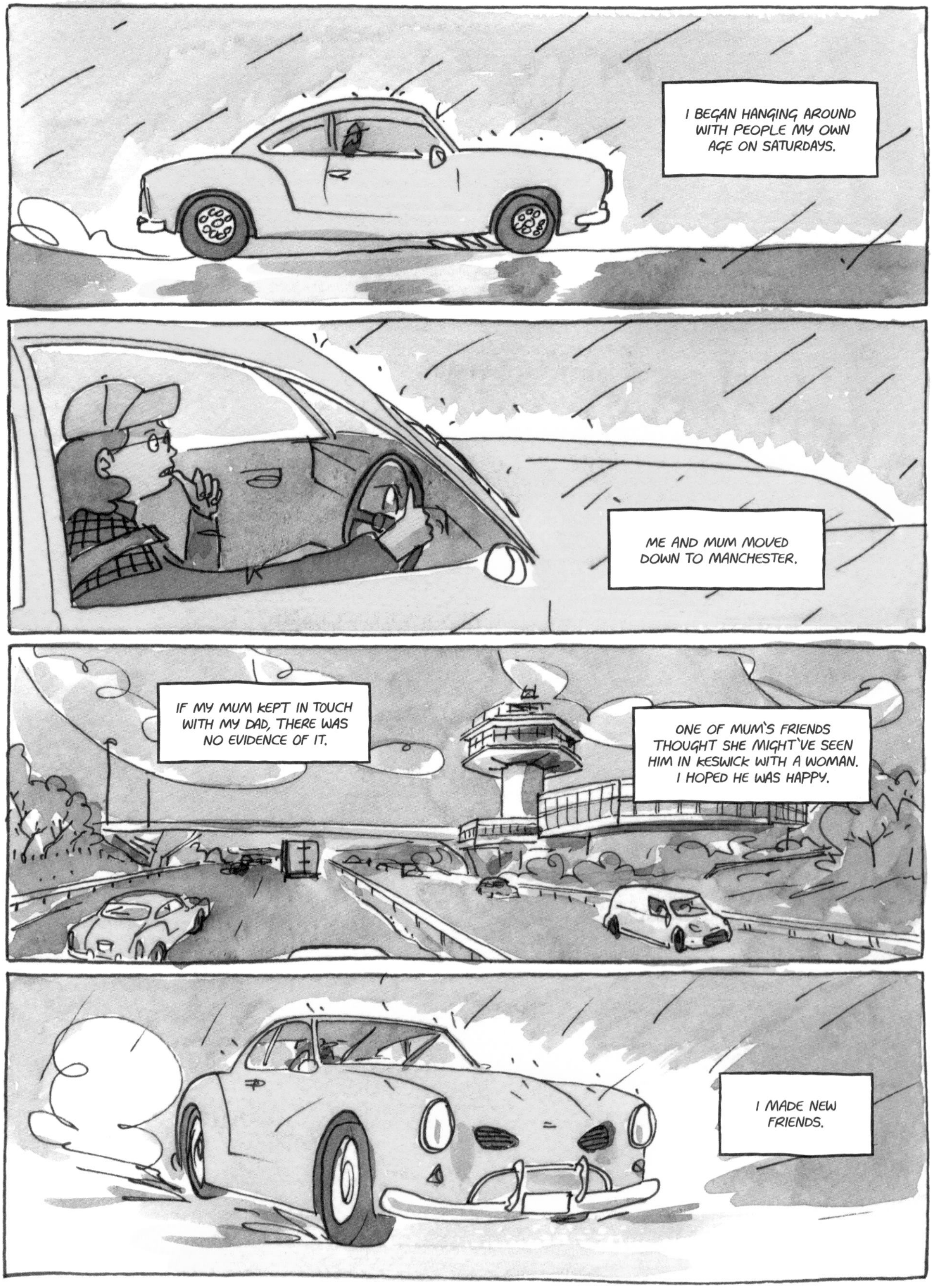
I BEGAN HANGING AROUND WITH PEOPLE MY OWN AGE ON SATURDAYS.
ME AND MUM MOVED DOWN TO MANCHESTER.
IF MY MUM KEPT IN TOUCH WITH MY DAD, THERE WAS NO EVIDENCE OF IT.
ONE OF MUM'S FRIENDS THOUGHT SHE MIGHT'VE SEEN HIM IN KESWICK WITH A WOMAN. I HOPED HE WAS HAPPY.
I MADE NEW FRIENDS.

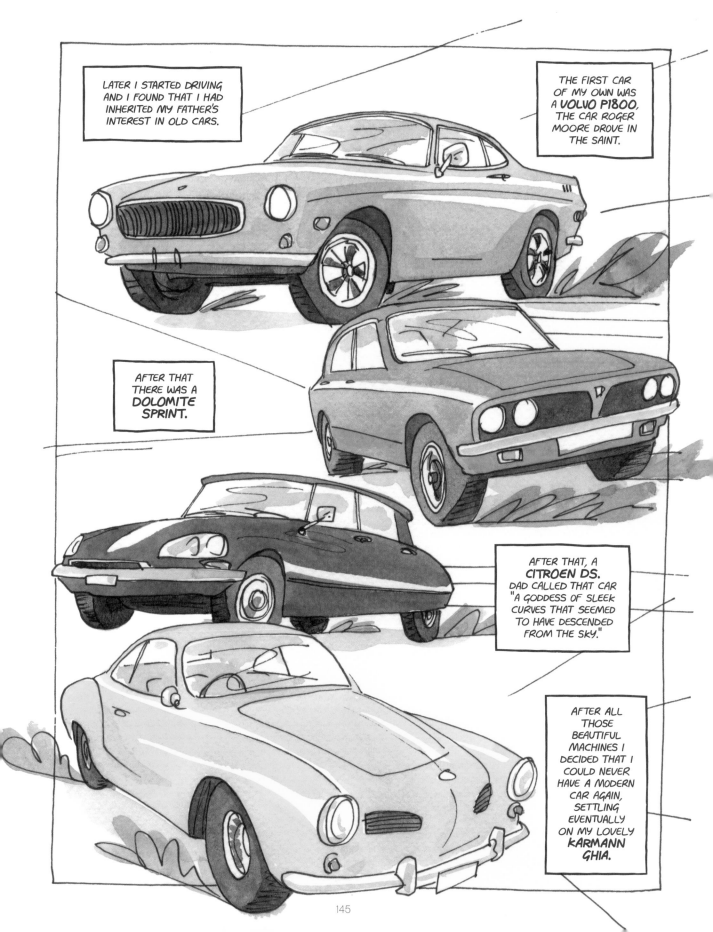

LATER I STARTED DRIVING AND I FOUND THAT I HAD INHERITED MY FATHER'S INTEREST IN OLD CARS.

THE FIRST CAR OF MY OWN WAS A *VOLVO P1800*, THE CAR ROGER MOORE DROVE IN THE SAINT.

AFTER THAT THERE WAS A **DOLOMITE SPRINT**.

AFTER THAT, A **CITROEN DS**. DAD CALLED THAT CAR "A GODDESS OF SLEEK CURVES THAT SEEMED TO HAVE DESCENDED FROM THE SKY."

AFTER ALL THOSE BEAUTIFUL MACHINES I DECIDED THAT I COULD NEVER HAVE A MODERN CAR AGAIN, SETTLING EVENTUALLY ON MY LOVELY *KARMANN GHIA*.

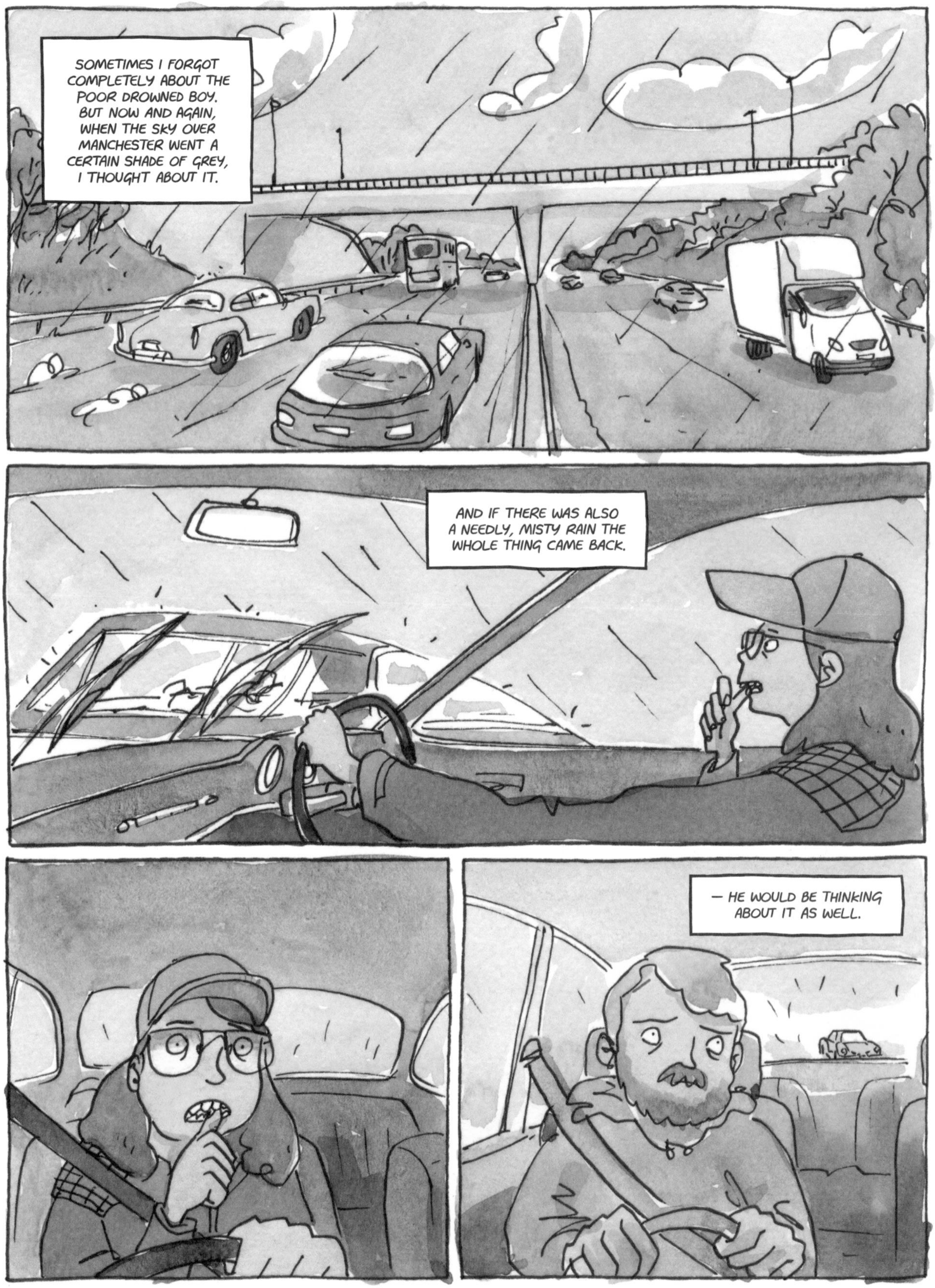
SOMETIMES I FORGOT COMPLETELY ABOUT THE POOR DROWNED BOY. BUT NOW AND AGAIN, WHEN THE SKY OVER MANCHESTER WENT A CERTAIN SHADE OF GREY, I THOUGHT ABOUT IT.
AND IF THERE WAS ALSO A NEEDLY, MISTY RAIN THE WHOLE THING CAME BACK.
— HE WOULD BE THINKING ABOUT IT AS WELL.

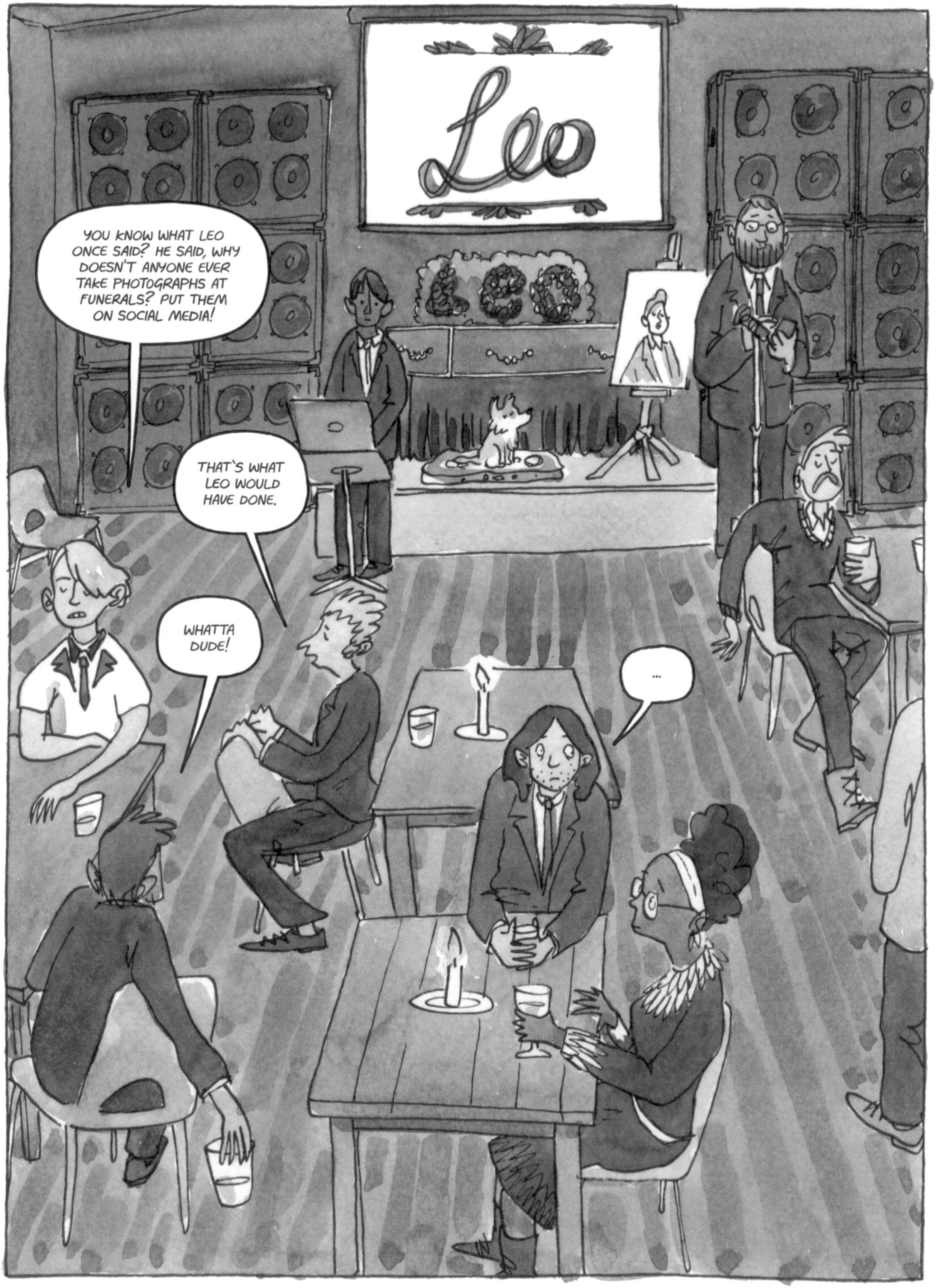
Leo
YOU KNOW WHAT LEO ONCE SAID? HE SAID, WHY DOESN'T ANYONE EVER TAKE PHOTOGRAPHS AT FUNERALS? PUT THEM ON SOCIAL MEDIA!
THAT'S WHAT LEO WOULD HAVE DONE.
WHATTA DUDE!
...

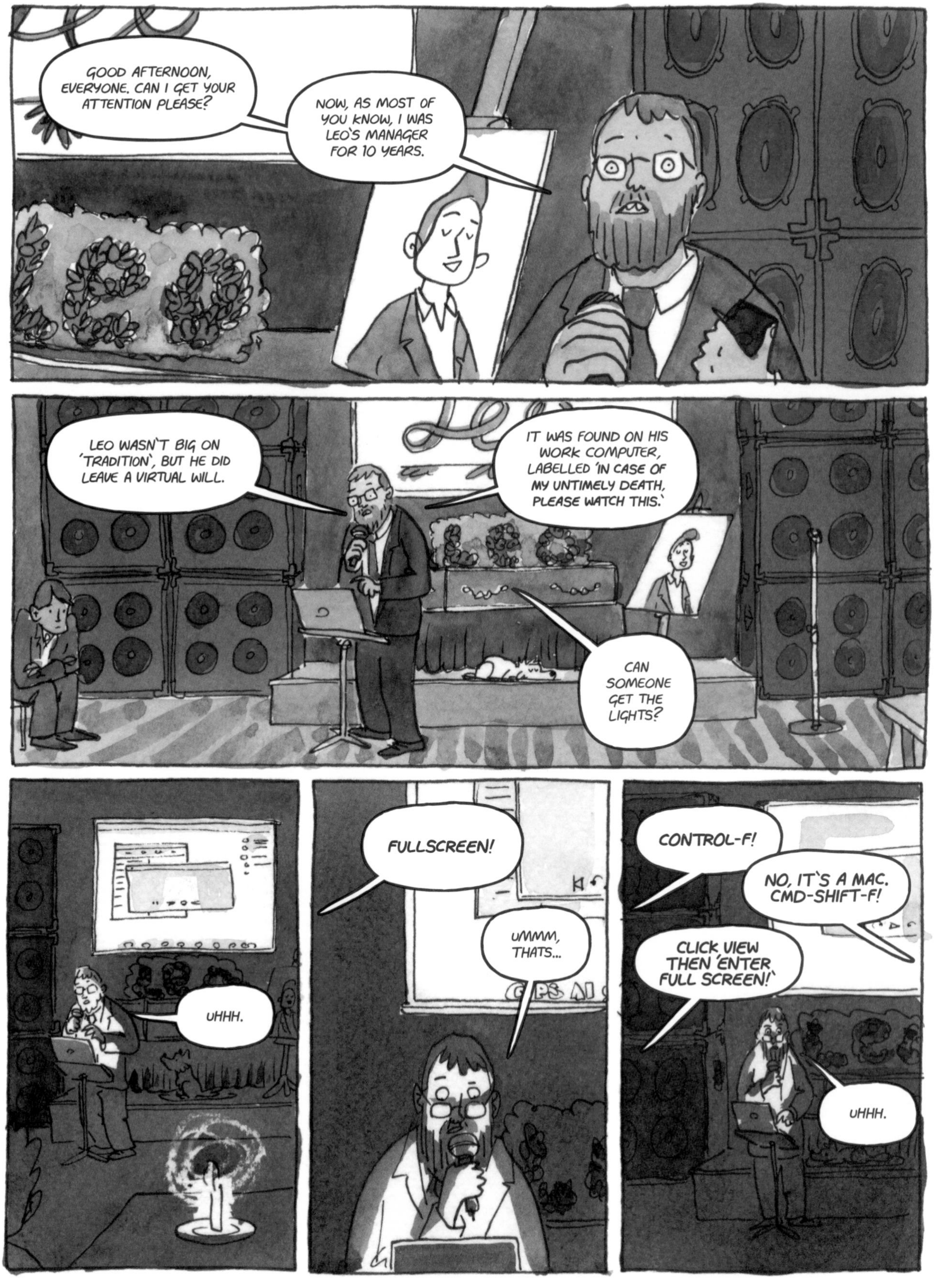
GOOD AFTERNOON, EVERYONE. CAN I GET YOUR ATTENTION PLEASE?
NOW, AS MOST OF YOU KNOW, I WAS LEO'S MANAGER FOR 10 YEARS.
LEO WASN'T BIG ON 'TRADITION', BUT HE DID LEAVE A VIRTUAL WILL.
IT WAS FOUND ON HIS WORK COMPUTER, LABELLED 'IN CASE OF MY UNTIMELY DEATH, PLEASE WATCH THIS.'
CAN SOMEONE GET THE LIGHTS?
UHHH.
FULLSCREEN!
UMMM, THATS...
CONTROL-F!
NO, IT'S A MAC. CMD-SHIFT-F!
CLICK VIEW THEN 'ENTER FULL SCREEN!'
UHHH.

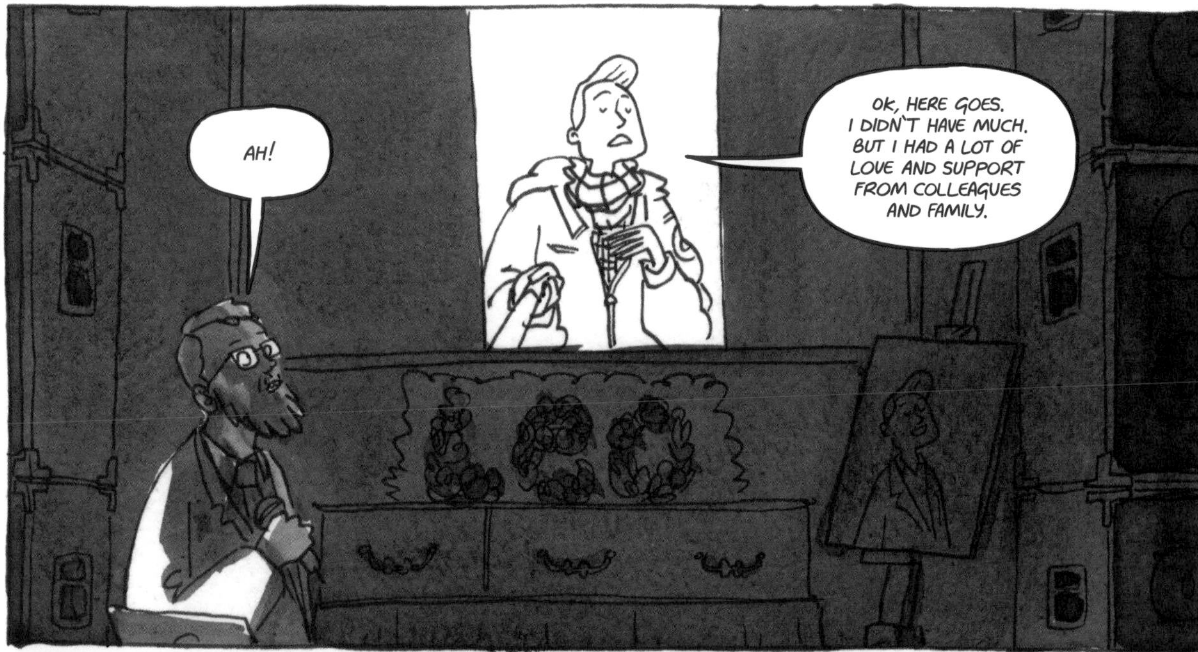
AH!
OK, HERE GOES. I DIDN'T HAVE MUCH. BUT I HAD A LOT OF LOVE AND SUPPORT FROM COLLEAGUES AND FAMILY.

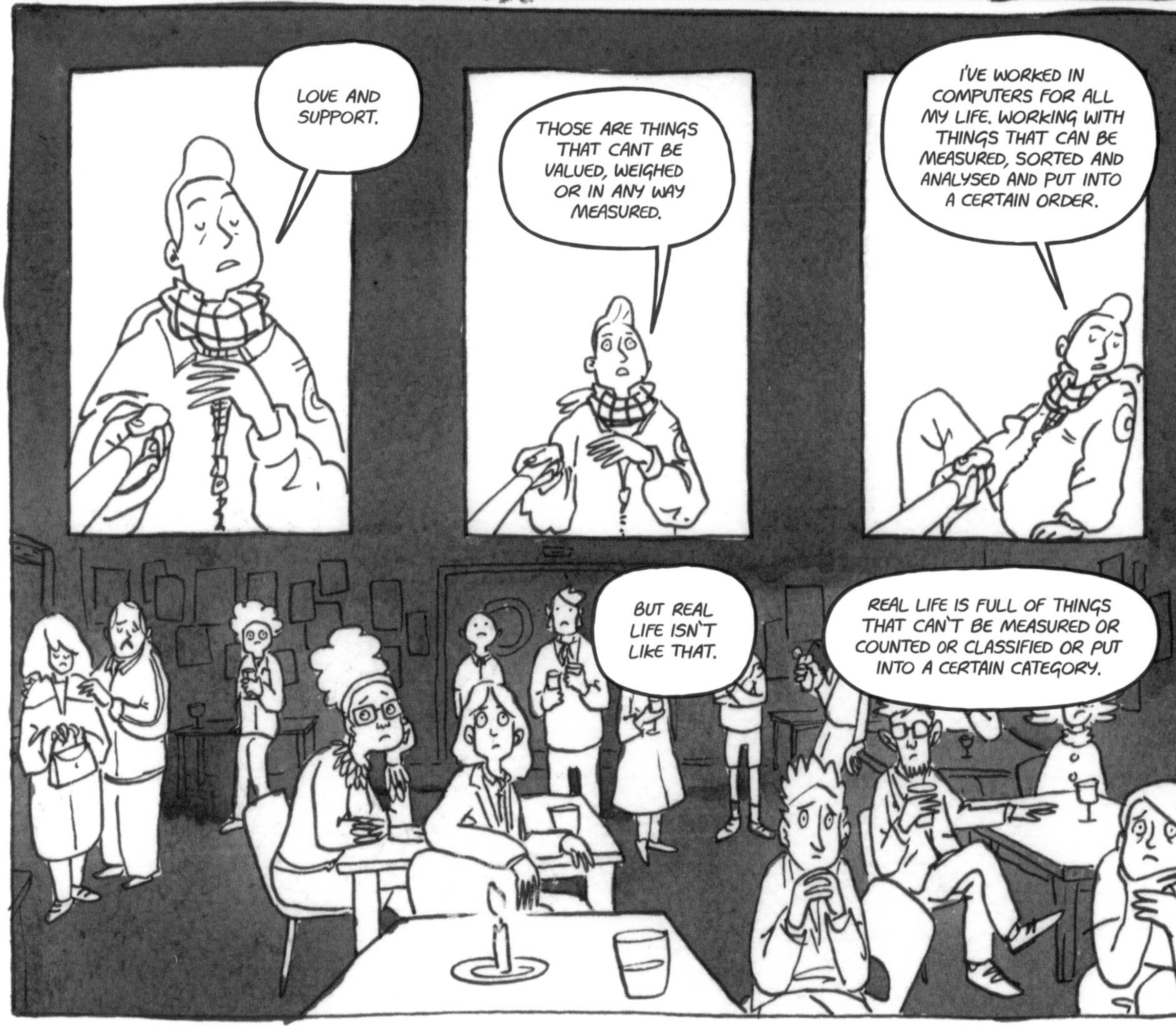
LOVE AND SUPPORT.
THOSE ARE THINGS THAT CANT BE VALUED, WEIGHED OR IN ANY WAY MEASURED.
I'VE WORKED IN COMPUTERS FOR ALL MY LIFE. WORKING WITH THINGS THAT CAN BE MEASURED, SORTED AND ANALYSED AND PUT INTO A CERTAIN ORDER.
BUT REAL LIFE ISN'T LIKE THAT.
REAL LIFE IS FULL OF THINGS THAT CAN'T BE MEASURED OR COUNTED OR CLASSIFIED OR PUT INTO A CERTAIN CATEGORY.

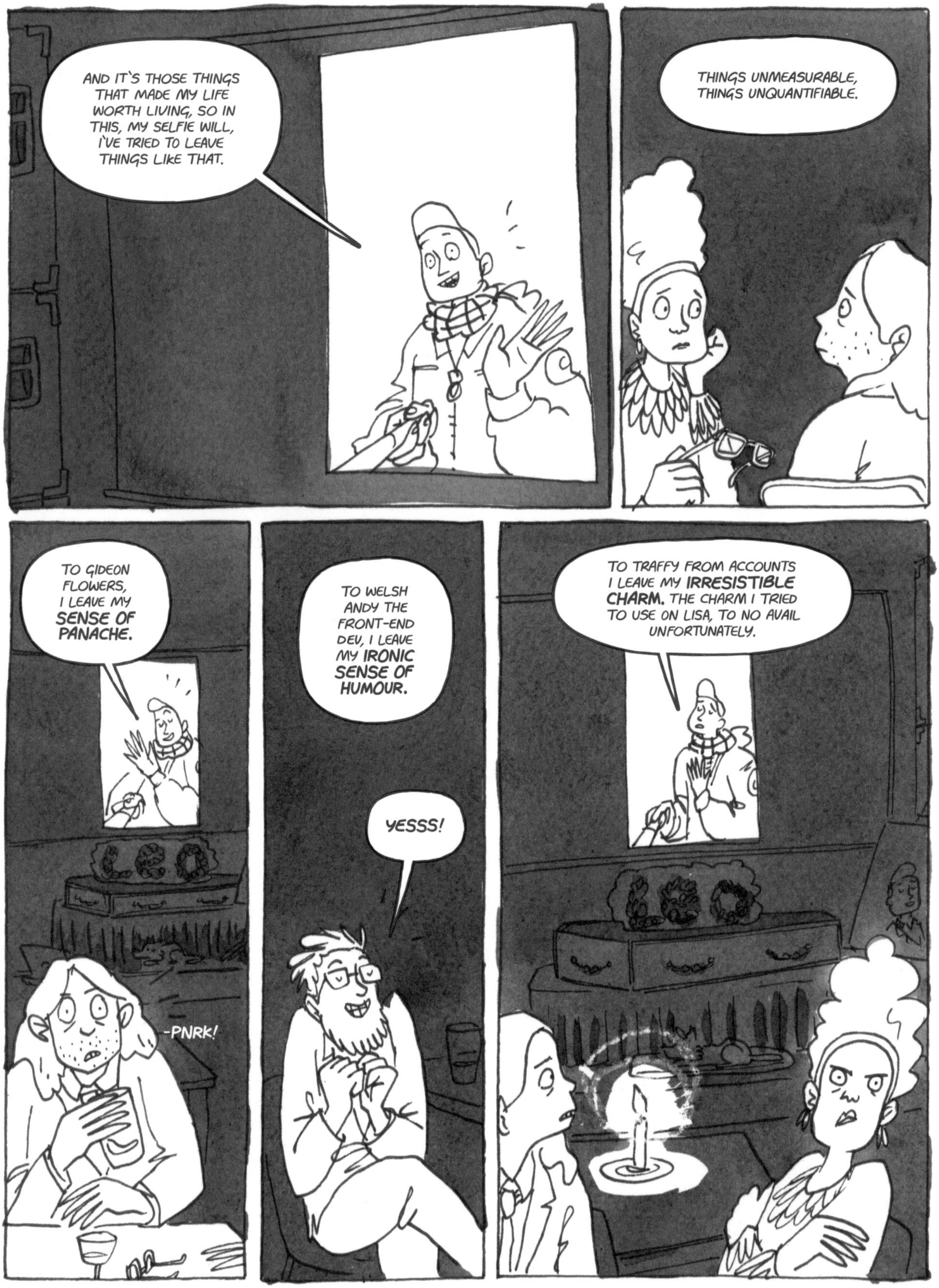
AND IT'S THOSE THINGS THAT MADE MY LIFE WORTH LIVING, SO IN THIS, MY SELFIE WILL, I'VE TRIED TO LEAVE THINGS LIKE THAT.
THINGS UNMEASURABLE, THINGS UNQUANTIFIABLE.
TO GIDEON FLOWERS, I LEAVE MY **SENSE OF PANACHE.**
-PNRK!
TO WELSH ANDY THE FRONT-END DEV, I LEAVE MY **IRONIC SENSE OF HUMOUR.**
YESSS!
TO TRAFFY FROM ACCOUNTS I LEAVE MY **IRRESISTIBLE CHARM.** THE CHARM I TRIED TO USE ON LISA, TO NO AVAIL UNFORTUNATELY.

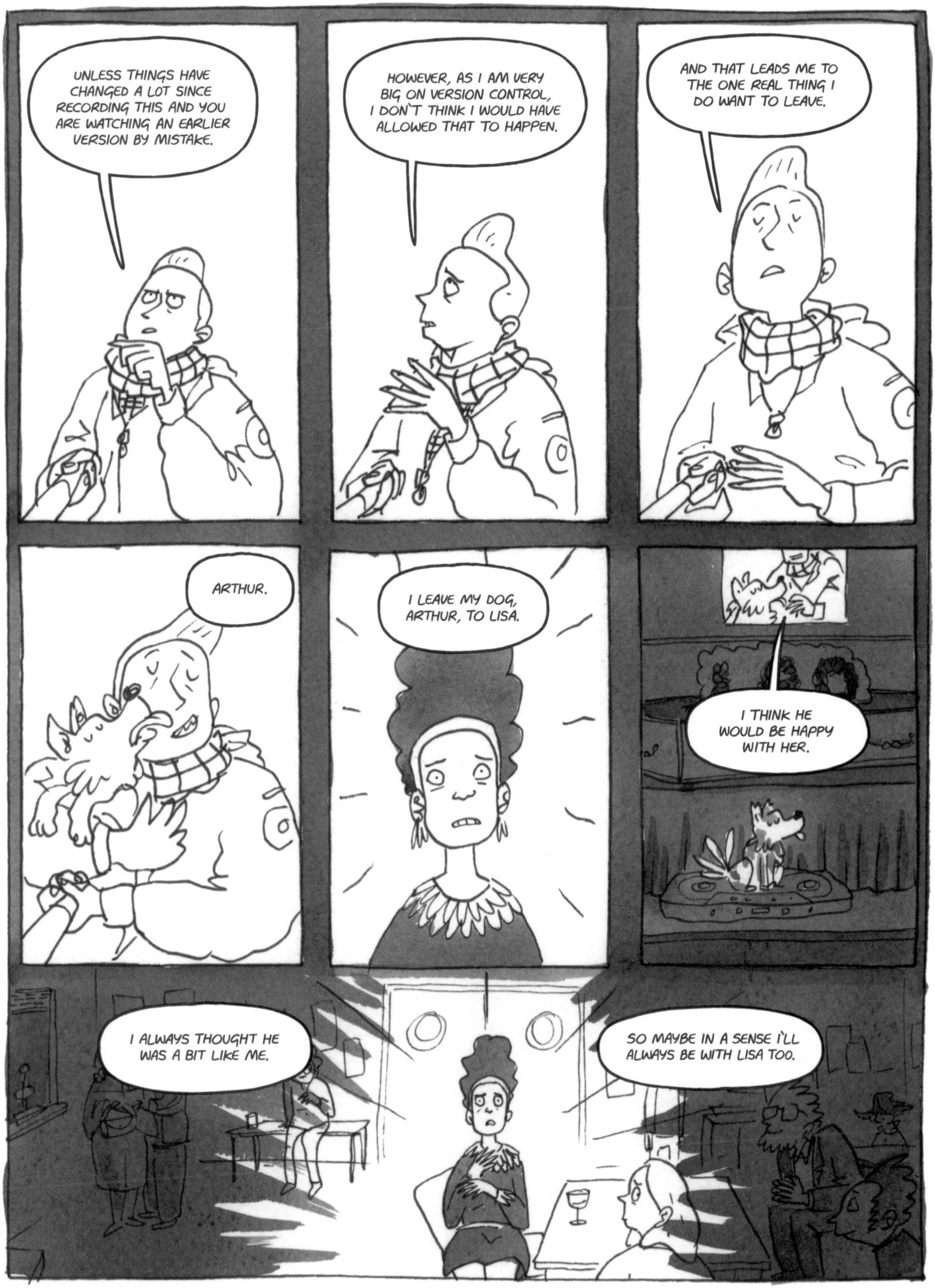
UNLESS THINGS HAVE CHANGED A LOT SINCE RECORDING THIS AND YOU ARE WATCHING AN EARLIER VERSION BY MISTAKE.
HOWEVER, AS I AM VERY BIG ON VERSION CONTROL, I DON'T THINK I WOULD HAVE ALLOWED THAT TO HAPPEN.
AND THAT LEADS ME TO THE ONE REAL THING I DO WANT TO LEAVE.
ARTHUR.
I LEAVE MY DOG, ARTHUR, TO LISA.
I THINK HE WOULD BE HAPPY WITH HER.
I ALWAYS THOUGHT HE WAS A BIT LIKE ME.
SO MAYBE IN A SENSE I'LL ALWAYS BE WITH LISA TOO.

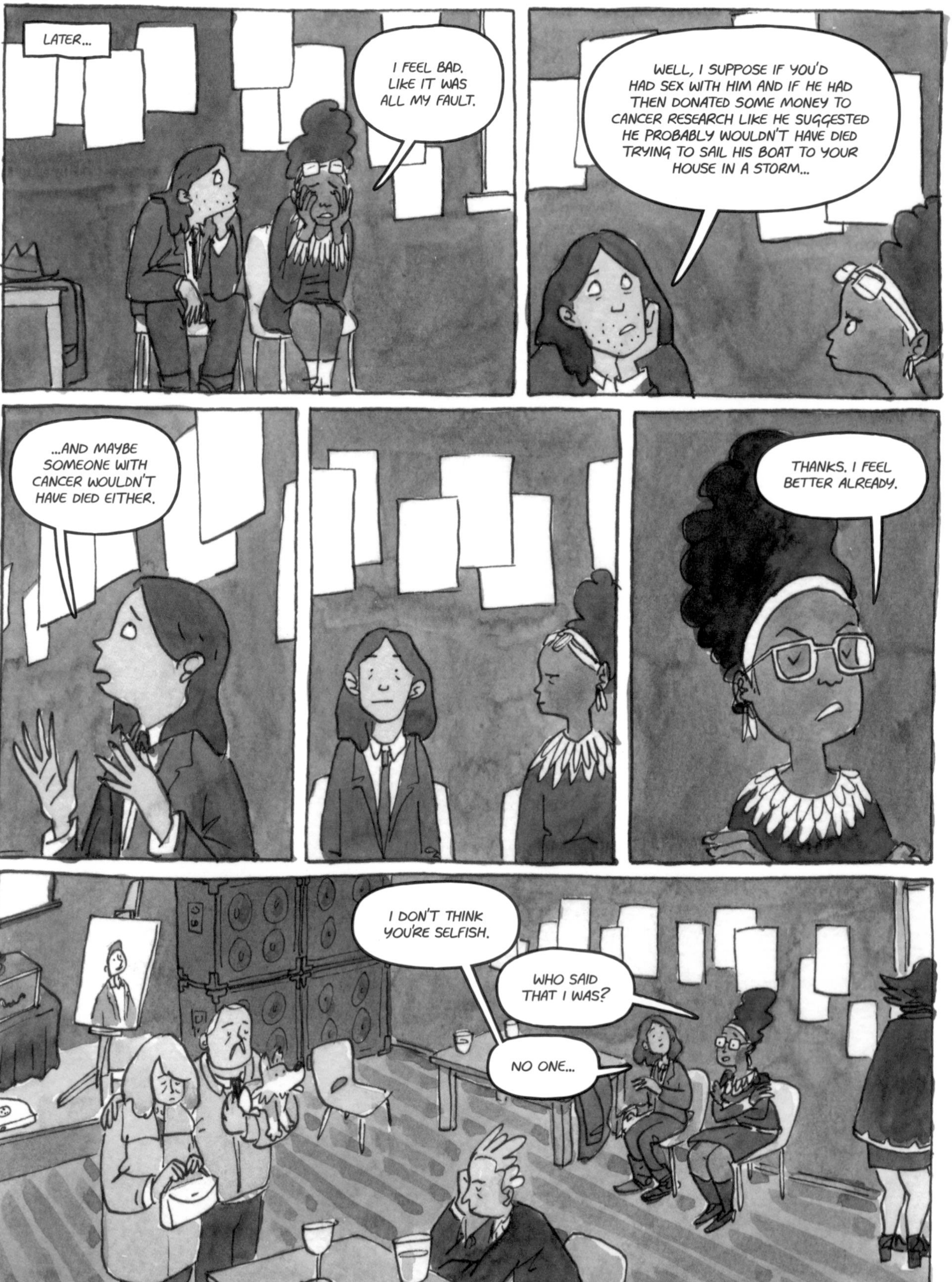
LATER...
I FEEL BAD. LIKE IT WAS ALL MY FAULT.
WELL, I SUPPOSE IF YOU'D HAD SEX WITH HIM AND IF HE HAD THEN DONATED SOME MONEY TO CANCER RESEARCH LIKE HE SUGGESTED HE PROBABLY WOULDN'T HAVE DIED TRYING TO SAIL HIS BOAT TO YOUR HOUSE IN A STORM...
...AND MAYBE SOMEONE WITH CANCER WOULDN'T HAVE DIED EITHER.
THANKS. I FEEL BETTER ALREADY.
I DON'T THINK YOU'RE SELFISH.
WHO SAID THAT I WAS?
NO ONE...

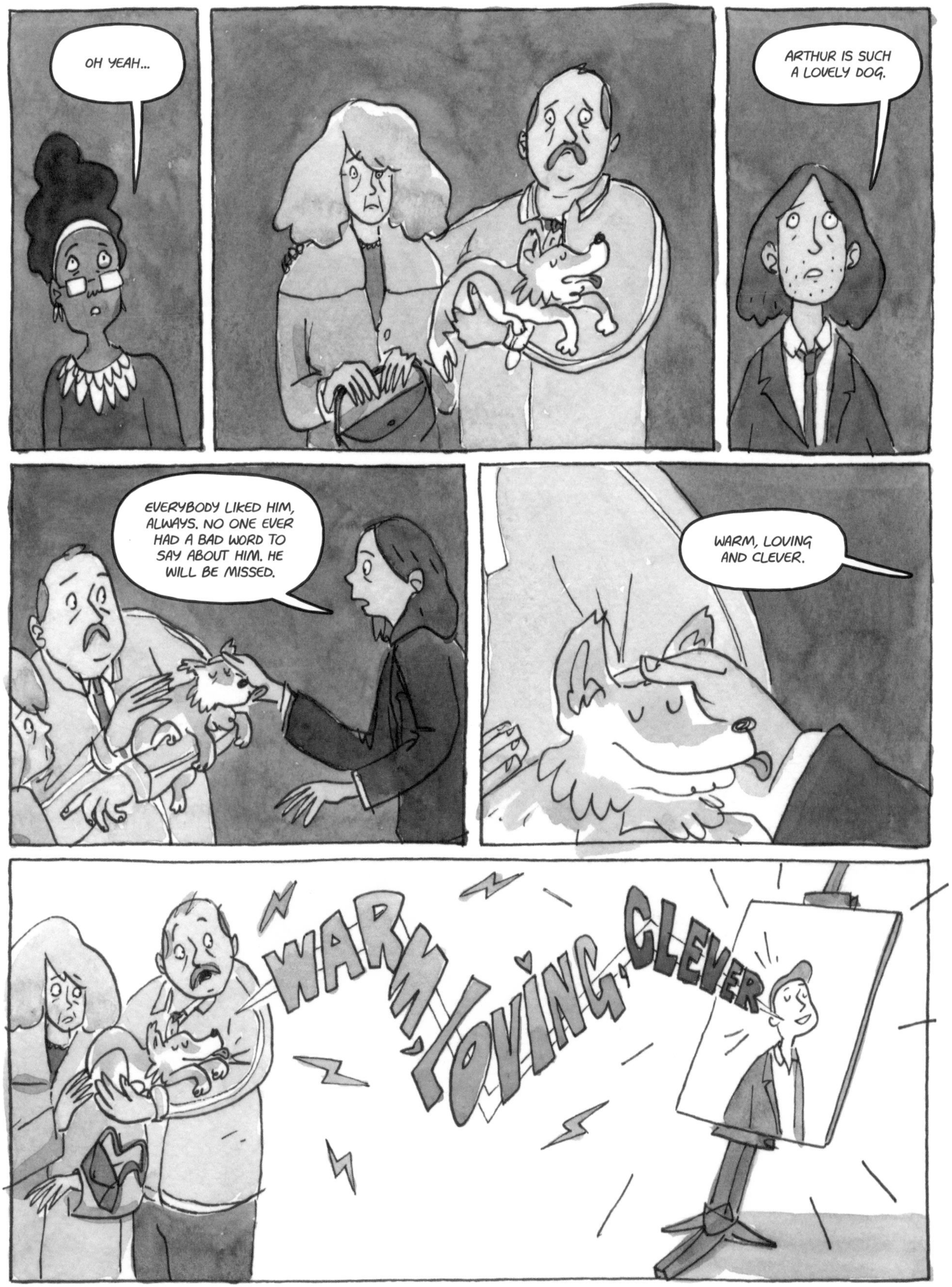
OH YEAH...
ARTHUR IS SUCH A LOVELY DOG.
EVERYBODY LIKED HIM, ALWAYS. NO ONE EVER HAD A BAD WORD TO SAY ABOUT HIM. HE WILL BE MISSED.
WARM, LOVING AND CLEVER.
WARM, LOVING, CLEVER

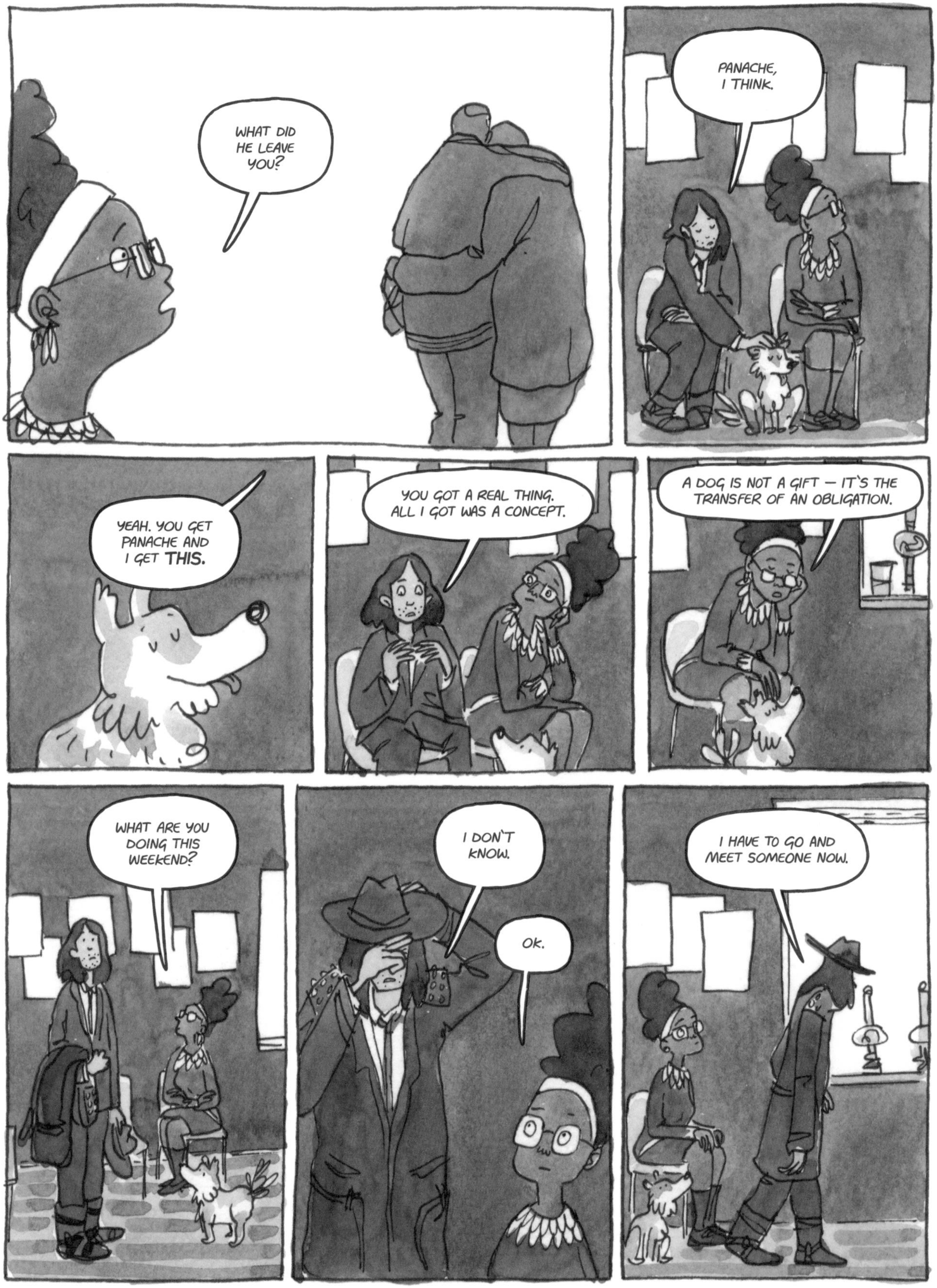
WHAT DID HE LEAVE YOU?
PANACHE, I THINK.
YEAH. YOU GET PANACHE AND I GET THIS.
YOU GOT A REAL THING. ALL I GOT WAS A CONCEPT.
A DOG IS NOT A GIFT — IT'S THE TRANSFER OF AN OBLIGATION.
WHAT ARE YOU DOING THIS WEEKEND?
I DON'T KNOW.
OK.
I HAVE TO GO AND MEET SOMEONE NOW.

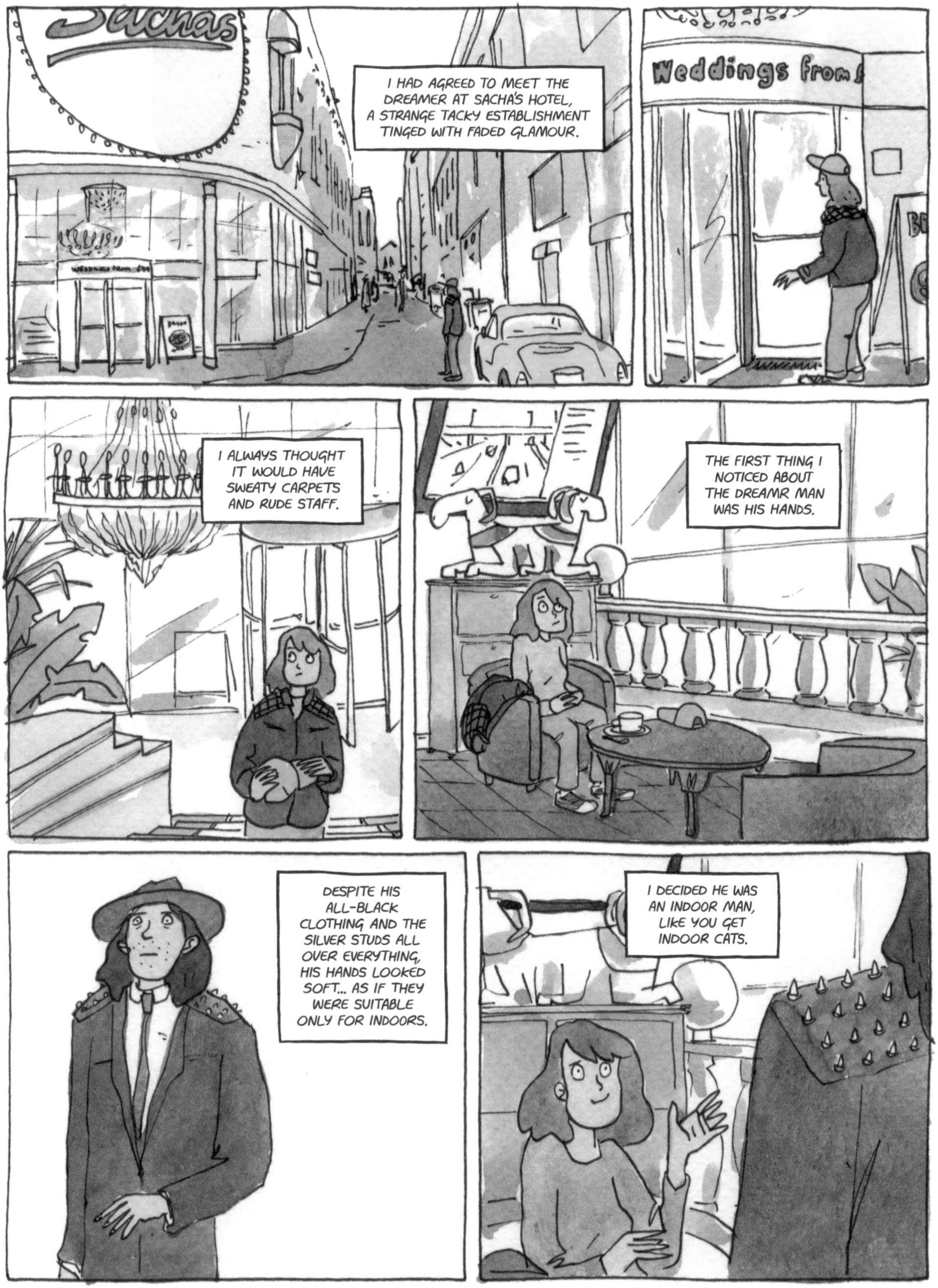
Sachas
I HAD AGREED TO MEET THE DREAMER AT SACHA'S HOTEL, A STRANGE TACKY ESTABLISHMENT TINGED WITH FADED GLAMOUR.
Weddings from
I ALWAYS THOUGHT IT WOULD HAVE SWEATY CARPETS AND RUDE STAFF.
THE FIRST THING I NOTICED ABOUT THE DREAMR MAN WAS HIS HANDS.
DESPITE HIS ALL-BLACK CLOTHING AND THE SILVER STUDS ALL OVER EVERYTHING, HIS HANDS LOOKED SOFT... AS IF THEY WERE SUITABLE ONLY FOR INDOORS.
I DECIDED HE WAS AN INDOOR MAN, LIKE YOU GET INDOOR CATS.

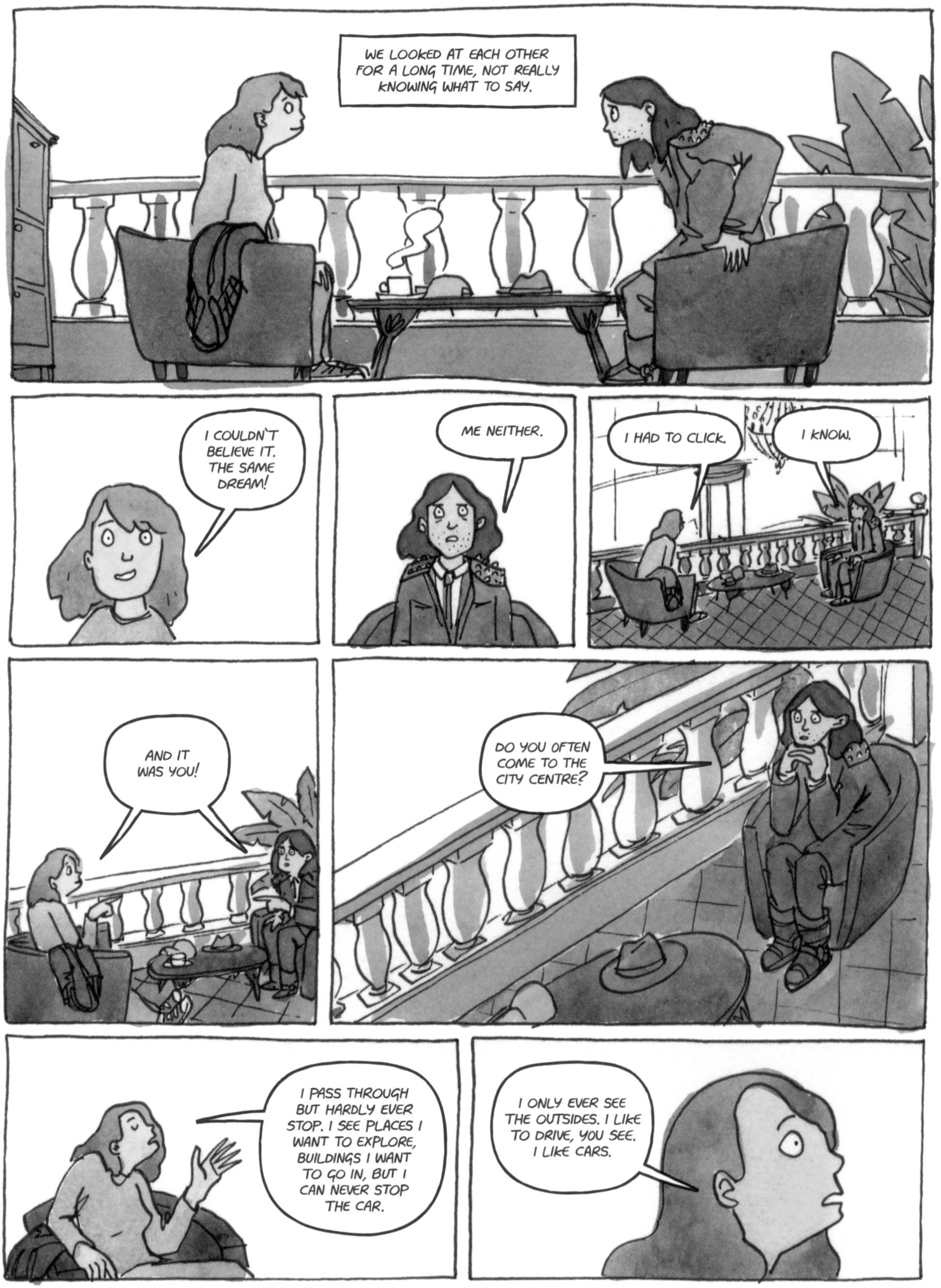

WE LOOKED AT EACH OTHER FOR A LONG TIME, NOT REALLY KNOWING WHAT TO SAY.
I COULDN'T BELIEVE IT. THE SAME DREAM!
ME NEITHER.
I HAD TO CLICK.
I KNOW.
AND IT WAS YOU!
DO YOU OFTEN COME TO THE CITY CENTRE?
I PASS THROUGH BUT HARDLY EVER STOP. I SEE PLACES I WANT TO EXPLORE, BUILDINGS I WANT TO GO IN, BUT I CAN NEVER STOP THE CAR.
I ONLY EVER SEE THE OUTSIDES. I LIKE TO DRIVE, YOU SEE. I LIKE CARS.

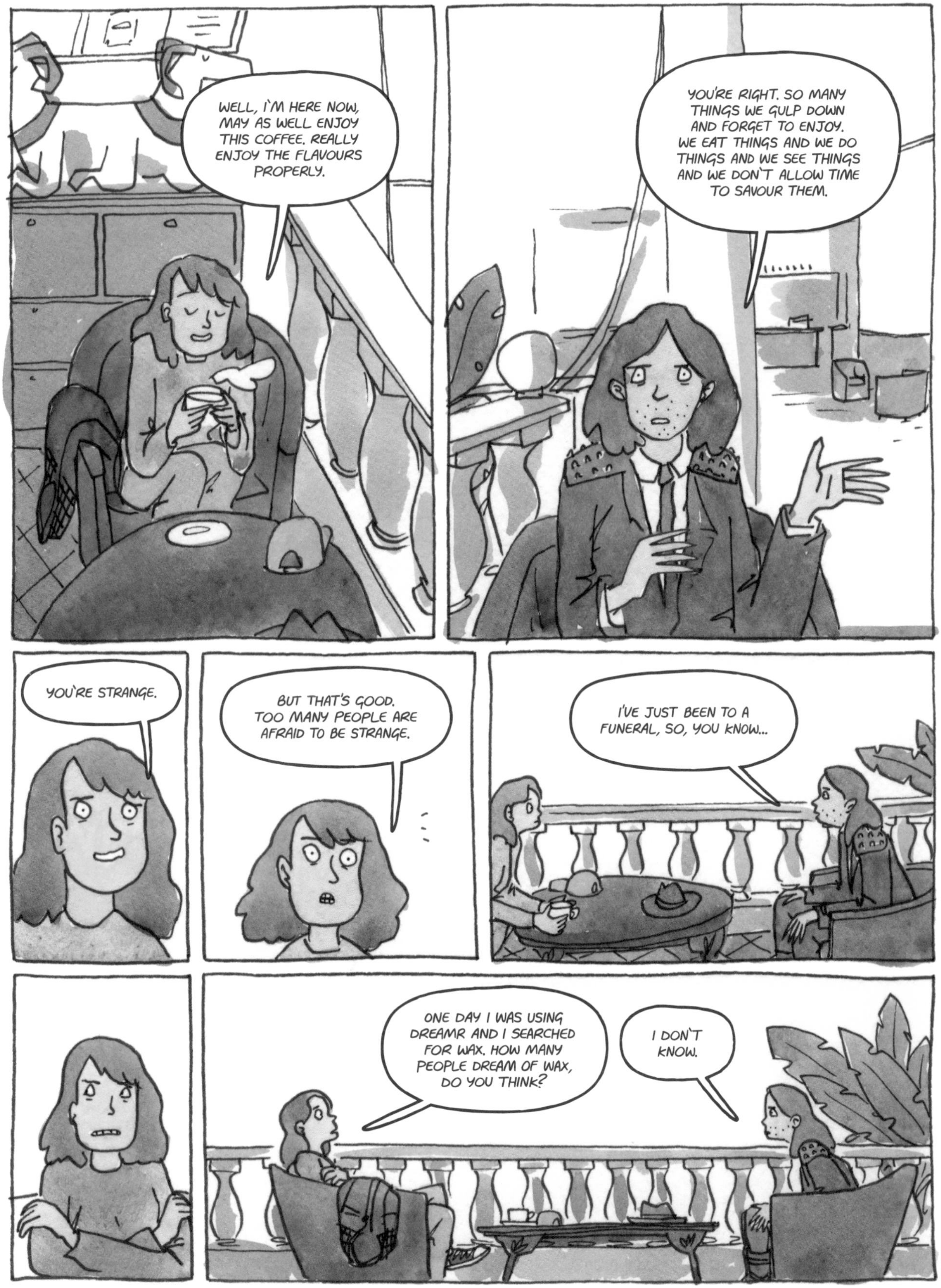
WELL, I'M HERE NOW, MAY AS WELL ENJOY THIS COFFEE. REALLY ENJOY THE FLAVOURS PROPERLY.
YOU'RE RIGHT. SO MANY THINGS WE GULP DOWN AND FORGET TO ENJOY. WE EAT THINGS AND WE DO THINGS AND WE SEE THINGS AND WE DON'T ALLOW TIME TO SAVOUR THEM.
YOU'RE STRANGE.
BUT THAT'S GOOD. TOO MANY PEOPLE ARE AFRAID TO BE STRANGE.
I'VE JUST BEEN TO A FUNERAL, SO, YOU KNOW...
ONE DAY I WAS USING DREAMR AND I SEARCHED FOR WAX. HOW MANY PEOPLE DREAM OF WAX, DO YOU THINK?
I DON'T KNOW.

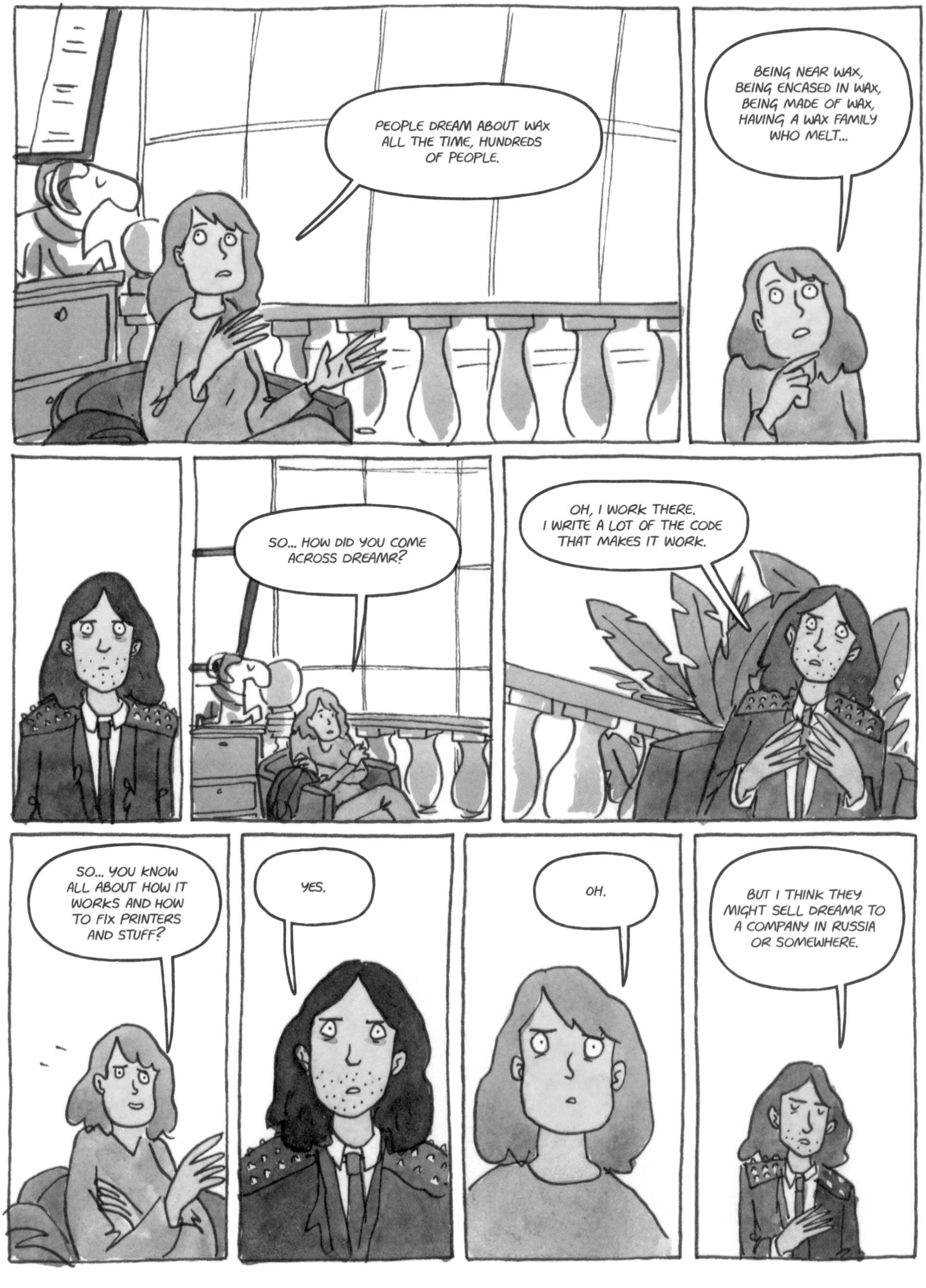
PEOPLE DREAM ABOUT WAX ALL THE TIME, HUNDREDS OF PEOPLE.
BEING NEAR WAX, BEING ENCASED IN WAX, BEING MADE OF WAX, HAVING A WAX FAMILY WHO MELT...
SO... HOW DID YOU COME ACROSS DREAMR?
OH, I WORK THERE. I WRITE A LOT OF THE CODE THAT MAKES IT WORK.
SO... YOU KNOW ALL ABOUT HOW IT WORKS AND HOW TO FIX PRINTERS AND STUFF?
YES.
OH.
BUT I THINK THEY MIGHT SELL DREAMR TO A COMPANY IN RUSSIA OR SOMEWHERE.

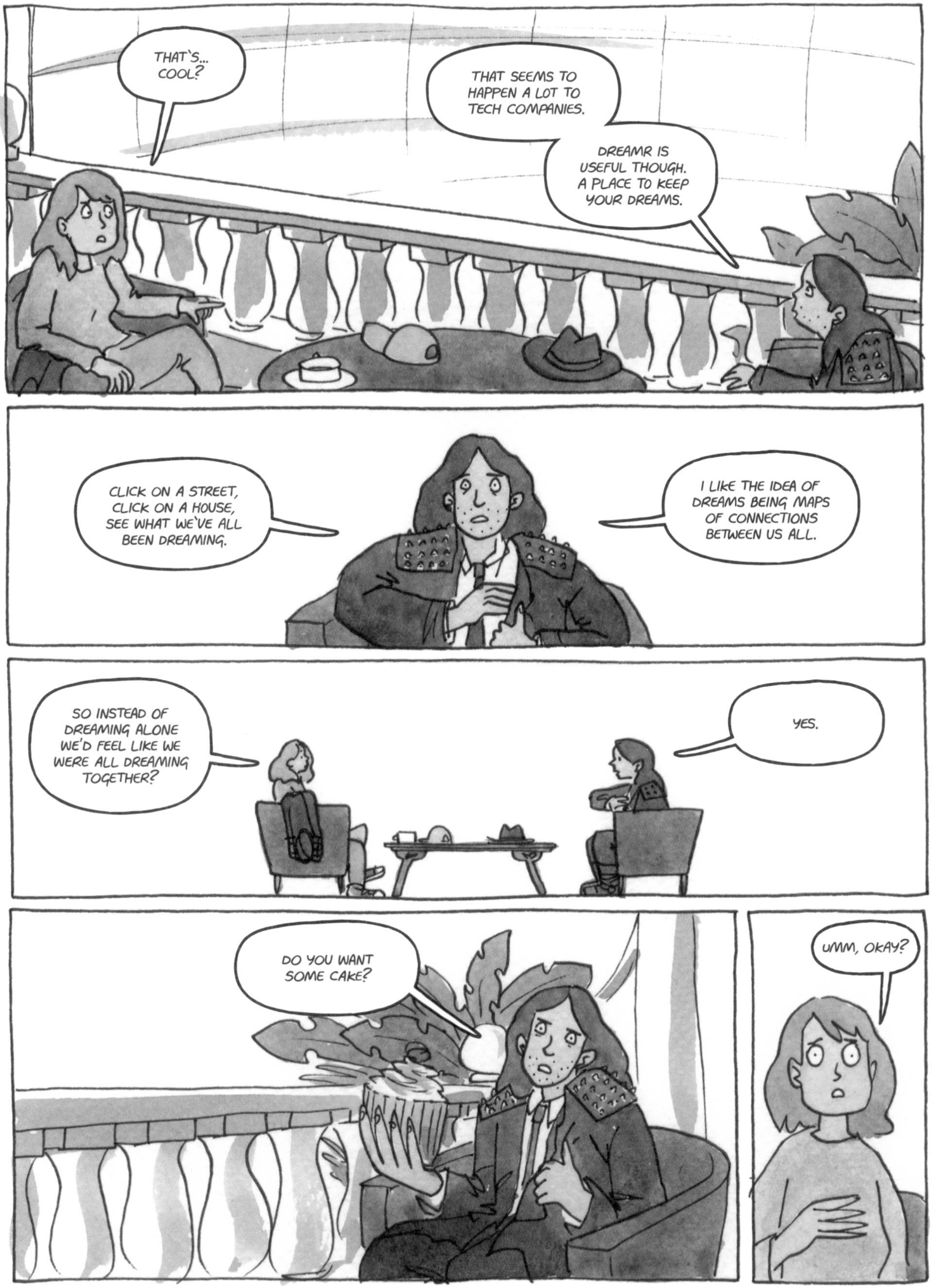
THAT'S... COOL?
THAT SEEMS TO HAPPEN A LOT TO TECH COMPANIES.
DREAMR IS USEFUL THOUGH. A PLACE TO KEEP YOUR DREAMS.
CLICK ON A STREET, CLICK ON A HOUSE, SEE WHAT WE'VE ALL BEEN DREAMING.
I LIKE THE IDEA OF DREAMS BEING MAPS OF CONNECTIONS BETWEEN US ALL.
SO INSTEAD OF DREAMING ALONE WE'D FEEL LIKE WE WERE ALL DREAMING TOGETHER?
YES.
DO YOU WANT SOME CAKE?
UMM, OKAY?

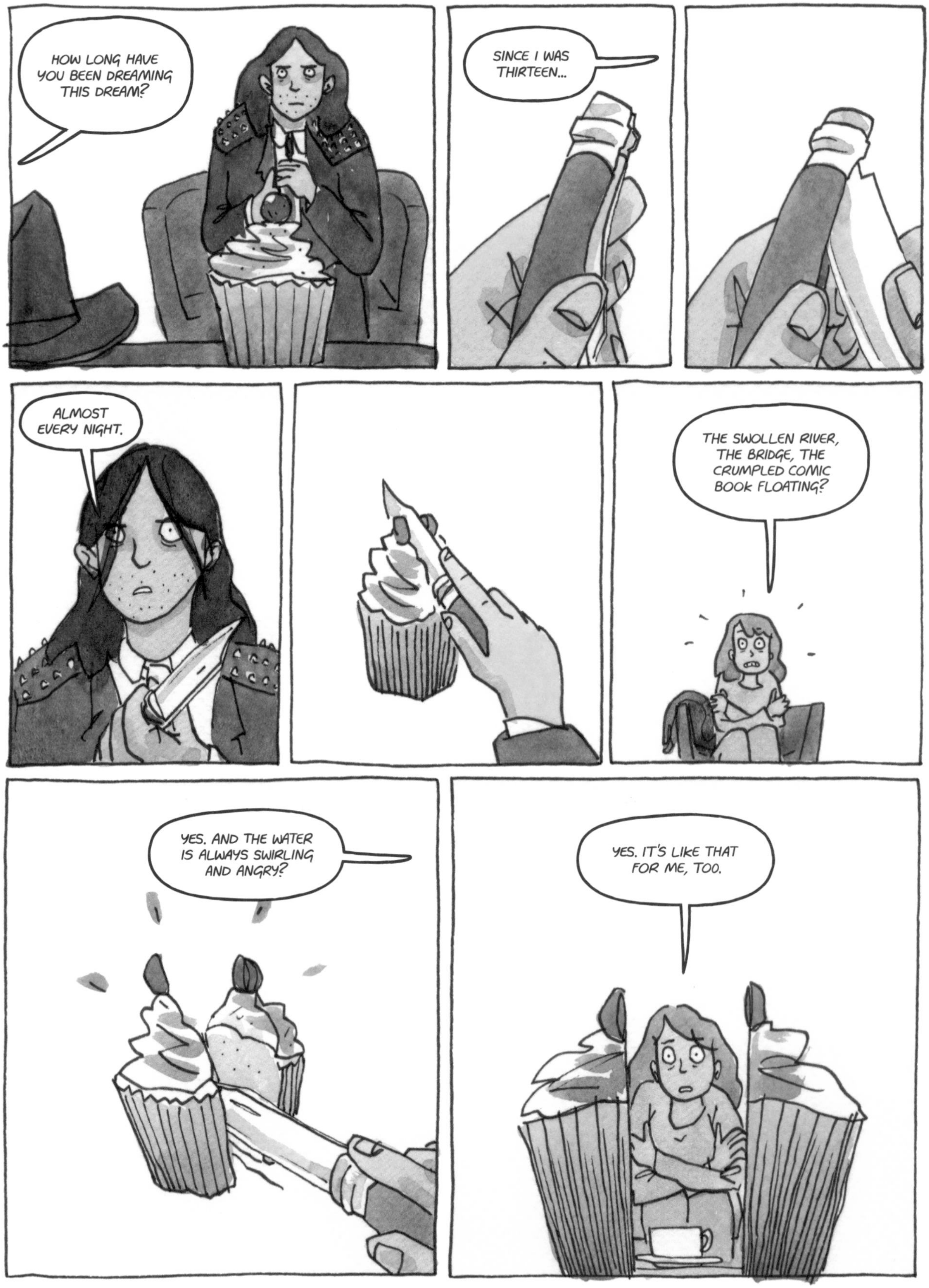
HOW LONG HAVE YOU BEEN DREAMING THIS DREAM?
SINCE I WAS THIRTEEN...
ALMOST EVERY NIGHT.
THE SWOLLEN RIVER, THE BRIDGE, THE CRUMPLED COMIC BOOK FLOATING?
YES. AND THE WATER IS ALWAYS SWIRLING AND ANGRY?
YES. IT'S LIKE THAT FOR ME, TOO.

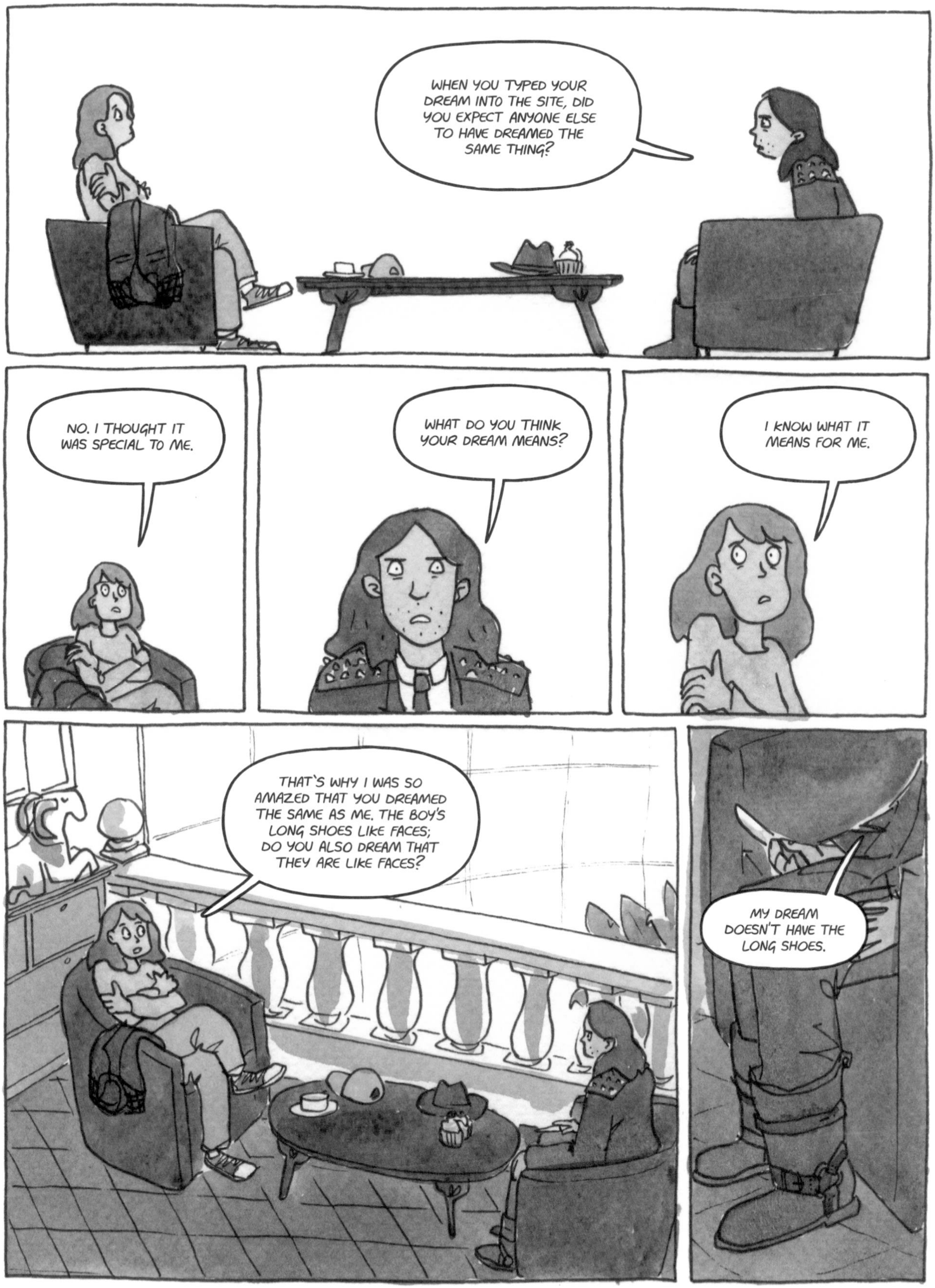
WHEN YOU TYPED YOUR DREAM INTO THE SITE, DID YOU EXPECT ANYONE ELSE TO HAVE DREAMED THE SAME THING?
NO. I THOUGHT IT WAS SPECIAL TO ME.
WHAT DO YOU THINK YOUR DREAM MEANS?
I KNOW WHAT IT MEANS FOR ME.
THAT'S WHY I WAS SO AMAZED THAT YOU DREAMED THE SAME AS ME. THE BOY'S LONG SHOES LIKE FACES; DO YOU ALSO DREAM THAT THEY ARE LIKE FACES?
MY DREAM DOESN'T HAVE THE LONG SHOES.

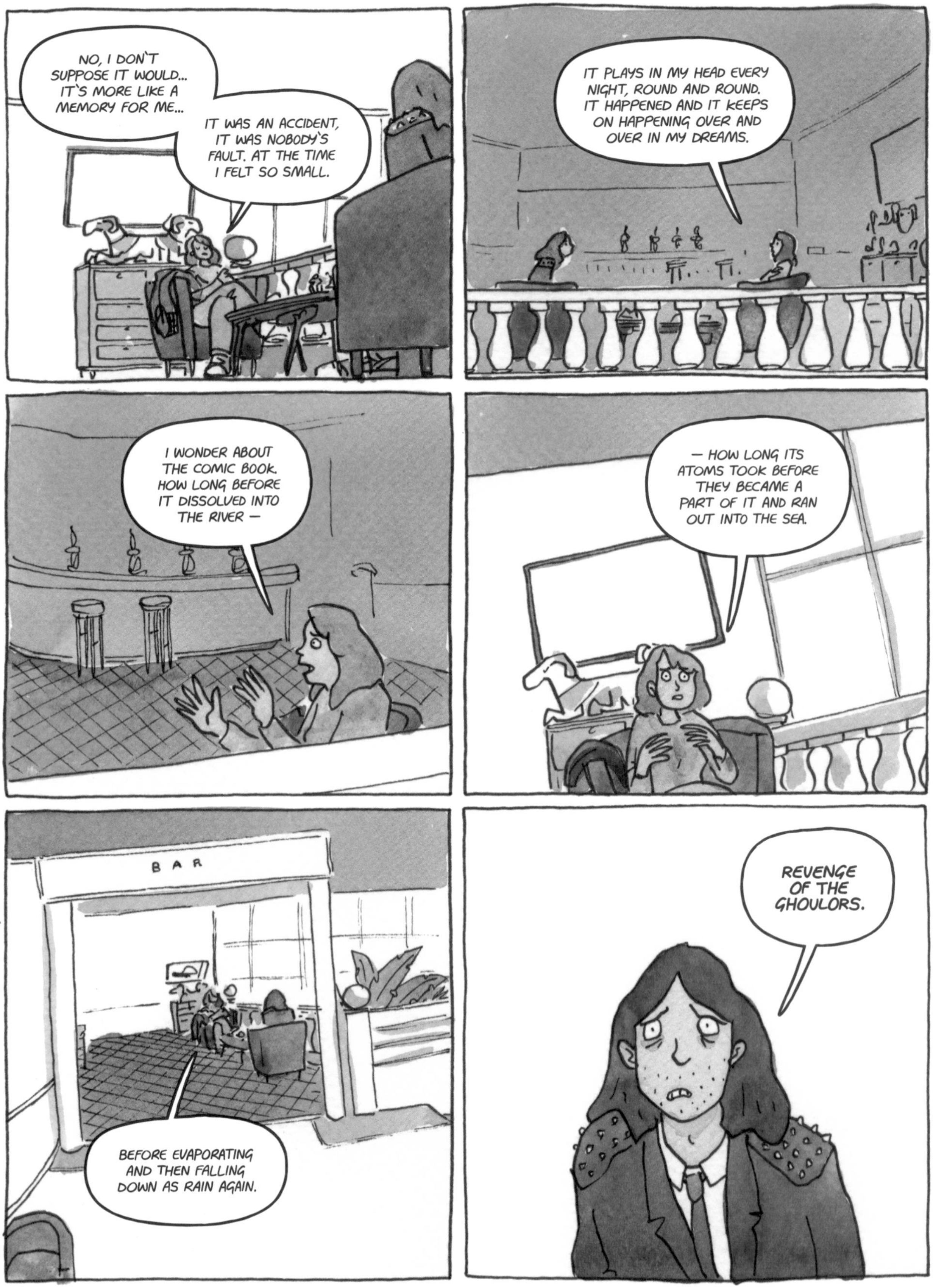
NO, I DON'T SUPPOSE IT WOULD... IT'S MORE LIKE A MEMORY FOR ME...
IT WAS AN ACCIDENT, IT WAS NOBODY'S FAULT. AT THE TIME I FELT SO SMALL.
IT PLAYS IN MY HEAD EVERY NIGHT, ROUND AND ROUND. IT HAPPENED AND IT KEEPS ON HAPPENING OVER AND OVER IN MY DREAMS.
I WONDER ABOUT THE COMIC BOOK. HOW LONG BEFORE IT DISSOLVED INTO THE RIVER —
— HOW LONG ITS ATOMS TOOK BEFORE THEY BECAME A PART OF IT AND RAN OUT INTO THE SEA.
BAR
BEFORE EVAPORATING AND THEN FALLING DOWN AS RAIN AGAIN.
REVENGE OF THE GHOULORS.

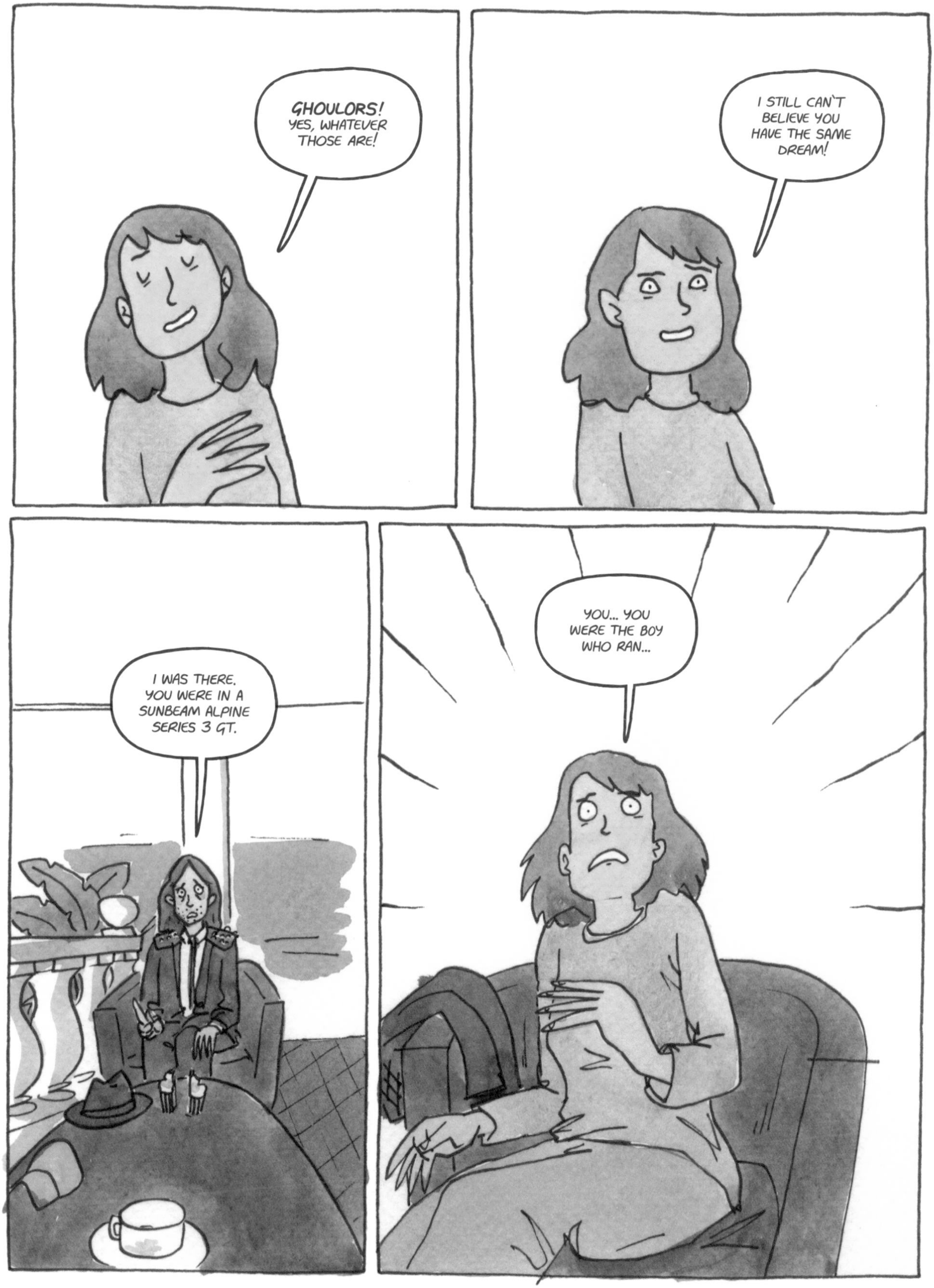
GHOULORS! YES, WHATEVER THOSE ARE!
I STILL CAN'T BELIEVE YOU HAVE THE SAME DREAM!
I WAS THERE. YOU WERE IN A SUNBEAM ALPINE SERIES 3 GT.
YOU... YOU WERE THE BOY WHO RAN...

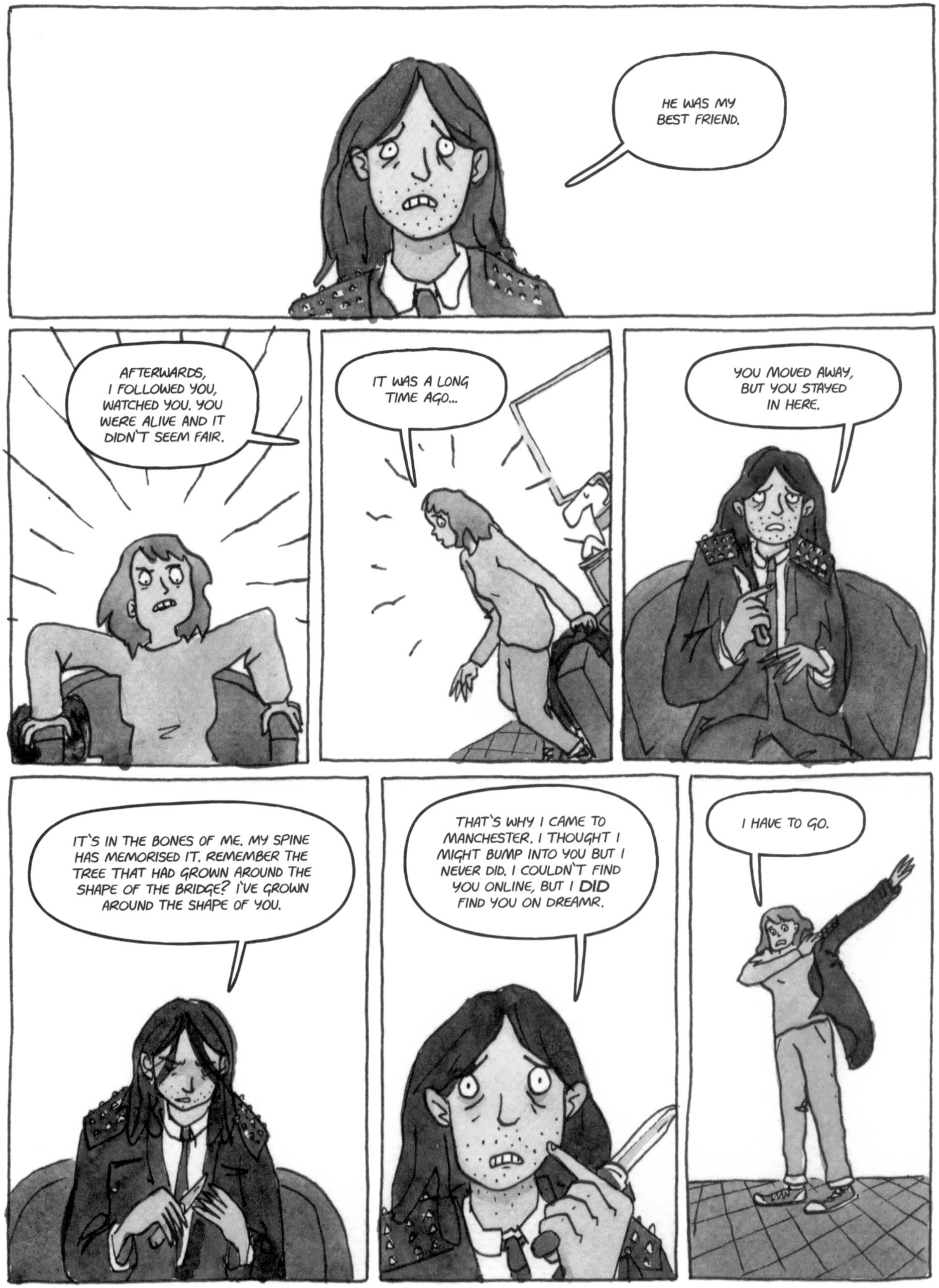
HE WAS MY BEST FRIEND.
AFTERWARDS, I FOLLOWED YOU, WATCHED YOU. YOU WERE ALIVE AND IT DIDN'T SEEM FAIR.
IT WAS A LONG TIME AGO...
YOU MOVED AWAY, BUT YOU STAYED IN HERE.
IT'S IN THE BONES OF ME. MY SPINE HAS MEMORISED IT. REMEMBER THE TREE THAT HAD GROWN AROUND THE SHAPE OF THE BRIDGE? I'VE GROWN AROUND THE SHAPE OF YOU.
THAT'S WHY I CAME TO MANCHESTER. I THOUGHT I MIGHT BUMP INTO YOU BUT I NEVER DID. I COULDN'T FIND YOU ONLINE, BUT I **DID** FIND YOU ON DREAMR.
I HAVE TO GO.

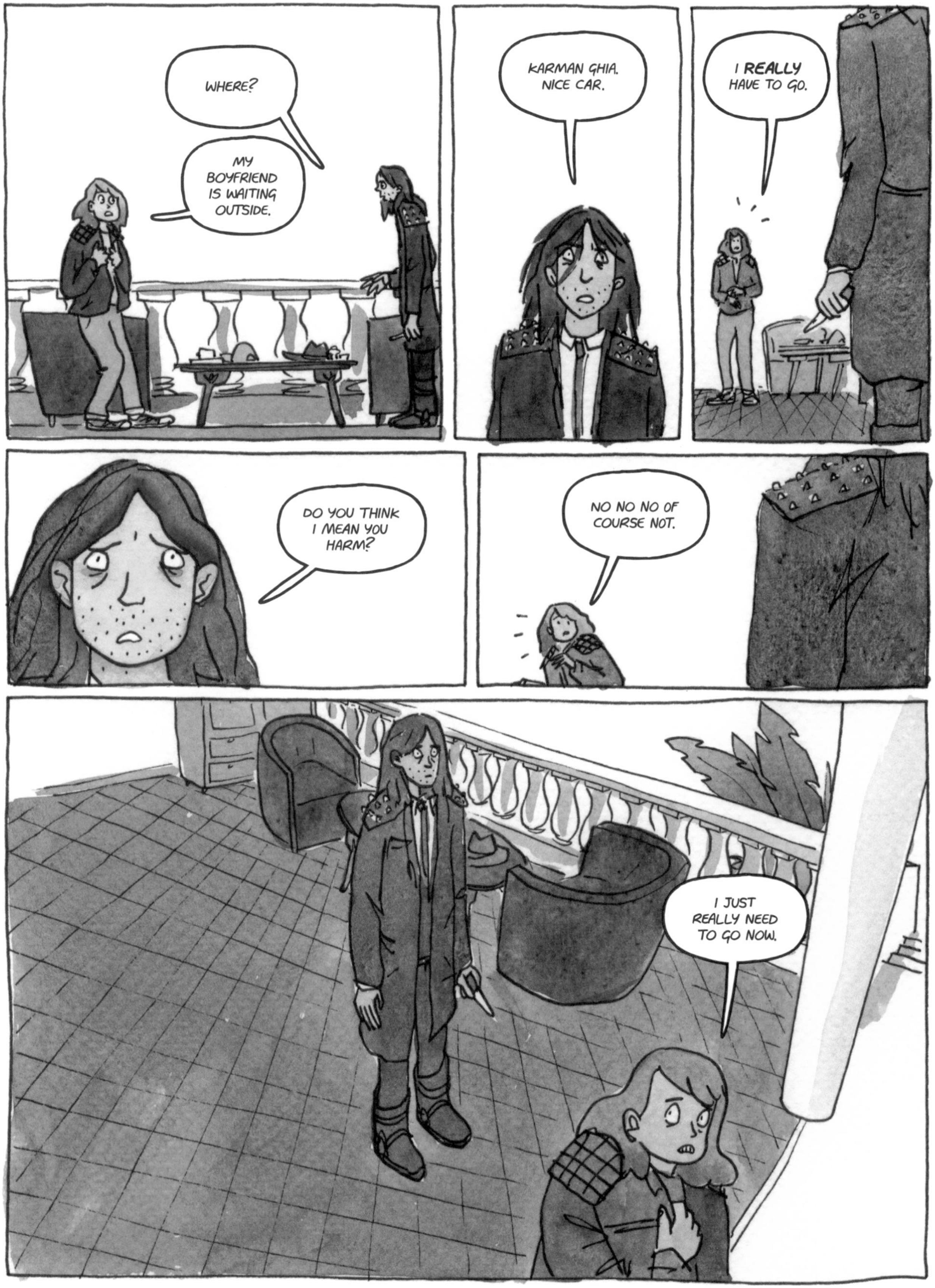
WHERE?
MY BOYFRIEND IS WAITING OUTSIDE.
KARMAN GHIA. NICE CAR.
I **REALLY** HAVE TO GO.
DO YOU THINK I MEAN YOU HARM?
NO NO NO OF COURSE NOT.
I JUST REALLY NEED TO GO NOW.

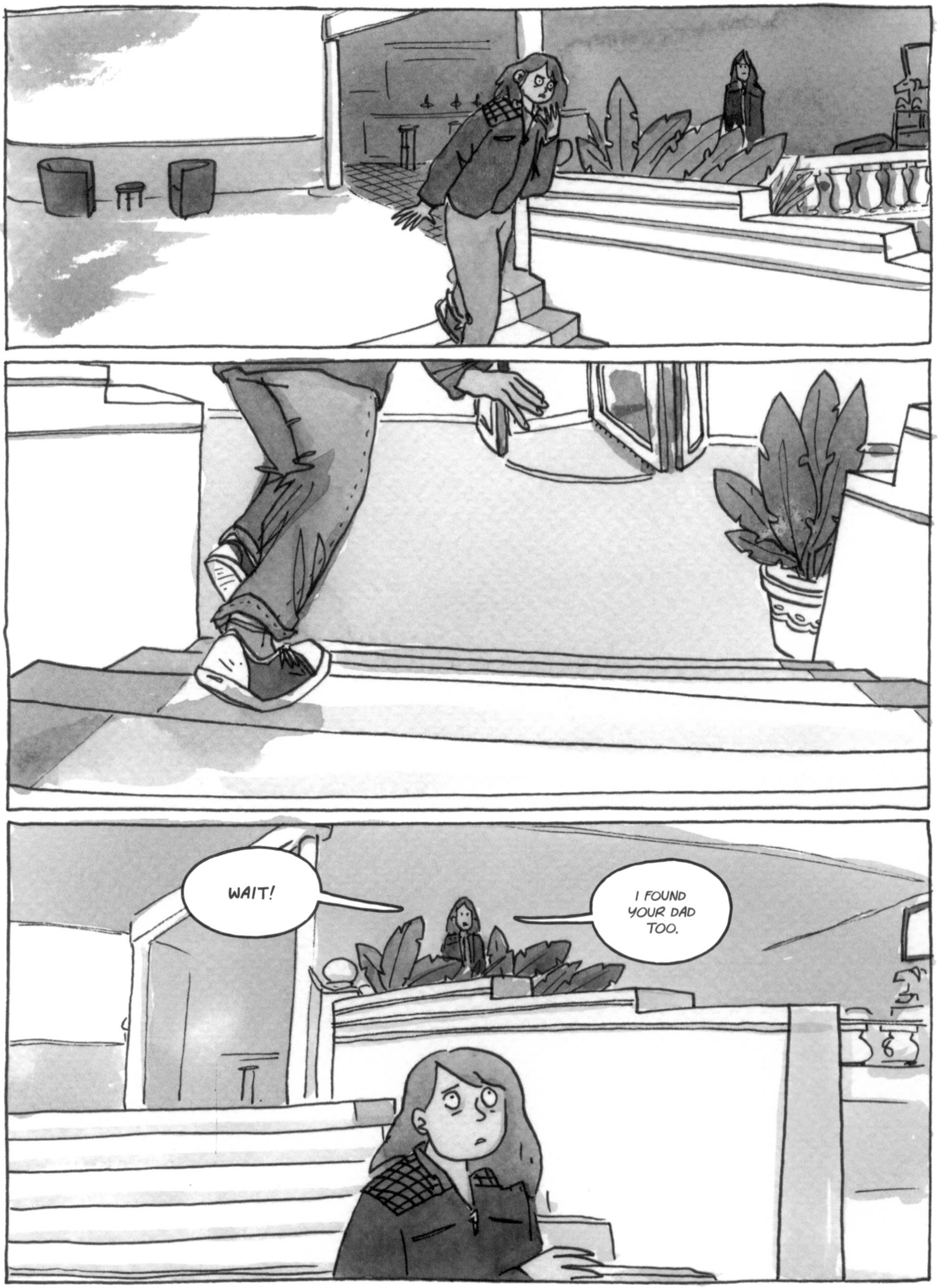
WAIT!
I FOUND YOUR DAD TOO.

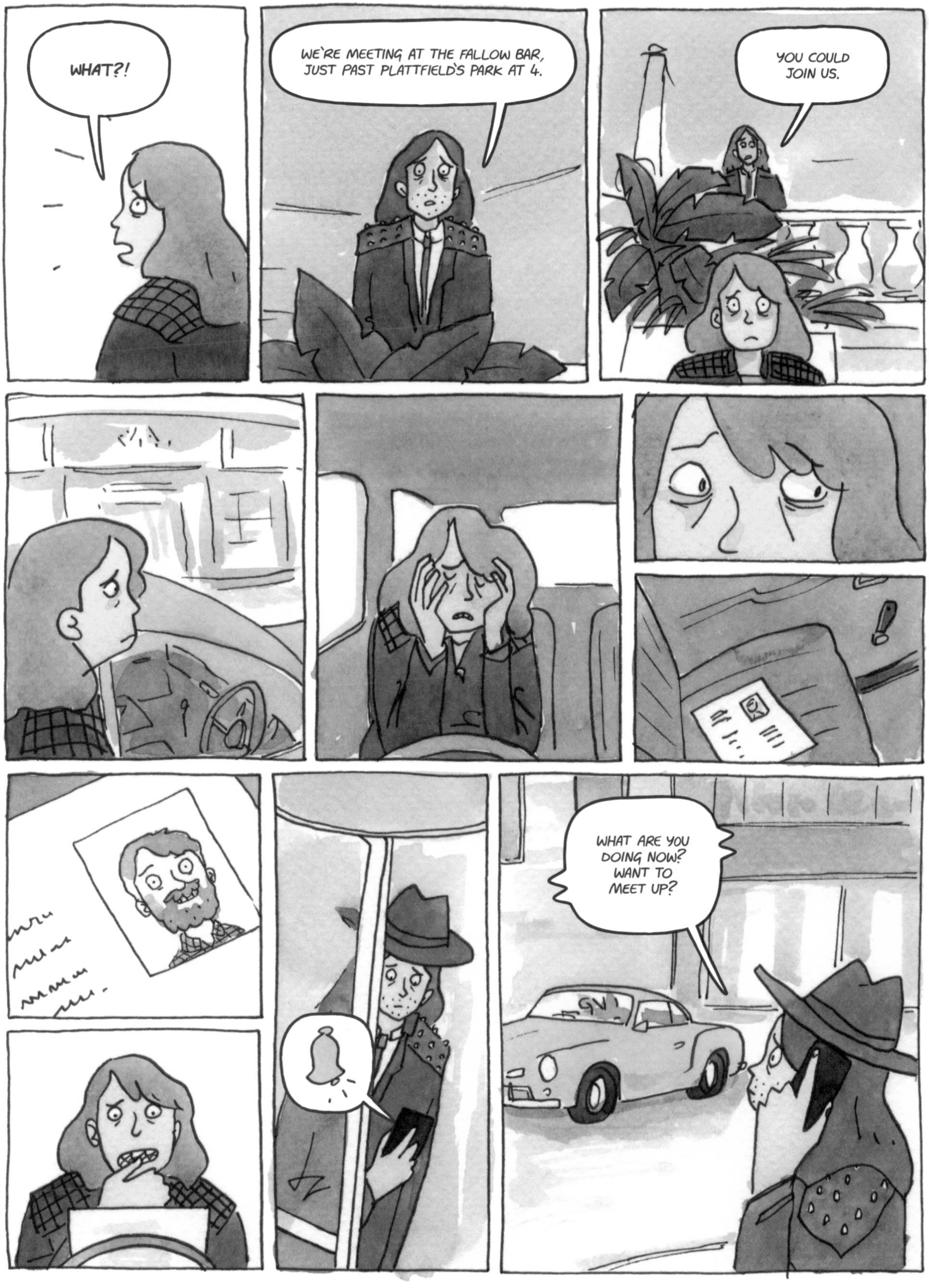
WHAT?!
WE'RE MEETING AT THE FALLOW BAR, JUST PAST PLATTFIELD'S PARK AT 4.
YOU COULD JOIN US.
!
WHAT ARE YOU DOING NOW? WANT TO MEET UP?

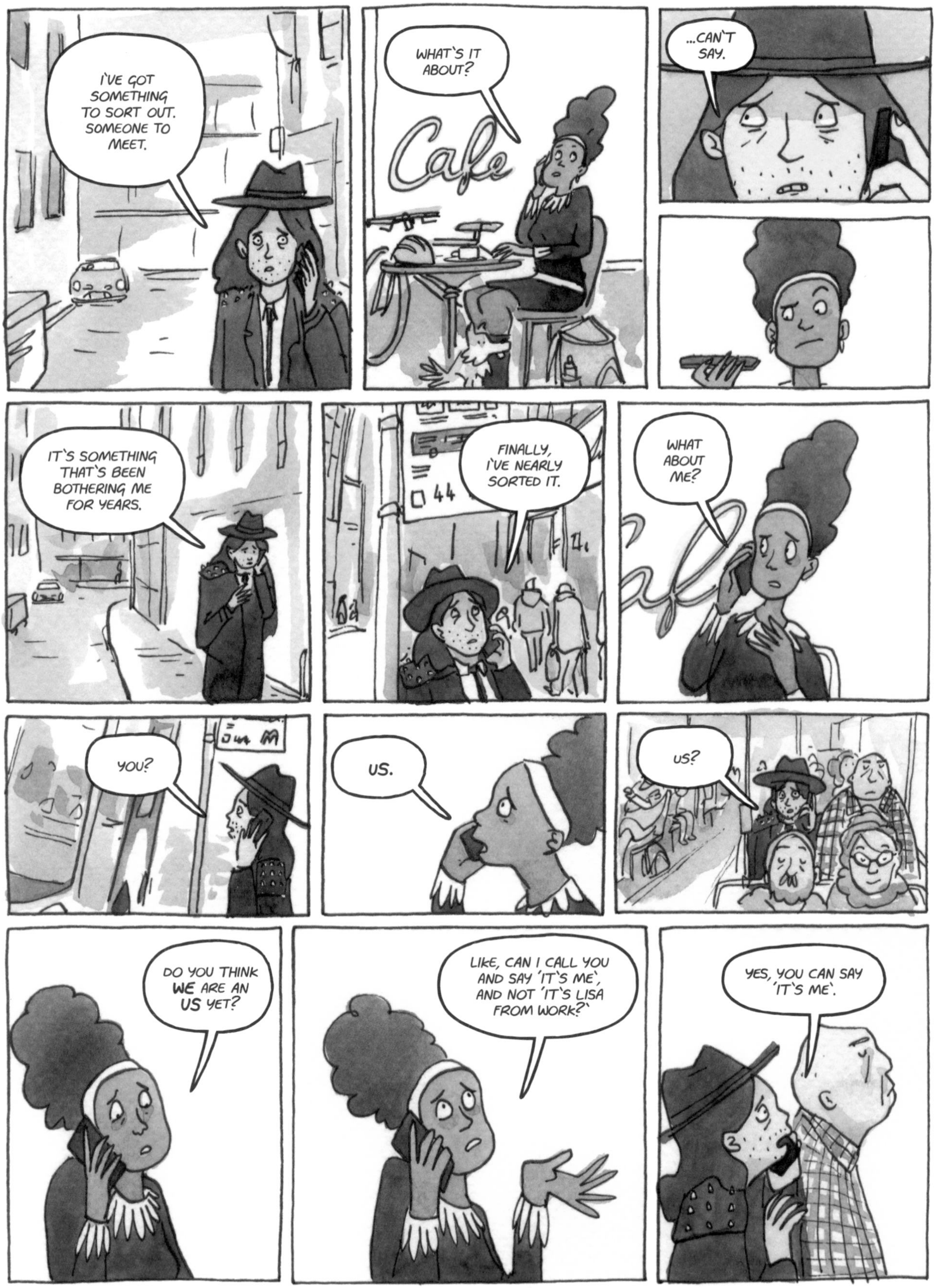
I'VE GOT SOMETHING TO SORT OUT. SOMEONE TO MEET.
WHAT'S IT ABOUT?
...CAN'T SAY.
IT'S SOMETHING THAT'S BEEN BOTHERING ME FOR YEARS.
FINALLY, I'VE NEARLY SORTED IT.
WHAT ABOUT ME?
YOU?
US.
US?
DO YOU THINK WE ARE AN US YET?
LIKE, CAN I CALL YOU AND SAY 'IT'S ME', AND NOT 'IT'S LISA FROM WORK?'
YES, YOU CAN SAY 'IT'S ME'.

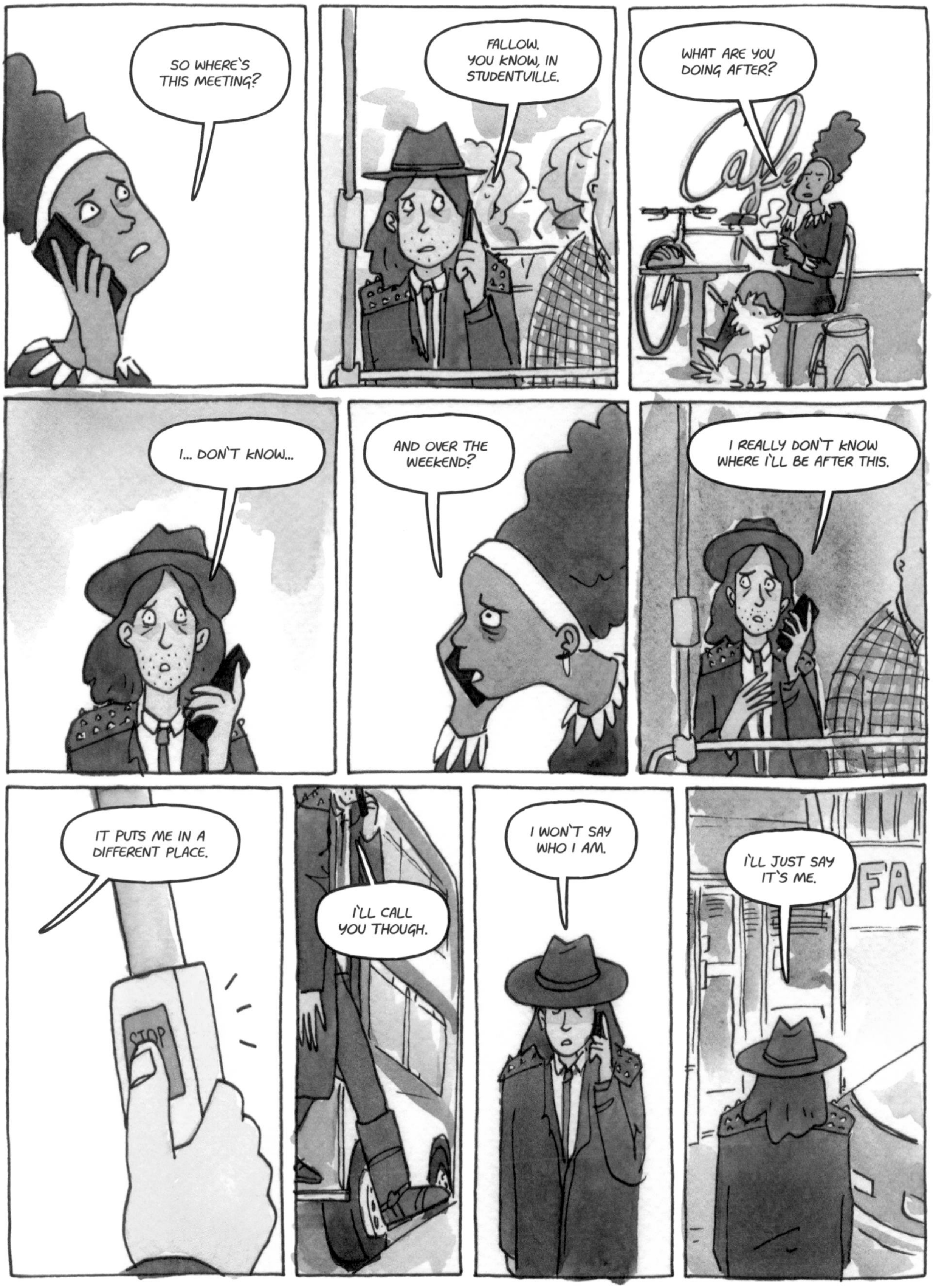
SO WHERE'S THIS MEETING?
FALLOW. YOU KNOW, IN STUDENTVILLE.
WHAT ARE YOU DOING AFTER?
Café
I... DON'T KNOW...
AND OVER THE WEEKEND?
I REALLY DON'T KNOW WHERE I'LL BE AFTER THIS.
IT PUTS ME IN A DIFFERENT PLACE.
STOP
I'LL CALL YOU THOUGH.
I WON'T SAY WHO I AM.
I'LL JUST SAY IT'S ME.
FA

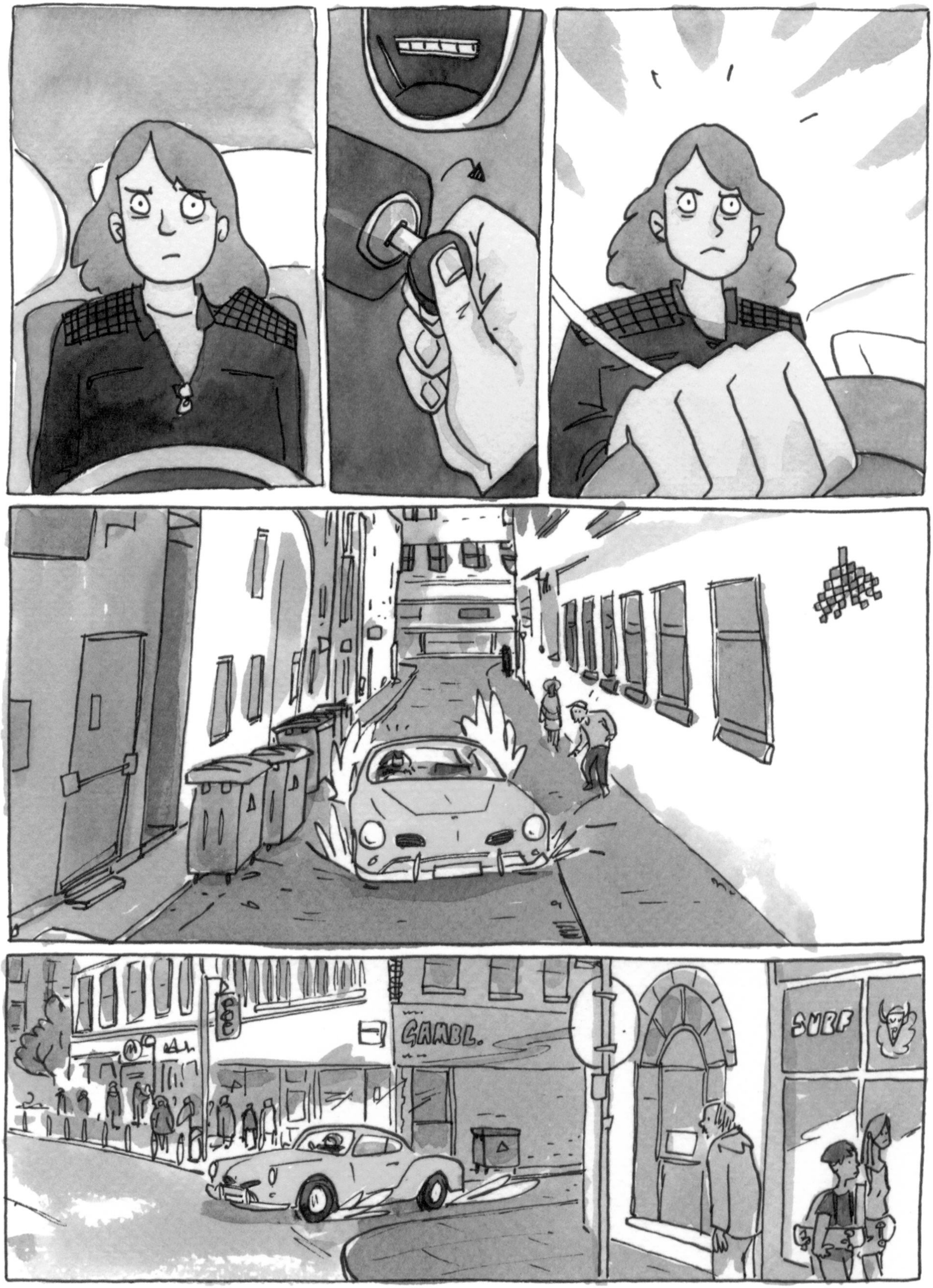
GAMBL.
SURF

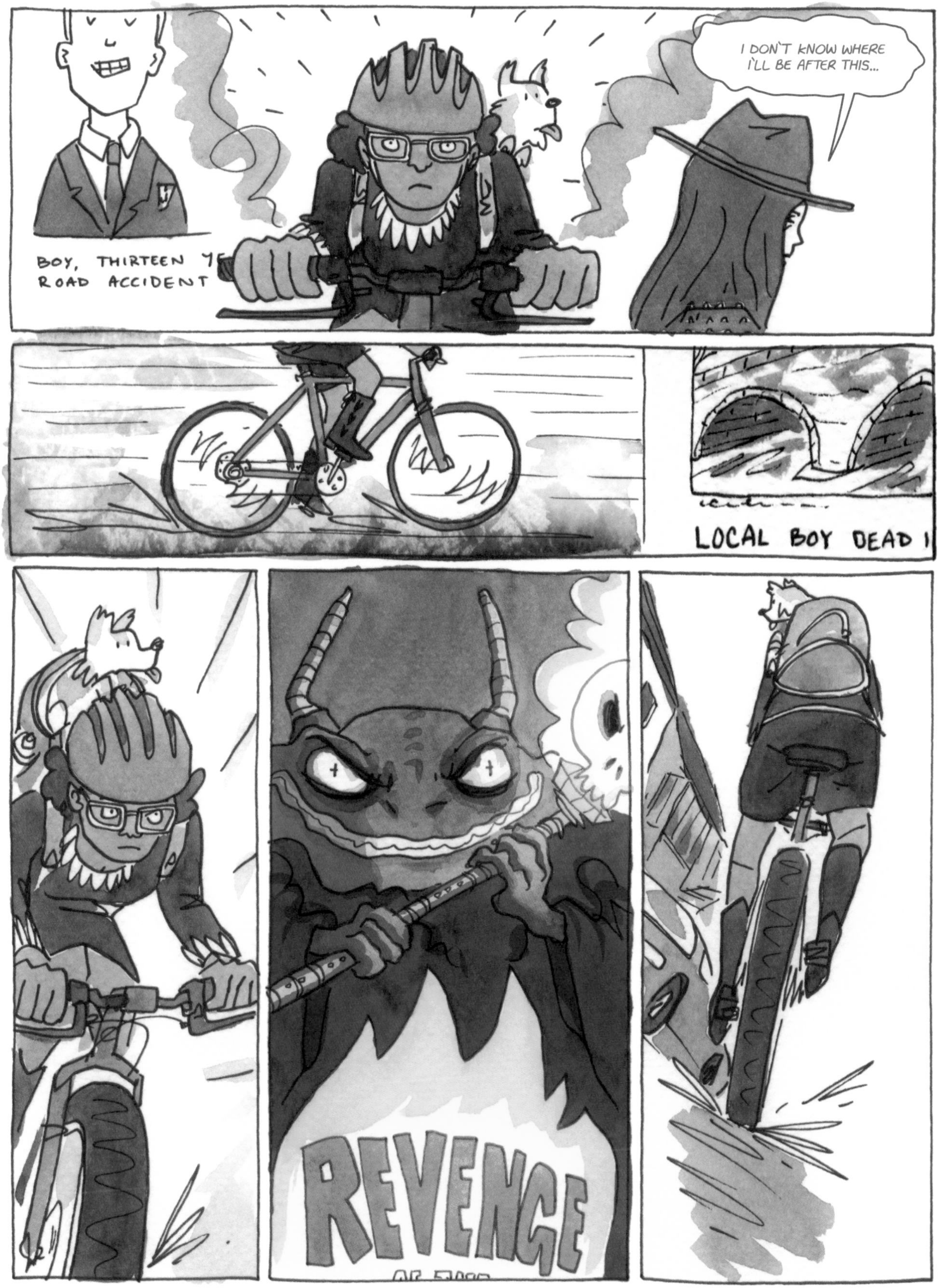
BOY, THIRTEEN YE
ROAD ACCIDENT
I DON'T KNOW WHERE I'LL BE AFTER THIS...
LOCAL BOY DEAD I
REVENGE

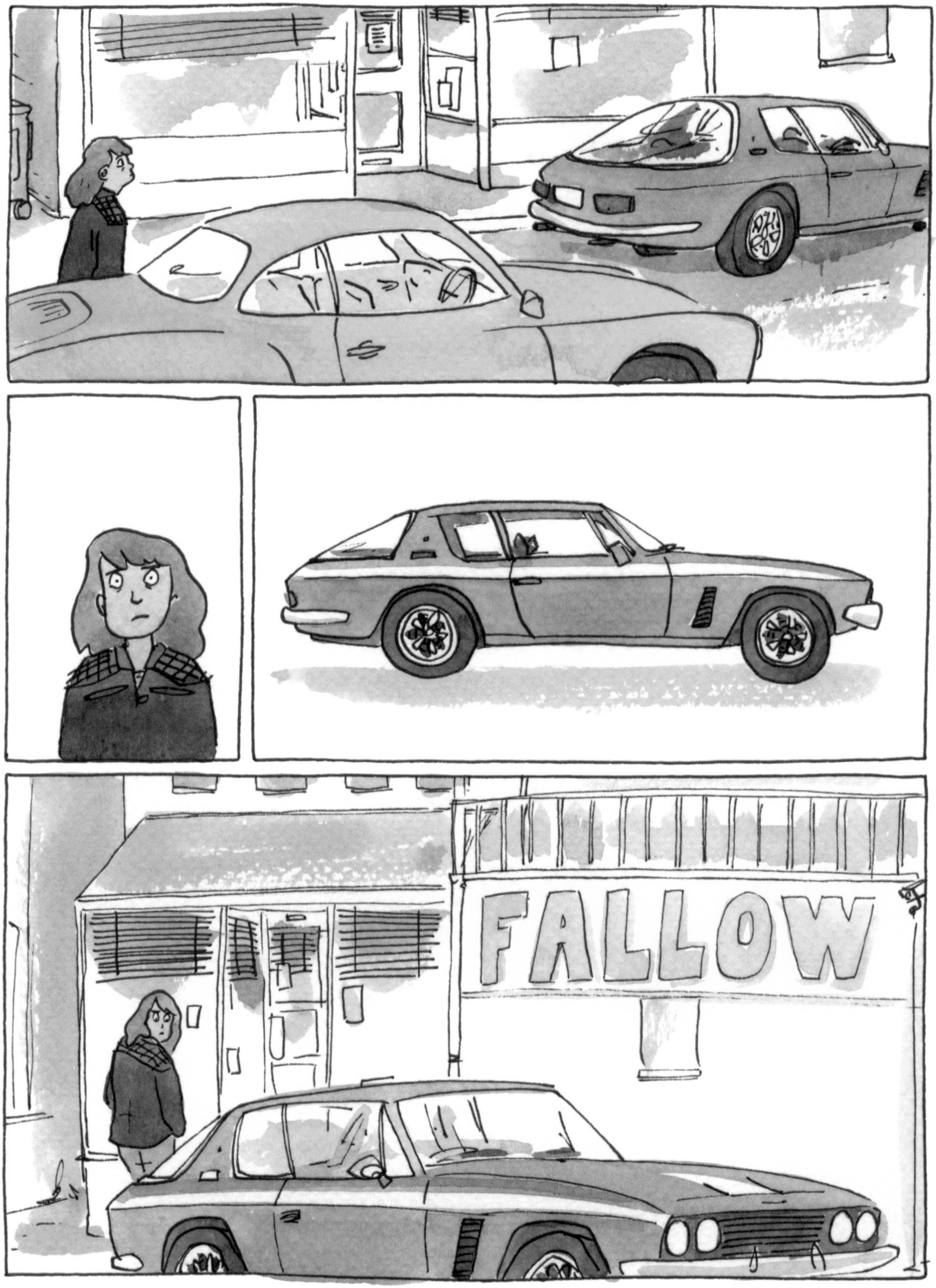
FALLOW

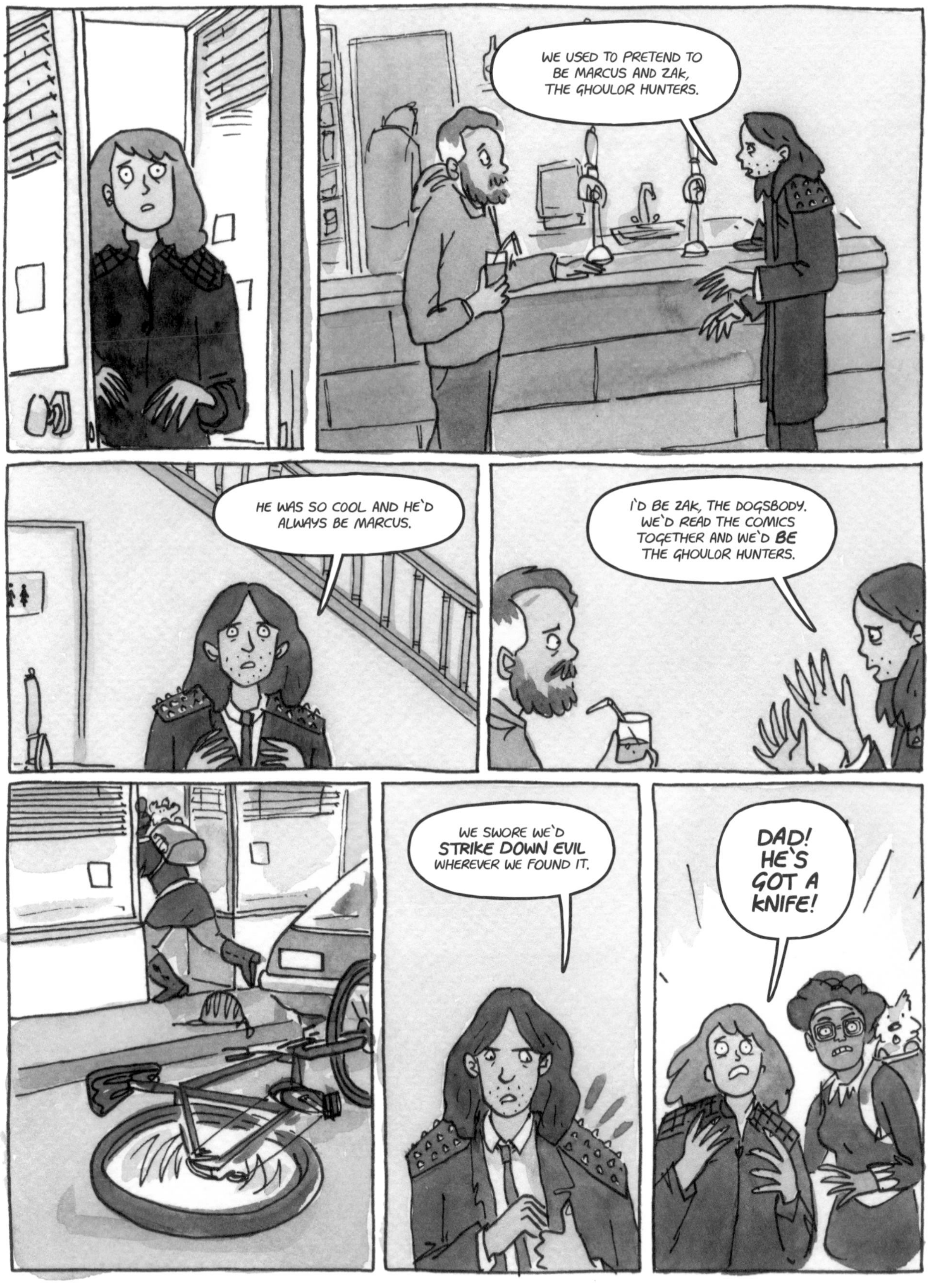
WE USED TO PRETEND TO BE MARCUS AND ZAK, THE GHOULOR HUNTERS.
HE WAS SO COOL AND HE'D ALWAYS BE MARCUS.
I'D BE ZAK, THE DOGSBODY. WE'D READ THE COMICS TOGETHER AND WE'D **BE** THE GHOULOR HUNTERS.
WE SWORE WE'D **STRIKE DOWN EVIL** WHEREVER WE FOUND IT.
DAD! HE'S GOT A KNIFE!

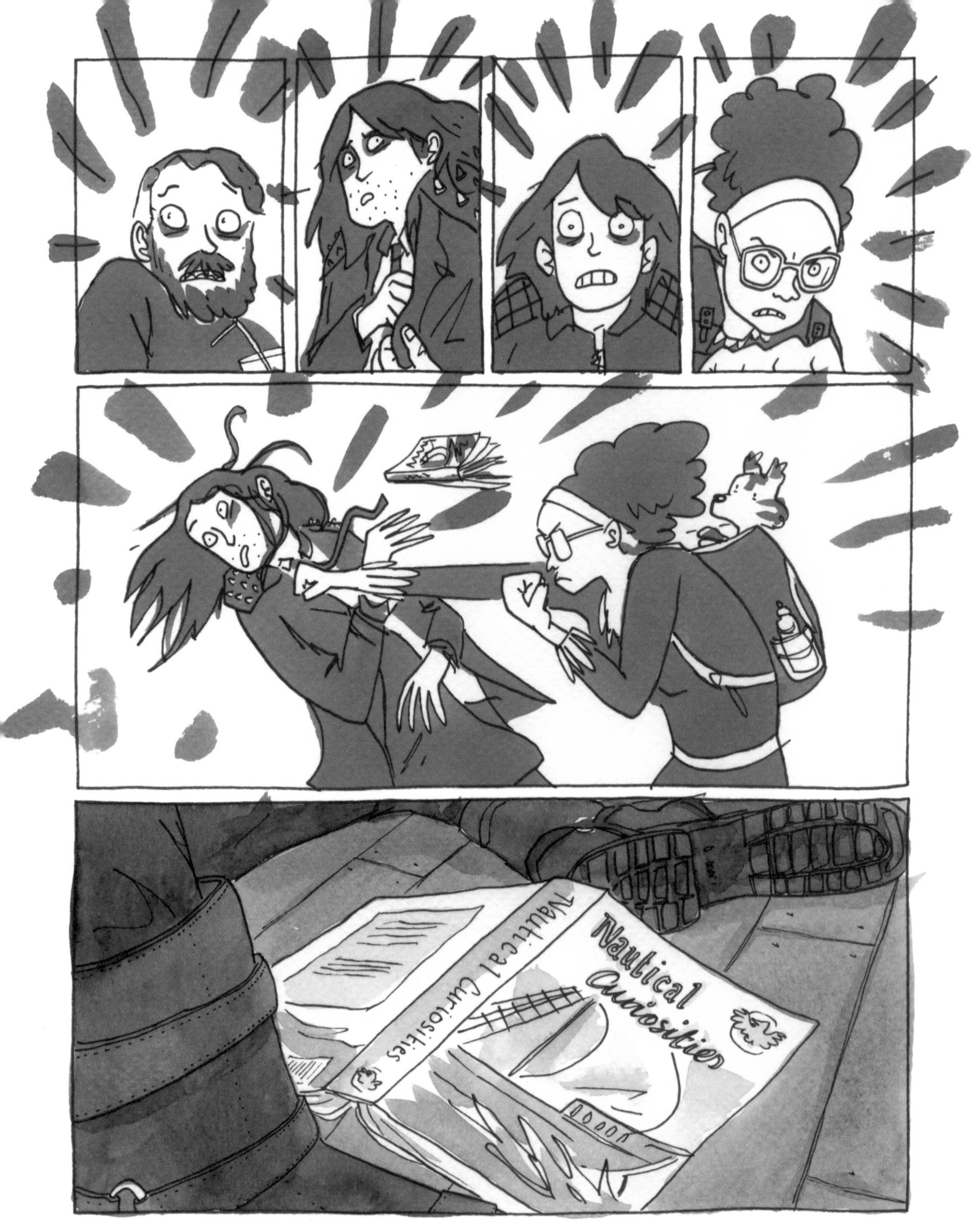
Nautical Curiosities
Nautical Curiosities

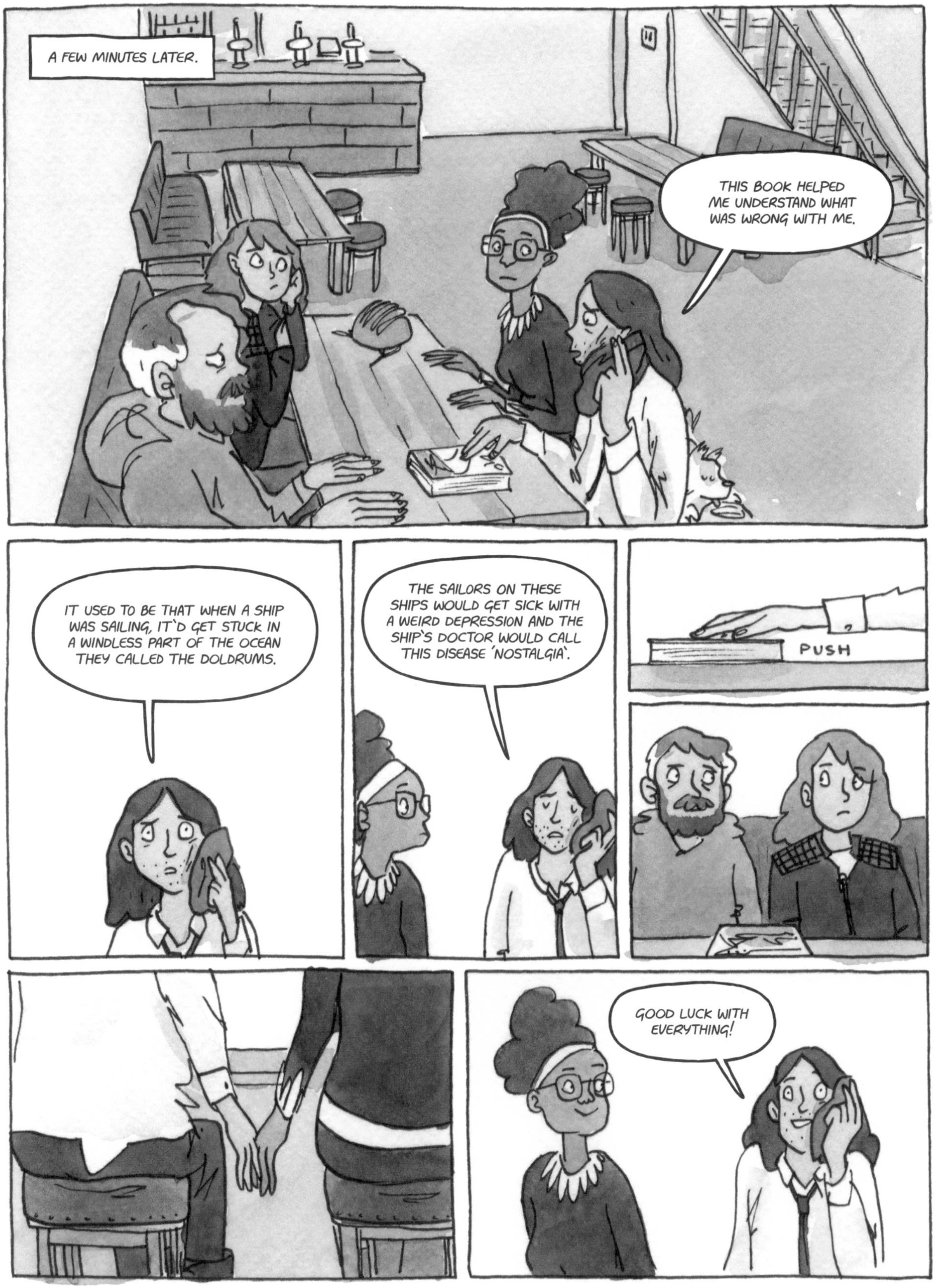
A FEW MINUTES LATER.
THIS BOOK HELPED ME UNDERSTAND WHAT WAS WRONG WITH ME.
IT USED TO BE THAT WHEN A SHIP WAS SAILING, IT'D GET STUCK IN A WINDLESS PART OF THE OCEAN THEY CALLED THE DOLDRUMS.
THE SAILORS ON THESE SHIPS WOULD GET SICK WITH A WEIRD DEPRESSION AND THE SHIP'S DOCTOR WOULD CALL THIS DISEASE 'NOSTALGIA'.
PUSH
GOOD LUCK WITH EVERYTHING!

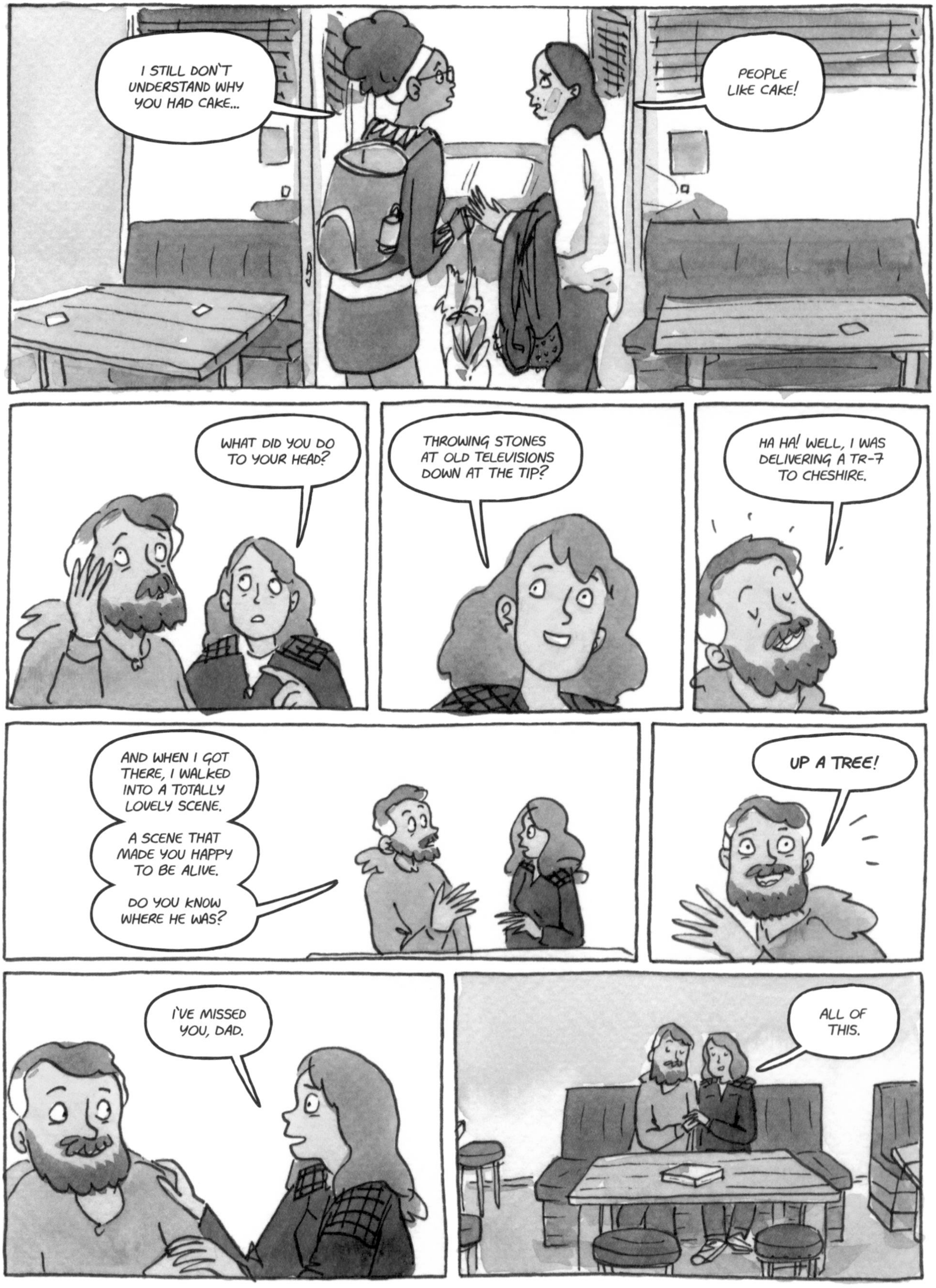
I STILL DON'T UNDERSTAND WHY YOU HAD CAKE...
PEOPLE LIKE CAKE!
WHAT DID YOU DO TO YOUR HEAD?
THROWING STONES AT OLD TELEVISIONS DOWN AT THE TIP?
HA HA! WELL, I WAS DELIVERING A TR-7 TO CHESHIRE.
AND WHEN I GOT THERE, I WALKED INTO A TOTALLY LOVELY SCENE.
A SCENE THAT MADE YOU HAPPY TO BE ALIVE.
DO YOU KNOW WHERE HE WAS?
UP A TREE!
I'VE MISSED YOU, DAD.
ALL OF THIS.

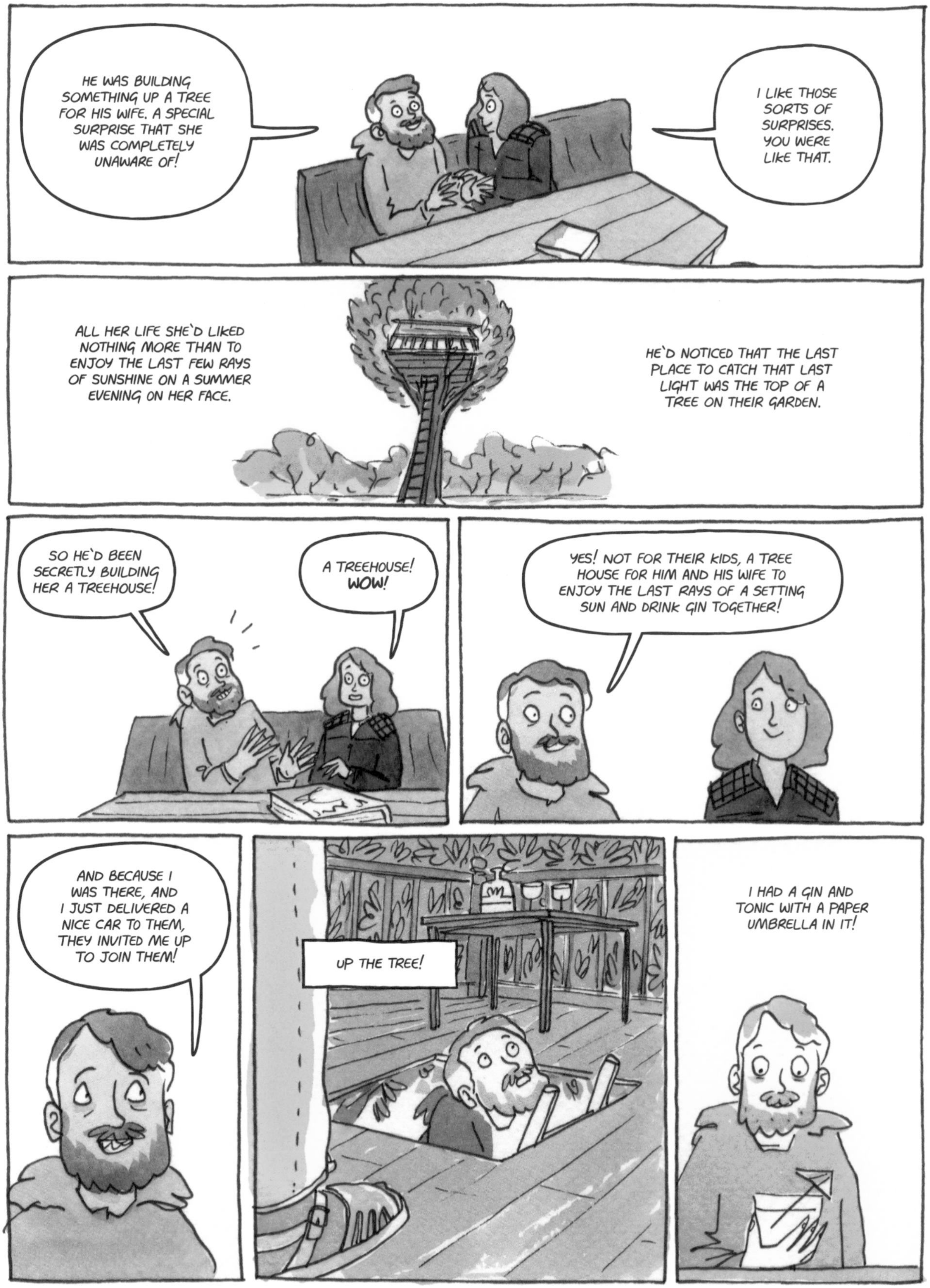

HE WAS BUILDING SOMETHING UP A TREE FOR HIS WIFE. A SPECIAL SURPRISE THAT SHE WAS COMPLETELY UNAWARE OF!
I LIKE THOSE SORTS OF SURPRISES. YOU WERE LIKE THAT.
ALL HER LIFE SHE'D LIKED NOTHING MORE THAN TO ENJOY THE LAST FEW RAYS OF SUNSHINE ON A SUMMER EVENING ON HER FACE.
HE'D NOTICED THAT THE LAST PLACE TO CATCH THAT LAST LIGHT WAS THE TOP OF A TREE ON THEIR GARDEN.
SO HE'D BEEN SECRETLY BUILDING HER A TREEHOUSE!
A TREEHOUSE! WOW!
YES! NOT FOR THEIR KIDS, A TREE HOUSE FOR HIM AND HIS WIFE TO ENJOY THE LAST RAYS OF A SETTING SUN AND DRINK GIN TOGETHER!
AND BECAUSE I WAS THERE, AND I JUST DELIVERED A NICE CAR TO THEM, THEY INVITED ME UP TO JOIN THEM!
UP THE TREE!
I HAD A GIN AND TONIC WITH A PAPER UMBRELLA IN IT!

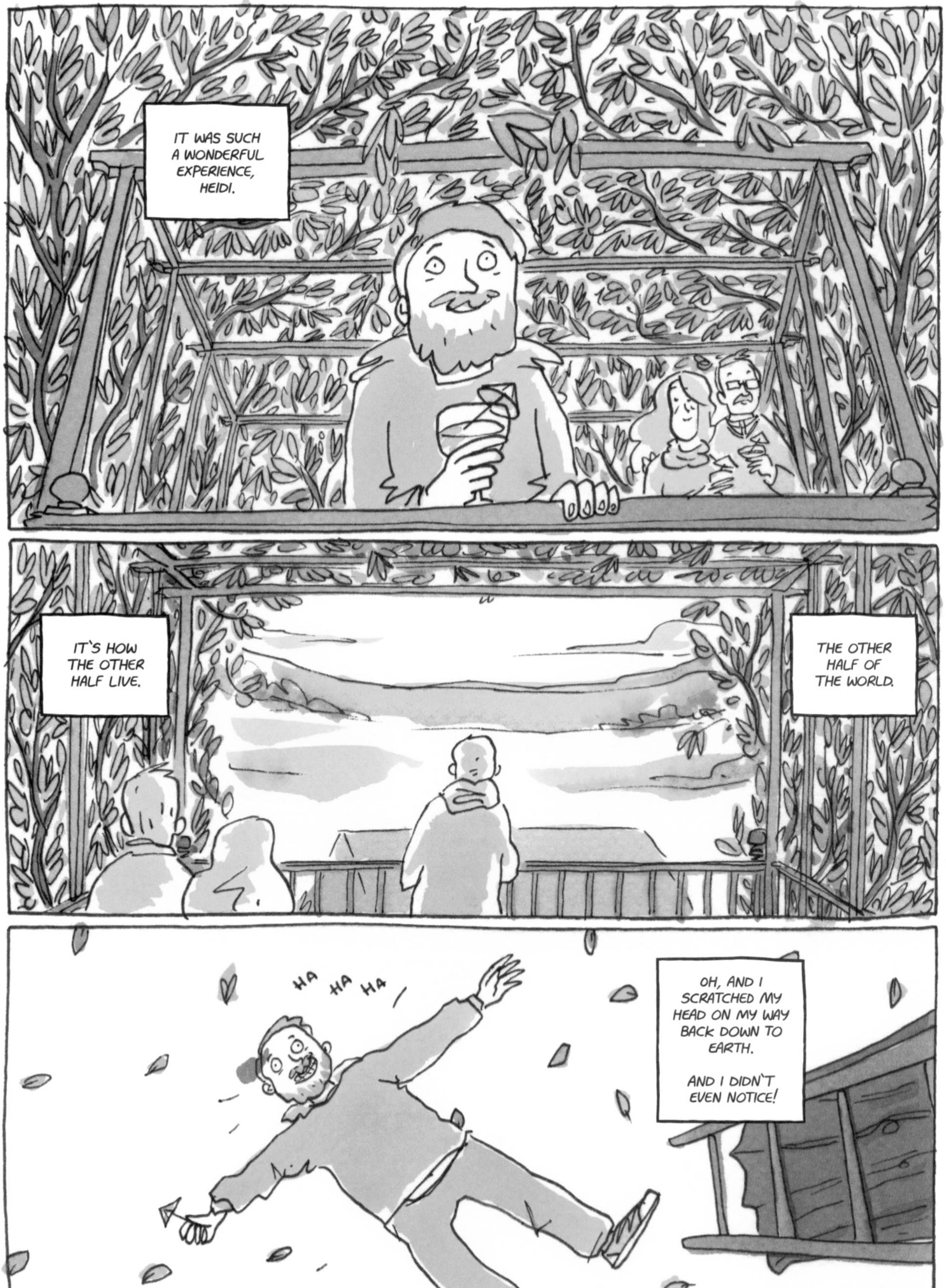
IT WAS SUCH A WONDERFUL EXPERIENCE, HEIDI.
IT'S HOW THE OTHER HALF LIVE.
THE OTHER HALF OF THE WORLD.
HA HA HA
OH, AND I SCRATCHED MY HEAD ON MY WAY BACK DOWN TO EARTH.
AND I DIDN'T EVEN NOTICE!

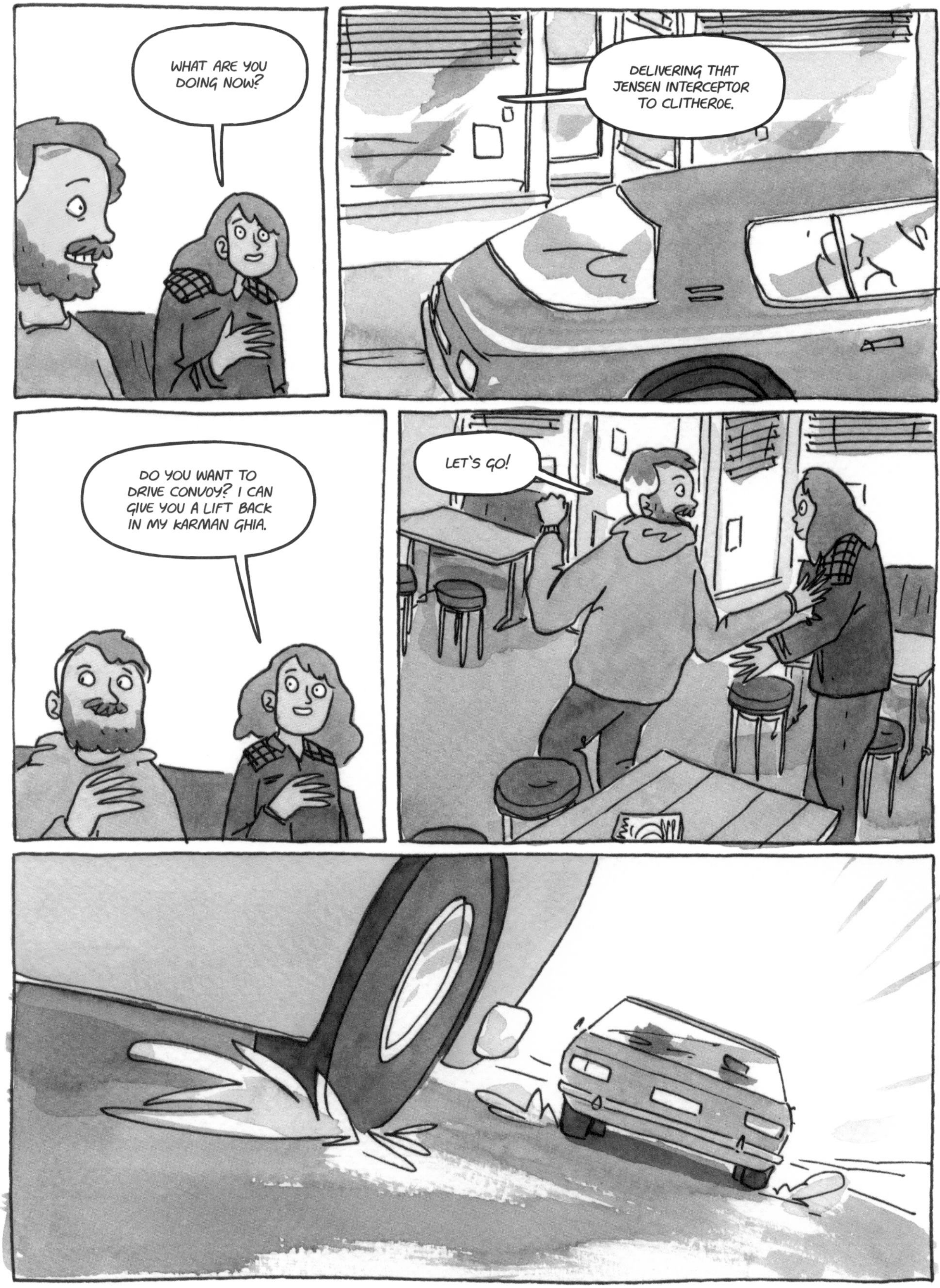
WHAT ARE YOU DOING NOW?
DELIVERING THAT JENSEN INTERCEPTOR TO CLITHEROE.
DO YOU WANT TO DRIVE CONVOY? I CAN GIVE YOU A LIFT BACK IN MY KARMAN GHIA.
LET'S GO!

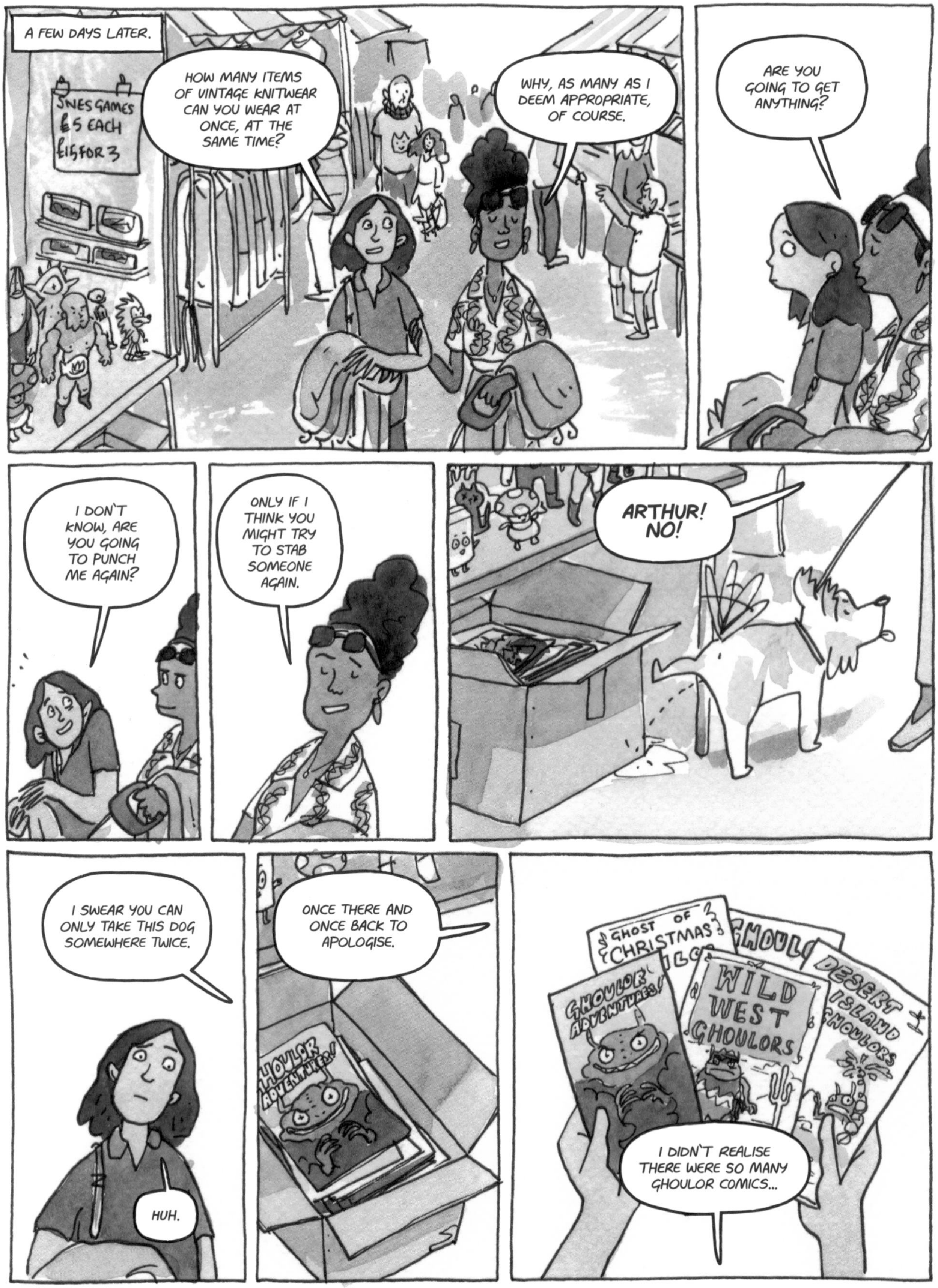

A FEW DAYS LATER.
SNES GAMES £5 EACH £15 FOR 3
HOW MANY ITEMS OF VINTAGE KNITWEAR CAN YOU WEAR AT ONCE, AT THE SAME TIME?
WHY, AS MANY AS I DEEM APPROPRIATE, OF COURSE.
ARE YOU GOING TO GET ANYTHING?
I DON'T KNOW, ARE YOU GOING TO PUNCH ME AGAIN?
ONLY IF I THINK YOU MIGHT TRY TO STAB SOMEONE AGAIN.
ARTHUR! NO!
I SWEAR YOU CAN ONLY TAKE THIS DOG SOMEWHERE TWICE.
HUH.
ONCE THERE AND ONCE BACK TO APOLOGISE.
HOULOR ADVENTURES!
GHOST OF CHRISTMAS
GHOULOR ADVENTURES!
WILD WEST GHOULORS
DESERT ISLAND GHOULORS
I DIDN'T REALISE THERE WERE SO MANY GHOULOR COMICS...

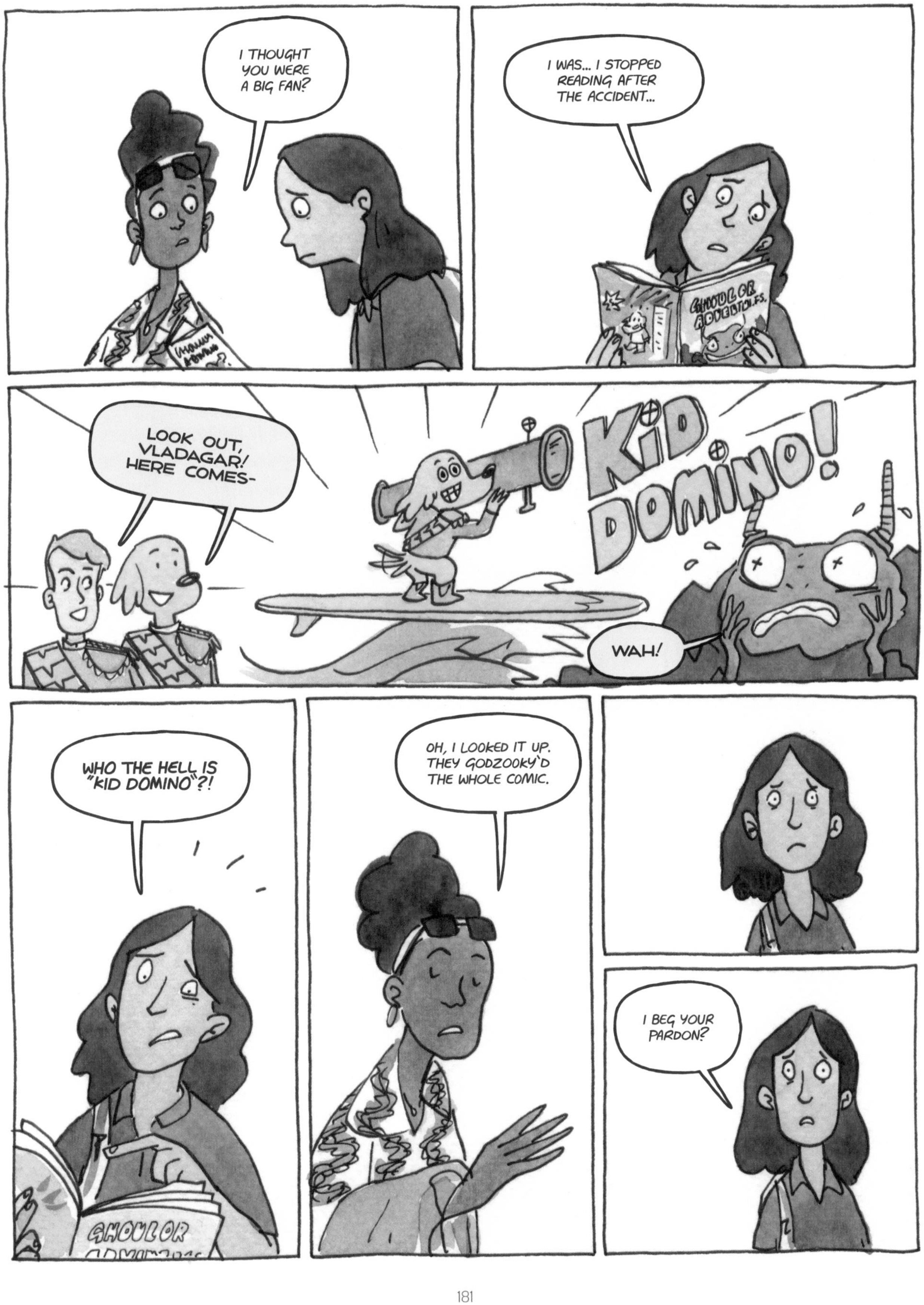
I THOUGHT YOU WERE A BIG FAN?
I WAS... I STOPPED READING AFTER THE ACCIDENT...
LOOK OUT, VLADAGAR! HERE COMES-
KID DOMINO!
WAH!
WHO THE HELL IS "KID DOMINO"?!
OH, I LOOKED IT UP. THEY GODZOOKY'D THE WHOLE COMIC.
I BEG YOUR PARDON?

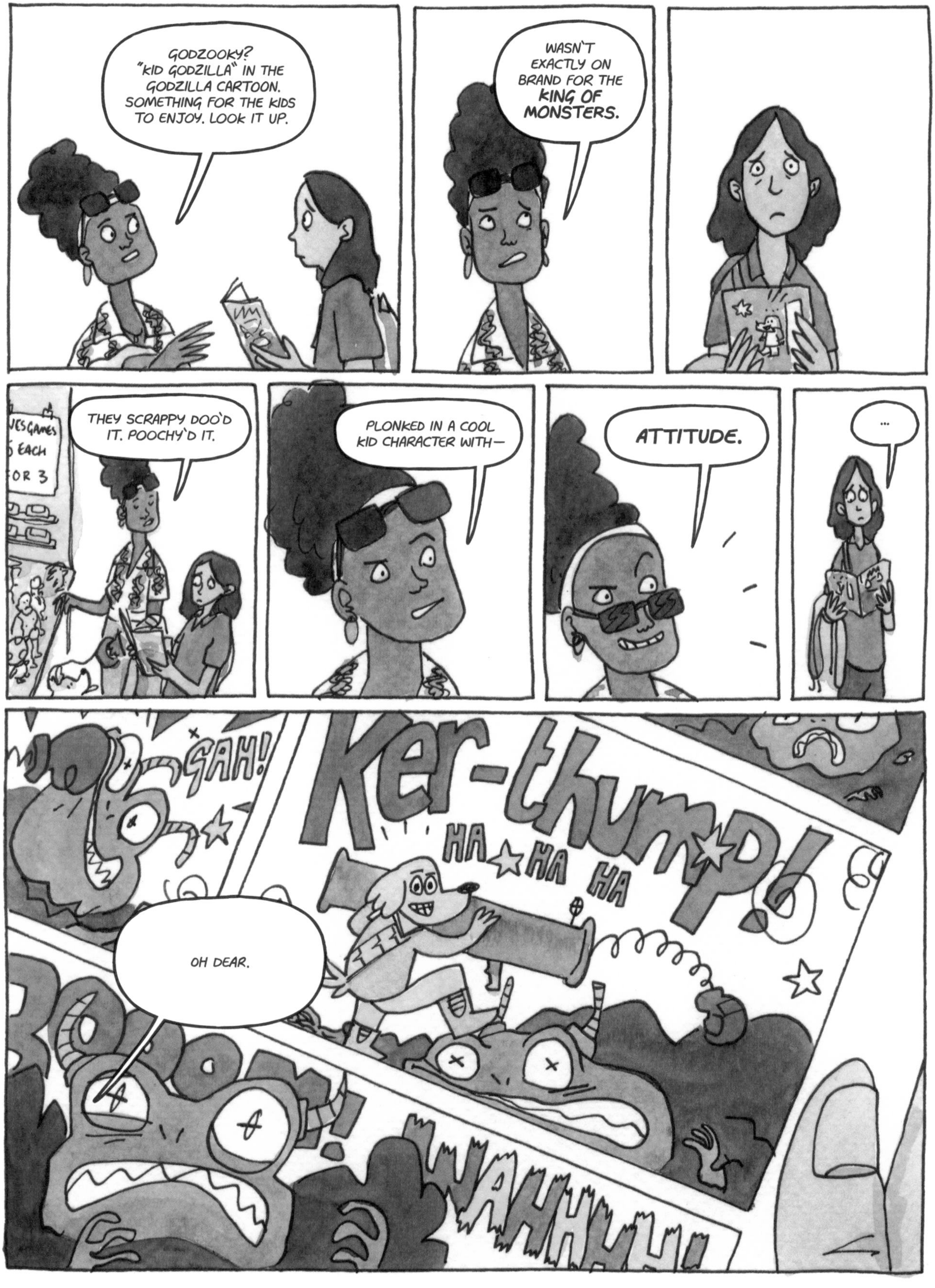
GODZOOKY? "KID GODZILLA" IN THE GODZILLA CARTOON. SOMETHING FOR THE KIDS TO ENJOY. LOOK IT UP.
WASN'T EXACTLY ON BRAND FOR THE KING OF MONSTERS.
THEY SCRAPPY DOO'D IT. POOCHY'D IT.
PLONKED IN A COOL KID CHARACTER WITH—
ATTITUDE.
...
GAH!
Ker-thump!
HA HA HA
OH DEAR.
WAHHHH!

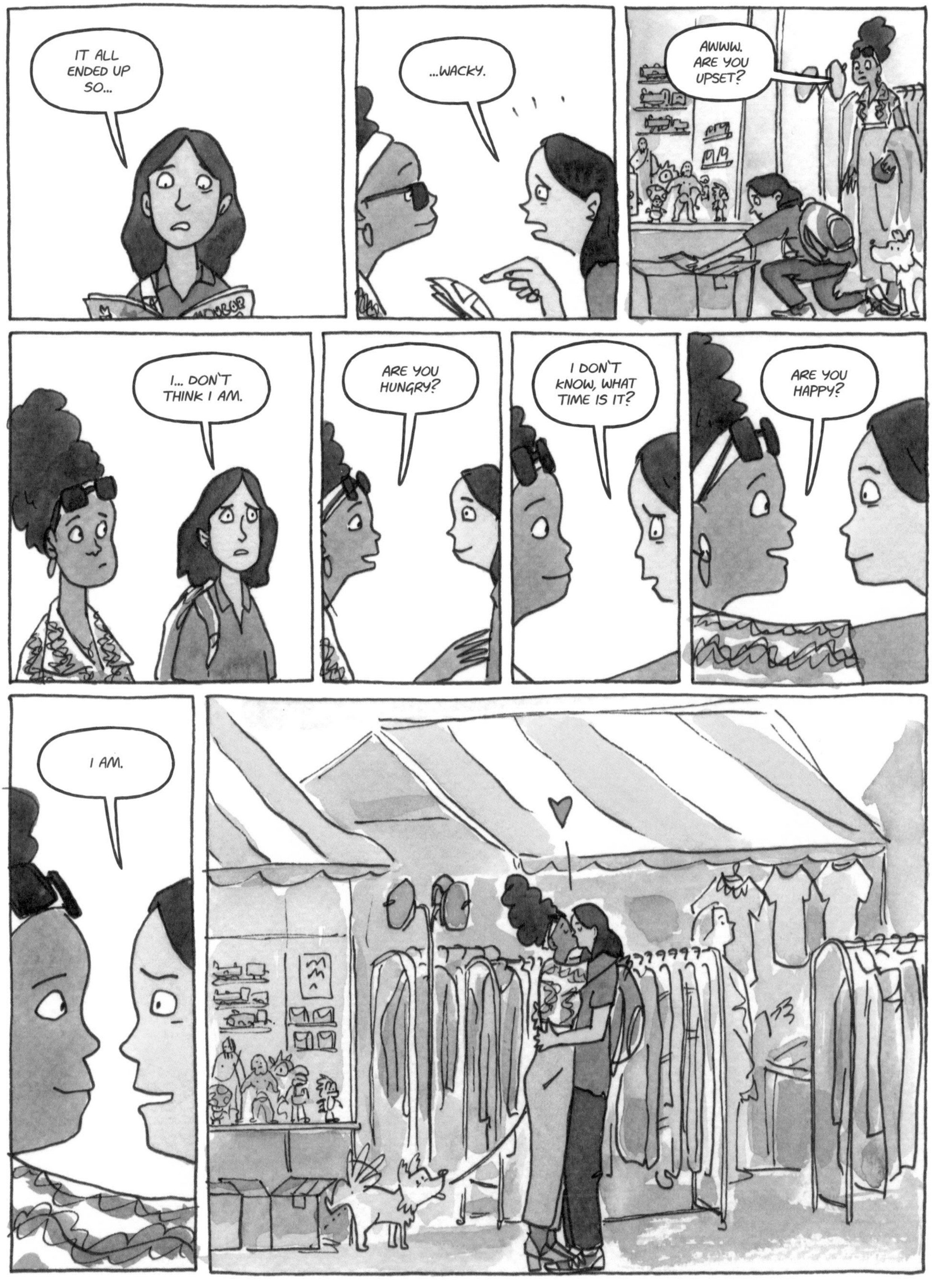
IT ALL ENDED UP SO...
...WACKY.
AWWW. ARE YOU UPSET?
I... DON'T THINK I AM.
ARE YOU HUNGRY?
I DON'T KNOW, WHAT TIME IS IT?
ARE YOU HAPPY?
I AM.

David Gaffney lives in Manchester, UK. He is the author of the novels *Never Never* (2008) and *All The Places I've Ever Lived* (2017), the short story collections *Sawn-Off Tales* (2006), *Aromabingo* (2007), *The Half-Life of Songs* (2010) and *More Sawn-Off Tales* (2013), and the graphic novel with Dan Berry, *The Three Rooms In Valerie's Head* (2018). *The Guardian* said: 'One hundred and fifty words by Gaffney are more worthwhile than novels by a good many others.'

davidgaffney.org

Dan Berry is a cartoonist, educator and podcaster from Shrewsbury, England. He is the creator of a number of comic books including *The Suitcase* (2012), *Carry Me* (2013), *Nicholas & Edith* (2015) and many more. He edited and contributed to the Eisner nominated anthology *24 by 7* (2018). He is also the host of the popular interview podcast *Make It Then Tell Everybody*.

thingsbydan.co.uk

Rivers is the second book by David Gaffney & Dan Berry, following **The Three Rooms In Valerie's Head**, also published by Top Shelf.